W9-CTJ-945

3DS MAX 6 FUNDAMENTALS

Ted Boardman

New
Riders

800 East 96th Street, 3rd Floor, Indianapolis, Indiana 46240

An Imprint of Pearson Education

Boston•Indianapolis•London•Munich•New York•San Francisco

3ds max 6 Fundamentals

Copyright © 2004 by New Riders Publishing

All rights reserved. No part of this book shall be reproduced, stored in a retrieval system, or transmitted by any means—electronic, mechanical, photocopying, recording, or otherwise—without written permission from the publisher, except for the inclusion of brief quotations in a review.

International Standard Book Number: 0-7357-1385-5

Library of Congress Catalog Card Number: 2003112027

Printed in the United States of America

First printing: February, 2004

08 07 06 05 04   7 6 5 4 3 2 1

Interpretation of the printing code: The rightmost double-digit number is the year of the book's printing; the rightmost single-digit number is the number of the book's printing. For example, the printing code 04-1 shows that the first printing of the book occurred in 2004.

Trademarks

All terms mentioned in this book that are known to be trademarks or service marks have been appropriately capitalized. New Riders Publishing cannot attest to the accuracy of this information. Use of a term in this book should not be regarded as affecting the validity of any trademark or service mark. 3ds max is a registered trademark of Discreet.

Warning and Disclaimer

Every effort has been made to make this book as complete and as accurate as possible, but no warranty of fitness is implied. The information is provided on an as-is basis. The authors and New Riders Publishing shall have neither liability nor responsibility to any person or entity with respect to any loss or damages arising from the information contained in this book or from the use of the CD or programs that may accompany it.

Associate Publisher
Stephanie Wall

Production Manager
Gina Kanouse

Acquisitions Editor
Elise Walter

Senior Project Editor
Sarah Kearns

Copy Editor
Keith Cline

Indexer
Lisa Stumpf

Proofreader
Sheri Cain

Composition
Ron Wise

Manufacturing Coordinator
Dan Uhrig

Cover Designer
Aren Howell

Media Developer
Jay Payne

Marketing
Scott Cowlin
Tammy Detrich
Hannah Onstad Latham

Publicity Manager
Susan Nixon

Dedication

I'd like to dedicate this book to Sally Turner, my long-time companion and friend who helps me stay on track.

Contents at a Glance

Table of Contents

About the Author

Currently, **Ted Boardman** is a traveling Discreet 3ds max and Autodesk 3D Studio VIZ training consultant. Ted is one of a handful of Authorized Discreet Training Specialists. Training sessions are custom classes designed to increase 3D modeling and animation productivity for a wide range of clients, from architecture, to aerospace, to television and computer gaming.

An integral part of Ted's training process is authoring and co-authoring books for New Riders Publishing on the production issues encountered in using 3ds max, including *3ds max 4 Fundamentals*, several books from the *Inside 3D Studio MAX* series, and *Inside 3D Studio VIZ 3*. Ted has contributed to several other books on the subject, as well as to Discreet advanced modules, and currently has a monthly column covering topics related to 3ds max at the http://www.cgarchitect.com web site.

Ted is an award-winning speaker at the annual Autodesk University symposium covering CAD and visualization topics and is founder of the Boston Area 3D Studio User Group.

Outside the 3D world, Ted has traveled, lived, and worked in Europe for many years, and for nearly 18 years ran a small architectural design/build firm that specialized in hand-cut Post and Beam structures. Long-distance bicycle travel and 28,000 miles of blue-water yacht deliveries served as a diversion from work for many years. Photography, painting, and opera are other interests.

Ted lives in Portsmouth, New Hampshire.

About the Technical Reviewers

These reviewers contributed their considerable hands-on expertise to the entire development process for *3ds max 6 Fundamentals*. As the book was being written, these dedicated professionals reviewed all the material for technical content, organization, and flow. Their feedback was critical to ensuring that *3ds max 6 Fundamentals* fits our readers' need for the highest-quality technical information.

Jon McFarland is the manager of the design department of a national developer/owner/manager of retail, office, residential, and entertainment complexes based in Cleveland, Ohio. His department's responsibilities include the creation of computer graphic stills and animations depicting proposed facilities and the incorporation of 3D models into photographs and videos.

In addition to his primary job, he teaches computer animation to graphic arts students at The Virginia Marti College of Fashion and Art, a small, accredited, college in Lakewood, Ohio, a suburb of Cleveland.

Jon spent seven years "blowin' stuff up" as a paratrooper in the U.S. Army. This naturally led to a career in computer graphics and animation that began in early 1990. He has a degree in mechanical engineering technology, but focuses his energy in the architectural visualization and animation fields.

Jon lives in Sheffield Lake, Ohio, and coaches baseball, soccer, and wrestling for his sons, Zachary and Jacob.

Tim Wilbers has been teaching at the University of Dayton in Ohio since 1983. He started working with digital imaging in 1986 and 3D computer modeling and animation on a professional basis in 1988. He started teaching digital imaging/photography courses in 1988 and began offering courses in 3D and developing a program for digital artists in 1992. Current activities include teaching three sequential courses in 3D and two in digital photography. He is also a Forum Assistant on Discreet's 3ds max user discussion web-board and is committed to making the creation of 3d com puter modeling and animation accessible to the greatest number of students and professionals. Living south of Dayton with his wife and son, he is known for over-feeding the native wildlife, including a small herd of white-tailed deer (six) in his front yard.

Acknowledgments

Without a good editing and production team, an author's work would be inconsistent and unreadable.

I would like to thank my technical editors, Jon McFarland and Tim Wilbers, for keeping me on track throughout the writing process and helping to clarify the learning objectives put forward in the exercises.

Thanks to the editing staff of Sarah Kearns and Keith Cline and the extensive production staff at New Riders Publishing for tying it all together into an attractive and readable book.

Thanks to Elise Walter at New Riders for keeping an eye on all of us.

Tell Us What You Think

As the reader of this book, you are the most important critic and commentator. We value your opinion and want to know what we're doing right, what we could do better, what areas you'd like to see us publish in, and any other words of wisdom you're willing to pass our way.

As an editor for New Riders Publishing, I welcome your comments. You can fax, email, or write me directly to let me know what you did or didn't like about this book—as well as what we can do to make our books stronger. When you write, please be sure to include this book's title, ISBN, and author, as well as your name and phone or fax number. I will carefully review your comments and share them with the author and editors who worked on the book.

Please note that I cannot help you with technical problems related to the topic of this book, and that due to the high volume of email I receive, I might not be able to reply to every message.

Fax: 317-428-3280

Email: elise.walter@newriders.com

Mail: Elise Walter
        Acquisitions Editor
        New Riders Publishing
        800 East 96th Street, 3rd Floor
        Indianapolis, IN 46240 USA

Introduction

Let's assume you decide to learn to play the violin. You start lessons this week, and by the end of the month, you want to have a concert at Carnegie Hall in New York City. Is that likely to happen? No, but it illustrates a point about learning 3ds max 6. As with any art form, you must start with the fundamentals. Then, using the lessons learned, you must build on that solid foundation and practice, practice, practice until you have developed a style of your own. Eventually, you will be ready for the Carnegie Halls of visualization and animation.

3ds max 6 has some powerful new features that enable users to increase productivity (through faster editing and enhanced functionality). As the title of this book implies, it covers some fundamentals of 3ds max 6, not necessarily topics that are only for first-time users of 3ds max 6, but for anyone who wants to be exposed to work methods and techniques that are fundamental to creating a scene in a timely manner.

Every level of user, from raw beginners to advanced users, can find information in this book that will help speed the day-to-day workflow.

The Concepts

In the first part of this book, I walk you through some of the traditional art concepts that have been used throughout the ages to create art that causes the viewer to make an emotional connection with the work, thereby conveying the goals of your story or presentation.

This book also covers the basic concepts important to the way 3ds max 6 functions to help you understand why a certain approach to modeling, materials, lighting, or animation helps you get the most from the software.

The Fundamentals

The discussions and exercises contained in this book walk you through the concepts and work methods that, although fundamental, are essential to an understanding of how 3ds max 6 functions. You also learn how to apply the basic knowledge to a workflow that increases your productivity.

In this book, you learn important fundamentals such as the following:

- The reference coordinate systems that enable you to manipulate objects in 3D space efficiently.
- Some concepts of working in 2D to create complex 3D scenes that can be edited quickly and easily.
- Reducing scene overhead to get the most out of the hardware you have available (which is one of the most important lessons presented in this book).
- How to make efficient materials to simulate complex geometry to increase rendering speed and to make your scenes unique.
- Applying lighting to scenes using the new radiosity and global illumination (methods that are cost-effective and convincing to the viewer).
- Fundamental animation techniques on which you can build your own techniques and styles.

As new users or users anxious to dive into the new features introduced in 3ds max 6, you will want to get stunning results as soon as possible from your new purchase.

Take the time to get a good grounding in these fundamental issues, and then the fancy work will come much more naturally to you as you dig deeper into the software.

The Exercises

The exercises in this book walk you step by step through a process similar to what you might encounter in a real-life project. The processes and methods are designed to help you form work habits that will be relevant whether you are a gamer, background artist, stage or set designer, or engineer.

Use the lessons learned from each exercise to come up with scenes of your own, incorporating the techniques and methods until you understand the process. Start with simple scenes that enable you to focus on understanding the concepts, and the fundamentals will quickly become part of your daily routine.

While you are completing the exercises, consider how you might apply the methods and techniques covered in your own line of work. An exercise can walk you through the creation of a building, for example, but you might be planning to use the same process to create the rough form of an automobile.

I hope that when you work on your own projects, you will not think, "I learned this or that from Ted Boardman." Instead, hopefully, the lessons you learn here will become an automatic reaction to challenges that you will face in your production schedules.

The Files and Content

The files included on the CD-ROM that accompanies this book include the files necessary for the exercises, but also other files in the ExtraFiles folder that are either more complete versions of the basic exercise files (such as the USS *Agamenticus*) or totally unrelated scenes, such as a pair of tech flashlights or an old brick brewery building. There are also rendered animations of the *Agamenticus* and its engine room.

Open all the files in this book and analyze how the objects were modeled, how the lights were placed, and how the materials and animation were created. Play with those scenes to come up with other approaches to improve them. Try to learn something new every day you work with 3ds max 6. Let these lessons become the foundation for your artistry.

The New Features

I've taken some different approaches to developing the scenes for the exercises, using as many of the new features in 3ds max 6 as practical, while remaining true to the fundamentals of 3ds max 6.

The editable poly editing features are introduced and used extensively in building the objects in the scenes.

Lighting is a new concept in 3ds max 6, and you learn to work with both global illumination and radiosity renderers. I have divided the exercises into three parts: the building of an 1860's ironclad boat called the USS *Agamenticus*, an outdoor scene of the shipyard where the boat was originally built, and an imaginary interior control center for the boat. My intention with this approach is to introduce you to the fundamentals of three very specific types of light-rendering scenarios: sunlight, light fixtures, and global illumination.

Animation also has been improved in 3ds max 6, and the animation exercises in this book walk you through the improvements and fundamental aspects of new animation features.

The Source

The exercises and work methods are derived from situations that arise in my max classes and during consulting. I try to make the exercises as real as possible while staying true to my teaching strategy.

Wherever 3ds max 6 takes you, good luck and have fun.

PART I

Introduction

CHAPTER 1

Workflow: Keeping the Process Running Smoothly

In This Chapter

Creating 3D scenes can be a complex task that can be accomplished much more efficiently with a little foresight and planning.

In this chapter, you learn some of the important factors to be aware of prior to starting a 3D project and some hints to remember during the execution of the project.

Some of the topics covered in this section include the following:

- **The chain of command**—Clearly define team members' responsibilities.
- **Needs assessment**—Determine the project scope and audience needs.
- **Storyboarding**—Create a visual outline of the project.
- **Choosing a team**—Select the right talent and capabilities for the specific project.
- **Set up a productive working environment**—Both equipment and training are critical to productivity.
- **Know when to stop**—Avoid the temptation to "tweak" the project into financial loss.
- **Develop office standards**—Written procedures and standards speed work.
- **Work in layers**—Layers, in this case, are compositing tools.
- **Cinematic animation techniques**—Watch film and TV for successful camera and editing methods.
- **Output capabilities**—Plan production to include a variety of output type possibilities.

Key Term

- **Storyboard**—A storyboard is a graphical outline that informs the team of the scope of the project.

Preparation and Planning

Before creating the first 3D element of a project, you should have a few basic organizational details settled. This ensures that all those involved know their responsibilities and have a good idea of the scope of the project and the time frame in which elements are to be completed.

Even the smallest projects with only one or two members of the staff benefit from a good plan going into production. When the project has more than a few collaborators, the planning stages become paramount to developing a solid outline that each team member can refer to as the work progresses.

It is unrealistic to think that, after developing a good plan of attack, nothing will change. 3D projects often seem to be in a constant state of change for a variety of reasons. However, the changes will be much less disruptive to the overall goals if those goals are spelled out for all involved.

Do not skip this step in the creation process to save time; doing so will be an exercise in false economy.

The Chain of Command

Critical communication paths between those who order the work, those who create the content, and those who present to the client must be established with each having an understanding of the available talent and resources.

Communications between the client and production staff, whether that is designers in-house or the actual client, will be something that will develop over time and constantly evolve as the whole visualization process matures. However, educating the client about the general process involved in creating the visualizations can smooth these communications. The client need not know specifically how scenes are created, but should know what types of requests will take time and which can be done quickly.

Letting the in-house client sit in on a half-day, hands-on training session with the 3D software can help him understand that there is no magic "make art" button on the computer and can give him better insight to some of the difficulties the production staff faces.

Regular short meetings between the production staff and the in-house "clients" can keep each team up-to-date on processes that either increase or hinder productivity from either side.

Needs Assessment

An important step in productivity is determining the scope and quality of work required to satisfy the client's expectations within the confines of time and budget.

Not every job that goes out the door requires photorealistic-quality images to communicate the important messages to the client. Feature films certainly need all the cutting-edge refinements technology has to offer, but public-service announcements to be shown on regional television might not have the same budget considerations and you will have to determine where you can trim production costs with the least effect on quality.

Flexible stages of production can help you avoid costly changes that require you to start from scratch. If modeling and details are too high early in the design development or if complete materials with high-resolution maps are applied to models, for example, it might focus unnecessary attention on decisions that are better left for later.

A better approach might be to rough out models much the same way a stone sculptor would and then go back to add details as they become necessary.

You could use highly compressed stand-in maps while developing the scenes to allow for faster test rendering, for instance, and then replace those with the quality maps near the end of the project.

Storyboarding

Storyboarding is the process of creating a graphic outline that illustrates the story and provides cues to production issues before any work begins on the project.

Storyboards can range from simple sketches to airbrushed or hand-painted panels that could be classified as works of art in their own right (see Figure 1.1).

For rendered still images, as an architectural visualization artist might require, the storyboard panels could contain the camera angles, direction, and notes describing specific colors or materials. Lighting scenarios and notes about the quality of lighting might prove to be helpful in storyboards, too.

Animation storyboards could contain the same information plus added notes and sketches referring to action in the scene. One storyboard panel per major action change in the animation motion would be a good place to start.

You might even include additional information pertaining to timing codes and dialogue or sound effects in the margins of the panels.

FIGURE 1.1   *High-quality storyboard panels by Andrew Paquette.*

If a storyboard is short and to the point, you can use just sheets of paper with several panels. For more complex projects, however, a large corkboard with individual panel sheets pinned in place gives a quick overview and is easy to change. Avoid the temptation to use sticky notepads—you might come back from lunch to find that a change in temperature or a breeze has caused your storyboard to scatter across the room like so many fall leaves in a storm.

The importance is not so much on the quality of the artwork of storyboards, but on how clearly it explains the scope and scheduling of the project.

Execution

Another crucial component of high productivity is planning the use of available talent and tools. Meet with team members and management to discuss some of the following topics before getting into actual production.

Choose a Team with Both Desire and Talent

Familiarize a broad range of personnel with the creation process and cultivate a pool of artists with a strong desire to apply the extra effort required to become proficient.

Forcing staff to become directly involved in the processes they are not comfortable with—be it modeling, lighting, materials, or animation—leads to bad office politics and pulls good talent from areas where they can be more productive.

Set Up a Productive Working Environment

Provide and maintain current and powerful computer systems. Hardware is a fixed-cost item and can be passed through the office, first as rendering stations, and then as clerical machines for years to come.

Do not, however, buy new hardware as the sole method of increasing productivity until you have mastered the art of scene optimization. Using new hardware as a fix for poor production practices is a waste of resources and time.

In a production office, pay particular attention to seating, lighting, and input devices. For example, a mouse and a tablet at each workstation can minimize stress and injury during long work sessions.

A clean, stable network system for network rendering can increase production (while requiring very little cost and maintenance).

Make sure that team members have an understanding of all the tools available to them before deciding on a production process. With a little practice, it will become habit to choose the right tool for the right job and you will avoid many of the pitfalls that come with forcing a tool to do a job for which it is not appropriate.

Know When to Stop

Focus on the elements of 3D production that will most impact the output and leave the rest by the wayside. For example, radiosity rendering might not add enough to your story line to justify the extra time involved in setting up or rendering (see Figure 1.2).

Do not use the technology for the sake of the technology alone.

Upon reaching a certain level of quality or communication value, it is important to be able to stop and move on to the next task. Perfection is an unobtainable goal—always worth striving for, but only up to the point where it becomes a burden on production.

FIGURE 1.2   *The image on the left, by the author, is of low quality and was made from scratch in about 4 hours. The image on the right, by Frances Gainer Davey, is very high quality and required about 16 hours to model the interior with furniture and accessories merged from other files.*

Integration and Output

You might be called upon to simultaneously create content for multiple uses. For example, you might be creating a computer game, but you will need higher-quality scenes for the marketing trailers and you might need even higher-quality still images.

Don't forget that more than one software package might be used to generate content. Therefore, you need appropriate converters and workflow methods to remain compatible throughout the project.

Develop Office Standards

Object-naming conventions, material and map libraries, and 3D object libraries are some of the standardized areas that can greatly enhance productivity.

Object naming cannot be stressed enough. Good naming control can provide an enormous return in productivity for a very minor cost.

Material naming standards and material library organization can also help avoid duplication of effort. Develop central depositories for maps and basic materials that are organized by category so that all users have easy access to a fundamental starting point to create custom materials for projects.

Work in Layers

Layers in this sense are elements such as background walls, mid-ground furniture, or foreground details that are based on distance from the camera or viewer.

Layers enable you to leave out detail to speed rendering, but also enable you to include detail as necessary to communicate information to the client. For example, you can simulate geometry that will not change with pre-rendered images for the background objects while modeling and manipulating the foreground objects.

Investigate compositing, the combining of 2D information in layers, with programs such as Discreet combustion or Adobe After Effects. Compositing might prove especially important in offices that use multiple software packages to generate content.

Layers also enable you to work discretely. For example, using layers, you can manipulate special image elements to modify shadows, reflections, or object color without having to re-render the entire 3D scene.

Cinematic Animation Techniques

Learn traditional film and television movement techniques so that you can develop and edit short-duration animations into a cohesive presentation.

These movement techniques will enable you to develop much smaller scenes with minimal camera movement—scenes that are easy to manage and that clients will find exciting and informative. Everyone wins!

Output Capabilities

Predetermine file types and image resolutions that will enable you to reuse content in a wide array of output types (for example, videotape and DVD, streaming media and web sites, and large-printed still images). Render all scenes to individual still image sequences and convert to compressed animation files as necessary.

Summary

Undoubtedly, more processes can be streamlined in a typical office to speed up content creation; if you can make use of several of the suggestions in this chapter, however, it will be a good beginning.

Start with an office-wide naming scheme and materials organization, and then focus on scene optimization (only modeling what you will see and making that as efficient as possible). All the while, focus on integrating a new spirit of communication between those who order the work and those who do the work to minimize the necessity of changes later in the production process.

Finally, consider the benefits that compositing and layering of scene elements provide to speed the workflow. It is not uncommon in film and video work to combine 30 or more layers that come from a variety of production sources into a single output image or animation. These methods will work equally well for architecture, computer gaming, film and television, and engineering fields.

CHAPTER 2

Important Fundamental Concepts in 3ds max 6

In This Chapter

In this chapter, you learn some of the important basic concepts that you need to know to fully understand the 3ds max 6 tools and processes.

Read through this chapter quickly for an overview of the processes, and then read through more slowly, experimenting with your own simple scenes to test the concepts in their basic form. After a little practice, you will find that you've incorporated these concepts into your daily work routine and your productivity will be enhanced without you having to think about what you are doing.

This chapter covers the following topics:

- **Coordinate systems**—The various ways to describe the three axes (X, Y, and Z) in 3D space.

- **Layers**—A method of organizing objects into common groups and assigning properties to those objects.

- **Setup and startup files**—Files that store parameters that you want to have active when creating new files.

- **Lofting**—A powerful modeling technique that requires a knowledge of basic concepts for an understanding of how to work efficiently.

Key Terms

- **Coordinate system**—Coordinate systems in 3ds max 6 define the directions of the X, Y, and Z axes as they relate to the 3D workspace.

- **Layers**—Layers are organizational entities used to select or set properties of sets of objects on the active layer.

- **Lofting**—Lofting is the modeling technique that creates 3D objects by extruding one or more 2D cross-section shapes along a 2D path.

Coordinate Systems in 3ds max 6

Users can easily identify with the World reference coordinate system in 3ds max 6 because it is defined by the default grid planes that show in the viewports when you start max. However, the World reference coordinate system is just the starting point for the possibilities for maneuvering and manipulating objects in 3D space.

I emphasize coordinate systems because one issue in 3ds max that I see as a fundamental hindrance to production for many users, both new and experienced, is a lack of understanding of the complete coordinate system.

> **tip**
>
> The World coordinate axes in 3ds max 6 follow common mathematical practice. If you were graphing on paper, X would be the horizontal axis and Y the vertical axis of the paper. 3D space is defined by the Z-axis, which projects off the paper toward you.

To use several important commands (the Align and Transform Type-In commands being the most notable), 3ds max 6 users must understand the various coordinate systems in the software. In both Align and Transform Type-In, you are asked to enter numeric data to align or array objects along the X-, Y-, or Z-axis. However, the direction of X, Y, or Z depends on the active coordinate system and the active viewport.

Reference Coordinate System

On the main toolbar menu, to the right of the Transform buttons, you will see a field with View in it by default. This is the reference coordinate system that is currently active. Click the View field and you see a pop-up menu of the different reference coordinate systems available (see Figure 2.1).

> **caution**
>
> There is also a View render window to the far right of the main toolbar that you do not want to change.

A simple walkthrough is provided here to illustrate some of the differences between the various reference coordinate systems. You can either try the exercises on your computer or, better yet, just read along to get the idea and then go to the computer and do the exercises. In any case, at some point, you should sit down and just play with very simple objects to get a feel for how the system works. As with many 3ds max 6 tools, don't try to learn this during a deadline crunch on a large project. With a little practice, the reference coordinate systems will become second nature and your productivity will increase accordingly. At the end of this section, you can read a summary of the attributes of each system.

note

Just performing a set of orchestrated steps is not conducive to learning a complex program such as 3ds max 6. It is far more important to use exercises as a guide to investigate a process (and after the exercises, you should immediately try your own version of the process).

Although numbered steps are necessary for many exercises in this book, it is best that you concentrate on learning the underlying concepts and processes presented.

FIGURE 2.1   *Menu showing available reference coordinate systems for 3ds max 6.*

Getting the Lay of the Land

Start with a new session of 3ds max 6. The display should be set to four viewports: Top, Front, Left, and Perspective. In the Top viewport, create a cylinder in the middle of the display (see Figure 2.2) and click the Zoom Extents All button, the upper-right button at the lower-right corner of the display (see Figure 2.3).

The following subsections provide descriptions and some exercises that highlight the individual reference coordinate systems that appear in Figure 2.1.

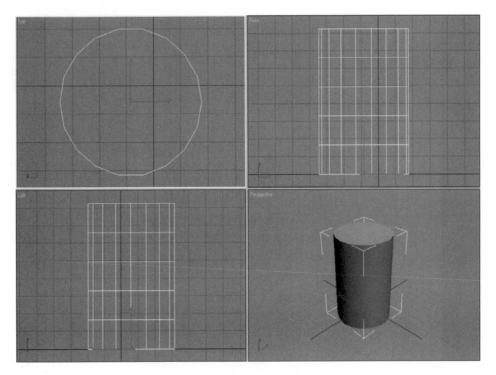

FIGURE 2.2   *All viewports fill with a cylinder.*

FIGURE 2.3   *Click the Zoom Extents All button, the upper-right button of the eight navigation buttons at the lower right of the display.*

View Reference Coordinate System

In the Top viewport, notice that the red and gray axis tripod at the bottom center of the cylinder shows positive X to the right, positive Y up, and positive Z out toward the viewer and that the current active reference coordinate system is set to View in the main toolbar (see Figure 2.4).

FIGURE 2.4   *The View reference coordinate system is the default setting found on the main toolbar.*

Right-click in the Front viewport to activate that viewport without deselecting the cylinder. Notice that the axis tripod adjusts to make the positive axis point in the same relative direction as was in the Top viewport when it was active. Right-click in the Left viewport to see a similar change. The axis tripod adapts itself to the orthographic viewports while in the View reference coordinate system so that positive X is always to the right, positive Y is always up, and positive Z is always out toward the viewer.

Now, right-click in the Perspective viewport and notice that the axis tripod corresponds to the World reference coordinate system by aligning with the Home grid. You can check it against the small tricolor tripod in the lower-left corner of each viewport that always indicates the World reference coordinate system. This is true for all nonorthographic viewports while in the View reference coordinate system—Perspective, User, Camera, and Light viewports.

Screen Reference Coordinate System

Right-click in the Top viewport to activate it, and then click View on the main toolbar and choose the Screen reference coordinate system from the list. Right-click in the other viewports and notice that the axis tripod behaves the same as it did in View mode.

The Screen reference coordinate system is exactly the same as View for orthographic viewports—positive X-axis to the right, Y up, and Z out. However, for nonorthographic viewports, the positive Z-axis points out of the screen toward the viewer. Use the Arc Rotate command, at the lower-right corner of the display, in the Perspective viewport, and watch the axis tripod move in the other viewports.

The Screen reference coordinate system enables you to move objects in space based on your line of site in nonorthographic viewports and proves useful for moving flying logos across the scene, for example.

World Reference Coordinate System

Right-click in the Top viewport and switch to the World reference coordinate system. Right-click in the other viewports and you can see that World reference coordinate system is always active for all viewport types.

Parent Reference Coordinate System

The next reference coordinate system in the list is Parent, which requires an object to be hierarchically

note

Hierarchical linking is beyond the scope of this fundamental exercise, but the option will be obvious to you when you use linking.

linked to another object in the parent/child relationship. In the Parent reference coordinate system, the child always uses the parents' Local reference coordinate system (discussed next).

Local Reference Coordinate System

Right-click in the Top viewport and choose Local in the reference coordinate system list. Right-click in the other viewports and the axis tripod is the same as it was for the World reference coordinate system. This is a coincidence because you created the cylinder in the Top viewport. Right-click in the Perspective viewport, click the Select and Rotate button on the main toolbar, and rotate the cylinder roughly 45 degrees in both the X and Y axes by picking and dragging on the red or green circle of the Rotate gizmo in the viewport (see Figure 2.5).

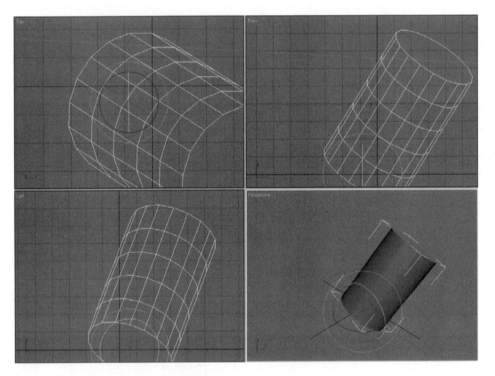

FIGURE 2.5   *Click the Select and Rotate button on the main toolbar and rotate the cylinder about 45 degrees in the X and Y axes.*

At this point, notice that even though you had the reference coordinate system set to Local, it switched automatically to View when you picked the Select and Rotate button. The current reference coordinate system is sticky for each transform: Move, Rotate, and Scale. After you set the reference coordinate system, it is retained for that transform until you change it again. The axis tripod also changes to the Transform gizmo when the transform buttons are picked.

tip

Get into the habit of constantly monitoring the reference coordinate setting and it will soon become an automatic reaction that you will not have to think about.

Right-click in the Top viewport, click the Select and Move transform button, and set the reference coordinate system to Local. Right-click in the other viewports and you can see that the Move Transform gizmo orients itself with the object as it was created (see Figure 2.6). Familiarize yourself with the Local reference coordinate system because it is an especially powerful production tool.

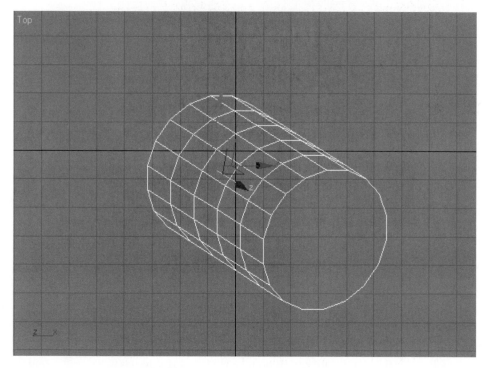

FIGURE 2.6   *In Local reference coordinate mode, the axis tripod and the Transform gizmo stay aligned with the object's creation axes.*

Grid Reference Coordinate System

The Grid reference coordinate system requires that you create a new Grid Helper object as the active work plane. Right-click in the Top viewport to activate it.

In the Create panel, Geometry rollout, click the Box button, and check the AutoGrid option just above the Box button to activate the feature. As you move your cursor over the cylinder, notice a tricolor cursor track the face normal of the face under the cursor. Hold the Alt key, and pick and drag a Box primitive on the end cap of the cylinder. Click the Select Object button on the main toolbar and select the new grid object at the top of the cylinder (see Figure 2.7).

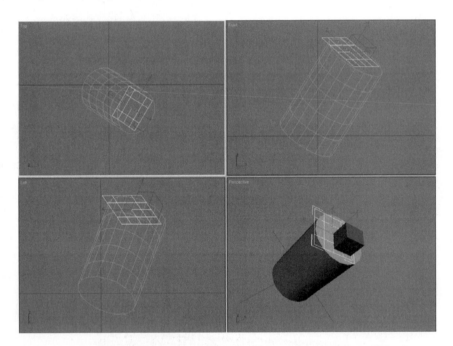

FIGURE 2.7   *You can create objects directly on any surface with the AutoGrid feature. Pressing Alt while you do this creates a permanent grid object in that plane.*

Holding the Alt key while creating an object in AutoGrid mode concurrently makes the new grid in the scene and makes it the active grid.

Click the Select and Move button and switch to the grid reference coordinate system, and the X, Y, Z axes of the grid are used for the current transform.

With the new grid object selected in the active viewport, right-click the grid and, in the pop-up menu, choose Activate HomeGrid to return to the default grid system. You can have as many of these grid helper objects as you want, but only one can be active at any time. You can reactivate the new grid at any time.

Pick Reference Coordinate System

In the Pick reference coordinate system, you can use the coordinate system of another object in the scene as the current system.

note

Face normals in 3ds max are invisible vectors that point perpendicular from any face. They are used as alignment tool aids and for face visibility, for example.

Right-click in the Top viewport to activate it and create a small sphere to one side of the cylinder. Click the Select and Rotate transform button, change the reference coordinate system to Pick, and pick on the cylinder in the Top viewport. The sphere is now using the cylinder's Local reference coordinate system axes directions. Also, Cylinder01 is added to the list of available reference coordinate systems.

Pivot Point Options

Another aid to production that goes hand in hand with the reference coordinate systems is the active Pivot Point type. Just to the right of the reference coordinate system window is a flyout menu with three choices of Pivot Point types. Choosing the bottom option, called Use Transform Coordinate Center, changes the rotation center to be at the base of the cylinder (see Figure 2.8).

note

Notice how the Rotate reference coordinate system is not aligned with the sphere, even though the sphere's Transform Gizmo is centered on its active pivot point.

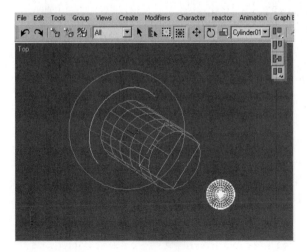

FIGURE 2.8   *Use the Use Transform Coordinate Center pivot point to rotate the sphere around the cylinder's Local axis pivot point.*

Use Pivot Point Center

In the Top viewport, select all the objects in the scene. With the Use Pivot Point Center option (top flyout button) set, notice that as you rotate the selection set, each object is transformed based on its current active reference coordinate system around its own individual pivot point rather than the center of the selection set. This is especially interesting when you are in Rotate mode.

Use Selection Center

Choose Use Selection Center (middle flyout button), and you see that the entire selection set of objects uses a single pivot point in the geometric center of the bounding box of the selected objects. This is most appropriate for rotations, also.

Use Transform Coordinate Center

The Use Transform Coordinate Center (bottom flyout button) uses the 0,0,0 Absolute World coordinate point except when the Pick reference coordinate system is active. The selected object then uses the Pick object's pivot point as its own.

Summary

The following list summarizes the attributes of the various reference coordinate systems:

- **View**—The axis tripod adapts itself to each orthographic viewport so that positive X-axis is to the right, positive Y-axis is up, and positive Z-axis is perpendicular out of the display. Nonorthographic viewports resort to using World reference coordinate system.
- **Screen**—Same as View in orthographic viewports. In nonorthographic viewports, the positive Z-axis always points at the viewer.
- **World**—This coordinate system always corresponds to the Absolute World coordinates.
- **Parent**—The child object uses the parent's Local coordinate system in a hierarchically linked parent/child relationship.
- **Local**—The coordinates always remain with the object as it was created, regardless of the object's rotation angle.
- **Grid**—Uses the active grid system's coordinate system.
- **Pick**—Uses the Local coordinate system of another object that is picked in the scene.

For the Align, Array, and Mirror commands in VIZ and max, always check the current active reference coordinate system to see which X-, Y-, and Z-axis is being used by the command. The mode is noted in the Align or Array dialog (see Figure 2.9).

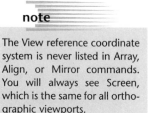

note

The View reference coordinate system is never listed in Array, Align, or Mirror commands. You will always see Screen, which is the same for all orthographic viewports.

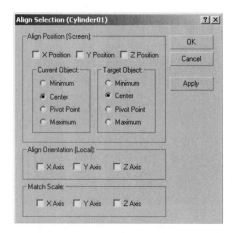

FIGURE 2.9   *The currently active reference coordinate system is shown in parentheses at the top left of the Align Selection dialog.*

Layers

Working in layers in 3ds max 6 is an important tool in a production environment. Although layers have been available in previous versions of 3ds max, version 6 offers improvements in workflow that make them more user friendly and useful.

Layers are organizational elements that contain objects that you place on the layer. You can then use the layers simply as selection tools that enable you to quickly select specific objects to transform them or to change the visibility of the layer's objects in the viewports or the renderer. You also can use layers to set the object properties or radiosity lighting properties for all objects currently on that layer, for example.

I do not want to rewrite the 3ds max 6 User Reference manual's layer information in this book, but do want to make you aware of the concept behind this production tool and to point out that essentially two places affect how layers are managed: the Layers Manager and the Object Properties dialog.

Layers Manager

Figure 2.10 shows the Layers Manager opened. The scene contains four layers, three with teapots, and the default layer with nothing on the layer.

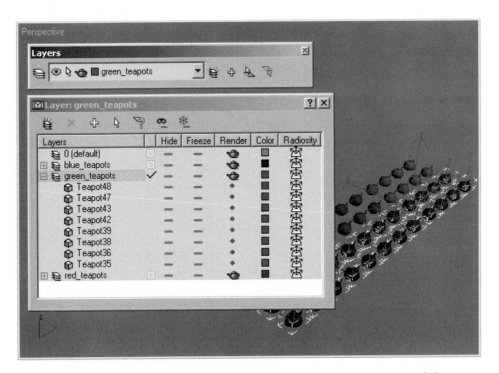

FIGURE 2.10   *The Layer menu and Layers Manager dialog opened to show some of the options available for creating and manipulating layers.*

This menu and dialog box enable you to create and manipulate layers, and to toggle properties such as the renderability, visibility, and radiosity settings of the Layers objects on or off.

I encourage you to use the 3ds max 6 Help files to further investigate layers and their functionality. Work with a simple file similar to this teapot example so that you learn the fundamentals of how the concept can be applied to your production workflow.

Object Properties Dialog

One issue that can be a bit confusing when first using layers in 3ds max 6 is that, by default, objects you create in max have their properties determined by the object settings, not by any layer settings. This means that no amount of layer manipulation will have any bearing on the properties of the objects on that layer until you enable the By Layer option for the object's properties.

Figure 2.11 shows the Object Properties General tab and Advanced Lighting tab. In the General tab, the Display Properties and Rendering Control of the selected objects have been set to By Layer control, whereas the Motion Blur in the General tab and the Geometric Object Properties in the Adv. Lighting tab are still set to the default By Object control.

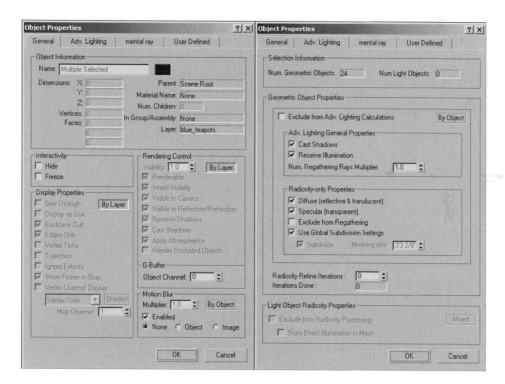

FIGURE 2.11   *For layer settings to affect objects, the properties must be changed from the default By Object to By Layer.*

Again, search the 3ds max 6 Help files for "using layers to organize a scene" for a more complete overview and more details on layers.

Settings and Startup Configuration

You can use several files in 3ds max 6 to enhance productivity (for example, 3dsmax.ini, maxstart.max, plugin.ini, and MaxStartUI.cui). You can use these files to store settings such as the units that are used (metric or U.S. standard units, for example) and menu and viewport layouts that max starts with when you open a new scene or reset the current scene.

Of these files, maxstart.max is the most important time-saving tool. Unlike the other setup files that have preset default values, it does not exist until you create it.

The maxstart.max file enables you to save the state of the workspace so that it comes up with the same settings each time you start a new file or reset the scene.

Although it would be possible to save a maxstart.max file that contains objects or lighting to load with each new file or reset action, you usually only want to change the viewport configurations to your preferences.

The maxstart.max file should be saved in the /3dsmax6/scenes subdirectory by default, but you can save it anywhere on your hard drive and use the Configure Paths dialog box to point to the location.

In Chapter 3, "Fundamental Modeling Techniques: The Building Blocks," you save a maxstart.max file that be used throughout this book.

Lofting Basic Concepts

In my view, lofting is the most powerful modeling tool in 3ds max, but one that is often underutilized because of some seemingly "strange" behavior when using it. The behavior is not really strange, but lofting is unlike any creation method you use in other software, so it requires that you know a few simple concepts for it to make sense.

But I Don't Speak the Language

To understand max lofting fully, you need to know the following terms:

- **Shape**—A shape is a 2D object in max. It might occupy 3D space as a helix shape does, but it does not have any surface information. A shape has a name and a color.

note

The term *lofting* comes from old ship-building practices where the patterns for ribs of a ship were all laid out in the upstairs loft of the ship builder's shop. Long, thin metal bands, or splines, were set on edge and bent to the curvature of the hull at given points along the keel. To hold the splines in place so that the lines could be traced on the patterns, the ship designer place heavy steel or lead "ducks" at the tangency points. To create the hull, the ribs (loft shapes) were then attached along the keel (loft path) and the planking was attached to form the hull (mesh object).

- **Spline**—A shape must contain at least one sub-object level spline, but a shape is a compound shape if it has more than one spline. For example, the Donut primitive is a compound shape made of two splines (that is, concentric circles).

- **Loft path**—The shape that defines the extrusion length of the loft object.

- **Loft shape**—The shape that defines the cross-sections of the loft object.

  A loft object can have only one closed or open spline as a path. A loft object can have an unlimited number of open or closed shapes as cross-sections.

  Each shape or path can have an unlimited number of vertices, and different shapes can have different numbers of vertices each.

  Each shape on a path must have the same number of splines. For example, you cannot loft a Circle and a Donut primitive on the same loft path.

- **Local reference coordinate system**—3ds max 6 has several different reference coordinate systems, as you learned earlier in this chapter, but the Local system is most important in lofting. Essentially, the Local system is the coordinate system of the shape as it is created. When you create a shape in any given viewport, the rule is that the local positive X-axis is to the right, the local positive Y-axis is up, and the local positive Z-axis is out toward the viewer. This Local reference coordinate system stays relative to the shape as the shape is rotated.

- **Pivot point**—The pivot point of a shape is usually positioned at the geometric center of the bounding box of the shape. It can be repositioned through the Hierarchy panel. The pivot point defines the apex of the X, Y, and Z axes of a shape.

- **First vertex**—Each spline has a first vertex indicated by a white box when in sub-object Vertex mode (see Figure 2.12). Open splines can have either end vertex as the first vertex, and closed splines can have any vertex as the first vertex.

The pivot point and first vertex are very important in the lofting process, and a lack of understanding of them is probably the prime reason for frustration while lofting.

The pivot point of the shape attaches to the first vertex of the path.

The orientation of the shape on the path is a bit more complex. I'll talk you through it here and show an example, then discuss it in more detail later. The local Z-axis of the shape aligns itself "down" the path, and the local Y-axis of the shape aligns with the local Z-axis of the path (see Figure 2.13).

tip

The first vertex of a shape can always be seen when in sub-object Vertex editing mode. However, you can view the first vertex at any time by selecting the shape(s), right-clicking and choosing Properties, and by checking Vertex Ticks in Display Properties. You must be in the default By Object mode, also.

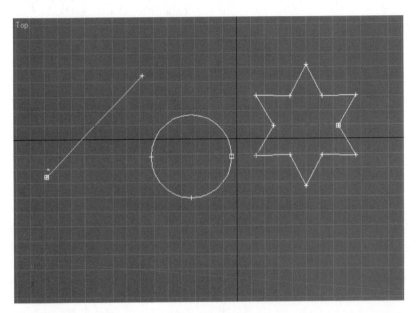

Figure 2.12 *Viewport showing white box indicating the first vertex of various shapes and the red X and Y axes tripod at the pivot point of the circle.*

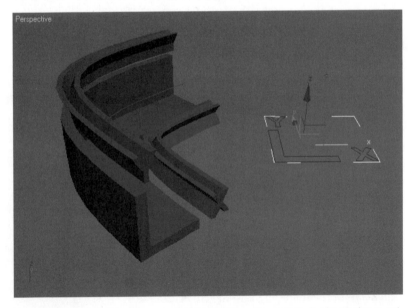

Figure 2.13 *Curved path and L shape created in the Top viewport. Loft object shows orientation of the shape on the path. You also can see the local axis directions of the 2D shapes as indicated by the Move Transform gizmo arrows.*

Lofting Options

The lofting process itself is simple enough, but a couple of options are worth mentioning. You can access lofting from the Compound Objects pull-down menu (via Create panel, Geometry, Compound Objects) (see Figure 2.14). You must have a valid 2D shape selected or the Loft button will be grayed out in the Object Type rollout.

The Creation Method rollout contains two options: Get Path and Get Shape. The usual workflow is to have the path selected and to use the Get Shape option. However, you could select the shape and use Get Path. The determining factor is that whichever object is selected remains in place and the other, shape or path, reorients and moves to the selected shape. Generally, I prefer to select the path and use Get Shape.

Just below Get Path and Get Shape are some very important options; Move, Copy, and Instance. The default is Instance. This means that a clone of the shape jumps to the path, not the original shape itself. The advantage of this option is that you can modify the original 2D shape and the lofted 3D mesh changes accordingly.

The Move option actually moves the original shape to the path, and Copy places a clone of the shape with no connection to the original (making either choice much less editable). I have never found the need to use either Move or Copy.

In Figure 2.15, most of the walls, glazing, and seating are lofted from 2D shapes, allowing for quick and easy editing.

As mentioned earlier, the fundamental process is simple enough, but you must understand more options to make an efficient lofting modeling choice.

FIGURE 2.14

The Loft panel with Name and Color, Creation Method, Path Parameters, and Skin Parameters rollouts expanded.

FIGURE 2.15   *This simple interior example uses lofting to create the walls and glazing at the left and right and elements of the seating. This allows for quick editing at the 2D shape level to make major changes to the 3D objects.*

The Importance of the First Vertex in Lofting

3ds max 6 builds the lofted mesh objects by first connecting the first vertex on each shape along the path and then building a mesh surface with the shape steps and path steps. Therefore, the relative position of the shape's first vertex determines the twisting of the object along the path.

To remove (or apply more) twisting, you must modify the loft object itself at sub-object level to rotate either of the shapes on the loft path—not the original shapes, mind you, but the instance clone of the shape that has attached itself to the loft path. Figure 2.16 shows a circle and a rectangle lofted along a straight-line path that illustrates the twisting that can occur.

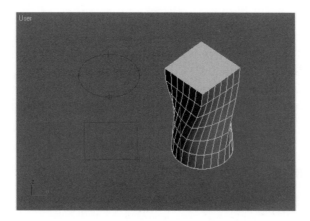

FIGURE 2.16   *Circle and rectangle shapes lofted along a straight line produce a twisted object because of the relative positions of first vertex of each shape.*

By modifying the lofted object at sub-object Shape level and rotating the circle on the loft path by 45 degrees around its local Z-axis, you can remove the twisting (see Figure 2.17).

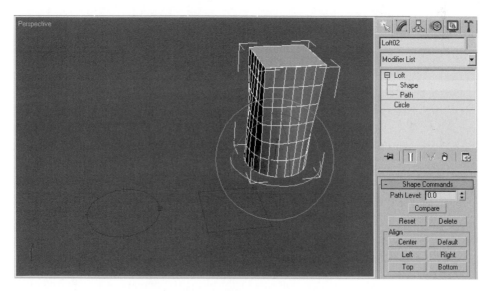

FIGURE 2.17   *By rotating the circle shape at the base of the loft object around its local Z-axis, you can easily remove or enhance the twist.*

Lofting Efficiency

If you want 3ds max 6 to be a cost-effective tool in your office, you *must* keep models as simple as possible. (Modeling overhead is the primary hindrance to production that I encounter in my training sessions.) Each vertex and face in a model uses valuable computer overhead, and you can quickly overwhelm even the most powerful systems and render them ineffective in an production scenario.

Lofting offers controls for adjusting mesh density of models while retaining the necessary details. First, you have to learn two new terms:

- **Shape steps**—Shape steps are intermediate points between vertices of the shape that define curvature in the connecting shape segment
- **Path steps**—Path steps have the same function between vertices on the path.

When a shape is lofted along a path, segments are created in the loft mesh for each vertex and path/shape step. These segments can clearly be seen in the preceding loft example, which has Edged Faces toggled on.

Right-clicking the selected loft object and going to the Object Properties dialog shows that the object has 332 faces. In the Modify panel, Skin Parameters rollout, there are two numeric fields: Shape Steps and Path Steps. Each is set to 5 by default in 3ds max 6.

Setting the path steps to 0 reduces the information that shows the curvature between the path's vertices. The object shows less definition in the transition from circular base to rectangular top (see Figure 2.18).

Increasing the path steps to 3 might give an acceptable level of detail depending on the distance from the camera or the background and leaves the overall face count at 236. You must be the judge of how much detail is enough, but you have the option to change it at any time to optimize the object for any occasion.

Reducing the shape steps to 0 of this loft object ruins the integrity of the object because the base is changed to a rectangular shape. A circle has four vertices and removing any intermediate steps that define curvature makes it rectangular (see Figure 2.19).

Increasing the shape steps to 3 might result in an acceptable mesh object with a total face count of 156, less than half the original 332 faces.

The important fact is that you can easily adjust the density of your lofted objects at any time to achieve an optimum balance between the detail of the object and the efficiency of the object, which is so critical to production.

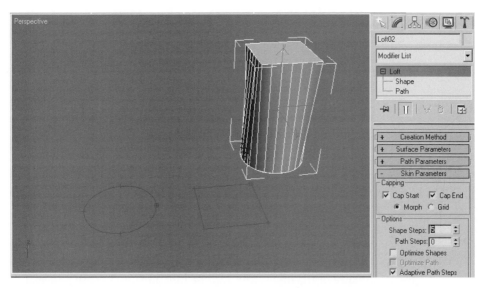

FIGURE 2.18   *Reducing the path steps from 5 to 0 reduces the definition of the transition from circular to rectangular along the length of the object. It reduces the number of faces from 332 to 92, with corresponding loss of visual detail.*

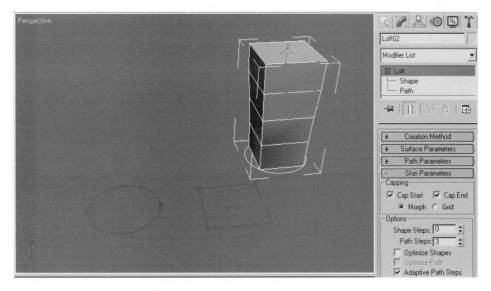

FIGURE 2.19   *Setting the shape steps to 0 completely ruins the integrity of the intended mesh by removing all curvature from the circular shape.*

Summary

In this chapter, you learned these fundamental concepts:

- **Reference coordinate systems**—A good understanding of the reference coordinate systems in 3ds max 6 is absolutely necessary to getting the most out of the software. It is essentially an easy system to learn but can be a bit confusing to new users. Take the time to practice on simple scenes and you will soon make it an integral part of your daily workflow.

- **Layers**—3ds max 6 has an updated and improved layer system that gives you added control for managing objects in your scenes.

- **Startup files**—You learned the principles of how to use maxstart.max files to standardize the configuration of the display layout of 3ds max 6. This will provide a smoother workflow when starting new scenes.

- **Lofting**—This chapter touched on the fundamental issues in lofting that are responsible for most confusion when initially learning to loft. Knowing about the importance of the first vertex and the functionality of path and shape steps will give you the basis you need to take full advantage of the power of lofting.

PART II

Outdoor Scene with Ship

CHAPTER 3

Fundamental Modeling Techniques: The Building Blocks

In This Chapter

In this chapter, you learn modeling techniques and processes that are among the most widely used and most important fundamental topics of using 3ds max 6:

- **Startup files**—By setting up of a standardized display space, you learn to smooth your workflow.

- **2D shapes**—Creating 2D shapes and converting them to 3D objects can be a flexible and efficient method of working. You learn about compound shapes and 2D sub-object editing methods.

- **Modifiers and the stack**—You also learn the important concept of how the 3ds max 6 modifier stack functions to allow flexible editing throughout the history of an object's creation.

- **Alignment tools and grid objects**—You perform exercises that illustrate some valuable ways to align objects to objects and build on specific planes in 3D space.

As with the other chapters in this book, step through the exercises provided to create, apply materials, and light scenes. But most importantly, stay focused on the lessons and concepts being introduced so that you can use them in your work.

Just doing the exercises will result only in a reading comprehension lesson if you do not stop to think about the process itself and imagine ways in which that process can work for you.

Key Terms

- **System units**—The internal mathematical units used for mathematical calculations. Options are U.S. Standard or Metric units.

- **Display units**—The manner in which system units are converted and displayed in numeric fields on the screen.

Standardizing Your Display Space

The exercises in this book will be much easier to follow if we standardize the units of measurement in the display, so the first thing you will learn is to set up a file that causes 3ds max 6 to open with specific settings each time.

The file is called the maxstart.max and does not exist on your system until you actually create it. After you save the file with the settings you want, it will be seen by max on startup or when you perform a Reset command from the File pull-down menu. There is only one maxstart.max file, and each time you open, edit, and save it, the changes will be in effect from that point on.

The first step in Exercise 3.1 is to check to see what the default system units are set to. For all U.S. copies of 3ds max 6, the system units are set to 1 unit = 1 inch. Again, the system units are used internally for all mathematical calculation and should be left alone unless you have very specific reasons to change this setting (for example, if you always work in metric units).

You will change the Grid Spacing settings and the viewport configuration for startup purposes, as well.

note

The units settings, for both system units and display units are stored in a file called 3dsmax.ini, which is in the \3dsmax6\ root directory. Information is automatically updated in this file when you change it.

Exercise 3.1   Creating a Settings Startup File

1. Open a new 3ds max 6 session. The default display should show four viewports with the Perspective viewport active as indicated by a yellow border around the viewport. The default Grid Spacing should be set at 10.0 generic units. If your display does not show four viewports, you can use the Min/Max Toggle button (Alt+W) (see Figure 3.1).

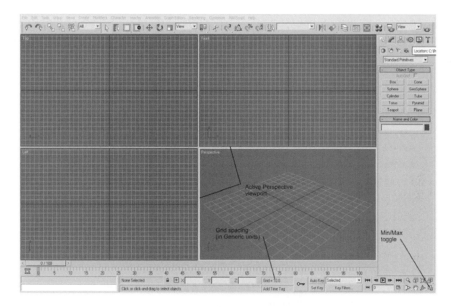

FIGURE 3.1   *The default display should show Grid spacing of 10.0 generic units and four viewports with the Perspective viewport active. The Min/Max Toggle button switches from a single to multiple viewport display.*

2. To change the System Units settings, click the Customize pull-down menu and choose Units Setup from the menu options (see Figure 3.2).

FIGURE 3.2   *To change the System Units setting, click the Customize pull-down menu and choose Units Setup.*

3. In the Units Setup dialog, click System Unit Setup and make sure that it is set to 1 Unit = 1.0 Inches in the System Unit Scale area (see Figure 3.3). Click OK to close the System Unit Setup dialog.

FIGURE 3.3   *Make sure that System Unit Scale is set to 1 Unit = 1.0 Inches and click OK to close this dialog.*

4. In the Units Setup dialog, pick the U.S. Standard radio button and set it to use Feet w/Fractional Inches. The default rounding value of the nearest 1/8 inch is fine (see Figure 3.4). Click OK.

note

The Default Units radio buttons in the Units Setup dialog are for numeric data entry only. If you type a number with no sign after it, 3ds max 6 treats it as feet. If you want to enter inches or feet and inches, you must use the appropriate single quote or double quote signs respectively. You can set the default for whatever makes the most sense in your production.

FIGURE 3.4   *Set the Display Unit Scale to U.S. Standard and Feet w/Fractional Inches to the nearest 1/8.*

5. Now, you set the World coordinate grid spacing that is visible in the four viewports. This grid can be used as a point of reference when creating objects or to snap to for accuracy when creating or moving objects. From the Customize pull-down menu, choose Grid and Snap Settings. In the Grid and Snap Settings dialog, click the Home Grid tab. Enter the following, as shown in Figure 3.5:

■ Grid Spacing = 1"

■ Major Lines Every Nth Grid Line = 12

■ Perspective View Grid Extent = 120

6. Close the Grid and Snap Settings dialog. From the File pull-down menu, choose Save As (see Figure 3.6) and name the file maxstart.max. The default \3dsmax6\ scenes\ subdirectory is fine. Now, any time you open 3ds max 6 or do a File, Reset from the pull-down menu, these settings are automatically loaded. Exit 3ds max 6.

note

The Grid Spacing is the minimum possible size of the grid, the Major Lines Every Nth Grid Line sets the number of grid lines before a darker line and it is the zoom factor that the grid will resize itself to when you zoom in and out of a viewport. The Perspective View Grid Extent is the size of the physical grid in the Perspective viewport—in this case, 120 inches (no sign needed). However, the usable grid actually extends to infinity.

note

You can place it in any subdirectory as long as you point to the subdirectory in the Customize, Configure Paths menu, General tab. In a larger production house, this might be on the main server (so that everyone starts with the same settings, for example).

FIGURE 3.5
Set the Grid Spacing to 1", Major Lines Every Nth Grid Line to 12, and Perspective View Grid Extent to 120.

FIGURE 3.6
From the File, Save As menu, name the file maxstart.max and save it into the default \3dsmax6\scenes subdirectory.

2D Shapes—A Foundation of Efficient Modeling

In this section, you learn a few important principles of working with 2D shapes that will be used as the basis for modeling more complex 3D objects. An understanding of the two principles—compound shapes and sub-object editing—will make quick work of many tasks that would be difficult without the fundamental knowledge of how the processes function. In Exercise 3.2, you create shapes that have no function other than to illustrate the principles that you will then apply to real models in the next section of this chapter:

- **Compound shape**—A compound shape is a shape made of two or more splines. You can use this principle to create very complex 3D objects that have voids and islands within the outer closed boundary of the shape.

- **Sub-object editing**—Each shape is comprised of three sub-objects: vertex, segment, and spline. A vertex is a nondimensional point in space, a segment is a line that connects two vertices, and a spline is an entity comprised of vertices and segments. A shape always has one spline, but can have an unlimited number.

The Principles of Compound Shapes

Compound shapes are just shapes with multiple spline sub-objects. Although the underlying principle is simple enough, the power inherent in the concept is one of the most productive you will learn.

Exercise 3.2   Creating Compound Shapes

1. Open a new 3ds max 6 session or go to the File pull-down menu and choose Reset.

2. If you're prompted to save any changes to the existing file, choose Yes, and place the file in an appropriate subdirectory if it contains any information you want to save. If you have nothing to save or if the prompt is "Do You Really Want to Reset," choose Yes.

3. Right-click in the Top viewport to activate it. Even though you can left-click in the viewport to activate the viewport, it is unwise to do so. You might be in a transform function and can inadvertently move or rotate an object. Always use right-clicking to activate new viewports.

4. In the Create panel, Shapes panel (see Figure 3.7), click the Rectangle button. In the Top viewport, drag a large rectangle. It is automatically named Rectangle01 and assigned a color.

5. Create another, smaller rectangle inside the first, similar to Figure 3.8. The new rectangle is named Rectangle02 and has a new color assigned to it. You can pick the object color swatch in the Create or Modify panel to open the Object color dialog. There, you can clear the Assign Random Colors check box to use a constant color for all new objects.

FIGURE 3.7
2D shapes are created from the Create panel, Shapes panel. Click the Rectangle button to create a rectangle in the Top viewport.

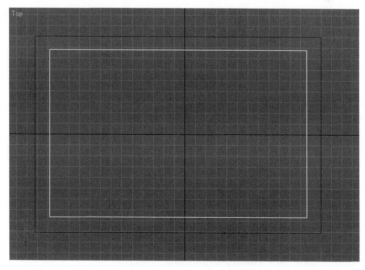

FIGURE 3.8   *Create another rectangle just inside the first rectangle in the Top viewport.*

6. On the main toolbar, click the Select by Name button (keyboard shortcut H), and you see Rectangle01 and Rectangle02 listed as objects in the scene. Highlight both rectangles in the Select Objects dialog (see Figure 3.9) and click the Select button in the dialog. Both rectangles will be white in the wireframe viewports and colored with white brackets in the shaded viewport to indicate that they are selected.

note

The colors are automatically and randomly assigned and are just for easier visualization in the viewports.

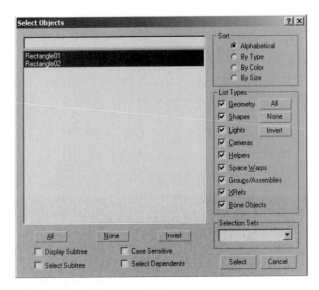

FIGURE 3.9   *Use the Select by Name button on the main toolbar to highlight both the names in the Select Objects dialog and click Select to select both rectangles in the scene.*

7. In the Modify panel, Modifier List, choose Extrude (see Figure 3.10). This turns the two shapes into two 3D objects with no thickness.

8. In the Modify panel, Parameters rollout, enter 2' in the Amount field and press Enter. This extrudes the 2 objects into boxes with a height of 2 feet (see Figure 3.11).

tip

You can also use the Select Object button (arrow on the main toolbar) to pick objects in the scene. Holding the Ctrl key while picking adds to or deselects from the selection set, whereas holding the Alt key while picking deselects objects only.

FIGURE 3.10 *With the two rectangles selected, go to the Modify panel, Modifier List, and choose Extrude. This applies an Extrude modifier with no thickness amount.*

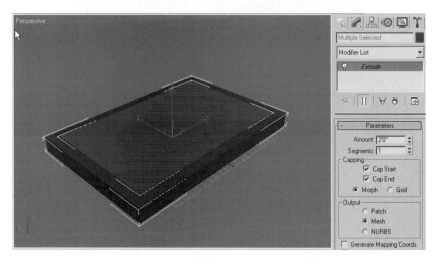

FIGURE 3.11 *In the Modifier panel, Parameters rollout, enter 2 in the Amount field and press Enter. You now have 2 boxes each 2 feet high.*

9. This is not a good situation in modeling, but illustrates a point on the importance of understanding how compound shapes function. What you have here are two simple rectangular shapes extruded to the same height and, in the Perspective viewport, you can clearly see that the software is having trouble showing the coincident surfaces at the top of the boxes. Just below the Extrude modifier in the Stack view, click the Remove Modifier from the Stack button, which looks like a trash can. You now have two shapes again: Rectangle01 and Rectangle02.

note

It is good to note here that each rectangle is a shape made up of one spline, four segments, and four vertices. Each has a name and a color associated with it.

10. Click the Select Object button and, in the Top viewport, pick the outer rectangle called Rectangle01. You now convert this shape from a parametric Rectangle primitive shape into an editable spline to enable you to work at sub-object level. In the Top viewport, right-click and, in the Convert To menu of the Quad menu, choose Convert to Editable Spline (see Figure 3.12). The Modify panel changes from a parametric rectangle menu to an editable spline menu.

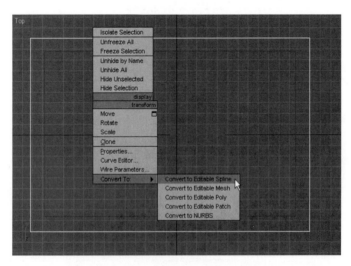

FIGURE 3.12 *By converting this shape from a parametric Rectangle primitive shape into an editable spline, you can work at sub-object level.*

11. In the Modify panel, Geometry rollout, click the Attach button (see Figure 3.13). In the Top viewport, move the cursor over the smaller rectangle and pick it when you see the Attach cursor (a cross with four circles and an arrow). Click the Attach button to disable it when you are done.

FIGURE 3.13   *In the Modify panel, Geometry rollout, click the Attach button. This enables you to pick other shapes in the scene to attach them to form a compound shape.*

12. On the main toolbar, click the Select by Name button. You have only one shape, called Rectangle01. The new compound shape is a shape made of two splines and has taken the name of the object to which the shape was attached. Click Cancel to close the Select Objects dialog.

13. In the Modify panel, Modifier List, choose Extrude, 2'0" remains in the Amount field from step #8 in the Amount field, and press Enter. Rather than the two boxes you had by extruding two shape, you now have a single box with a hole through it (see Figure 3.14).

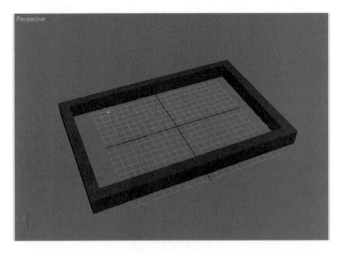

FIGURE 3.14 *An extruded compound shape, a shape made from more than one spline, becomes a box with a hole through it.*

This process is simple, yet powerful. You have just learned a simple example, but you can use it in much more complex situations.

The splines can be nested inside each other as many levels as you want. The object is solid from the outside shape until it finds an island, at which point, it becomes a void. Then, if there is another island inside the void, it becomes a solid, and so on. Figure 3.15 shows a complex example of the concept.

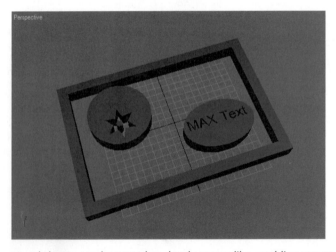

FIGURE 3.15 *Compound shapes can be nested as deeply as you like, enabling you to create complex objects with a simple principle.*

Again, practice with simple examples at first, working toward more complex nested shapes, to learn how the process works. Soon, it will become an important part of your daily workflow.

The Principles of Sub-Object Editing

Like compound shapes, the principle of sub-object editing itself is simple enough. You learn the basics of some of the sub-object editing available with 2D shapes in Exercise 3.3, but be aware that sub-object editing can be found throughout 3ds max 6. For example, 3D objects can be edited at sub-object level and many modifiers can be manipulated at sub-object level. Later exercises and chapters in this book give you practical experience editing at various sub-object levels.

Exercise 3.3   The Basics of Sub-Object Editing

1. From the File pull-down menu, choose Open (see Figure 3.16), click the No button when asked "Do You Want to Save Your Changes?," and open the file on the CD-ROM called Ch03_Compound_shape01.max. From the File pull-down menu, choose Save As and, in the Save File As dialog, choose an appropriate subdirectory on your computer and click the plus sign button just to the left of the Save button (see Figure 3.17). This step saves a new file with the name incremented (that is, Ch03_Compound_shape02.max).

FIGURE 3.16
From the File pull-down menu, choose Save As. This enables you to save a file with a new name.

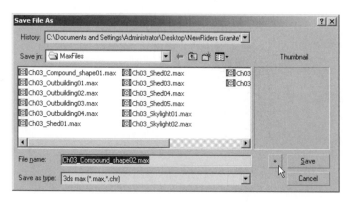

FIGURE 3.17   *In the Save File As dialog, you point to a subdirectory on your computer and click the plus sign button to increment the filename as it saves the new file.*

2. In the Top viewport, select the Rectangle01 object. This is an extruded compound shape that you can easily edit at sub-object level. In the Modify panel, Stack view, click the plus next to Editable Spline to expand the levels. Highlight Spline in the list (see Figure 3.18).

tip

Clicking the Customize pull-down menu, Preferences, Files tab enables you to choose Increment on Save. This means that saving a file always creates a new file with an incremented name regardless of the command you use to save. This can be a great tool in production, where you might have to return to a previous state in your editing. You can clean up the hard drive to purge unnecessary files when the project is finished.

FIGURE 3.18   *Select Rectangle01 in the Top viewport and, in the Modify panel, Stack view, expand the stack and highlight Spline.*

3. In the Top viewport, select the small circle spline in the middle of the star spline. It becomes red in the display when selected. On the main toolbar, click the Select and Move button and move the spline to the space above the ellipse spline (see Figure 3.19). You have now edited the shape at sub-object spline level.

4. To exit sub-object mode, click Editable Spline in the stack, and then pick on Extrude in the stack to return to the top editing level. The 3D cylinder created by extruding the circle is now above the ellipse.

warning

Do not click the box with the minus sign to the left of editable spline because it only collapses the view of sub-object levels. You must pick on the Editable Spline to exit sub-object mode. The text changes from yellow to gray and the sub-object symbol to the right of Editable Spline disappears to indicate you are out of sub-object mode.

If you remain in sub-object mode, you won't be able to select other objects in your display. This is a common mistake with new users.

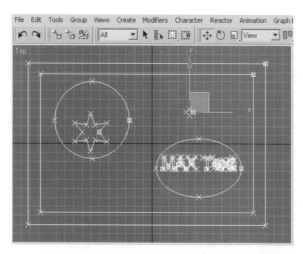

FIGURE 3.19   *In the Top viewport, select the circle spline within the star spline. Click Select and Move on the main toolbar and move it to the space above the ellipse spline.*

5. Now, you change the nesting level of the circle. In the Modify panel, Stack view, highlight sub-object Spline again. Move the circle spline inside the large circle and just above the star. Exit sub-object mode by clicking Editable Spline, and then click on Extrude to return to the top of the stack. The 3D object now has a circular hole above the star rather than a cylinder because you changed the nesting level of the circle (see Figure 3.20).

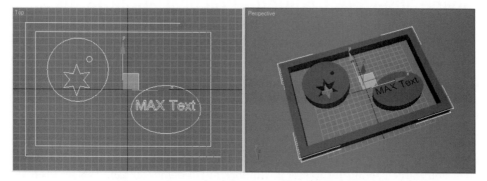

FIGURE 3.20   *By moving the small circle spline into the large circle spline, you change the nesting level and the spline is now a hole rather than a cylinder. The process starts as a solid from the outer spline and works inward to an island, where it becomes a void to the next island, which again becomes a solid.*

6. Take the time to experiment with this example by editing at the three sub-object levels. Try selecting a vertex, for example, right-click with the cursor over the vertex, and try the different corner types found in the Quad menu (see Figure 3.21)—Bézier Corner, Bézier, Corner, and Smooth—to change the tangency at the selected vertices.

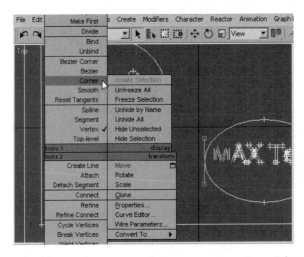

FIGURE 3.21 *In Vertex sub-object mode, you can select one or more vertices, right-click a vertex, and change the tangency to affect the curvature in and out of the vertex.*

2D Shape Sub-Object Editing—Practical Applications

Now, you now learn more practical application of shape sub-object editing and how to use modifiers to turn the shapes into 3D objects as buildings for a mid-1800s shipyard.

At this point, concentrate on the process of working with 2D to create 3D rather than exactly what it is you are creating as a final object. It is important to get a feel for the workflow and the editing capabilities. The objects you create will make a large boat shed that will be used in the shipyard scene.

Along with practicing the 2D shape creation and editing, you will gain some practice in applying some of the alignment tools and reference coordinate system information you learned about in Chapter 2, "Important Fundamental Concepts in 3ds max 6."

Editing a Compound Shape for the Front of a Boat Shed

In Exercise 3.4, you edit a parametric rectangle shape to form the outline of the front and back walls of a large boat shed (see Figure 3.22).

FIGURE 3.22   *You will use sub-object editing and modifiers to create and edit a boat shed.*

The beauty of working with a 2D compound shape is that it is very easy to make changes at the 2D level to affect the more complex 3D object, especially when it comes to adding openings through the object, such as door and window openings.

Remember that even though you are building walls in these examples, you could use the same principles and methods to create the back plate of a computer case or perhaps the instrument panel of an aircraft or to model a chain-link fence. Learn the tools and use your imagination.

note

Notice that the front wall is symmetrical left and right—its outline is made of straight lines and has few corner points. Starting with a rectangle shape, adding and moving points on its outline results in an economical model that is easy to construct.

Exercise 3.4   2D Sub-Object Editing

1. Open the file called Ch03_Shed01.max on the CD-ROM. From the File pull-down menu, choose Save As, point to an appropriate subdirectory on your hard drive, and use the plus sign button to save a new file with the name incremented to Ch03_Shed02.max.

2. Right-click in the Front viewport to activate it. On the main toolbar, click the Select Object button and pick shed_shape, the blue Rectangle shape, in the viewport. You will now learn a new method of accessing sub-object level editing for 2D shapes. In the Modify panel, Modifier List, choose the Edit Spline modifier (see Figure 3.23).

note

Much like selecting the object, right-clicking, and converting to an editable spline, the Edit Spline modifier gives you access to sub-object editing. However, it is still possible to drop to the Rectangle level in the Stack view to change the parameters of the rectangle.

If the Edit Spline modifier is used to change the topology of the rectangle—to add a vertex, for example—you can no longer make changes below that point in the editing history without affecting the integrity of the object.

The Edit Spline modifier also takes up more memory space, which makes it less efficient. You will learn through experience when it is prudent to convert to an editable spline or to use the Edit Spline modifier. There are no hard-and-fast rules.

FIGURE 3.23   *Select the rectangle in the Front viewport and, in the Modify panel, Modifier List, choose the Edit Spline modifier.*

3. You now edit the rectangle to the shape of the shed's gable end. First, add vertices to the top horizontal segment and the two vertical sides with the Divide option. In the Modify panel, Stack view, click the plus sign left of Edit Spline to expand it. Highlight Segment in the list. In the Front viewport, pick the top horizontal segment. It turns red when selected. In the Modify panel, Geometry rollout, position the cursor in the empty space between the options and use the hand cursor to scroll the panel upward until you find Divide (see Figure 3.24). The Divide number is set to 1. Click the Divide button (only once) and you can see a new vertex appear in the middle of the selected segment.

4. In the Front viewport, select one of the vertical segments, hold the Ctrl key, and pick the other vertical segment to add it to the selection set. Only both vertical segments should be red. In the Modify panel, Geometry rollout, set the Divide number to 3 and click the Divide button. Three new vertices should be equally spaced along each vertical segment (see Figure 3.25).

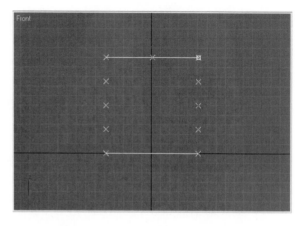

FIGURE 3.25

Select the 2 vertical segments, set the Divide number to 3, and click the Divide button. This adds three equally spaced vertices to those segments.

FIGURE 3.24

In sub-object Segment mode, select the top horizontal segment in the Front viewport and, in the Modify panel, Geometry rollout, click the Divide button to add a new vertex in the middle of the segment.

caution

You must first have the correct segments select, then set the Divide number, and then click the Divide button. The order is important to get the correct results.

If you make a mistake, use the Undo button on the main toolbar to get back to step 3 of this exercise and try again.

5. In the Modify panel, Stack view, highlight Vertex to enter Vertex sub-object mode. In the Front viewport, select one of the upper-corner vertices, hold the Ctrl key, and select the other upper-corner vertex (see Figure 3.26).

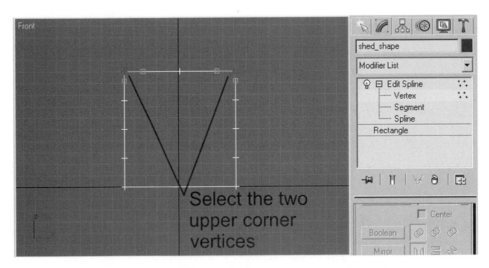

FIGURE 3.26   *In Vertex sub-object mode, select the two upper-corner vertices of the rectangle in the Front viewport.*

6. You now use the Select and Move tool in conjunction with Transform Type-In to move the vertices downward by exactly 24 feet. On the main toolbar, click the Select and Move button. In the status bar at the bottom center of the display, toggle the Absolute Mode Transform Type-In to Offset Mode Transform Type-In (see Figure 3.27). Highlight the Y numeric field to the right of the toggle, enter –24, and press Enter to finalize the command. The numeric field shows 0'0" to show no offset from the current position, but the vertices should look like Figure 3.28.

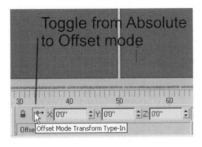

FIGURE 3.27   *Toggle the Absolute Mode Transform Type-In button to Offset Mode Transform Type-In.*

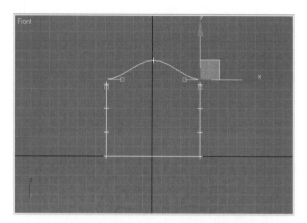

FIGURE 3.28 *In the Transform Type-In numeric field for the Y-axis, enter –24 and press Enter. The two corner vertices will move exactly 24 feet in the negative Y-axis of the Front viewport.*

7. Notice that the sloped segments are curved, which is something you don't want for your roof. The reason is that the vertices of the shape have tangency set to Bézier Corner type. In the Front viewport, pick one of the green handles of the left-corner vertex and move it around. You can adjust the curvature of the segments. Don't worry if you distort the shape. On the main toolbar, click the Select Object button and, in the Front viewport, click and drag a selection window around the entire shape to select all vertices. Right-click in the viewport and choose Corner from the tools1 Quad menu. All curvature is removed from all vertices (see Figure 3.29).

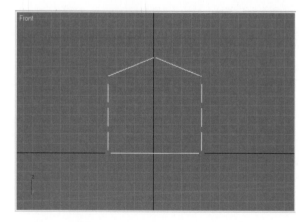

FIGURE 3.29 *Select all vertices of the shape, right-click in the viewport, and choose Corner from the tools1 Quad menu. This removes all curvature from the shape.*

8. Now, move vertices to create sloped walls, eaves, and a short vertical wall segment near the base. In the Front viewport, select the third vertex from the bottom on the left-vertical side (see Figure 3.30). On the main toolbar, click the Select and Move button. In the status bar, X-axis Transform Type-In numeric field, highlight 0'0" and enter 12. Highlight the Y-axis field, enter 34, and press Enter. This moves the vertex up and under the roof line to form a sloped wall and eave (see Figure 3.31).

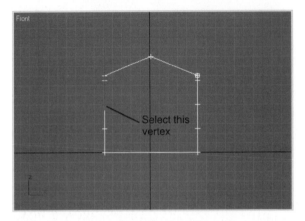

FIGURE 3.30   *In the Front viewport, select the third vertex from the bottom on the left vertical side.*

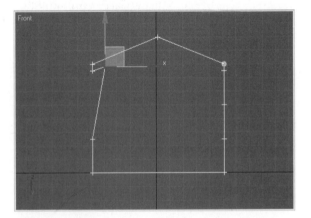

FIGURE 3.31   *Move the selected vertex using Offset Mode Transform Type-In 12 feet in the positive X-axis and 34 feet in the positive Y-axis of the Front viewport.*

9. On the main toolbar, click the Select Object button and select the third vertex from the bottom on the right side. Click the Select and Move button on the main toolbar. Enter –12 in the X-axis Transform Type-In numeric field and 34 in the Y-axis field and press Enter to move the vertex left and up.

10. Drag a selection window around the two vertices second from the bottom, enter –20 in the Y-axis numeric field, and press Enter. This forms the gable end of your boat shed (see Figure 3.32).

caution

It is important to move the vertices in the Front viewport for this exercise. Because of the active View reference coordinate system (see Chapter 2), each viewport can have the X, Y, and Z axes pointing in different directions.

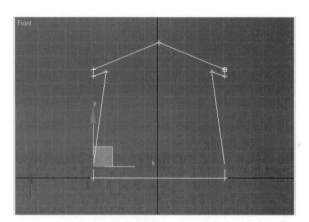

FIGURE 3.32 *Move the two vertices second from the bottom –20 feet in the Y-axis.*

11. The shed should be narrower at the top than it is currently. To fix this, select all the roof vertices and scale them in toward the center. This requires a change Scale type from Uniform to Non-uniform and of the Pivot option to Use Selection Center; otherwise, the vertices try to scale on each of their own centers, not the center of the selection, and scale in two directions rather than just horizontally (X-axis). Click the Select Object button on the main toolbar and, in the Front viewport, drag a selection window around the seven roof vertices. Click and hold the Select and Uniform Scale button and choose the Select and Non-Uniform Scale button from the flyouts (see Figure 3.33). This enables you to scale in only the X-axis.

note

Notice that you have selected vertices with the Select Object button while you were in the Select and Move command. It is not necessary to select first and then to move, but use caution that you do not accidentally move something while trying to select when using Select and Move.

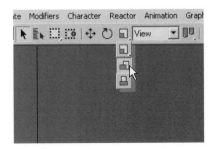

FIGURE 3.33   *Click and hold the Select and Uniform Scale button and choose the Select and Non-Uniform Scale button from the flyouts.*

12. On the main toolbar, click and hold the Use Pivot Point Center button and choose Use Selection Center button. The Scale Transform gizmo centers itself in the geometric center of the selection set of vertices (see Figure 3.34).

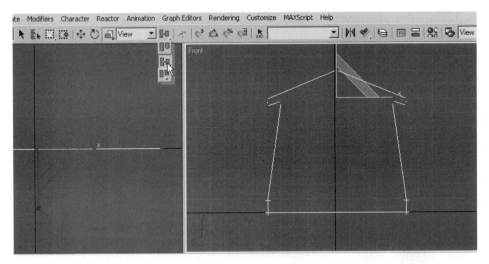

FIGURE 3.34   *Switch from Use Pivot Point Center to Use Selection Center to allow scaling about the geometric center of the selected vertices.*

13. In the Front viewport, move the cursor over the X-axis leg of the Transform gizmo so that it turns yellow. Click and drag the mouse to the left so that you scale the vertices in the X-axis only. As you are scaling, you can read the amount of X-axis scaling in the X-axis numeric field on the status bar. Scale to 75 percent and release the mouse button. The shape should look similar to Figure 3.35.

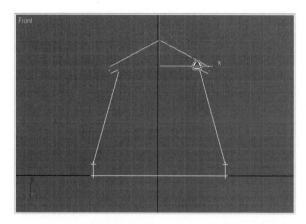

FIGURE 3.35   *Non-uniformly scale the roof vertices to 75 percent of their original size in the X-axis only. As you are scaling, you can read the amount in the X-axis numeric field on the status bar.*

14. In the Modify panel, Stack view, click Edit Spline to highlight it in gray. This exits sub-object mode and is an important step to get into the habit of performing after sub-object edits. On the main toolbar, click the Select Object button to exit Non-Uniform Scale mode. In the File pull-down menu, choose Save (Ctrl+S) to save the file. It should already be named Ch03_Shed02.max.

You have learned sub-object editing and transformed vertices to create a gable end shape of a boat shed. It is important to note that all transforms were done in the Front viewport for consistent directions for the X, Y, and Z axes that are controlled by the current View reference coordinate system. Scaling vertices is done with the Use Selection Center option to keep from scaling in on their individual centers. Using the Use Pivot Point Center would have no effect because a vertex is a point in space with no dimensions. You also used the Scale Transform gizmo to ensure that you only scaled in one axis.

Reusing Existing Geometry

In Exercise 3.5, you learn to make use of existing geometry in the gable end shape to build the walls of the shed. To re-create the necessary splines to match the gable end would be time-consuming and open to potential error, so you extract data from the existing shape to reuse.

The key is to extract what you need without affecting the underlying shape that will become the gable end. This is done with a Detach option at the sub-object level. You learned in Chapter 2 that you could easily attach shapes to shapes and detach, as the name would imply, is just the opposite. The detached sub-object entities become new shapes with a distinct name and color.

You can either detach entities and remove them from the original or detach copies, leaving the original intact.

Exercise 3.5   Using Detach to Extract Data from Shapes

1. Open the file called Ch03_Shed02.max on the CD-ROM or from the preceding exercise. From the File pull-down menu, choose Save As, point to an appropriate subdirectory on your hard drive, and use the plus sign button to save a new file with the name incremented to Ch03_Shed03.max.

2. Right-click in the Front viewport to activate it. Click the Select Object button on the main toolbar and pick the shed_shape object in the Front viewport. In the Modify panel, Stack view, highlight the Segment sub-object level. In the Front viewport, click and drag a selection window that includes or touches all segments except the bottom horizontal segment (see Figure 3.36).

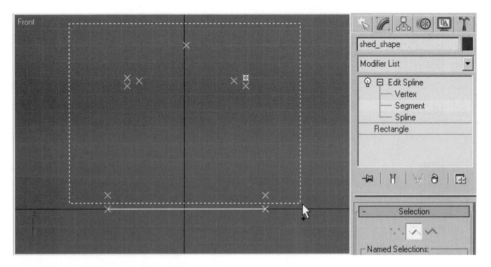

FIGURE 3.36   *In Stack view, enter Segment sub-object level and, in the Front viewport, click and drag a window including or touching all but the bottom horizontal segment.*

3. In the Modify panel, near the bottom of the
Geometry rollout, you see a Detach button with
three optional check boxes to the right. Check the
Copy option (see Figure 3.37). Click the Detach
button to bring up the Detach dialog. Enter
wall_shape01 in the Detach As field and click
OK (see Figure 3.38). In the Stack view, click
Edit Spline to exit sub-object mode. Edit Spline
turns gray.

tip

On the main toolbar, a toggle
button is three buttons over to
the right from the Select
Object button. By default, it is
a dotted box with a sphere half
in it. This is Crossing mode for
selection windows; any object
inside or touching the selection window is selected. If you
toggle the button to Window
mode, only objects completely
inside the window are selected.

FIGURE 3.37 *Make sure to check the Copy option below the Detach
button before clicking Detach.*

FIGURE 3.38 *After checking the Copy option, click the Detach button
and name the new shape wall_shape01 and click OK.
This detaches the selected segments into a new shape
independent of the original.*

caution

It is important to check the
Copy option before clicking
Detach to leave the underlying
data intact.

4. On the main toolbar, click the Select by Name button (H) and double-click
wall_shape01 in the list to select it (see Figure 3.39). The shape is open and, if
extruded to a 3D object, would have no thickness. You change it to a closed shape
to create 2-foot-thick walls. In Stack view, expand Editable Spline, and highlight
Spline sub-object level. In the Front viewport, click the shape. It has only one
spline, which turns red when selected.

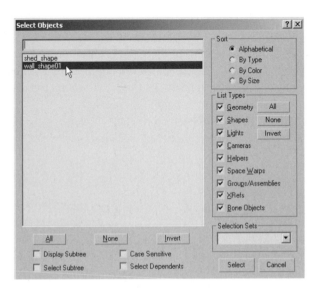

FIGURE 3.39   *Select the new shape in the Select Objects dialog.*

5. In the Modify panel, Geometry rollout, enter 2 in the Outline numeric field and press Enter. The shape becomes a closed shape with a width of 2 feet (see Figure 3.40). In the Stack view, click Editable Spline to exit sub-object mode.

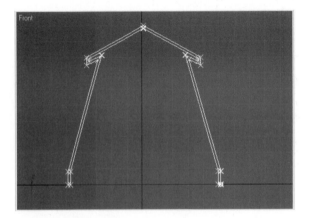

FIGURE 3.40   *In the Modify panel, Geometry rollout, enter 2 in the Outline numeric field and press Enter to create a closed spline with a 2-foot width.*

caution

For this exercise, *do not* pick the Outline button itself. To use the Outline button, click it, and then click the spline and drag to manually set the width.

6. Now, convert this shape to 3D walls. Make sure you are out of sub-object mode. In the Modify panel, Modifier List, click Extrude. In the Modify panel, Parameters rollout, enter 300 in the Amount field and press Enter. The side walls and roof of a 300-foot shed have been created. Click the Zoom Extents All button in the lower-right corner of the display to zoom out in all viewports (see Figure 3.41).

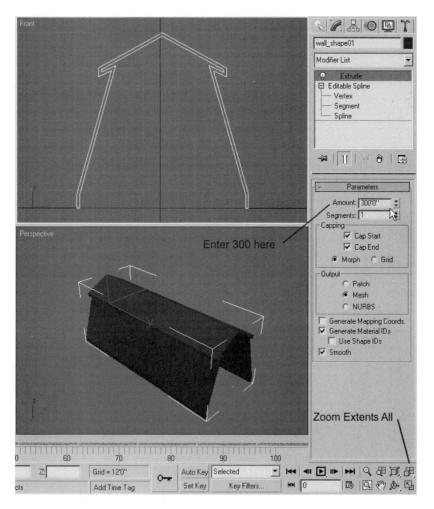

FIGURE 3.41 *Apply an Extrude modifier to the wall_shape01 shape and enter 300 in the Amount field. Use Zoom Extents All to view the new 3D object in the viewports.*

7. Save the file; it should already be named Ch03_Shed03.max.

You have extracted data from an existing shape to retain the integrity and sizing, and then modified it with Outline for width, and extruded it to a 3D set of walls and roof. Knowing how to use the Detach option with Copy can make the creation of new objects easier and can increase your confidence regarding the size and location of the new data.

Cloning and Alignment

Exercise 3.6 introduces you to the process of cloning objects in 3ds max 6. When you detached the segments in Exercise 3.4 as a copy, it was a form of cloning, the only one available at sub-object level. Objects, however, can be cloned in three ways:

- **Copy**—Has no connection with the original.
- **Instance**—Has a two-way connection with the original. Edit either one and the other also changes.
- **Reference**—Changes made to the original pass to the reference clone, but edits to the clone are not passed back; that is, it's a one-way connection.

In the case of your gable end walls, you want them both to have a large door and a window that will always be the same size in each wall. An instance clone enables you to make this to happen.

Instance and reference clones also have a smaller memory footprint than the original and can therefore save computer resources.

You also learn to use the Align tool in 3ds max 6, which is an incredibly productive tool. Its use requires you to be familiar with the reference coordinate systems explained in Chapter 2, so it might be wise to review that chapter before proceeding.

Exercise 3.6   Cloning, Aligning, and More Sub-Object Editing

1. Open the file called Ch03_Shed03.max on the CD-ROM or from the preceding exercise. From the File pull-down menu, choose Save As, point to an appropriate subdirectory on your hard drive, and use the plus sign button to save a new file with the name incremented to Ch03_Shed04.max.

2. You first make a solid gable wall for the shed and edit the door and window in later. This illustrates the power of cloning and sub-object editing in a production environment with frequent changes. On the main toolbar, click the Select by Name button and double-click shed_shape in the list to select it. In the Modify panel, Modifier List, choose Extrude and, in the Parameters rollout, enter 2 in the

Amount field, and press Enter. The shape is now a solid gable wall, 2 feet thick. Rename this object at the top of the Modify panel to **Gable01**.

3. One way to clone this object is to choose Clone from the Edit pull-down menu. This displays the Clone Options dialog. Make sure that the Instance radio button is checked and that the name has automatically been incremented to Gable02 (see Figure 3.42). Click OK and you have two gable walls in exactly the same position in the scene. Notice in the Modify panel that the new Gable02 is the selected object.

tip

Naming objects is very important, especially when working with others. Always name objects soon after creation with a name that is unique and makes some sense in the context of the scene or the type of object that it is.

Using capital letters for 3D objects and lowercase for 2D objects is a good way to separate the objects in selection lists. You need to check the Case Sensitive sorting option in the list to enable the function.

Devise your own naming scheme and stick to it to increase productivity.

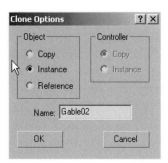

FIGURE 3.42   *You can clone objects from the Edit pull-down menu. The Instance option creates a connection between the clone and the original. Editing either one affects the other, and the clone uses fewer computer memory resources.*

4. Select the wall_shape01 object and rename it Wall01. You now align Gable02 to the other end of the long wall object. Select Gable02. Right-click in the Perspective viewport to make that viewport active while keeping the Gable02 object selected. On the main toolbar, click the Align button and, in the Perspective viewport, pick the Wall01 object to call the Align Selection (Wall01) dialog. Because you are in the Perspective viewport and the reference coordinate system is set to View, the Align tool is using the World coordinates to define the X, Y, and Z axes. Review Chapter 2 if necessary. The Gable02 needs to move in the negative Y-axis to align to the other end of the Wall01. Check the Y Position check box in the Align Selection dialog. Check the Minimum radio buttons for both the current object and target object (see Figure 3.43). This aligns the farthest point of the bounding box of Gable02 with the farthest point of the bounding box of Wall01 in the negative Y-axis for perfect alignment. Click OK to finish the command.

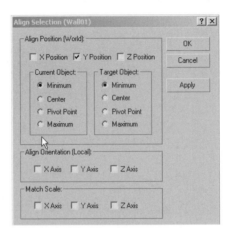

FIGURE 3.43 *With the Align tool, you can quickly align objects by their bounding boxes. The current object is the object you have selected; the target object is the object you pick to align to. You must know the reference coordinate system to make sense of the directions of the three axes for each viewport and coordinate system.*

5. You now discover that you need a window in both gable walls. You accomplish this by editing at sub-object level and attaching a rectangle to create a compound shape. In the Front viewport, select Gable01. You can select it by picking on the same spot at the edge of the gable end and cycling through the three objects or by using Select By Name. You edit this wall because it is on the grid plane defined by the black lines passing through the 0,0,0 World coordinate. It is important that the compound shape have all its splines in the same plane for this example. In the Create panel, Shapes panel, click the Rectangle button and drag any rectangle in the Front viewport. In the Modify panel, Parameters rollout, enter 16 in the Length and Width fields of Rectangle01.

6. Click the Align button on the main toolbar and pick the wall objects in the Front viewport. You must click a visible line to pick the object. In the Align Selection dialog, check both the X Position and Y Position option and check Center in the Current and Target Object columns to align the rectangle, as shown in Figure 3.44. Click OK. It doesn't matter which 3D object you align to in the X and Y axes of the Front viewport because they all have a common center.

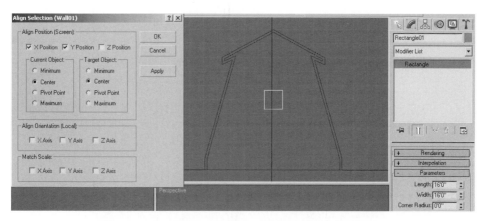

FIGURE 3.44   *Using the Align tool in the Front viewport, align the rectangle to either of the three 3D objects to be centered in the X and Y axes.*

7. In the Front viewport, select Gable01. You might have to use the Select by Name button. In the Modify panel, Stack view, highlight Edit Spline. Your gable walls disappear. In the Geometry rollout, click the Attach button and, in the Front viewport, pick the edge of the new rectangle. In the Modify panel, Stack view, highlight Extrude to return to the top of the stack; you see that you have a window in each of the gable walls (see Figure 3.45).

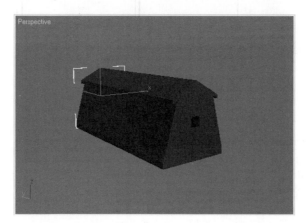

FIGURE 3.45   *Attaching a new shape to create a compound shape for one wall creates a window opening in that wall and, in any instance, clones of that wall. The power of this process cannot be underestimated.*

8. The next step is to create a large door opening in both ends so that the boat can move in and out. This a similar process to adding the window, except you do not want the door to have a threshold. You create the rectangle for the opening, attach it, and Boolean subtract it from the outer shape of the building. In the Front viewport, create a rectangle with a length of 50 feet and a width of 70 feet. Use Align to align it to one of the 3D objects center to center in the X-axis only. Review steps 5 and 6 of this exercise if you have problems.

9. On the main toolbar, click the Select and Move button and move the rectangle in the Y-axis of the Front viewport so that it is near the window but overlapping the bottom of the walls (see Figure 3.46).

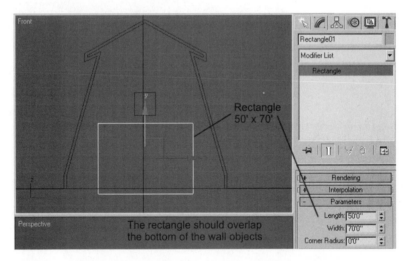

FIGURE 3.46 *Create a 50-foot length by 70-foot width rectangle, center it to the walls in the X-axis of the Front viewport, and move it in the Y-axis to overlap the walls at the bottom.*

10. In the Front viewport, select Gable01. In the Modify panel, Stack view, highlight Edit Spline. In the Geometry rollout, click the Attach button and pick the edge of the rectangle in the Front viewport. Click Attach again to exit the mode.

11. In the Stack view, highlight Spline sub-object level. In the Front viewport, pick the outer spline of the shape; it defines the side walls and the roof. You won't see it turn red in the Front viewport because other objects are in the way, but you should see it red in the other wireframe viewports. Near the middle of the Geometry rollout, toggle the Subtraction button of the Boolean operation. Click the Boolean button to highlight it yellow and move the cursor over the rectangular spline in the Front viewport. When the Subtraction cursor shows (see Figure 3.47), click the rectangle to subtract it from the outer spline.

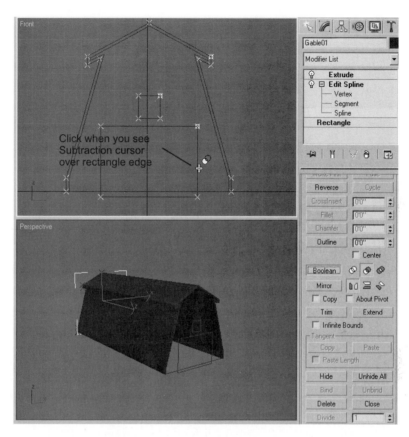

FIGURE 3.47 *Select the outer spline of Gable01. In the Modify panel, Geometry rollout, toggle the Subtraction button for Boolean operations. Click the Boolean button and pick the rectangle in the Front viewport when you see the Subtraction cursor.*

12. Click the Select Object button to exit the Boolean mode. In the Stack view, highlight Edit Spline to exit sub-object mode, and click Extrude to return to the top of the stack. You now have a large door opening with no threshold (see Figure 3.48).

13. Save the file; it should already be called Ch03_Shed04.max. You now have a shed with two gable ends with openings.

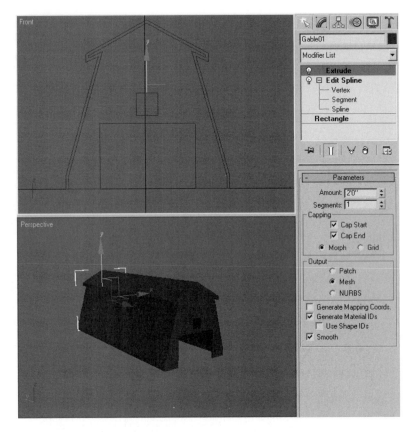

FIGURE 3.48   *Exit Boolean mode and return to the Extrude modifier level of the Stack view. Each gable wall will have a large door opening with no threshold.*

By using the power of editing 2D shapes at sub-object level in the Modifier stack and combining that power with the concept of instance cloning, you have an extremely productive workflow that is both efficient and flexible. These examples are simple, but you can apply the same process to more complex scenarios.

Extract 2D Data from 3D Mesh Objects

Exercise 3.7 is a bit more complex than necessary to create a simple box object that will act as the floor of the shed. The reason for doing it this way is to introduce you to more important sub-object editing commands, both on 2D and 3D objects.

You learn to extract 2D entities from a 3D mesh and clean them up to make them into a 3D floor object. Another topic covered is vertex welding, which is something you will need to use often in 3ds max 6 modeling.

Exercise 3.7   Extracting Data from 3D Objects and More 2D Editing Tools

1. Open the file called Ch03_Shed04.max on the CD-ROM or from the preceding exercise. From the File pull-down menu, choose Save As, point to an appropriate subdirectory on your hard drive, and use the plus sign button to save a new file with the name incremented to Ch03_Shed05.max.

2. Right-click in the Perspective viewport to activate it. On the main toolbar, click the Select Object button and select Wall01, the long wall and roof object. In the Tools pull-down menu, choose Isolate Selection (Alt+Q). This hides all other objects in the scene so that you can concentrate on working with just the selected object(s). Move the Warning: Isolated Selection dialog to the upper right of the display. Click the Min/Max Toggle button at the lower right of the display to fill the display with the Perspective view. Right-click the Perspective label at the top left of the viewport and choose Wireframe (see Figure 3.49).

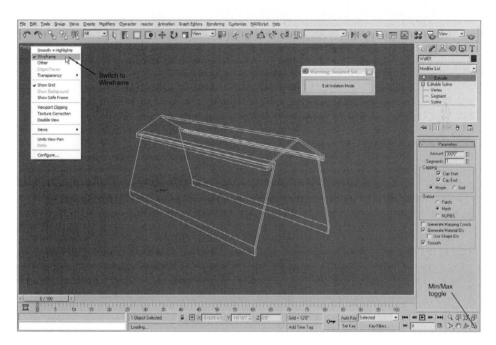

FIGURE 3.49   *Select Wall01 and use Isolate Selection to hide all other objects. Min/Max Toggle button for a single viewport and switch to Wireframe viewing.*

3. Now, add a modifier to the 3D object that allows sub-object editing. Make sure the Wall01 is selected and, in the Modify panel, Modifier List, choose the Edit Mesh modifier. In the Stack view, expand Edit Mesh and highlight Edge sub-object level.

Zoom in to the left-front corner of Wall01 and select the long and short outer edges. Use Ctrl to add to a selection set. Press the Spacebar to lock the selection. A padlock button turns yellow on the status bar (see Figure 3.50). Locking a selection keeps you from accidentally selecting something else in the next step.

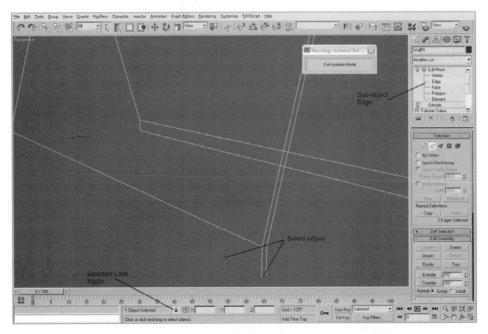

FIGURE 3.50   *Zoom in to the left front of Wall01. Apply an Edit Mesh modifier to Wall01 and go to Edge sub-object level in Stack view. Using Ctrl to add to a selection set, select the long and short edges of the left side of the wall.*

4. Use the Arc Rotate button (Alt+mouse wheel) to view Wall01 from the opposite corner. Press the Spacebar to unlock the selection. Hold the Ctrl key and select the long and short edges of this side. You should see that 4 Edges Selected appears at the bottom of the Selection rollout. In the Modify panel, Edit Geometry rollout, click the Create Shape from Edges button (see Figure 3.51).

5. In the Create Shape dialog, change the name to **Floor** and check the Linear radio button to eliminate any curvature in the new shape (see Figure 3.52).

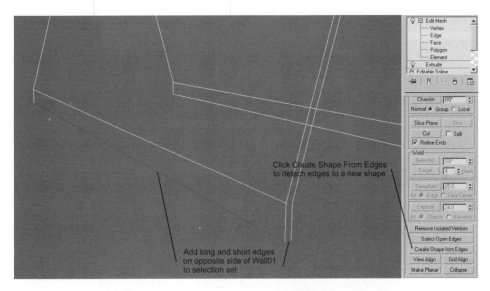

FIGURE 3.51 *Use Arc Rotate to view Wall01 from the opposite corner, and press the Spacebar to unlock the selection. With the Ctrl key down, select the long and short outer edges from this side of Wall01 and click the Create Shape from Edges button in the Edit Geometry rollout.*

6. In the Modify panel, Stack view, highlight Edit Mesh to exit sub-object mode. Click the Remove Modifier from the Stack button just below Stack view. You no longer need the modifier after the shape has been detached (and, besides, it requires extra memory resources).

7. In the Select by Name (H) dialog, double-click Floor. In the Tools pull-down menu, choose Isolate Selection (Alt+Q) so that you only have the 2D shape called Floor in the viewport. Use the Min/Max Toggle to return to a four-viewport display, right-click in the Top viewport, and use Min/Max Toggle to fill the display with it. Use Region Zoom to fill the Top viewport with the top end of the Floor shape.

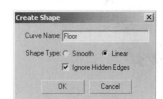

FIGURE 3.52
Rename the new shape Floor in the Create Shape dialog and check the Linear radio button to eliminate any curvature that may be present.

8. In the Spline sub-object level, click the Extend button in the Geometry rollout and pick the right end of the short horizontal segment at the top left of the shape. You see the Extend cursor (see Figure 3.53). This extends the segment to the next segment in its path. Pan the viewport upward and do the same to the short horizontal segment at the bottom of the shape. Click the Extend button to exit the mode.

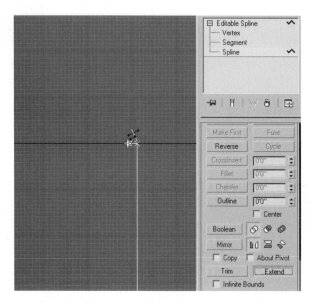

FIGURE 3.53   *Go to Spline sub-object level. In the Geometry rollout, click the Extend button and pick the left end of the short horizontal segment at the top right of the shape.*

9. The shape appears to be a closed rectangle, but it isn't. If you were to extrude it now, it would have no top or bottom surface because it is an open shape. You must first weld the vertices to create a closed shape. Zoom Extents All so that you can see the entire shape in the Top viewport. In Stack view, go to Vertex sub-object mode. Drag a selection window around all vertices and you see that you have six vertices selected. In the Geometry rollout, enter 1 (1 inch) in the Weld numeric field and click the Weld button (see Figure 3.54). This welds all vertices in the selection that are within 1 inch of any other selected vertices, combining them into a single vertex and closing the shape.

FIGURE 3.54
Welding vertices combines all selected vertices within a threshold distance into a single vertex. This closes the open shape so that it can be extruded as a solid box.

10. In the Stack view, highlight Editable Spline to exit sub-object mode. In the Modify panel, Modifier List, choose the Extrude modifier. If you Min/Max Toggle to see all viewports, and then Zoom Extents All, you see that the shape has not extruded to give it thickness, but has slid along its length (see Figure 3.55). This is caused by the local axis

being derived from the shape created in the Front viewport. This is a common event that keeps new users from using Create Shape from Edges, but it is easy to fix.

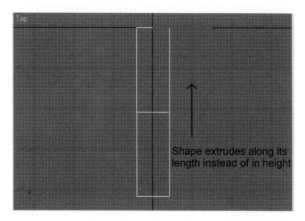

FIGURE 3.55   *Applying an Extrude modifier to this shape slides it instead of giving it thickness because of the local Z-axis of the object from which it was derived.*

11. Click the Remove Modifier from the Stack button to remove the Extrude modifier. In the Top viewport, from the Create panel, Shapes panel, create a line anyplace inside the rectangle (its local Z-axis pointing toward you). In the Modify panel, Geometry rollout, click the Attach button and pick the rectangle in the Top viewport. Click the Attach button again to exit that mode. This creates a compound shape with its local Z-axis determined by the line. In the Modify panel, Stack view, expand the line and highlight Spline sub-object level. In the Top viewport, pick the line to turn it red and press Delete on the keyboard. The rectangle now has a new local Z-axis pointing toward you in the Top viewport. It also has assumed the name Line01, so change it back to Floor. Exit sub-object mode.

12. In the Modifier List, choose Extrude and you will have a box 300 feet high. In the Parameters rollout, change the Amount to –2 and the floor becomes 2 feet thick in the negative Z-axis. Click the Exit Isolation Mode button in the dialog to see the other objects in the scene. The shed now sits on a slab floor (see Figure 3.56).

13. Save the file. It should already be called Ch03_Shed05.max and consists of a shed on a slab floor that can be easily edited at any time. You have not actually created any 3D objects for this exercise, but have converted 2D shapes to 3D objects with modifiers.

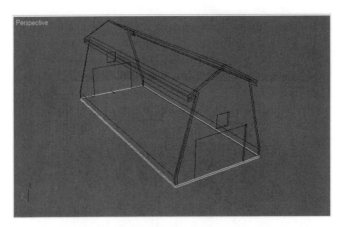

FIGURE 3.56   *Extruding the Floor in the negative Z-axis and exiting Isolation mode shows a shed on a slab floor.*

Yes, it was a roundabout exercise, but you learned some valuable lessons, such as creating 2D shapes from existing 3D mesh objects and some important sub-object editing commands, such as vertex welding. You learned to lock and unlock selection sets with the Spacebar, which enables you to navigate viewports without accidentally losing the selection set.

You also learned that it is possible to create shapes with a Z-axis direction that gives unexpected results when converted to 3D mesh. This can happen with shapes imported from other vector software packages, as well, but it is easy to correct when you recognize the problem.

Modifiers and the Modify Stack

In this section, you learn more about the modifiers available in 3ds max 6 and how to manipulate the modifier stack (that is, the history of changes you have made to objects in the scene).

Although there are modeling methods in which you do not use modifiers and the modifier stack, it is the most flexible and safe way to work if you expect possible changes in the design later in the process.

In the next three exercises, you create some simple background outbuildings using only 2D shapes and modifiers. You then edit copies of the buildings with a series of modifiers that enable you to edit only

tip

If you do not expect changes to be made in the design, you have a boss or client whom you never want to lose! Welcome to Nirvana.

specific portions of the buildings and, finally, you learn about a modifier that is imperative to know about when scaling objects.

As in previous exercises, the objects you build are relatively simple so that you can concentrate on learning the workflow and concepts presented.

Exploring the Bevel Modifier

A modifier that is extremely simple in its design, but is still a powerful tool for general modeling and adding important detail to make scenes more convincing, is the Bevel modifier. It's basically an advanced Extrude modifier that enables you to bevel the extrusion sides inward or outward.

Exercise 3.8   The Bevel Modifier

1. Open the file called Ch03_Outbuilding01.max on the CD-ROM. From the File pull-down menu, choose Save As, point to an appropriate subdirectory on your hard drive, and use the plus sign button to save a new file with the name incremented to Ch03_Outbuilding02.max.

2. In the Perspective viewport, select the rectangle called out_building01. The name is in lowercase because the object is a 2D shape. In the Modify panel, Modifier List, choose Bevel. The rectangle changes to a solid flat plane. Rename the object Out_building01, the capital letter indicating that the object is now 3D.

3. In the Modify panel, Bevel Values rollout, you see three levels of Height and Outline values. The Height setting is exactly like the Extrude modifier: It extrudes the shape in the positive or negative local Z-axis. The Outline setting is how much that new height level is beveled in toward or away from the geometric center of the shape.

4. In the Level 1 Height numeric field, enter 10 and press Enter. The shape now has a height of 10 inches. Click Zoom Extents All to view the object fully in all viewports (see Figure 3.57).

5. In the Bevel Values rollout, check Level 2 to activate it. Enter 1 in the Height for Level 2 and press Enter. The object extrudes another foot in the Z-axis from the top of the Level 1 height. Enter 1 in the Level 2 Outline field and press Enter. The top of Level 2 is now 1 foot larger in all directions, resulting in a 45-degree bevel outward (see Figure 3.58).

caution

Do not choose the Bevel Profile modifier in the Modifier List. You learn about that modifier in Chapter 4, "Shipbuilding 101: The Making of a Boat."

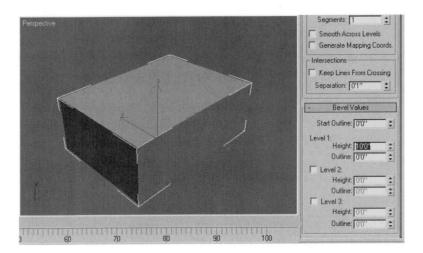

Figure 3.57 *Entering a value in the Level 1 Height field is the same as applying an Extrude modifier.*

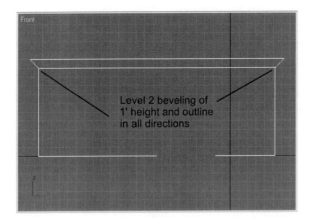

Figure 3.58 *Adding Level 2 with a Height and Outline amount of 1 foot results in a 45-degree outward beveling atop the 10-foot box.*

6. In the Bevel Values rollout, check Level 3 and enter a Height of 6 and an Outline of –11. The object is 6 feet higher, but the bevel is inward with the negative amount in the Outline field. This results in the appearance of a simple building with trim and a hip roof (see Figure 3.59). This detail might be sufficient for background buildings in your scene. It is easily adjustable and very efficient.

7. Save the file; it should already be named Ch03_Outbuilding02.max.

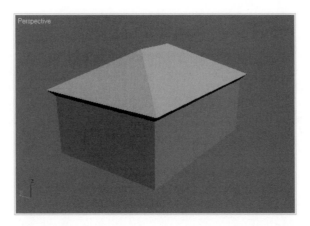

FIGURE 3.59 *A simple rectangle with a Bevel modifier can be made to represent a small building with a hip roof. It is easily edited at anytime and is efficient.*

With a Level 1 height of 1 foot, this object could be just the roof of a building with a fascia, trim, and hip roof. Use your imagination. Open a new 3ds max scene and play with different shapes and different bevel settings to see how many possible variations you can think up. Experimenting with tools makes them easier to use in production.

Editing 3D Mesh at Sub-Object Level

In the Exercise 3.9, you learn to apply a stack of modifiers that enable you to make changes beyond the capability of the Bevel modifier while retaining some ability to move up and down the modifier stack to edit at various points of the history. You also learn to rename modifiers in the stack for clarity, which can be especially important in a collaborative environment and a new method of cloning objects.

Exercise 3.9   Sub-Object Editing of 3D Mesh

1. Open the file called Ch03_Outbuilding02.max on the CD-ROM or from the preceding exercise. From the File pull-down menu, choose Save As, point to an appropriate subdirectory on your hard drive, and use the plus sign button to save a new file with the name incremented to Ch03_Outbuilding03.max.

2. Select Out_building01 in the Perspective viewport. You will leave this building intact and clone a copy that will be modified. On the main toolbar, click the Select and Move button. In the Perspective viewport, hold the Shift key and move the cursor over the X-axis arrow of the Transform gizmo. The arrow shaft highlights yellow. Click the shaft, and then drag a clone of the building in the positive X-axis direction. In the Clone Options dialog, make sure the Copy radio button is selected and that the name has been incremented to Out_building02 (see Figure 3.60). Click OK. Remember, a copy clone has no connection with the original.

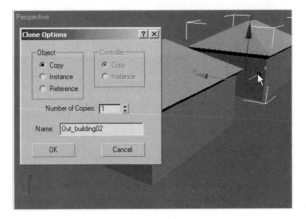

FIGURE 3.60 *Holding the Shift key while transforming an object is a way to clone objects. Using the Transform gizmo enables you to clone only in the axis you want.*

3. Now, you edit the new building to add a clerestory roof while retaining some ability to make changes to the edits. To cut clutter in the display, go to Tools pull-down and choose Isolate Selection (Alt+Q), and then click Zoom Extents All. In the Modify panel, Bevel Values rollout, enter –8 in the Level 3 Outline field. This flattens the top of the roof.

4. Because the Bevel modifier has only three levels available and because it can only be applied to 2D shapes, you need to use some other form of modifier to change this existing roof. First, apply a Mesh Select modifier that only enables you to select at the sub-object levels of a mesh object. The beauty of Mesh Select is that it uses very little computer resources, so you can use many without

note

All mesh objects in 3ds max 6 have triangular faces. The viewport is simplified by hiding the diagonal edges of the triangles where it makes sense. Polygon sub-object level is any set of triangular faces bordered by a visible edge when viewed in Wireframe mode. In the preceding step, you selected two triangular faces, for example.

affecting performance. In the Modify panel, Modifier List, choose Mesh Select. In Stack view, expand Mesh Select and the highlight Polygon sub-object level. In the Perspective viewport, pick the flat area at the top of the roof. It highlights red when selected (see Figure 3.61).

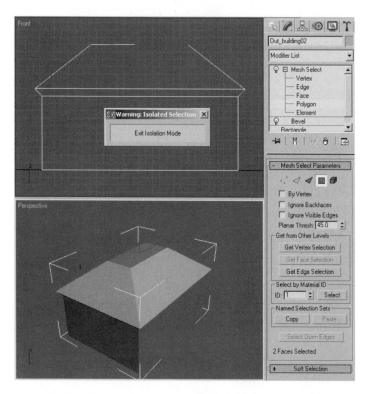

FIGURE 3.61 *The Mesh Select modifier can be used to select sub-object sets of mesh objects. This modifier has no editing capability by itself. Use it to select the horizontal polygon at the top of the roof.*

5. You can now apply a modifier to the stack that will operate on only the selection set below it—in this case, the polygon at the top of the roof. While remaining in Polygon sub-object mode, go to the Modifier List and choose the Face Extrude modifier. In the Modify panel, Parameters rollout, enter 36

tip

The Face Extrude modifier does not use the Display unit rules for data entry. All numeric values in the Amount field are in decimal inches. However, you can always override the Display units by typing the sign you want in the numeric field. If you want to enter metric amounts, for example, you could type in 200mm and the amount would be converted to current units.

in the Amount field and press Enter. The selected Polygon has been extruded 36 inches by moving the selected faces and creating new faces on all sides (see Figure 3.62).

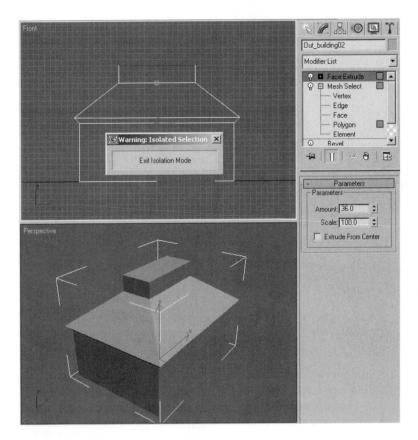

FIGURE 3.62 *A Face Extrude modifier applied above a Mesh Select operates only on the faces selected by the Mesh Select.*

6. You need to add some trim and the roof plane to this clerestory roof. You can just keep adding Mesh Select modifiers and Face Extrude modifiers until you have the desired results. In the Modify panel, Modifier List, choose Mesh Select again, go to Polygon mode, and you should see that the top polygon is still selected. Apply a new Face Extrude modifier, set the Amount to 6 and the Scale to 108. This results in a beveling effect similar to the Bevel modifier. Apply another Mesh Select and go to Polygon mode. Apply another Face Extrude and enter 24 in the Amount and 1 in the Scale. This last Face Extrude applies a peaked roof (see Figure 3.63).

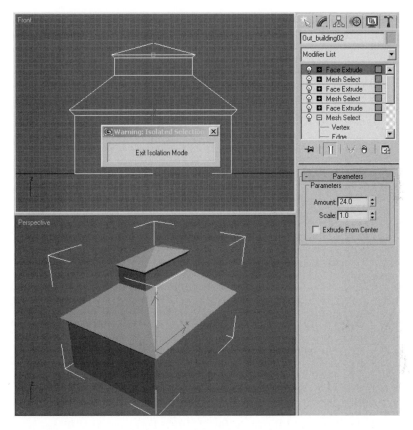

FIGURE 3.63 *By applying two more Mesh Select and Face Extrude modifier combinations you can build a clerestory roof on top of the existing mesh object.*

7. To change the height of the clerestory, go to the Stack view and highlight the lowest Face Extrude in the stack. When you do so, you get a Warning dialog that says your changes at this level might cause unexpected results (see Figure 3.64). This is because it is possible to apply edits that change the topology in a way that any modifier above that point will not understand. In this case, you will be okay, but you should pick the Hold/Yes option in the Warning dialog. This saves the entire file to a hidden file on the hard drive and you can use the Edit pull-down, Fetch option to get it back at any time. Click Hold/Yes. In the

In the Edit pull-down menu, you can use the Hold option or the Fetch option at any time to save and retrieve files from the hold buffer file on the disk. Each time you click Hold, it overwrites any information already in the buffer; each time you click Fetch, it retrieves only what was last stored in the buffer. It is a great tool when you are experimenting with changes.

Modify panel, Parameters rollout, change the Amount from 36 to 24. In Stack view, return to the top Face Extrude modifier.

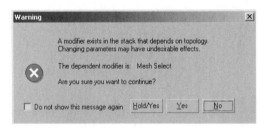

FIGURE 3.64   *Dropping below topology change levels in the Modifier stack produces a warning that further changes might have unexpected results. You can click the Hold/Yes button to save the current file that can be retrieved with the Fetch command if something goes wrong.*

8. In the Modify panel, Modifier List, choose Mesh Select one more time, but do not go into any sub-object mode. This "caps" off the modifier stack so that any subsequent modifiers act on the entire object, not just the last selection in the stack.

9. Select the Face Extrude modifier just below the top Mesh Select and click Hold/Yes in the Warning dialog. Right-click the Face Extrude and choose Rename from the menu. Use the right-arrow key on the keyboard to place the cursor at the far right of Face Extrude and edit it to read Face Extrude-Peak (see Figure 3.65). Return to the top of the stack.

10. Exit Isolation mode by clicking the Exit Isolation Mode button in the Warning: Isolated Selection dialog. Click Zoom Extents All to zoom out to all objects in all viewports. Save the file; it should already be called Ch03_Outbuilding03.max.

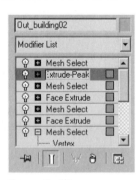

FIGURE 3.65
You can rename modifiers in the stack by highlighting the modifier, right-clicking it, and choosing Rename from the menu. This enables you to append the name with some meaningful hint that clarifies what the modifier does. Avoid the temptation to change the modifier name itself; just append info to it.

New Modifiers and Scaling in 3ds max 6

In Exercise 3.9, the rectangular clerestory roof came to a peak, which makes the roof pitch unequal, something that would never be built. Although you don't need to be a stickler for accuracy for this file, you will correct the roof issue and learn about a new modifier called XForm and about general scaling in 3ds max 6.

Exercise 3.10   XForm Modifier and Scaling Issues

1. Open the file called Ch03_Outbuilding03.max on the CD-ROM or from the preceding exercise. From the File pull-down menu, choose Save As, point to an appropriate subdirectory on your hard drive, and use the plus sign button to save a new file with the name incremented to Ch03_Outbuilding04.max.

2. In the Front viewport, select Out_building02. On the main toolbar, click Select and Move. Hold the Shift key and move Out_building02 in the positive X-axis (to the right), using the arrow on the Transform gizmo far enough so that it is off-screen. Release the mouse button, make sure Copy is checked in the Clone Options dialog and that the object is named Out_building03. Click OK.

3. In the Tools pull-down menu, choose Isolate Selection (Alt+Q) and click Zoom Extents All. The modifier stack has a Mesh Select modifier at the top that you applied to cap the sub-object selections to return control to the whole object. You can use this Mesh Select modifier for the next step. Expand the top Mesh Select modifier and highlight Vertex sub-object mode. In the Front viewport, drag a selection window around the very peak of the roof to select the four vertices (see Figure 3.66) that you scaled down to 1 percent in the preceding exercise. You will non-uniformly scale these in the X-axis to equalize the roof pitches.

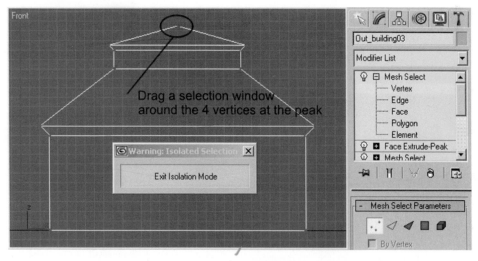

FIGURE 3.66   *Using the existing Mesh Select modifier at the top of the stack, go to Vertex sub-object mode and drag a selection window around the four vertices at the peak of the roof.*

4. If you try to pick the Select and Uniform Scale button on the main toolbar, you notice that all the Transform buttons are grayed out. A Mesh Select modifier can be used only to select sub-object entities and contains no editing commands. To get around this, you need to add an XForm modifier to the vertices. XForm stands for "transform." In the Modifier List, choose XForm.

5. On the main toolbar, click and hold the Uniform Scale and Scale button and choose Select and Non-Uniform Scale from the flyouts (see Figure 3.67).

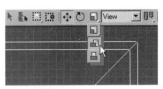

FIGURE 3.67
Select the Non-Uniform Scale button by holding on Select and Uniform Scale and choosing it in the flyout buttons.

6. On the main toolbar, set the transform center option to Use Selection Center so that the vertices don't scale on their own axes (see Figure 3.68). In the Front viewport, click the X-axis restrict arrow of the Transform gizmo and drag to the right until the roof pitch is approximately 45 degrees. See Figure 3.69. Again, accuracy is not so important here. As you drag the cursor to the right, it disappears off the screen and automatically wraps itself to the other side, so you continue to scale without releasing the mouse.

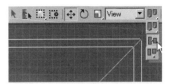

FIGURE 3.68
Set the transform center option to Use Selection Center so that the vertices don't scale on their own axes.

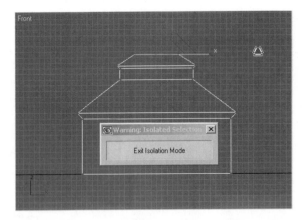

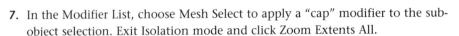

FIGURE 3.69   *In the Front viewport, click the X-axis restrict arrow of the Transform gizmo and drag to the right until the roof pitch is approximately 45 degrees.*

7. In the Modifier List, choose Mesh Select to apply a "cap" modifier to the sub-object selection. Exit Isolation mode and click Zoom Extents All.

8. Save the file; it should already be named Ch03_Outbuilding04.max.

You have used an XForm modifier to transform—scale, in this case—sub-object selections made with a Mesh Select modifier.

Alignment Tools and Grids

In this section, you learn a couple of new alignment options and how the reference coordinate systems can be put to practical use during alignment.

You also learn about grid helper objects in 3ds max 6. These physical grid planes can be treated similarly to other objects in a max scene, but they are only visible in the viewports and are never rendered in your final images. Learning to use these grids and experiencing how they relate to reference coordinate systems can speed your modeling and editing significantly.

Alignment and grids are also another of the elusive tools in max that just don't make much sense without a fundamental knowledge of the reference coordinate systems.

After you perform these basic exercises that introduce you to the functionality of alignment tools and grids, I encourage you, as always, to experiment with extremely simple scenes until you get a feel for the tools and they become part of your workflow without having to think about them.

warning

Never scale objects in 3ds max! You should always use the XForm modifier whenever you scale entire objects in 3ds max 6. It is an option when at sub-object level because transforms at sub-object level take place in the modifier stack at the appropriate time.

The way 3ds max is designed, it evaluates the modifier stack from the bottom up. The base object is evaluated first, the modifiers are evaluated in order, and finally the transforms are evaluated.

Move and Rotate transforms do not change the topology of objects, so always evaluate correctly. Scale, especially non-uniform scale, does change the topology of objects. Using an XForm modifier and scaling it forces the scale values to be evaluated at the proper point in history and is a foolproof way to scale objects.

You might not see the results of this issue until long after you have done the scaling directly on an object, so always use this method to be safe.

Using Face Normals as an Alignment Tool

Face normals are invisible vectors pointing perpendicular from any face in 3ds max 6. Basically, if a vector points toward the viewer in a viewport or rendered image, the face is visible. If the face normal vector points away, the face is invisible. However, you can take advantage of these face normals as an alignment tool. In Exercise 3.11, you learn to use the face normal of a skylight to align it to the surface of your shed roof. You also learn to use the Snap controls and Local reference coordinate system to make adjustments to the position for accurate placement of the skylight on the surface.

Exercise 3.11   Normal Align and Snap Commands

1. Open the file called Ch03_Skylight01.max on the CD-ROM. From the File pull-down menu, choose Save As, point to an appropriate subdirectory on your hard drive, and use the plus sign button to save a new file with the name incremented to Ch03_Skylight02.max.

2. This file is a copy of the shed from earlier exercises and there is a skylight on the World coordinate system grid at the corner of the shed. You will place that skylight on the roof surface. In the Perspective viewport, select the Skylight01 object at the front corner of the shed. On the main toolbar, click the Select and Rotate button and move the cursor over the X-axis (red) restrict circle on the Transform gizmo. When it turns yellow, click and hold, and then move the mouse to rotate the Skylight01 so that you can clearly see the bottom, about –110 degrees (see Figure 3.70). You might want to maximize the Perspective viewport to better see what you are doing.

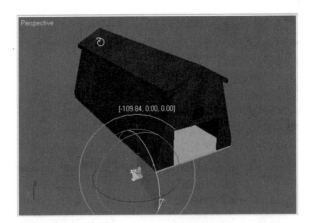

FIGURE 3.70   *Rotate the Skylight01 about –110 degrees in the X-axis to clearly see the bottom. This is the surface that you will align to the roof surface nearest you in Perspective viewport.*

3. All objects in your scene have the face normals pointing outward from the center of the object or, in the case of the side walls that have thickness, out from the space between the outer and inner surface. Otherwise, you would not be able to see the objects. You use the face normals on the bottom of the skylight to align to the face normals of the roof surface. This is a multi-step process that requires a

little hand-eye coordination, but it is simple enough to get the hang of quickly. On the main toolbar, click and hold the Align button and choose Normal Align from the flyouts (see Figure 3.71).

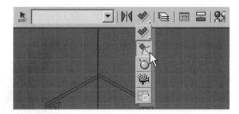

FIGURE 3.71   *On the main toolbar, click and hold the Align button and choose Normal Align from the flyouts.*

4. In the Perspective viewport, move the Normal Align cursor over the selected Skylight01 until you see the cross-hairs show, and then click and hold on Skylight01. While holding the left mouse button and moving the cursor slightly, you should see a blue vector indicating the face normals (see Figure 3.72).

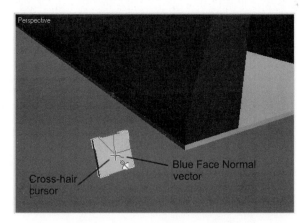

FIGURE 3.72   *While holding the left mouse button and moving the cursor, position the blue face normal vector near the center of the bottom of Skylight01.*

5. Release the left mouse button and move the cursor to the roof surface. Click and hold on the roof surface and move the new green vector near the front center of the roof plane (see Figure 3.73).

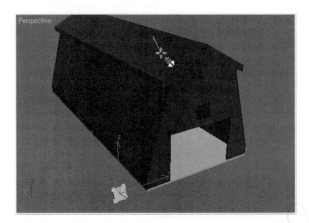

FIGURE 3.73   *Release the left mouse button, and then click and hold on the roof surface to position a green vector in the center front of the roof plane.*

6. Release the left mouse button and Skylight01 matches its bottom surface to the roof surface and a Normal Align dialog appears (see Figure 3.74). Click OK to accept the current position.

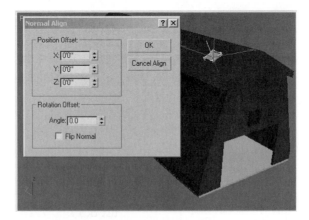

FIGURE 3.74   *Releasing the left mouse button causes Skylight01 to align its bottom surface to the roof surface. Clicking OK in the Normal Align dialog accepts the current position.*

7. The skylight is now sitting flat on the roof surface, but you now adjust its position to a known point so that you can more accurately move it into a final position. You use Snap tools for this process. The pivot point of Skylight01 is at the center

of the bottom faces. You move the skylight to the front peak of the roof using both Pivot Point and Vertex Snap options. The pivot point of the skylight is snapped to the vertex of the roof. The skylight is then in a known position and can be move accurately from there. On the main toolbar, right-click the Snap Toggle button (magnet with a 3). In the Grid and Snap Settings dialog, click the Clear All button, and then check Pivot and Vertex options (see Figure 3.75). Close the dialog.

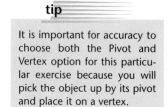

tip

It is important for accuracy to choose both the Pivot and Vertex option for this particular exercise because you will pick the object up by its pivot and place it on a vertex.

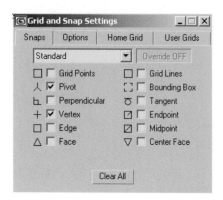

FIGURE 3.75   *Right-click the Snap Toggle button and, in the Snap and Grid Settings dialog, set snaps to Pivot and Vertex only.*

8. It will be easier to see what you are doing if you switch to Wireframe viewport mode. Right-click the Perspective label in the upper left of the viewport and choose Wireframe from the list. You must also click the Snap Toggle button to activate it. Just setting the options does not automatically turn it on. In the Perspective viewport, zoom in closely to the skylight and peak. On the main toolbar, click the Select and Move button to toggle it on. As you move the cursor over the skylight, you see either a light blue vertex tick or a larger cyan pivot indicator, depending on which the cursor is closer to. You want the large cyan pivot indicator visible in your viewport (see Figure 3.76).

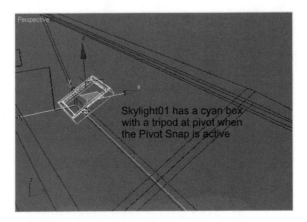

FIGURE 3.76   *While in Select and Move mode, you can grab the Skylight01 by its pivot point when you are in Pivot Snap mode and the cursor is nearest the pivot and the cyan box should show in the viewport.*

9. With the large cyan pivot indicator visible, hold the left mouse button, and drag the cursor near the vertex at the front of the roof peak. It snaps to the vertex when you see the cyan tick (see Figure 3.77). Release the mouse button and the object is positioned with its bottom center on the vertex. The orientation remains aligned with the roof plane.

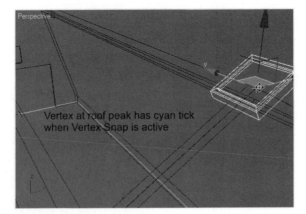

FIGURE 3.77   *Dragging the cursor to the vertex at the front of the roof peak displays a cyan tick when the snap is active. Release the mouse button and the skylight will be in position.*

10. You now use Offset Mode Transform Type-In to move the skylight to an exact distance from the peak. In the Perspective viewport, with View reference coordinate system active, the X and Z axes are not aligned with the roof plane, so the Transform Type-In won't allow the skylight to move parallel to the roof surface. On the main toolbar, pick the View window and choose Local from the menu (see Figure 3.78). Turn Snap Toggle off on the main toolbar.

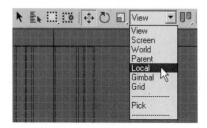

FIGURE 3.78   *Setting the current reference coordinate system to Local for the Skylight01 has the X, Y, and Z axes aligned with the roof plane. Positive X runs back along the ridge, and positive Y runs down the eave.*

11. On the status bar, click the Absolute Mode Transform Type-In button to toggle to Offset mode (see Figure 3.79). Enter 20 in the X-axis numeric field, 20 in the Y-axis numeric field, and press Enter. Right-click the Perspective label in the viewport and switch back to Smooth+Highlights shading. Skylight01 is now in position on the roof (see Figure 3.80).

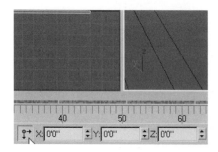

FIGURE 3.79
Toggle Absolute Mode Transform Type-in to Offset Mode Transform Type-in, and then move the Skylight01 20 feet in the positive X and Y axes.

FIGURE 3.80
Skylight01 is now positioned exactly where you want it and is flush with the roof surface.

12. Save the file; it should already be called Ch03_Skylight02.max.

The Normal Align command makes use of the face normal vectors of each 3D face to enable you to match normal to normal to place objects on other objects. In this case, it gave proper orientation of the skylight to the roof, but you learned to use Snap options to specifically place objects based on geometry attributes. This positioned the skylight at a known point on the shed. You were then able to move the skylight an exact amount in a desired plane by using the Transform Type-in and the Local reference coordinate system.

Understanding the concepts in this exercise enables you to work faster and more accurately, thus increasing your production.

AutoGrid Feature and Grid Helpers

As mentioned earlier in this chapter, grid helper objects can be treated much like any object in the scene, except that they will never render in the final image.

Although you can go to Create panel, Helpers panel, and create a grid object in your scene, you will learn a more automatic way to model directly on surfaces with the option of creating a grid object or not.

AutoGrid in 3ds max 6 is a feature that again uses the face normals of surfaces to define the current work plane. So far, all the objects you created in the exercises have been created on the planes in space defined by the black lines that run through the 0,0,0 coordinate of the World coordinate space.

In Exercise 3.12, you learn to create and modify a grid on a surface, use the Grid reference coordinate system to position objects, and then you learn to return to the default World coordinate system grids.

Exercise 3.12   Using AutoGrid and Grid Helpers for More Control

1. Open the file called Ch03_Skylight02.max on the CD-ROM or from the preceding exercise. From the File pull-down menu, choose Save As, point to an appropriate subdirectory on your hard drive, and use the plus sign button to save a new file with the name incremented to Ch03_Skylight03.max.

2. This is the shed scene with the skylight from Exercise 3.11. In this exercise, you learn how AutoGrid works, but you are only experimenting at this point and might not want to commit to the changes. You might remember the Hold command from when navigating the Stack view and dropping below a modifier that has changed topology. You answered Hold/Yes to a Warning dialog to save the scene in a buffer file on the hard drive. In the Edit pull-down menu, choose Hold.

3. In the Perspective viewport, zoom so that you can see most of the roof plane and skylight. In the Create panel, click the Box primitive button and check AutoGrid in the Object Type rollout (see Figure 3.81).

4. In the Perspective viewport, as you move the cursor over the shed and the skylight, you see that the tripod is adapting itself to the face normal of the face it is over. When the cursor is over the roof plane the skylight sits on, click and drag a new box object; you see a grid appear on the roof surface (see Figure 3.82). When you click to finalize the height of the box, the grid disappears; the box has now been created directly on the roof surface.

FIGURE 3.81
First, click the Box button, and then check AutoGrid in the Create panel, Object Type rollout.

FIGURE 3.82   *With AutoGrid turned on, you can click and drag a new box on the roof surface.*

5. You do not need a box on the roof surface, only the grid object it used. To get rid of the box and return the scene to the state before you started this experiment, go to the Edit pull-down menu and choose Fetch. Click Yes when a dialog appears asking whether it is OK to fetch the file from the hold buffer. You are now back to where you were when you clicked Hold.

6. Create the box on the roof plane again with AutoGrid, but this time, hold the Alt key as you drag the box on the roof. The grid object remains, and the AutoGrid option is checked off in the Object Type rollout. Press the Delete key to delete the box; it was only used to create the grid on a surface.

7. On the main toolbar, click the Select Object button and pick the grid in the Perspective viewport. It highlights white like other objects. In the Modify panel, Parameters rollout, set the Grid Spacing to 4 and press Enter. The new grid has 4-foot spacing that you could snap to if you set your snap to grid points or grid lines. The size of the grid object is not so important. It is only a visual aid, but the grid extends in the plane to infinity. Anything you create is on the work planes defined by the location of 0,0,0 of this object.

tip

The information is still in the hold buffer and remains there until you pick Hold again. You could start a new experiment and Fetch back the old information at any time.

It is a good idea to use the File, Save keyboard shortcut (Ctrl+ S), because then you have the information stored in two places in case something goes wrong.

8. You now use this grid to array the skylight across the roof at specific intervals. In the Perspective viewport, select Skylight01. On the main toolbar, click the Select and Move button and change the reference coordinate system from Local to Grid.

9. On the main toolbar, right-click the Snap Toggle button and, in the Grid and Snap Settings dialog, click Clear All, and then check only Grid Points. Close the dialog and, on the main toolbar, toggle Snap on.

10. To better see what you are doing, go to the Views pull-down menu and choose Save Active Perspective View. This enables you to get back to this view. In the Perspective viewport, right-click the Viewport label, choose Views, Grid, Top (see Figure 3.83) from the cascading menu to show the Grid view in the viewport. Zoom in the Grid (Top) viewport so that you can see the grid and the skylight.

11. In the Grid viewport, select Skylight01, hold the Shift key, click on the lower-left corner of the skylight so you see the cyan Snap indicator, and move 20 feet to the left. You can read on the status bar when the X-axis numeric field reads –20'0". The Move operation is snapping to the 4-foot grid points, but you have to keep the skylights aligned horizontally because, by default, the Transform gizmo is overridden by the Snap settings.

12. In the Clone Options dialog, check Instance and enter 10 in the Number of Copies field. When you click OK, you get an array of 11 skylights each spaced 20 feet from the other (see Figure 3.84).

13. To return to the Perspective view, right-click in the Grid viewport if it is not already active, press P, and, in the Views pull-down menu, choose Restore Active Perspective View.

FIGURE 3.83 *By right-clicking the Perspective viewport label, you can choose Views, Grid, Top to look directly down on the new grid.*

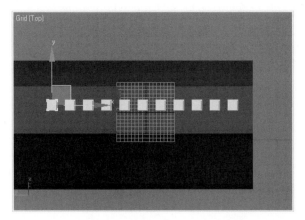

FIGURE 3.84 *Using a grid object with 4-foot spacing and moving the skylight while snapping to grid points enables you to create an array of instanced skylights across the roof.*

14. To return to the World coordinate grid system, click the Select Object button on the main toolbar and pick the grid object on the roof. Right-click and choose Activate HomeGrid from the Quad menu (see Figure 3.85). The grid object is still in the roof plane, but remains inactive until you select it and right-click to activate again. Click the Snap Toggle button to turn it off.

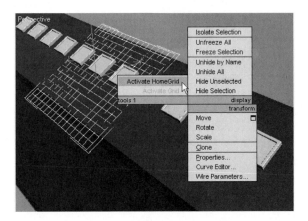

FIGURE 3.85   *You can switch back to the default World coordinate grid by selecting the current grid object, right-clicking, and choosing Activate HomeGrid from the Quad menu.*

15. Save the file; it should already be called Ch03_Skylight03.max.

AutoGrid enables you to create 3D primitive objects or 2D shapes on any surface based on the face normal under the cursor when you start the creation process. The temporary grid disappears when the creation is complete. An alternative is to hold the Alt key when using AutoGrid; in which case, a permanent grid object is created with the object or shape. The new grid can define a new reference coordinate system and can be adjusted in size and spacing for more control. You can switch back to the default World coordinate grid system by deactivating the current grid or by deleting it.

Summary

In this chapter, you learned modeling techniques and processes that, although not the most exciting and flashy features, are very important to a smooth workflow in 3ds max 6. Some of the concepts and methods you learned include the following:

- **Startup files**—By setting up a standardized display space, you learned to smooth your workflow. This can be especially true in a collaborative work environment.

- **2D shapes**—Creating 2D shapes and converting them to 3D objects can be a flexible and efficient way to work. You learned about compound shapes and 2D sub-object editing methods. With compound shapes, you can create complex objects that would be very difficult to build otherwise.

- **Modifiers and the stack**—You learned the important concept of how the 3ds max 6 modifier stack functions to allow flexible editing throughout the history of an object's creation. Individual modifiers can be adjusted or removed from the stack.

- **Alignment tools and grid objects**—You performed exercises that illustrated some valuable ways to align objects to objects and build on specific planes in 3D space. Alignment relies heavily on your knowledge of reference coordinate systems that you learned about in Chapter 2.

CHAPTER 4

Shipbuilding 101: The Making of a Boat

In This Chapter

In this chapter, you learn more modeling techniques that enable you to use a background image as a guide for editing. You also learn a few new modifiers and some new alignment techniques for placing objects along complex paths. In this chapter, you create several scenes and then learn to merge them into a single file. Some of the topics covered in this chapter include the following:

- **Background images**—You can use maps or images in viewports as a background to use as a guide when modeling.

- **Editable polygons**—Converting 3D mesh objects to editable polygons results in four-sided faces, where possible, rather than the triangular faces of mesh objects and introduces new tools for editing.

- **Symmetry modifier**—This modifier enables you to create half an object and, in one operation, mirror, trim, and weld the two halves together.

- **Spacing tool**—This tool makes it possible to place equally spaced clones between two points or along a complex path.

- **More modifiers**—You learn to use the Bevel Profile and Lathe modifiers to create easily editable objects from 2D shapes.

- **Merge files**—An efficient workflow, especially in a collaborative environment, can result from creating small manageable files and then merging them into a single scene.

This chapter requires you to do a fair amount of hand editing in the exercises. Read the exercises first to see the direction the process will take, and then go back and do the steps slowly and carefully. With a little practice, it will become second nature to quickly trace over and edit using background images.

Key Terms

- **Background image**—A picture or map that can be viewed as a backdrop to any viewport. It is not part of the rendering, but only a template to be used as a modeling guide.

- **Editable polygon**—An editable polygon has faces with four sides compared to the triangular faces of a mesh object. There are also new tools available when modifying editable polygon objects.

- **Box modeling**—A term used to describe a modeling technique in which you start with a primitive object, such as a box, and add edges and polygons to create more complex objects.

- **Renderable spline**—2D shapes can have attributes set that give them 3D thickness in the scene.

Primitive Objects and Editable Poly: A Starting Point

In Chapter 3, "Fundamental Modeling Techniques: The Building Blocks," you worked with 2D shapes and 3D mesh objects. While editing the 3d mesh objects, you applied modifiers that enabled you to select sub-object level, Vertex, Edge, Face, Polygon, or Element entities. A polygon within a 3D mesh is defined as any set of triangular faces bordered by a visible edge.

Editable polygon, or *editable poly* as it is also known, is a different type of editing object. Instead of triangular faces, it builds the surface with quads whenever possible. It is primarily designed for computer gaming engines to more easily keep information stored in vertices in a more controlled manner. However, editable poly objects have sub-object levels of Vertex, Edge, Border, Polygon, and Element and have a very different set of editing tools available; these tools can prove to be very efficient and fast to work with.

The downside to working with editable poly is that there is no history to navigate when trying to make changes. After you commit to a change and move on to other edits, it can be very difficult to modify those changes.

Figure 4.1 shows two objects in wireframe mode with all edges visible. The object back and left was converted to an editable poly, and the foreground object is an editable mesh. You can see that the only triangular faces in the editable poly are in the rounded end, where they are absolutely necessary to describe the curved surface.

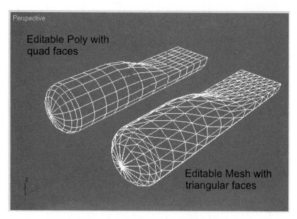

FIGURE 4.1   *You can see editable poly on the left and editable mesh on the right. Editable poly uses quad faces where possible, whereas the editable mesh always uses triangular faces.*

As mentioned, the editing tools are also different for the two object types, both in the tools available and in the manner in which they are applied. Figure 4.2 shows an overview of the Modify panels for each object type.

You will work mostly with editable poly objects in this chapter because the tools lend themselves well to modifying against a background object to create a clean, efficient object that accurately depicts the form of the object you are tracing.

The exercises in this chapter walk you through several repetitions of editable poly editing while creating the boat hull, starting with a simple Box primitive object.

note

There is an EditMesh modifier that you can apply to any 3D object to allow the same functionality as editable mesh. It can be removed or disabled from the object if necessary, returning you to a point in the editing history before the modifier.

There is no Edit Poly modifier; after you convert an object to editable poly and made changes, you are committed to those changes.

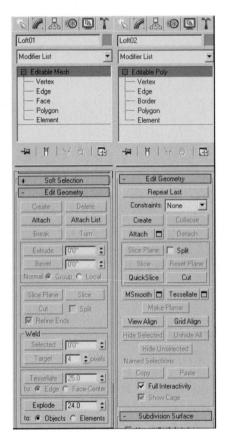

FIGURE 4.2   *Modify panel for editable mesh on the left and for editable poly on the right. Different tools are available for each object type.*

Box Modeling from a Background Image

The boat you will be re-creating is the USS *Agamenticus,* an ironclad warship built in Portsmouth, New Hampshire, in 1865. You can find photos, more information, and links about the *Agamenticus* and similar ships at `http://www.history.navy.mil/ photos/sh-usn/usnsh-a/agament.htm`, a public web site of the Department of the Navy. Figure 4.3 shows the completed 3ds max 6 model.

This boat will not be historically or physically accurate, but you will learn a modeling process that you can apply to many different objects from boats, planes, or furniture, to more organic objects such as characters.

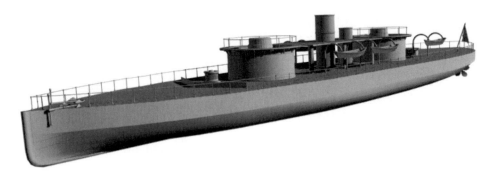

FIGURE 4.3   *An example of the model of the USS* Agamenticus *that you will be building in this chapter.*

The background image you use as a guide to the modeling is a set of hull plans from a similar class of boat, although not of the USS *Agamenticus* itself. The boat is long enough so that the plans are broken into the bow and stern lines with the connecting hull section to be interpolated as a straight line.

> **note**
>
> The bow is the front of the boat, the stern is the back of the boat, and the keel is the main structural element that runs the length of the bottom of the boat.

The boat plans are typical hull plans consisting of vertical station lines and horizontal water lines. You will edit a box to match the curvature defined by the intersections of these lines, real or interpolated, to form the shape of the hull. If you are not familiar with hull design, work slowly at first, making sure you understand why you are moving entities of the box, not just moving them because it is written in the steps.

I've created boat hulls through various modeling techniques such as lofting, spline and patch techniques, and NURBS modeling, and none has proven so fast and efficient as Box modeling (as it will be for you, after you learn to read the hull design plans).

This chapter is a good one in which to practice using the Hold and Fetch commands found in the Edit pull-down menu, as well as the Save keyboard shortcut of Ctrl+S. These options enable you to go back if you mess up during the process.

Background Images and Box Modeling Techniques

You first learn to set up a scene with background images in the various viewports and trace those images by editing an editable poly object at sub-object levels. The bow section and stern section are built separately in the scene, and are then attached later in this chapter.

Exercise 4.1   Configuring for Background Images in Viewports

1. Open the file called Ch04_BoatHull01.max on the CD-ROM. From the File pull-down menu, choose Save As, point to an appropriate subdirectory on your hard drive, and use the plus sign button to save a new file with the name incremented to Ch04_BoatHull02.max. There is nothing in this scene, but it ensures that you are using correct units and viewport settings.

2. In the Views pull-down menu, choose Viewport Background (Alt+B). In the Viewport Background dialog, click the Files button and, from the CD-ROM, open Hull_plan.jpg. In the Aspect Ratio area, check the Match Bitmap radio button and make sure that Lock Zoom/Pan is checked. For the Apply Source and Display To area, check the All Views radio button (see Figure 4.4). Matching the bitmap aspect ratio is important to keep the image from distorting when it tries to fit different viewport layouts. Lock Zoom/Pan enable you to zoom and pan while the image retains its relative size. Apply to All Views causes the image to show in each viewport. Click OK.

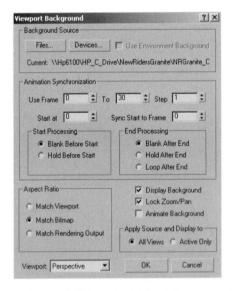

FIGURE 4.4   *In the Viewport Background dialog, check Match Bitmap, Lock Zoom/Pan, and All Views options for this exercise.*

3. Right-click the viewport label of each ortho viewport, Top, Front, Left, and clear the Show Grid option. Then, right-click the Perspective viewport label and clear

both Show Grid and Show Background. You will use a clean Perspective viewport to keep track of the modeling progress. Then, set each viewport to use Smooth + Highlights shading (see Figure 4.5). The menu closes each time you change an option, so you must right-click the viewport label each time.

tip

This is a good point at which to use the keyboard shortcut Ctrl+S to save the file with the current name (and to use the Edit pull-down menu, Hold option for added safety).

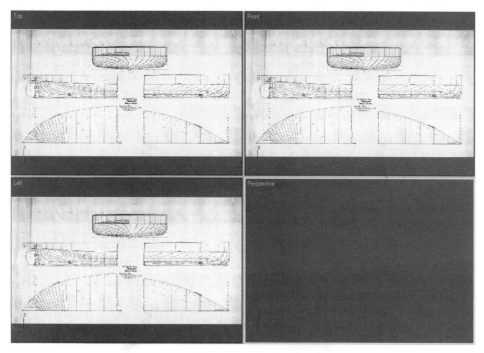

FIGURE 4.5   *Right-click the viewport labels of the ortho viewports, Top, Front, and Left, and clear the Show Grid options. Right-click the Perspective viewport label and clear Show Grid and Show Background.*

4. Right-click the Perspective label and choose Configure in the menu. In the Viewport Configuration dialog, check the Rendering Options feature called Display Selected with Edged Faces (see Figure 4.6). Click OK. This action causes objects selected in shaded viewports to automatically show both the shaded faces and the wireframe edges, making sub-object editing much easier.

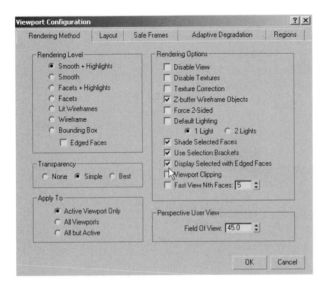

caution

Using background images in viewports often can use large amounts of memory when trying to zoom or pan in the viewports. You will see warning dialogs asking if you want to continue. Turning off the viewport Show Background image for the zoom or pan operation, and then turning it back on again, keeps the warning dialog from slowing the process.

FIGURE 4.6   *Right-click the Perspective viewport label and choose Configure. In the dialog, check the option called Display Selected with Edged Faces for simultaneous shaded and wireframe views of only the selected objects.*

5. Activate the Top viewport and use Zoom and Pan to center the bow plan in the viewport (see Figure 4.7).

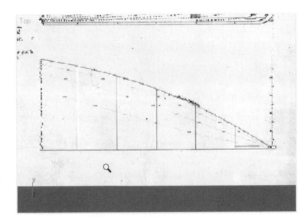

FIGURE 4.7   *In the Top viewport, use Zoom and Pan to roughly center the bow plan in the viewport.*

6. In the Create panel, Geometry panel, click the Box button in the Object Type rollout and drag a box to cover the bow plan drawing. In the Modify panel, Parameters rollout, set the Length to 4' 8", the Width to 12'4" and the Height to 3'0". Rename the object Bow01.

7. You cannot see the plan below the box to make sure the alignment is close. Right-click the box and choose Properties in the Quad menu. In the Object Properties dialog, Display Properties area, check the See Through option (see Figure 4.8). Click OK.

tip

The options you set in the Viewport Configuration dialog pertain to all viewports, only the active viewport, or all but the active viewport, depending on the option checked in the Apply To area of the Viewport Configuration dialog.

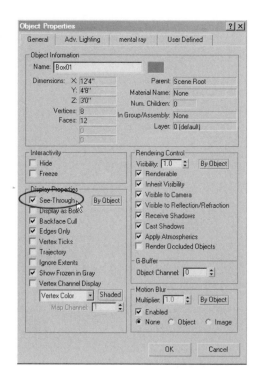

FIGURE 4.8   *Right-click the box in the Top viewport and choose Properties in the Quad menu. Check the See-Through option in the Display Properties area.*

8. On the main toolbar, click the Select and Move button and, in the Top viewport, move the box to align it with the bow plan as best you can, remembering that accuracy is not so important in this exercise (see Figure 4.9).

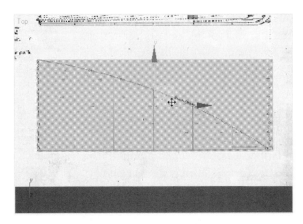

FIGURE 4.9   *Using the Select and Move tool from the main toolbar, you can easily position the semitransparent box in the Top viewport over the bow plan.*

9. Right-click the box again and choose Convert To and Convert to Editable Poly from the cascading menu (see Figure 4.10). In the Modify panel, rename the box Bow01.

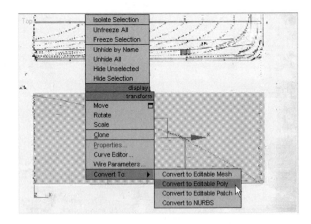

FIGURE 4.10   *Right-click the box to Convert to Editable Poly from the cascading menu.*

10. Save the file; it should already be named Ch04_BoatHull02.max.

By loading a background image in each of the ortho viewports and setting it to respect the original aspect ratio of the image, you can position objects quite accurately over the background with ease. The ability to change the properties of an object to See-Through helps this process.

Slicing Station Lines

In Exercise 4.2, you slice the Bow01 box at each station line, lines that run vertically through the hull, in the Top viewport. A tool called Quick Slice enables you to quickly slice through the object to create new vertices and edges that will define new polygons in the object. These can then be further edited to form the bow of the hull.

Exercise 4.2   Modifying an Editable Poly to Slice at Station Lines

1. Open the file called Ch04_BoatHull02.max on the CD-ROM or from the preceding exercise. From the File pull-down menu, choose Save As, point to an appropriate subdirectory on your hard drive, and use the plus sign button to save a new file with the name incremented to Ch04_BoatHull03.max.

2. You can use Figure 4.11 as a reference for where the seven slices will be taken; there are two slices on the right side for the keel and stem of the boat.

note

The background image is undoubtedly scanned from old paper drawings, leaving something to be desired in the quality. Follow the steps carefully and interpolate where it looks like a line might be, even if you cannot clearly see it.

You should also use Edit, Hold after each slice in case something goes wrong and you need to get back to a point where you know the model is correct.

note

You might have to turn on Display Selected with Edged Faces for this viewport to see the results of the following steps. It is already active in Perspective viewport, depending on the options you set in Exercise 4.1, step 4.

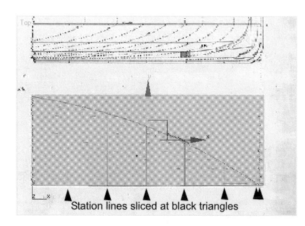

Figure 4.11   *The black triangles indicate where the station lines are in the plan. Notice that there are two triangles on the right side to create a stem and keel slice.*

3. Right-click in the Top viewport to activate it and click the Min/Max Toggle (Alt+W) at the lower right of the display to maximize the Top viewport. Make sure Bow01 is selected. In the Modify panel, Stack View, expand Editable Poly and highlight Edge sub-object level. In the Edit Geometry rollout, click the QuickSlice button (see Figure 4.12).

4. In the Top viewport, pick Bow01 on the lower edge where it intersects with the first station line. Move the mouse and you see a red slice line through the box. Move the cursor over the station line near the top to ensure a vertical slice, and click to finalize the step (see Figure 4.13). If the slice was successful, click the Hold option in the Edit pull-down menu.

FIGURE 4.12
When in sub-object Edge mode, click QuickSlice in the Modify panel, Edit Geometry rollout.

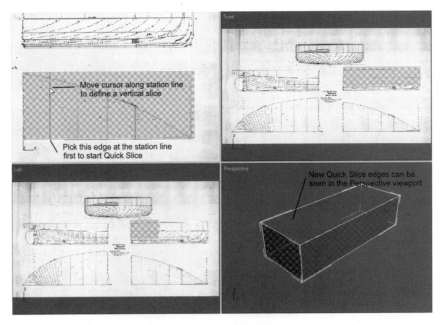

FIGURE 4.13   *Use the QuickSlice command to slice from the bottom edge of the box in the Top viewport where it meets the first station line. Then, move the cursor along the station line and click when the new red slice line is vertical.*

5. Repeat step 4 for each of the other six station lines, creating two near the right edge to form the stem and keel. Remember to use Edit, Hold after each Quick Slice in case something goes wrong so that you can use Fetch to return to the last good action. The box should look like Figure 4.14.

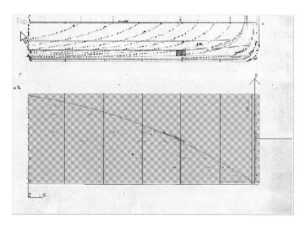

FIGURE 4.14   *Use QuickSlice to create a total of seven new station lines in Bow01.*

6. In the Modifier panel, Stack view, highlight Editable Poly to exit sub-object mode. Save the file. It should already be named Ch04_BoatHull03.max.

The editable poly QuickSlice command provides a great way to slice new edges and vertices in a 3D object.

warning

The QuickSlice plane is always perpendicular to your line of sight in the viewport. For this reason, it is dangerous to use QuickSlice in a nonorthographic viewport unless you are absolutely sure of what you are doing.

Moving Vertices to Form the Hull Shape

In Exercise 4.3, you learn to move selection sets of vertices to make Bow01 match the curve of the hull plan as seen from the top. You learn about Ignore Backfacing, a command that is helpful in the following exercises.

Exercise 4.3   Ignore Backfacing and Vertex Editing

1. Open the file called Ch04_BoatHull03.max on the CD-ROM or from the preceding exercise. From the File pull-down menu, choose Save As, point to an appropriate subdirectory on your hard drive, and use the plus sign button to save a new file with the name incremented to Ch04_BoatHull04.max.

2. Select Bow01 in the Top viewport. In the Modify panel, Stack view, highlight the Vertex sub-object level. The vertices of the new slice edges highlight red in the viewports. Make sure Select Object is highlighted on the main toolbar and click any-place in the Top viewport to deselect all vertices. The vertices are now blue. In the Modify panel, Selection rollout, be sure that the Ignore Backfacing option check box is clear (see Figure 4.15). As seen in the Top viewport, each blue tick represents two vertices, one at the upper and another at the lower edge. If Ignore Backfacing is checked, it is impossible to select the lower vertex and the editing will not be correct. You will need to check the option in later exercises.

FIGURE 4.15
Make sure that the Ignore Backfacing check box is clear so that you can select vertices on the back side of the box as seen in the Top viewport.

3. On the main toolbar, click the Select and Move button. In the Top viewport, drag a selection window on the vertices second from the left, top edge (see Figure 4.16).

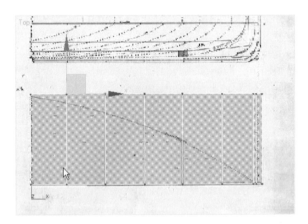

FIGURE 4.16   *While in Select and Move mode, drag a selection window to select the two vertices in this area.*

4. Move the cursor over the Y-axis restrict arrow of the Transform gizmo and move the two vertices downward until they meet the curved edge of the drawing (see Figure 4.17).

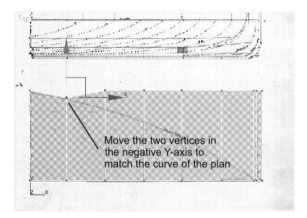

caution

Just picking the two vertices will be impossible, because one is directly above the other. You must use a window selection area with Ignore Backfacing off to select them.

Move the two vertices in the negative Y-axis to match the curve of the plan

FIGURE 4.17   *Move the pair of vertices in the negative Y-axis to meet the curve of the plan.*

5. Repeat step 4 for each pair of vertices along the upper edge in the Top viewport. Zoom in on the Top viewport to see what you are doing, but do not be obsessive about accuracy. The last two pairs should match the stem in the drawing (see Figure 4.18).

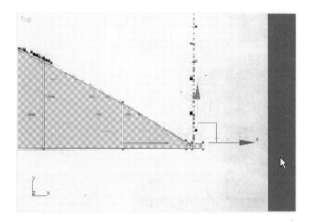

FIGURE 4.18   *Move each pair of vertices to match the curve of the hull plan. Watch that you match the stem on the right.*

6. In the Modify panel, Stack view, highlight Editable Poly to exit sub-object mode. Save the file; it should already be called Ch04_BoatHull04.max.

Slicing the Water Lines

Exercise 4.4 is similar to Exercise 4.2 and gives you more practice with QuickSlice. However, you learn to switch viewports and align the model with another view of the plans. Remember that this is a 3D model, so working in one view is highly impractical. You should always work in the viewport that gives you the most control over your modeling. This is another reason to learn your reference coordinate systems well, because the directions of the X, Y, and Z axes can change in each viewport and coordinate system combination.

Exercise 4.4   Slicing the Horizontal Water Lines

1. Open the file called Ch04_BoatHull04.max on the CD-ROM or from the preceding exercise. From the File pull-down menu, choose Save As, point to an appropriate subdirectory on your hard drive, and use the plus sign button to save a new file with the name incremented to Ch04_BoatHull05.max.

2. Activate the Front viewport by right-clicking in it, and then zoom and pan to view the side drawing of the boat's bow section. You first align and resize the Bow01 to fit the plan.

3. In the Front viewport, select Bow01 and, on the main toolbar, click Select and Move. Move Bow01 in the X and Y axes to align the right and bottom edges to the drawing. In the Modify panel, Stack view, highlight level. Drag a selection window around pairs of vertices in the top row and, using the Y-axis restrict arrow of the Transform gizmo, move the vertices to match to top of the drawing (see Figure 4.19).

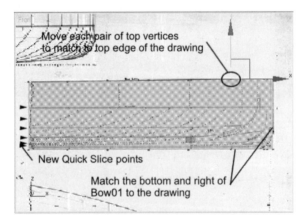

FIGURE 4.19 *Match the bottom and right edges of Bow01 to the plan and, at Vertex sub-object level, move pairs of vertices in the top row to match the plan.*

tip

Whether you zoom with the Zoom button at the lower right of the display or you use the mouse wheel, holding the Ctrl key increases the zoom factor and speed, and holding the Alt key diminishes the effects, offering more control.

4. Right-click the Front viewport label and make sure the Edged Faces option is checked in the menu. This enables you to see the edges and shaded object simultaneously. In the Modify panel, Stack view, highlight Edge sub-object level. In the Edit Geometry rollout, click the QuickSlice button. In the Front viewport, use QuickSlice to cut six horizontal water lines as indicated by the black arrows in Figure 4.19. Click the left edge of Bow01 first, and then move the cursor to the right along the drawing line to create a horizontal slice along each water line or parallel to them. Use Edit, Hold after each slice so that you have a way to back up, other than Undo, if you make a mistake. Pick the QuickSlice button to disable it when you finish all six slices. The final slice pattern for station lines and water lines should look like what's shown in Figure 4.20.

note

The second new slice from the top does not fall on a water line in the drawing. It is perfectly acceptable to interpolate between water lines to give more points to describe a smooth hull if you think it is necessary. Keep in mind, however, that efficiency is of prime importance in modeling, and the detail must justify the extra overhead.

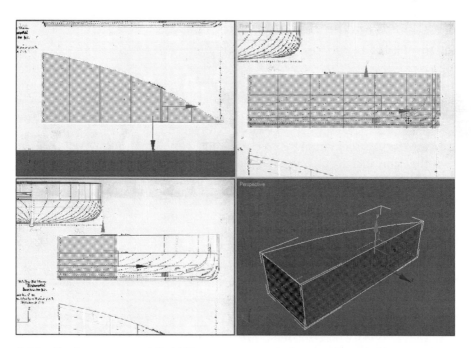

FIGURE 4.20 *You have now used QuickSlice to create vertical station lines and horizontal water lines in Bow01.*

5. In the Modify, Stack view, highlight Editable Poly to exit sub-object mode. Save the file; it should already be named Ch04_BoatHull05.max.

Forming the Hull Curvature

In Exercise 4.5, you learn to edit at Vertex level to move the vertices at the intersection of station lines and water lines to match the curvature of the hull as described in the end drawings of the boat. First, you rotate Bow01 in the Top viewport and then, in the Front viewport, align it with the drawing as viewed from the bow. You then learn to select single vertices and move them into place without affecting vertices in the background that need to stay in place. Make sure you review the steps first to have a clear understanding of what this will accomplish and why you must pick vertices carefully. You then move pairs of vertices to form the curve of the bow.

Exercise 4.5   Moving Vertices at the Intersection of Station Line and Water Line to Fit the Hull Curvature

1. Open the file called Ch04_BoatHull05.max on the CD-ROM or from the preceding exercise. From the File pull-down menu, choose Save As, point to an appropriate subdirectory on your hard drive, and use the plus sign button to save a new file with the name incremented to Ch04_BoatHull06.max.

2. Click the Select Object button on the main toolbar and, in the Top viewport, select Bow01. You must first rotate it so that it matches up with the end view of the hull in the Front viewport. On the main toolbar, click the Angle Snap toggle, and then right-click Angle Snap to see that it is set to 5 degrees. Click the Select and Rotate button on the main toolbar (see Figure 4.21). Close the Grid and Snap Settings dialog.

3. In the Top viewport, rotate Bow01 in the Z-axis –90 degrees. Rotate will be snapping in 5-degree increments, and you can read the angle in the Transform Type-In fields at the bottom center of the display. The point of the bow faces downward, as shown in Figure 4.22.

note

As mentioned at the beginning of this chapter, the boat plans used here do not represent the full length of the boat. The bow and stern sections are depicting the areas of maximum curvature and the midsection of the boat is presumed to be a fairly straight-line interpolation. The end-view drawings represent the boat looking both forward and aft with the outer edges being the widest point of the hull. Therefore, Bow01 does not match the width of the hull drawing as seen from the front, so it will be the centerline you will use as the matching edge.

note

Again, you might have to turn on Display Selected with Edged Faces for this viewport to see the results of the following steps. It is already active in Perspective viewport, depending on the options you set in Exercise 4.1, step 4.

note

You might want to right-click on the Top viewport label and clear Show Background to make this faster.

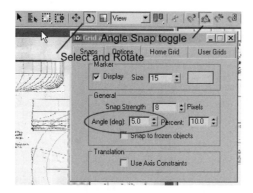

FIGURE 4.21   *Click, and then right-click the Angle Snap toggle on the main toolbar. You see that the default angle is 5 degrees. Close the Grid and Snap Settings dialog and click the Select and Rotate button on the main toolbar.*

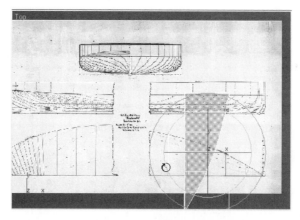

FIGURE 4.22   *Using Angle Snap, you can rotate Bow01 in the Top viewport in 5-degree increments. Read the angle in the Transform Type-In fields until it is rotated –90 degrees. The bow will point downward.*

4. Right-click in the Front viewport to activate it. On the main toolbar, click Select and Move and move Bow01 to match the center of the end drawing. The right side of the drawing is looking from the bow toward the stern. The left side is looking from the stern forward. Match the bottom of Bow01 to the very bottom of the keel projection (see Figure 4.23).

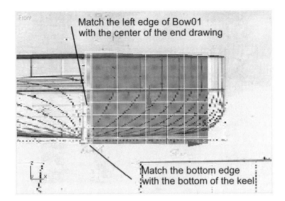

Figure 4.23 *In the Front viewport, move Bow01 to match the left edge to the enter of the end view and the bottom edge to the bottom of the keel.*

5. Now, move pairs of vertices in the Front viewport to form the keel of the boat. Zoom in to the bow area in the Top and Perspective viewports to see the curved side of the boat, and zoom in close in the Front viewport to see the whole Bow01 (see Figure 4.24). Edit, Hold at this point.

caution

You are about to move vertices in a very specific manner. It would be wise to use the Edit, Hold option frequently.

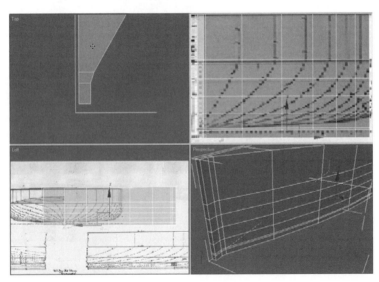

Figure 4.24 *In the Top viewport, zoom close to the bow; in the Front viewport, zoom to view Bow01; in the Perspective viewport, Arc Rotate and zoom to see the curved side of the boat.*

6. In the Modify panel, Stack view, highlight Vertex sub-object mode. Make sure the Ignore Backfacing check box is clear in the Selection rollout. In the Front viewport, click carefully in empty space to deselect all vertices, and then drag a window around the third pair of vertices from the bottom left of Bow01. You should see two vertices selected at the bottom of the Selection rollout of the Modify panel (see Figure 4.25).

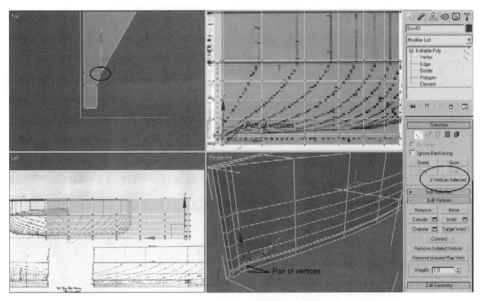

FIGURE 4.25   *Drag a selection window around the pair of vertices third from the bottom left in the Front viewport.*

7. In the Front viewport, move the pair of selected vertices left (negative X-axis; use the Transform gizmo) until they are behind the second pair from the left. This defines the width of the keel. Continue from left to right until you have moved all the pairs to build a straight keel (see Figure 4.26). You can Arc Rotate in the Perspective viewport to see the keel clearly.

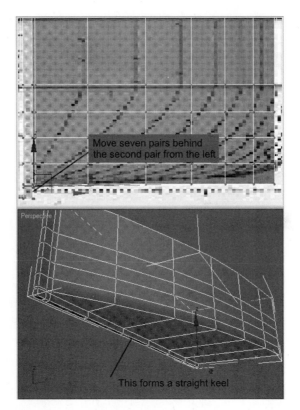

Move seven pairs behind
the second pair from the left

This forms a straight keel

FIGURE 4.26 *Move the pair of selected vertices in the negative X-axis behind the second pair from the left. Repeat this for each pair to the right to form a keel.*

8. Now, move individual vertices so they follow the curvature lines of the drawing in the Front viewport. They do not have to be on the curve lines, but you use those as a guide. The top two rows of vertices and the left two columns of vertices do not get moved because they form the gunwales and keel of the boat. To avoid vertices that might be behind the model as you view it in the Front viewport, check the Ignore Backfacing check box in the Selection rollout of the Modify panel. Start with the fourth column from the left and move the four vertices from the bottom, one at a time, in the negative X-axis, to match the curve nearest that column (see Figure 4.27).

9. Working from left to right, move the subsequent vertices in the negative X-axis to match their closest curve in the drawing. Bow01 should take on the shape of the hull, as shown in Figure 4.28. Use Edit, Hold often so that you can use Edit, Fetch to recover from any mistakes. The first time you do this, it might seem complex, but when you understand the process, you will be able to perform it quickly.

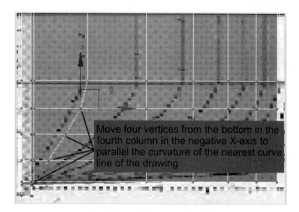

FIGURE 4.27   *Move the four bottom vertices of the forth column from the left to match the drawing curve nearest to it. You do not need to be on the curve; just keep the line parallel.*

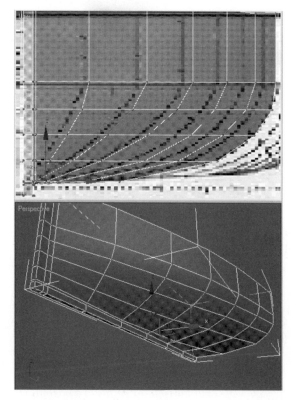

FIGURE 4.28   *Move the bottom four vertices of the other columns to match the curvature of their corresponding curve in the drawing.*

10. Now, clean up the curvature of the bow from the side view. Click Editable Poly in the Stack view to exit sub-object mode and, in the Left viewport, move Bow01 to match the right edge and bottom of the side drawing and zoom in on the lower-right corner (see Figure 4.29).

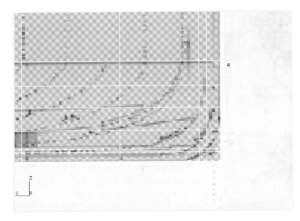

FIGURE 4.29   *In the Left viewport, move Bow01 to align the right and bottom edge to the drawing and zoom in.*

11. In the Modify panel, Stack view, highlight Vertex. In the Selection rollout, clear the Ignore Backfacing check box. In the Left viewport, select pairs of vertices at the intersections near the bottom right of the bow and move them in the negative X-axis to follow the curvature of the drawing. You need to select by window to get the two vertices, front and back, at each intersection. You have 14 pairs to move (see Figure 4.30).

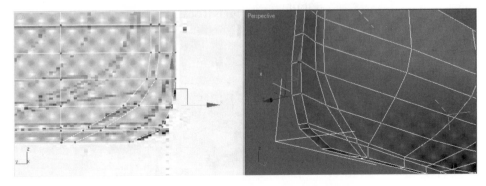

FIGURE 4.30   *Move 14 pairs of vertices in the negative X-axis to match the curvature of the drawing at the lower right of the bow in the Left viewport.*

12. Highlight Editable Poly in the Stack view to exit sub-object mode. Save the file; it should already be called Ch04_BoatHull06.max.

Resizing and Positioning the Bow and Stern to Full Scale

In Exercise 4.6, you open a new file that has the stern section modeled in the same way as Bow01, and both have been rotated and aligned to match the center edges and bottoms and to butt them together. Although the drawing was matched closely for the creation of the two objects, no scale relates the parts to the drawing. The determination has been made that scaling both objects by 500 percent closely represents the true size of the boat.

tip

You don't have to make everything in real-world sizes in 3ds max, but it is prudent to do so, especially with collaborative work. If your boat is only a few inches long, it will still look correct until you match it to someone else's scene that is in real units.

Exercise 4.6   Scaling and Positioning the Boat Sections

1. Open Ch04_Boat01.max from the CD-ROM. This file has the stern section, so do *not* use the file from the preceding exercise. Save the file to your hard drive with the name Ch04_Boat02.max. The file has a bow and stern section and the background image has been turned off (see Figure 4.31).

2. You now scale the bow and stern sections by 500 percent to make them close to real-world sizes. You learned in the preceding chapter that you should *never* scale objects in 3ds max because of the modifier stack evaluation order. Always apply an XForm modifier to the object and scale the modifier. In the Perspective viewport, select Bow01. In the Modify panel, Modifier List, choose XForm. On the main toolbar, click the Select and Uniform Scale button. In the status bar, toggle from Absolute Mode Transform Type-In to Offset Mode Transform Type-In and enter 500 in the X: numeric field—the only one available in Uniform Scale, it scales in all axes (see Figure 4.32). Press Enter. Bow01 fills the viewports. In the Modifier panel, Stack view, highlight XForm to exit sub-object Gizmo mode.

caution

The XForm modifier is the only modifier that automatically switches to sub-object mode. You must remember to exit sub-object mode before proceeding after you make adjustments.

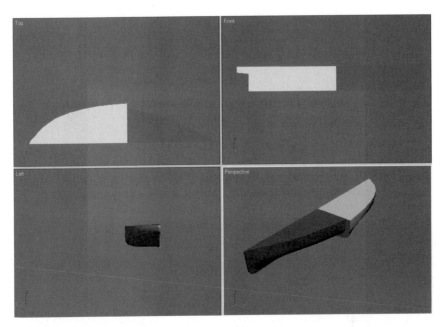

FIGURE 4.31   *The bow and stern sections of the boat with Show Background turned off.*

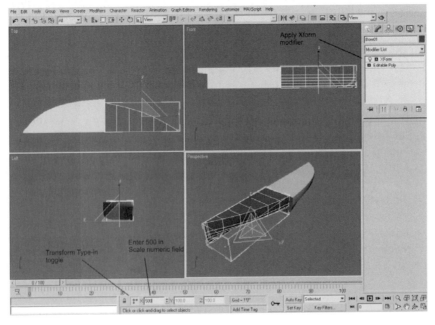

FIGURE 4.32   *Apply the XForm modifier and scale it 500 percent uniformly in all three axes.*

3. In the Perspective viewport, select Stern01 and repeat Step 2 to resize it by 500 percent. Click Zoom Extents All to fill the viewports with the objects, and you see they are out of alignment because they have different scaling centers.

4. Use the Align tool to realign them. In the Perspective viewport, make sure that Stern01 is selected. On the main toolbar, click the Align button and, in the Perspective viewport, click Bow01. Align is using the World coordinate system to determine the axes. In the Align Selection dialog, check the X Position check box. In the Current Object column, check Maximum, and check Minimum in the Target Object column. This aligns the butt ends. Click the Apply button to set the alignment and reset the check boxes, but remain in Align. Check Y Position and Z Position and check Minimum in both Current and Target Object columns (see Figure 4.33). Click OK.

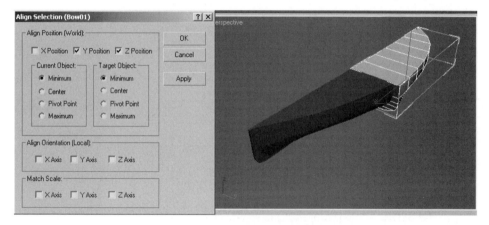

FIGURE 4.33 *Use the Align command to align Stern01 to Bow01.*

5. Select both objects in the Perspective viewport, right-click, and choose Convert To and Convert to Editable Poly in the Quad menu. This collapses the modifier stack to "bake in" the scaling of the XForm modifier.

6. Select only Bow01 and, in the Modify panel, Edit Geometry rollout, click the Attach button and pick Stern01 in the Perspective viewport. This attaches the two objects into a single editable poly. Click the Attach button to deactivate it and rename the object Hull01.

7. Save the file; it is already named Ch04_Boat02.max.

Setting Up the Boat Length

You have attached the two Editable Poly objects into a single editable poly object, but you realize that the boat is not the right length. In Exercise 4.7, you learn about sub-object Element editing and you clean up Hull01 to prepare to make it a continuous object.

Exercise 4.7   Element Sub-Object Editing

1. Open the file called Ch04_Boat02.max on the CD-ROM or from the preceding exercise. From the File pull-down menu, choose Save As, point to an appropriate subdirectory on your hard drive, and use the plus sign button to save a new file with the name incremented to Ch04_Boat03.max.

2. You have one object in the scene. If you select Hull01 in the Top viewport, go to the Utilities panel, and click Measure; you see that the bounding box dimensions—that is, the outside dimensions—are reported at the bottom and that the length is 131 feet (rounding up to the nearest foot; see Figure 4.34).

3. If you click the File pull-down menu and choose Summary Info from the menu, you see notes have been added in the Description area about the boat sizes (see Figure 4.35). The current length is 131' and the commissioned length from the notes is 258'6". Close the Summary Info dialog. This means the bow section must be moved 125'6" to in the positive X-axis of the Top viewport to be the correct overall length.

FIGURE 4.34

Use the Utilities panel, Measure tool to find information about the selected object.

4. In the Modify panel, Stack view, highlight Element sub-object level. In the Top viewport, pick the bow end (right), and the entire element that was defined by attaching two objects together turns red. Click the Select and Move button to activate it, make sure Offset Mode Transform Type-in is toggled on, and enter 125.5 in the X-axis numeric field in the status bar. Press Enter and the bow moves to the right. Click Zoom Extents All. Exit sub-object mode and open the Utilities panel. The overall length of Hull01 in the Measure panel is now 256'6" when rounded up.

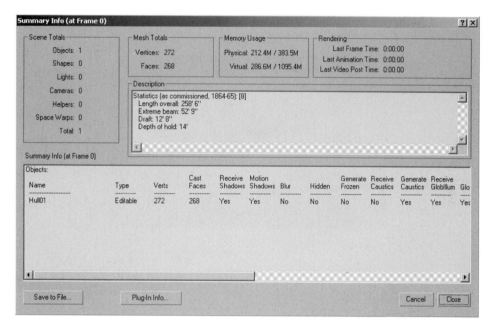

FIGURE 4.35   *From the File pull-down menu, choose Summary Info to see notes that have been entered to describe the size of the original boat.*

5. Now, remove faces from the flat areas to open the hull for connecting and welding in the next exercise to close the gap between bow and stern. In the Modify panel, Stack view, highlight Polygon sub-object mode. On the main toolbar, click the Select Object button, click in a blank area in the Top viewport to deselect everything, and toggle from crossing selection mode to window selection mode. Drag a selection window that includes only the flat inside ends of each element (see Figure 4.36). Press the Delete key to delete the end caps of the sections. Exit sub-object mode.

6. Save the file. It is already called Ch04_Boat03.max.

note

Looking at the stern section to the right in the Perspective viewport, notice that the backside of the boat seems to have disappeared. It has not. You are seeing the effect of face normals. Face normals that point toward the viewer are visible; face normals that point away are invisible.

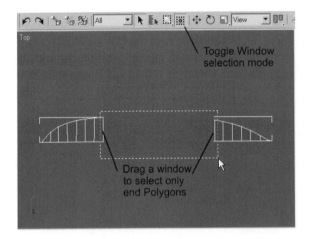

FIGURE 4.36   *In sub-object Polygon, using window selection mode, drag a window to include only the end caps of each hull section.*

Adding Segments to the Hull and Closing the Gap

In Exercise 4.8, you learn to add segments to the hull by cloning edges. You then weld the vertices from stern to bow to close the gap and make the hull one closed 3D object. You've already learned about welding selection sets of vertices into a common vertex that is at the geometric center of the selected shape vertices in Chapter 3, Exercise 3.7. In this exercise, you weld individual mesh vertices to target vertices. This ensures that one of the vertices, the target vertex, remains in place, which offers another level of control.

Exercise 4.8   Edge Cloning and Target Welding of Vertices

1. Open the file called Ch04_Boat03.max on the CD-ROM or from the preceding exercise. From the File pull-down menu, choose Save As, point to an appropriate subdirectory on your hard drive, and use the plus sign button to save a new file with the name incremented to Ch04_Boat04.max.

2. Select Hull01 and in the Modify panel, Stack view, highlight Edge sub-object level. In the Top viewport, drag a selection window around the right end edges of the stern section (see Figure 4.37).

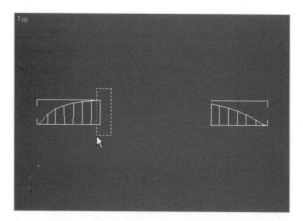

FIGURE 4.37   *In Edge sub-object level, drag a selection window around the right edges of the stern section as seen from the Top viewport.*

3. On the main toolbar, click the Select and Move button. Hold the Shift key and move the selected edges in the positive X-axis about ? of the way across the gap. This clones the edges and creates new faces. Repeat this three more times, each about the same distance until the gap is almost closed (see Figure 4.38).

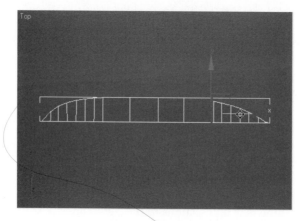

FIGURE 4.38   *Clone the edges four times to make four new segments that almost close the gap.*

4. Activate the Perspective viewport and zoom in on the gap between the bow and stern section. Highlight Vertex sub-object mode in the Stack view. In the Edit Vertices rollout, click the Target Weld button. In the Perspective viewport, click and drag from the back top vertex on the stern to the corresponding vertex on the bow. You see a dotted line when you are dragging (see Figure 4.39). Release the mouse button and the vertices are welded.

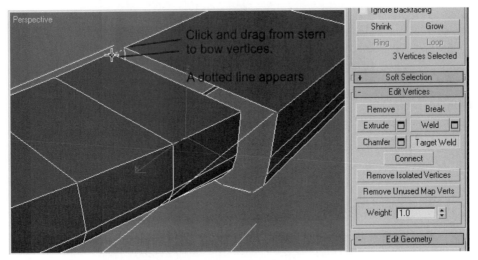

FIGURE 4.39   *In Edit Vertices rollout, click Target Weld button. Drag from the stern vertex to the corresponding bow vertex.*

5. Repeat step 4 to weld all the vertices around the hull gap. You have to Arc Rotate to view them, and it is easier if you maximize the Perspective viewport. Click the Target Weld button when you finish to disable it. Go to Select and Move and carefully move the vertices in the Y-axis of the Perspective viewport to "fair" or smooth out the curvature of the new hull sections to the stern and bow (see Figure 4.40).

6. Exit sub-object mode and save the file. It is already called Ch04_Boat04.max.

Don't worry. There is a finished half hull waiting if you hopelessly mess this one up. You sometimes need to practice a bit working in the Perspective viewport before it feels natural.

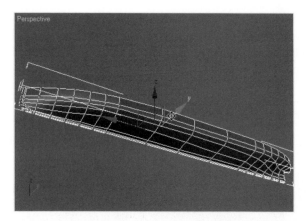

FIGURE 4.40 *Target Weld the vertices of the stern to corresponding vertices of the bow all around the gap. Then, move the new vertices in the Y-axis of the Perspective viewport to "fair" the lines and smooth the transition.*

Smoothing Groups

In Exercise 4.9, you learn about an important concept called *smoothing*. The viewport display and the renderers have the capability of making the edge between two adjacent faces a hard edge or a smooth, blended edge.

This is all controlled by smoothing groups. It is simple: If two adjacent faces share a common smoothing group number, the edge is smoothed. Otherwise, the edge is seen as a sharp, faceted line.

Smoothing group numbers can be assigned to selected faces at sub-object level or by applying a Smooth modifier. Smoothing group numbers can also be automatically applied based on the angle at the shared edge.

Objects are also automatically assigned smoothing group numbers at creation time based on various rules.

In Exercise 4.9, you select sets of polygons and assign smoothing group numbers at sub-object level to form hard edges in the hull where you want them.

Exercise 4.9   Applying Smoothing Group Numbers at Polygon Level

1. Open the file called Ch04_Boat04.max on the CD-ROM or from the preceding exercise. From the File pull-down menu, choose Save As, point to an appropriate subdirectory on your hard drive, and use the plus sign button to save a new file with the name incremented to Ch04_Boat05.max.

2. Right-click the viewport labels for Top, Front, and Left, and set the viewport to wireframe mode. Activate the Perspective viewport and make sure nothing is selected in the scene. Notice that the bow and stern appear smooth, whereas the midsection looks faceted (see Figure 4.41). Select Hull01.

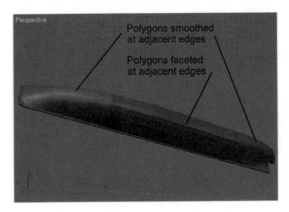

FIGURE 4.41 *The bow and stern appear smooth, but the midsection of the hull is faceted. This is caused by the smoothing group assignments of the polygons.*

3. Right-click in the Left viewport to activate it. In the Modify panel, Stack view, highlight Polygon. Make sure Ignore Backfacing is clear in the Selection rollout. On the main toolbar, click the Select Object button and make sure you are in window selection mode. In the Left viewport, drag a selection window to include all top-deck polygons (see Figure 4.42). The top deck turns red and you should see 19 polygons selected in the Selection rollout.

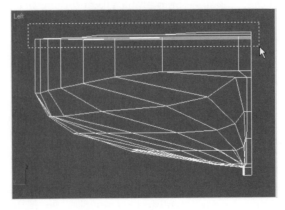

FIGURE 4.42 *In window selection mode, drag a window to select all the top-deck polygons in the Left viewport.*

4. In the Modify panel, Polygon Properties rollout, click the Clear All button, and then pick the 1 button in the Smoothing Groups matrix (see Figure 4.43). The 1 button becomes highlighted in yellow. All the selected polygons are assigned smoothing group 1, and their edges smooth to each other.

5. On the main toolbar, toggle the selection mode to crossing. In the Left viewport, drag a crossing window through the gunwale polygons (see Figure 4.44). Remember that crossing selects all entities within or touching the window. Window mode selects all entities completely within the windows. In the Polygon Properties rollout, click Clear All, and then highlight the 2 button in the matrix.

FIGURE 4.43
In the Polygon Properties rollout, click the Clear All button, and then highlight 1 in the Smoothing Groups matrix to assign Smoothing Group 1 to each selected polygon.

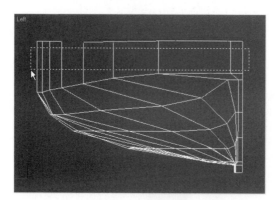

FIGURE 4.44   *On the main toolbar, toggle to crossing selection mode and drag a window through the gunwale polygons.*

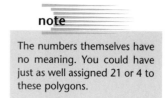

note

The numbers themselves have no meaning. You could have just as well assigned 21 or 4 to these polygons.

6. To make the next selection easier, select faces by the previously assigned smoothing group numbers and then add to the selection set. In the Polygon Properties rollout, click the Select by SG button. In the Select by Smooth Groups dialog, highlight 4, 5, 6, 7 (see Figure 4.45). Click OK. This selects all other polygons that have had these groups assigned automatically at creation. In the Front viewport, hold the Ctrl key and drag a crossing window through the bottom polygons of new the midsection (see Figure 4.46).

FIGURE 4.45
In the Select by Smooth Groups dialog, highlight 4, 5, 6, 7.

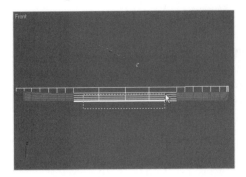

note

You will probably find it easier to use all viewports and zoom in and out as necessary to select all the faces. Take your time; if you make mistakes, click in a clear area and start again. Creating selection sets is something you will do all the time in 3ds max 6, and after a little practice, it becomes a natural process.

FIGURE 4.46   *Hold the Ctrl key and drag a crossing window through the bottom polygons of the new midsection.*

7. In the Polygon Properties rollout, click the Clear All button, and highlight 3 in the Smoothing Groups matrix.

8. In the Left viewport, click in empty space to deselect all, and use crossing window with the Ctrl key to select all the polygons of the keel, including the vertical polygons at the bow (see Figure 4.47). This also selects most of the flat faces that cap the center of Hull01. That is okay. In Polygon Parameters, click Clear All, and assign 4 to the selection. Click Editable Poly in Stack view to exit sub-object mode and click in empty space in the Perspective viewport. You see clear edges in the shaded view at the transition point of smoothing groups (see Figure 4.48).

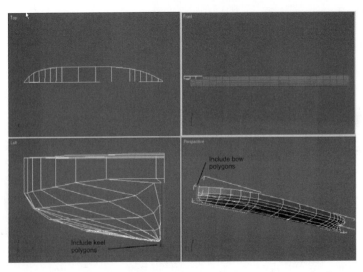

FIGURE 4.47   *Using a crossing window selection and the Ctrl key, create a selection set for the keel and bow stem.*

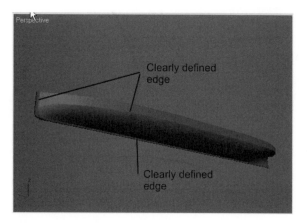

FIGURE 4.48   *Exit sub-object mode and clear the selections to see clearly defined edges at the transition of smoothing groups.*

9. Save the file. It is already named Ch04_Boat05.max.

Making the Hull Whole

So far, you succeeded in creating a beautiful half hull of your boat quite easily. So now it's time to create the other half, right? No...no need to do that. You could copy this half with the Mirror command, and then go through the process of trimming and welding, but there is a better way: the Symmetry modifier.

In Exercise 4.10, you apply the Symmetry modifier to mirror, trim, and weld in one operation. It also enables you to adjust the trim point just where you want it at any time.

Exercise 4.10   Applying a Symmetry Modifier to Create a Whole Hull

1. Open the file called Ch04_Boat05.max on the CD-ROM or from the preceding exercise. From the File pull-down menu, choose Save As, point to an appropriate subdirectory on your hard drive, and use the plus sign button to save a new file with the name incremented to Ch04_Boat06.max.

2. In the Top viewport, select Hull01. In the Modify panel, Modifier List, choose Symmetry. You see that the hull mirrors itself along the X-axis, but the new object has two bows and the stern is completely gone. This is the trimming and welding action (see Figure 4.49).

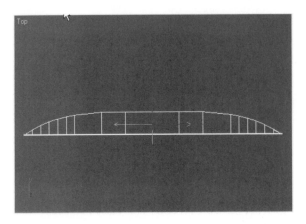

FIGURE 4.49   *Applying the Symmetry modifier to the hull mirrors it in the X-axis and trims the stern.*

3. In the Modify panel, Parameters rollout, check the Mirror Axis Y radio button. The hull now mirrors down the center along the keel axis. In the Left viewport, you can see that the keel is missing, however (see Figure 4.50).

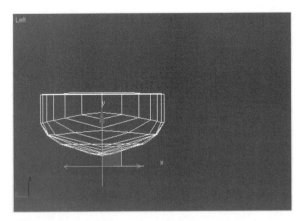

FIGURE 4.50   *Mirroring in the Y-axis completes the hull correctly, but cuts off the keel.*

4. In the Modify panel, Stack view, expand the Symmetry modifier and highlight the Mirror sub-object level. This puts you into move mode and the mirror plane turns yellow in the viewport. In the Left viewport, click and drag the X-axis Transform gizmo arrow and move the half hull to the right until you separate the two halves (see Figure 4.51).

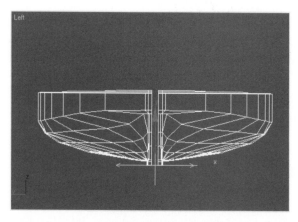

FIGURE 4.51   *Moving the mirror plane in sub-object Mirror far enough in the positive X-axis of the viewport separates the two hull halves.*

5. Move the mirror plane back just far enough for the halves to slightly overlap and you will have a complete hull with trimming and welding handled by the modifier. In Stack view, exit sub-object Mirror mode by clicking Symmetry. The result is a well-defined boat hull, as shown in Figure 4.52.

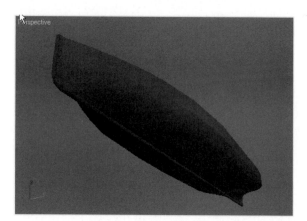

FIGURE 4.52   *Exit sub-object mode for the Symmetry modifier and you have a complete hull object.*

6. Save the file. It should already be called Ch04_Boat06.max.

Building Superstructure with New Modifiers

In this section, you learn to work with new modifiers to build the elements that make up the superstructure of the boat—turrets, smokestacks, railings, and stanchions, for example.

You also learn about an alignment tool called the *Spacing tool*, which enables you to place clones of objects along complex 2D shapes.

Finally, you merge the parts into a single file to finish the boat.

Bevel Profile Modifier

The first modifier in this section of the book that you will learn about is the Bevel Profile modifier. In Chapter 3, you used a modifier called Bevel that enabled you to extrude and outline a 2D shape up to three levels. Although the Bevel modifier has an option to apply curved outlined areas, it is a bit difficult to control. The Bevel Profile modifier comes to the rescue. It requires two 2D shapes—a base shape and a profile shape—the modifier is always applied to the base shape. You can think of the profile shape as a complex extrusion and outlining path that will define the height of the new 3D mesh.

In Exercise 4.11, you create a gun turret that sits on the deck of the boat. The 2D shapes have already been created for you. The turret itself has a 23-foot diameter inside dimension, is 10 inches thick, and has a 3-inch base at the bottom.

Exercise 4.11   Creating a Turret with Bevel Profile

1. Open the file called Ch04_Turret01.max on the CD-ROM. From the File pulldown menu, choose Save As, point to an appropriate subdirectory on your hard drive, and use the plus sign button to save a new file with the name incremented to Ch04_Turret02.max.

2. In the file are three 2D shapes: turret_inside_radius, turret_profile, and bracket_shape. The Bevel Profile modifier will be applied to turret_inside_radius and use turret_profile as the profile. In the Perspective viewport, select the large circle called turret_inside_radius. In the Modify panel, Modifier List, choose Bevel Profile. The circle becomes a shaded flat surface in the Perspective viewport. In the Modify panel, Parameters rollout, click the Pick Profile button (see Figure 4.53).

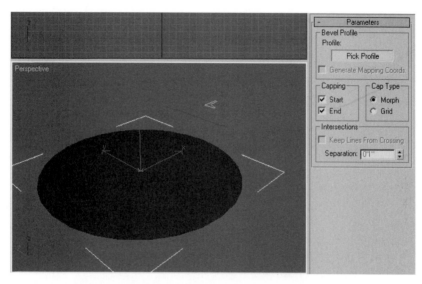

FIGURE 4.53   *Apply a Bevel Profile modifier to the circle and it turns to a shaded flat plane in the Perspective viewport. It is no longer a 2D object.*

3. In the Perspective viewport, pick the turret_profile line and the 3D turret grows from the grid plane (see Figure 4.54). In the Utilities panel, click the Measure button. The dimensions are shown as 23' in X- and Y-axis, and 12' in the Z-axis. This means the outside diameter is 23 feet. This is because the first vertex of the profile attaches itself to the base shape. Not to worry—because of the functionality of the modifier stack, it is easy to add the extra thickness to make it larger.

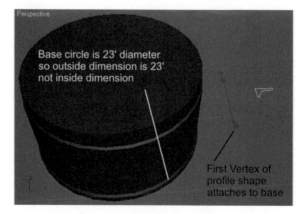

FIGURE 4.54   *The first vertex of the profile attaches to base shape. In this object, the outside diameter is 23 feet. You must increase the size.*

4. In the Perspective viewport, select the turret 3D mesh. In the Modify panel, Stack view, highlight the Circle at the bottom of the stack. In the Parameters rollout, change the Radius to 12'7" (10" + 3" extra). In Stack view, highlight Bevel Profile to return to the top of the stack. In the Parameters rollout, clear the check boxes for Capping, both Start and End. This reduces the number of faces from 332 to 280. Rename the object Turret01 in the modifier stack.

5. You now create a top cap for the turret, optimize it, and align the two. Activate the Top viewport. In the Create panel, Geometry panel, click Cylinder in the Object Type rollout. Pick and drag any size cylinder in the Top viewport. In the Modify panel, Parameters rollout, set the Radius to 15' and Height to 3". In the Perspective viewport, notice that the new cylinder has a more prominent segmented outer edge and it has height segments that add unnecessary detail (see Figure 4.55).

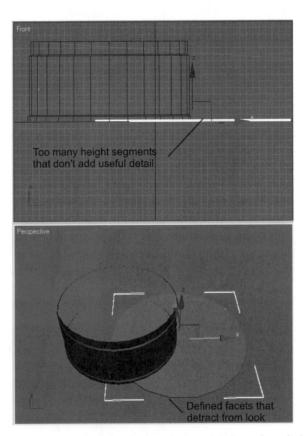

FIGURE 4.55   *This cylinder has too much detail where it doesn't help and too little where it is noticeable.*

6. In the Modify panel, Parameters rollout, enter 1 in Height Segments and 28 in Sides numeric fields. The cylinder now looks much better and has about half the faces (112 versus 216). Always try to be aware of any optimizations you can uses while modeling.

7. Now, align the cap to the top center of the turret. Make sure Cylinder01 is selected and the Perspective viewport is active. On the main toolbar, click the Align button. Pick the Turret01 in the Perspective viewport. In the Align Selection dialog, check X, Y, and Z Position check boxes and make sure Center is checked in both columns to align the object's geometric center to geometric center. Click the Apply button to set the alignment, to clear the check boxes, and remain in Align. Check the Z Position check box and check Minimum in the Current Object column and Maximum in the Target Object column to place the cylinder centered on top of the turret. Click OK.

8. Save the file; it is already called Ch04_Turret02.max.

New Alignment Tools

In Exercise 4.12, you learn to align an object's positive Z-axis to a viewport. This orients the bracket shape so that it can be easily aligned under the cap.

Exercises 4.12   Viewport Align Option

1. Open the file called Ch04_Turret02.max on the CD-ROM or from the preceding exercise. From the File pull-down menu, choose Save As, point to an appropriate subdirectory on your hard drive, and use the plus sign button to save a new file with the name incremented to Ch04_Turret03.max.

2. Activate the Front viewport and select the bracket_shape 2D object. You can use Select by Name on the main toolbar to make selecting easier. On the main toolbar, click and hold on Align and choose Align to View from the flyouts (see Figure 4.56).

3. The shape aligns its local Z-axis to point from the viewport (see Figure 4.57). Click OK. In the Modify panel, Modifier List, choose Extrude and enter 3" in the Amount field to give the shape thickness. Rename the object Bracket01.

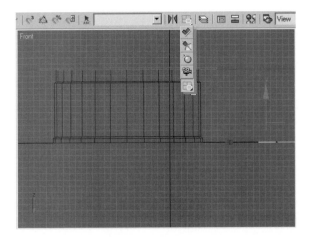

FIGURE 4.56   *On the main toolbar, choose the Align to View button from the flyouts.*

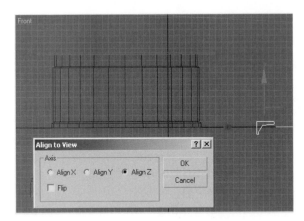

FIGURE 4.57   *Click OK in the Align to View dialog so the shape's local Z-axis points out from the viewport.*

4. Now, center it to Cylinder01 and align it flush to the outside edge. In the Front viewport, make sure Bracket01 is selected. On the main toolbar, click and hold Align to View and choose Align from the flyouts. In the Front viewport, pick Cylinder01. In the Align Selection dialog, check Y Position, Maximum in Current Object, and Minimum in Target Object. Click Apply. Check Z Position and Center in both columns. Click Apply. Click X Position and Maximum in both columns. Click OK. The bracket is now positioned where you want it, holding up the cap (see Figure 4.58).

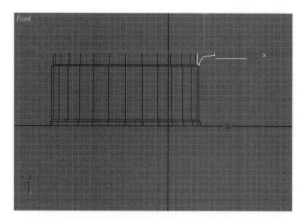

Figure 4.58 *With a series of quick alignments, the bracket is positioned precisely where you want it and in the correct orientation.*

5. Save the file. It is already called Ch04_Turret03.max.

Creating a Circular Array of Objects

In Exercise 4.13, you learn how to make a circular array of cloned objects around the center of another object, and you use Angle Snap to keep accurate spacing. This is another example of the power of reference coordinate systems. You also learn a handy tip about performing calculations in 3ds max 6.

Exercise 4.13   Arraying Clone

1. Open the file called Ch04_Turret03.max on the CD-ROM or from the preceding exercise. From the File pull-down menu, choose Save As, point to an appropriate subdirectory on your hard drive, and use the plus sign button to save a new file with the name incremented to Ch04_Turret04.max.

2. Activate the Top viewport and select Bracket01. On the main toolbar, click and hold on the View reference coordinate system and choose Pick from the menu (see Figure 4.59). In the Top viewport, pick either the Cylinder01 or Turret01. The name of the object appears in the window, and they both share a common center from this view.

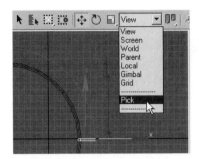

FIGURE 4.59   *Change the reference coordinate system from View to Pick and pick either Turret01 or Cylinder01 in the Top viewport.*

3. On the main toolbar, click and hold on the Use Pivot Point Center button, which is located to the right of the reference coordinate system window, and choose Use Transform Coordinate Center, the bottom flyout. Click the Select and Move button (if it is not already) and you see the Transform gizmo in the center of the turret. This is now the rotation center of Bracket01.

4. On the main toolbar, click the Select and Rotate button. It sets the reference coordinate system back to View. Pick on View and choose Turret01, which is now an entry in the menu. Set to Use Transform Coordinate Center again to use the turret center.

5. Set the Angle Snap option to get 14 evenly spaced brackets. On the main toolbar, click and then right-click the Angle Snap Toggle button. In the Grid and Snap Settings dialog, you see the Angle is set to 5.0 degrees. You have 14 objects in a 360-degree circle. Highlight the numeric field for Angle. Press Ctrl+N to call the Numerical Expression Evaluator. Enter 360/14 in the field, and the result is reported on the line below (see Figure 4.60). Click the Paste button and the result is entered in the numeric field. Close the Grid and Snap Settings dialog.

6. Make sure the Select and Rotate is still toggled on, hold the Shift key for cloning, and rotate the bracket in the Z-axis one detent, 25.71 degrees (see Figure 4.61). In the Clone Options dialog, check the Instance radio button, enter 13 in the Number of Copies field, and click OK. You now have 14 evenly spaced and correctly oriented brackets supporting the cap (see Figure 4.62).

7. Save the file; it is already called Ch04_Turret04.max.

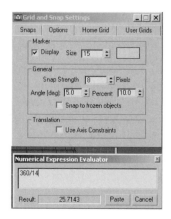

FIGURE 4.60   *Highlight any numeric field and press Ctrl+N to call the Numerical Expression Evaluator for performing math functions in 3ds max 6.*

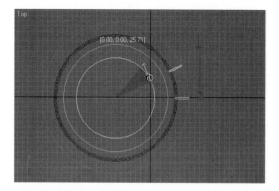

FIGURE 4.61   *Hold the Shift key and rotate the bracket in the Z-axis one detent of the Angle Snap.*

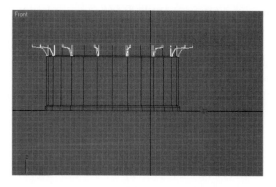

FIGURE 4.62   *The cloned brackets are correctly spaced and oriented.*

The Lathe and Shell Modifiers

Your boat needs a smokestack, so in Exercise 4.14, you create one from a single 2D shape and a couple of modifiers: Lathe and Shell.

The Lathe modifier "spins" a 2D shape about an adjustable center to create a 3D mesh. Once created, you will make a "mistake" and convert the object from a shape with the modifier to an editable mesh. Upon learning that the smokestack should have had a thickness to it, something that would have been easily accomplished by editing the 2D shape with the Lathe modifier, you apply the Shell modifier to create a similar effect.

Exercise 4.14   Creating a Smokestack with Thickness

1. Open the file called Ch04_SmokeStk01.max on the CD-ROM. From the File pull-down menu, choose Save As, point to an appropriate subdirectory on your hard drive, and use the plus sign button to save a new file with the name incremented to Ch04_SmokeStk02.max.

2. The file contains a single shape called smokestack_profile. You could use this shape in conjunction with a circle to create a stack similar to the way you created the turret in Exercise 4.13. Instead, however, you use the Lathe modifier. In the Perspective viewport, select smokestack_profile. In the Modify panel, Modifier List, choose Lathe. The result is an object that is too thin for the boat because the center of the Lathe is the geometric center of the shape.

3. In the Modify panel, Stack view, expand the Lathe modifier, and highlight Axis. This enables you to change the position of the lathing axis to edit the object. On the main toolbar, click Select and Move and, in the status bar, you see that Offset Mode Transform Type-In is toggled off. Click the button to toggle from Absolute to Offset mode. In the X field of Transform Type-In, enter –4 and press Enter. You now have an 8-foot diameter stack with no thickness or end caps (see Figure 4.63). In the Stack view, click Lathe to exit sub-object mode.

4. Right-click in the Perspective viewport twice, once to activate it and again to call the Quad menu. In the Quad menu, choose Convert To, and then choose Convert to Editable Mesh from the cascading menu. The Lathe modifier is gone and the object is a simple editable mesh. However, your client thinks it should have some thickness.

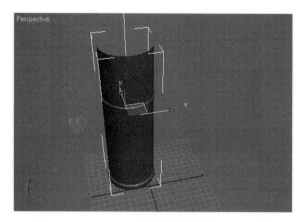

FIGURE 4.63 *Applying a Lathe modifier to a shape and adjusting the position of the axis at sub-object level results in a tube with no thickness.*

5. In the Modifier List, choose Shell. The default settings make the smokestack 1 inch thicker to the outside. In the Parameters rollout, enter 3 in the Inner Amount and 0 in the Outer Amount (see Figure 4.64). Now, the extra thickness is toward the inside. The Shell modifier could add significantly to the face count of objects, so use it wisely.

6. Rename the object Smokestack01 and save the file. It is already called Ch04_SmokeStk02.max.

Spacing Tool and Renderable Splines

In this section, you learn to use a 2D shape to distribute objects in an equally spaced pattern along the shape. This enables you to add stanchions or posts that will support a safety railing around the deck of the boat at roughly a 6-foot spacing.

This is a great tool for placing light poles along a street, spikes on a dogs collar, or ducks in a row, for example.

FIGURE 4.64
The Shell modifier gives single surface objects a thickness inward or outward.

Then, to actually create the railing itself, you align a copy of the path to the top of the stanchions and make it renderable. Any 2D shape can be made renderable, which applies a circular cross-section by default with the radius and detail you set. It is normally only visible at render time, but you also can have it visible in the viewports.

All forms of ropes and wires or spider webs could be created easily by enabling renderable splines.

Spacing Stanchions on the Deck

Exercise 4.15 walks you through the steps of placing vertical stanchions at roughly 6-foot centers around the outside of the deck of the boat. The shape has already been created by extracting 2D data from the hull and resizing and moving it into position. The Stanchion01 object is just a cylinder that has been edited at sub-object level. The original object is left in place and clones are distributed along the path. You align the original at the bow at the end of the exercise, but generally, it would be deleted after the spacing operation.

Exercise 4.15   Using the Spacing Tool to Distribute Objects

1. Open the file called Ch04_Monitor01.max on the CD-ROM. From the File pull-down menu, choose Save As, point to an appropriate subdirectory on your hard drive, and use the plus sign button to save a new file with the name incremented to Ch04_Monitor02.max.

2. In the Perspective viewport, select Stanchion01. It might be easiest to use Select by Name because it is a relatively small object and difficult to pick. In the Tools pull-down menu, choose Spacing Tool. In the Spacing Tools dialog, you can either pick two points in a viewport to have a number of evenly spaced objects or you can pick a path. You should click the Pick Path button and, in the Perspective viewport, pick the shape at the top outer edge of the hull (see Figure 4.65). The button now reads rail_path.

3. With Stanchion01 still selected, click the Align button on the main toolbar. Press H to call the Pick Object dialog and double-click rail_path in the list. In the Align Selection dialog, check X, Y, and Z Position to align Center to Center. Click Apply. In the Align Selection dialog, check Z Position, Minimum in Current Object, and Maximum in Target Object. Click Apply. Click X Position and Stanchion01 should move to the tip of the bow (see Figure 4.67). Click OK.

4. Save the file. It should already be called Ch04_Monitor02.max.

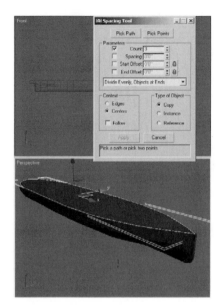

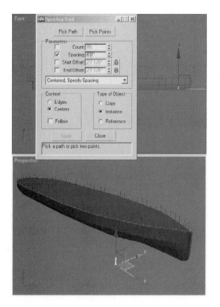

FIGURE 4.65 *Select Stanchion01 and then choose Spacing Tool in the Tools pull-down menu. Click the Pick Path button in the Spacing Tool dialog and pick the shape at the top of the deck.*

FIGURE 4.66 *Set the Spacing Tool to use rail_path with 6-foot spacing between instance clones.*

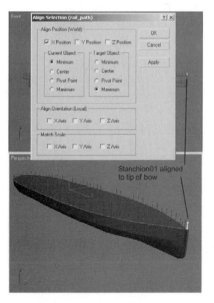

FIGURE 4.67 *Use the Align tool to place Stanchion01 at the tip of the bow.*

A Renderable Spline at a Safety Railing

Normally, shapes do not show up in any rendered image, but sometimes, it is helpful to have a shape be treated as an object—in the case of ropes and wires, for example. In Exercise 4.16, you learn to enable the renderable spline settings for a clone of the rail_path shape that has been aligned with the top of the stanchions. You then learn to optimize the resulting object.

Exercise 4.16   Assigning Shape Thickness in Renderings and Viewports

1. Open the file called Ch04_Monitor02.max on the CD-ROM or from the preceding exercise. From the File pull-down menu, choose Save As, point to an appropriate subdirectory on your hard drive, and use the plus sign button to save a new file with the name incremented to Ch04_Monitor03.max.

2. In the Perspective viewport, select rail_path at the top of the deck. In the Edit pull-down menu, choose Clone. In the Clone Options dialog, select the Copy radio button and rename the object Safety_rail (see Figure 4.68). Click OK. You choose Copy because Instance would make both renderable when you apply the setting.

3. The cloned copy becomes the selected object. On the main toolbar, click the Align button and, in the Perspective viewport, pick the Stanchion01 at the tip of the bow. Check Z Position and set Current Object to Maximum and Target Object to Maximum. Click OK.

4. In the Modify panel, Rendering rollout, enter 2" in the Thickness field and 6 in the Sides field. The default 12 sides to the object is much too dense for the detail you need. Check the Renderable option and check Display Render Mesh (see Figure 4.69). This last option enables you to view the 3D mesh in the viewports.

5. Save the file. It is already called Ch04_Monitor03.max.

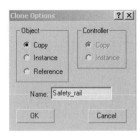

FIGURE 4.68
With Edit, Clone, make a copy of the rail_path shape and call it Safety_rail.

FIGURE 4.69
Set the shape to be visible in the renderings and the viewports, and optimize the number of sides to fit the detail needed.

tip

If you have many renderable spline objects in the scene, it would be wise to leave Display Render Mesh off. Turning it on could slow viewport performance significantly.

Merging Objects from Other 3ds max Files

You have created objects such as turrets and smokestacks that you will now merge into this scene and align in place on the deck of the boat. The original files remain intact and there will be no connection to the merged objects. Merging is often used when collaborating with other artists, but it also is useful for keeping scenes manageable in any office.

File Merging and 3ds max Groups

In Exercise 4.17, you merge objects from the turret file you created earlier, and then you use the Hold command to store the file in a buffer so that you can experiment will aligning the turret to the deck. It won't work as you might expect, so you will fetch the file back and learn about groups in 3ds max 6.

Exercise 4.17   Merging and Grouping Objects

1. Open the file called Ch04_Monitor03.max on the CD-ROM or from the preceding exercise. From the File pull-down menu, choose Save As, point to an appropriate subdirectory on your hard drive, and use the plus sign button to save a new file with the name incremented to Ch04_Monitor04.max.

2. In the File pull-down menu, choose Merge and find the file called Ch04_Turret05.max on the CD-ROM. You only want the 3D mesh objects from this scene so, in the Merge dialog, List Types area, click the None button to clear all the "type" check boxes, and then check Geometry to show a list of only 3D mesh objects. At the bottom of the dialog, click the All button to highlight the list (see Figure 4.70). Click OK to merge the objects.

3. On the main toolbar, enter Turret in the Named Selection Sets window and press Enter. This enables you to reselect the merged objects using this name (see Figure 4.71).

4. In the Edit pull-down menu, choose Hold to save the scene to a file. On the main toolbar, click Align and, in the Perspective viewport, pick Hull01. In the Align Selection dialog, check X, Y, Z Position, and Center for both Current and Target Objects. Click OK. This makes a mess of things because the center of each individual piece is aligned with the center of the hull. In the Edit pull-down menu, click Fetch, and then answer Yes in the dialog.

5. The turret objects are no longer selected. Click the drop-down arrow to the right of the Named Selection Sets window on the main toolbar and choose Turret in the list to select them again. In the Group pull-down menu, choose Group. Name the group Turret in the Group dialog (see Figure 4.72). Click OK.

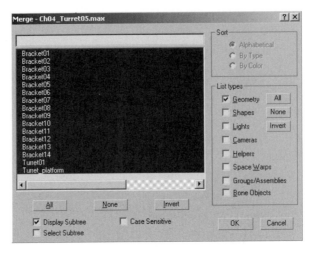

FIGURE 4.70   *Set the Merge list to show geometry only, highlight all in the list, and click OK to merge.*

FIGURE 4.71   *Enter Turret in the Named Selection Sets window of the main toolbar and press Enter. Pressing Enter after typing the name is important to make it final.*

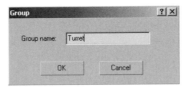

FIGURE 4.72   *From the Group pull-down menu, choose Group and name this group Turret.*

6. In the Perspective viewport, align the group with the Hull01, center to center in the three axes, and notice that each object keeps its original relationship to the others in the group. In the Align Selection dialog, click Apply. Check Z Position and Minimum in the Current column and Maximum in the Target column. Click OK. On the main toolbar, click the Select and Move button. On the status bar, toggle Offset Mode Transform Type-In and enter –3" in the Z field. Press Enter. This moves the turret to the surface of the deck, which is not the same as the maximum point of the hull bounding box because of some curvature in the deck.

7. In the Transform Type-In X field, enter 40 and press Enter to move the turret forward. In the Edit pull-down menu, choose Clone. Check the Instance option and click OK to clone the group. In the Transform Type-In X field, enter –80 and press Enter. You now have two turrets on the deck (see Figure 4.73).

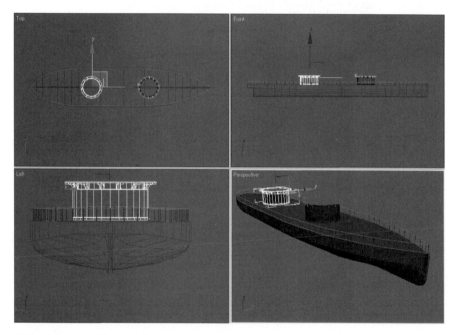

FIGURE 4.73   *Move the Turret01 forward and clone it as an instance. Then, move the clone to the rear of the deck.*

8. In the File pull-down menu, choose Merge and find Ch04_SmokeStk02.max on your hard drive or on the CD-ROM. In the Merge dialog, highlight Smokestack01 and click OK.

9. In the Perspective viewport, align the stack to sit on the deck at the center of the hull using the same process as step 6, but instead of moving it down the 3 inches, you can align to a turret body using Minimum to Minimum in the Z-axis.

10. Save the file. It is already called Ch04_Monitor04.max.

You now have a hull with turrets and a smokestack, which, if you look back and review the process, was quite easy to create. It might seem like a long time since you started, but with a little practice, you could do it again quickly.

Most important is that you learned tools and techniques that can be applied to your own work.

Summary

You can apply the topics you learned in this chapter, both tools and methods, throughout your own work. The topics covered in this chapter included the following:

- **Background images**—You learned to use maps or images in viewports as a background to use as a guide when modeling.

- **Editable polygons**—You learned to convert 3D mesh objects to editable polygons, resulting in four-sided faces, where possible, rather than the triangular faces of mesh objects; you also learned new tools that are available when editing the editable polygons.

- **Symmetry modifier**—This modifier, you learned, enables you to create half an object and, in one operation, mirror, trim, and weld the two halves together.

- **Spacing tool**—As you learned, this tool enables you to place equally spaced clones between two points or along a complex path.

- **New modifiers**—You learned to use the Bevel Profile modifier and the Lathe modifier to create easily editable objects from 2D shapes.

- **Merge files**—Another valuable lesson you learned is to create small manageable files and then merge them into a single scene. This process can result in an efficient workflow for you, especially in a collaborative environment.

CHAPTER 5

Creating Convincing Terrain

In This Chapter

In Chapter 4, "Shipbuilding 101: The Making of a Boat," you learned to display background images and use those images as a guide for editing an existing model to add detail and shape it into a recognizable object. You were not concerned with a scale factor until after the modeling was finished and you could apply scale the model to match its real-world size.

In this chapter, you set up a scene that enables you to trace the contour lines of a background image of a topological map. You roughly trace the map with straight-line segments first, and then adjust the detail and smooth it out later. Finally, you use the Compound Object Terrain tool to surface the contour lines for an accurate landscape object.

You also learn in this chapter to create efficient trees for use in larger landscape scenes. Although there are trees in the Create, AEC Extended, Foliage panel in 3ds max and there are plenty of third-party options for creating 2D "billboard" and 3D trees, those options are not always ideal. The 3D trees tend to be very dense geometry and can slow production a lot, and the 2D trees cannot be viewed from an angle much higher than 30 degrees above the horizon. These exercises also teach you some important new tools that can be applied to other modeling tasks.

This chapter also introduces XRef commands, which enable you to reference objects from other scenes into your current scene. This is similar to File, Merge, except the XRef objects share a connection with the original file. Change the original file and the object you have XRef'd into your scene with change accordingly. Some of the topics covered in this chapter include the following:

- **Setting a scale from background maps**—You learn to trace a background map and retain the scale for relatively accurate terrain modeling.

- **Terrain compound object**—Exercises show you how to convert contour lines into landscape meshes.

- **Normalize Spline**—Learning to use this modifier helps you control vertex placement on 2D shapes.

- **Skydome**—You learn to create a hemisphere that accepts maps to simulate the sky in outdoor scenes.

- **ShapeMerge Compound**—You learn to cut new edges into mesh objects with 2D shapes to define new modeling or material boundaries.

- **Scatter compound object**—You learn to make efficient, low-polygon trees and distribute them in large-scale landscape scenes.

- **XRef objects**—Cross-referencing objects from other files merges the object into the current scene with a one-way editing connection from the original to the reference.

This chapter reviews some of the techniques you learned in previous chapters and takes them to another level for higher productivity.

Key Terms

- **XRef**—Importing objects from other scenes can be done with XRef objects or XRef Scene from the File pull-down menu, leaving a connection from the original to the referenced copy in your scene.

- **ShapeMerge**—This enables you to project 2D shapes into 3D surfaces to cut new edges and define new faces.

- **Safe frame mode**—This viewport attribute enables you to match the viewport aspect to the rendered output size. It is intended for matching output to television devices, but can be used in background image tracing.

- **Flip face normals**—This enables you to control the visibility of faces or polygons changing the direction the face normal points.

Tracing Contour Maps to Create 3D Terrain: The Process

In this section, you learn to set up a background image and trace the contour lines needed to create a landscape object.

It is important to set a scaling factor at the beginning so that you have continuity between the lateral sizes of the landscape and the height of the contours. The process involves determining the actual size of a feature in the map you will trace—in this case, a small island in the river.

You then create a temporary box and resize it to the dimensions of the island. Then, you zoom and pan so that the box covers the island in the background image. Objects you trace over the background image will now be to relatively accurate scale.

As you trace over the contour lines, you assign names based on the elevation of the contour. Lines that represent the river bottom will be identified as such so that they can be moved to a negative height to represent land below sea level.

You will not be using the file from this exercise to actually create the landscape in the following exercises, but you will use one that has already been traced. This is just for consistency throughout the rest of the chapter, but please don't skip this part; it is an important step to learn in the process. With a little practice, you can create accurate landscapes quickly for any sites for which you have maps available as background images.

Setting Up for Tracing Background Topographical Maps

In Exercise 5.1, you open a topographical map as a background image and adjust it for proper aspect ratios in the viewports. You then learn to zoom and pan to set a scale that matches real-world sizes. The contours of this map are at 20-foot intervals.

Again, this setup file teaches you the process for when you use your own files. In subsequent exercises in this chapter, you use a file that has already been prepared so that everything remains consistent throughout the exercises.

Exercise 5.1   Setting Up a Background Image for Tracing

1. Open the file called Ch05_MapTrace.max on the CD-ROM. From the File pull-down menu, choose Save As, point to an appropriate subdirectory on your hard drive, and use the plus sign button to

note

The reason why scale is more important in this example than in the boat plans you traced for Chapter 4 is that scale makes it easier to move the contour lines you trace to the proper elevation, because you are starting at a known point.

save a new file with the name incremented to Ch05_MapTrace01.max. The scene has a topographical map displayed as the background image in the Top viewport.

2. Place your cursor over the intersection of the four viewports until you see the resize cursor. Click and drag to the right to resize the four viewports. Release the mouse button and the viewports resize with the background image stretching to fit the new viewport (see Figure 5.1). This obviously creates problems for accurate tracing. In the Views pull-down menu, choose Viewport Background. In the Viewport Background dialog, check Match Bitmap in the Aspect Ratio area. This returns the image to its original aspect ratio to keep it accurate (see Figure 5.2). The Display Background and Lock Zoom/Pan options should already be checked.

> **note**
>
> You might get a Missing External Files error if the background image cannot be found. Use the Customize pull-down menu, Configure Paths option to locate the file on your CD-ROM.

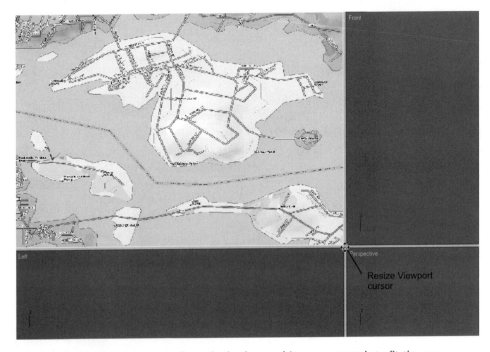

FIGURE 5.1   *Resizing the viewport allows the background image to stretch to fit the new aspect ratio.*

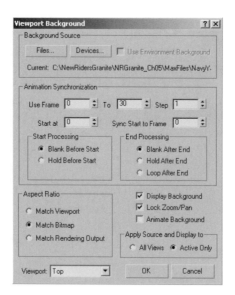

FIGURE 5.2   *In the Views pull-down menu, choose Viewport Background and set the Aspect Ratio to Match Bitmap to keep the image at the proper aspect for accurate tracing.*

3. Right-click in the Top viewport to activate it and use the Min/Max toggle at the lower right of the screen or Alt+W from the keyboard to fill the display. Again, the map retains its proper aspect.

4. Using the original map, the size of Clarks Island at the center right of the map was determined to be 650 feet horizontally by 525 feet vertically. In the Create panel, Geometry panel, click Box and create any size box in the Top viewport. In the Modify panel, Parameters rollout, enter 525 in the Length and 650 in the Width fields, respectively. The height is not important for this exercise. The viewport will fill with this large box. Click Zoom Extents All to fill the display with the box. The Background Image seems to disappear, but it has actually resized itself to a very small image. In the Views pull-down menu, choose Reset Background Transform to fill the display with the image again.

5. In the Views pull-down menu, click Viewport Background and, in the Viewport Background dialog, clear Lock Zoom/Pan. In the Top viewport, zoom out and move the box until it is centered over Clarks Island. You can right-click the viewport label and switch to wireframe mode to make it easier to see what you are doing (see Figure 5.3).

tip

To return the viewports to the default configuration, place the cursor over the intersection, right-click, and pick Reset Layout.

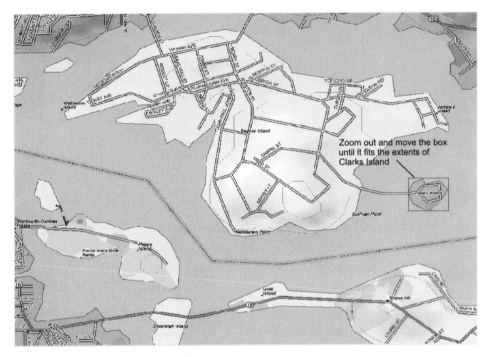

FIGURE 5.3   *After unlocking Zoom/Pan in the Viewport Background dialog, use the Zoom tool and position the box until it fits the extents of Clarks Island.*

6. In the Viewport Background dialog, check Lock Zoom/Pan again. Use Views, Reset Viewport Transform if the view changes. In the Views pull-down menu, choose Save Active Top View. This stores the current view in a buffer and enables you to restore the view should you mess it up. Each viewport can be stored in this manner. Zoom and pan in the Top viewport to fill the display with the large island (Seavey Island) in the middle of the image. Now, you can hide or delete the box at Clarks Island.

7. In the Create panel, Shapes panel, click the Line button in the Object Type rollout. In the Creation Method rollout, select Drag Type Corner radio button (see Figure 5.4). This means that all line segments will be straight with no curvature. This makes tracing faster by eliminating the chance of creating curvature by mistake.

caution

Zooming and panning in a locked viewport can use large amounts of memory and you might get a warning message. If you have limited resources on your computer, keep the zooming and panning to an absolute minimum.

FIGURE 5.4   *In the Create panel, Shapes panel, click Line and toggle the Corner radio button in the Drag Type area.*

tip

You will get better results if you go to Customize pull-down menu, Preferences, Viewports tab and make sure you are using Software Z-Buffer video drivers.

Work slowly at first—the image is a typical map that you might trace and, because 3ds max 6 only shows a proxy image in the viewport, the lines can be difficult to see.

Pick as few points as you can to describe the contours as accurately as you deem necessary. For example, three points can define most curves, one at each tangent of the curve and another at the apex of the curve. Larger sweeping curves may require more points, but keep them to a minimum.

8. In the Top viewport, trace the outside edge of Seavey Island with a close line and name it seavey00_01. The name seavey lets you know where the line is, 00 is the elevation, and 01 means it's the first line at elevation 00 for this island. An island with two hilltops would have at least two contours at some elevations, for example.

9. Trace the next contour lines toward the interior of the island at the 20-foot contours. Name them seavey20_01 and seavey20_02. Continue until all the lines are traced, zooming and panning as necessary. When you are finished, the Top viewport looks similar to Figure 5.5 if you turn off the background image. The riverbed contours are a "best guess" just to drop the riverbed below the islands.

10. You do not need to save this file. In the exercise in which you create the actual terrain, you use contours that have already been traced to make sure that everyone is using the same information. The first time you perform these steps, the process seems cumbersome. With a little practice, however, it will make sense, enabling you to create more complex terrain quickly.

tip

If you are using a graphics card with OpenGL drivers, you might be able to configure 3ds max 6 in the Customize pull-down menu, Preferences, Viewports tab for a better-quality background image. Each card/driver combination is different.

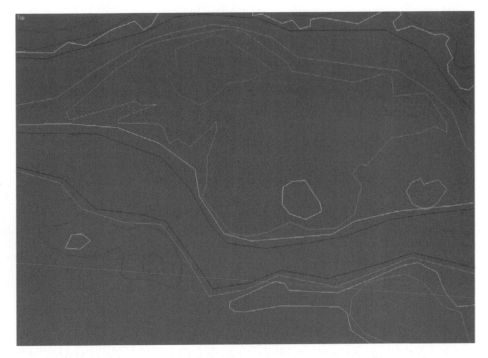

FIGURE 5.5   *Trace all the landmasses and contours that you need to complete your ter-rain. In this example, the contours are a "best guess" to drop the surface below the islands.*

Creating the Terrain, Water, and Sky

In this section, you complete several exercises that take the traced contour lines, move them into the correct elevations, and skin over the contours with a surface to represent your terrain. You also learn to smooth the straight-line segments by adjust-ing tangents and to adjust vertices of the contour shapes for a more regular face dis-tribution over the surface with a Normalize Spline modifier.

You then create and position a Plane primitive that will become the water surface for the river.

Finally, you create a hemisphere that acts as the sky for your scene and place a camera looking from the river toward the shore, where your boat launch site will be.

Preparing the Traced Contour Lines

The contour lines have been traced from the background image and have been named according to location and elevation as the lines were traced. In Exercise 5.2, you select and move the contours into their proper elevation in the World Z-axis.

Exercise 5.2   Setting the Contours to Proper Elevation

1. Open the file called Ch05_Terrain01.max on the CD-ROM. From the File pull-down menu, choose Save As, point to an appropriate subdirectory on your hard drive, and use the plus sign button to save a new file with the name incremented to Ch05_Terrain02.max. The scene has a topographical map displayed as the background image in the Top viewport with the contours on the World coordinate plane.

2. Right-click in the Perspective viewport to activate it and maximize the viewport to fill the display. Click the Select by Name button on the main toolbar and select all the shapes with 20 in the name, except for the river shapes (see Figure 5.6).

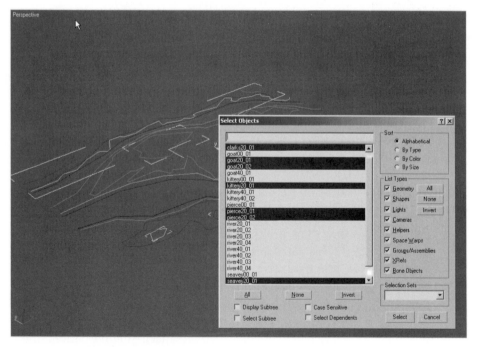

FIGURE 5.6   *Use Select by Name on the main toolbar to select all shapes with 20 in the name, except for the river shapes.*

3. On the main toolbar, click the Select and Move button. On the status bar, enter 20 in the Transform Type-In Z-axis field and press Enter. The selected contours move up 20 feet in the positive Z-axis.

4. In the Select by Name dialog, select all shapes with 40 in the name, except for the river shapes. Enter 40 in the Z-axis Transform Type-In and press Enter.

5. In the Select by Name dialog, select all shapes for river20 and enter –20 in the Z-axis Transform Type-In.

6. Select all the river40 shapes and enter –40 in the Z-axis. All the contours should now be at the proper elevation to create an accurate terrain.

7. Save the file, it should already be named Ch05_Terrain02.max.

Adjusting and Surfacing the Contours

In Exercise 5.3, you attach the individual contour shapes into a single compound shape. Although this step is not required for the terrain compound object to surface the contours, it will make it easier to adjust the position of the vertices for more control over the density of the surface mesh and the regularity of the face layout.

tip

It doesn't matter whether the Transform Type-In is set to Absolute mode or Offset mode, because the elevations are based on the World coordinate plane at elevation 0.

If you started at elevation 2000, for example, it would be important to use Offset Mode Transform Type-In to move the contours a relative distance from the tracing plane or to use the complete elevation in the name, such as 2040, and enter those numbers in the field.

note

Because this is fairly flat coastal terrain over a large area, the elevation changes are not significant. It is common practice in landscape visualization to exaggerate terrain elevations to make the hills more pronounced for easier reading in the final renderings. You won't do that for these exercises, however.

Exercise 5.3   Adjusting the Contours and Creating the Terrain

1. Open the file called Ch05_Terrain02.max on the CD-ROM or from the preceding exercise. From the File pull-down menu, choose Save As, point to an appropriate subdirectory on your hard drive, and use the plus sign button to save a new file with the name incremented to Ch05_Terrain03.max.

2. In the Perspective viewport, select any contour line. Right-click in the Viewport and, from the Quad menu, choose Convert To, and Convert to Editable Spline. In the Modify panel, Geometry rollout, click the Attach Multiple button. In the Attach Multiple dialog, click the All button to select all shapes in the scene. Click

Attach to create a compound shape, a shape with multiple splines. In the Modify panel, rename the object Landscape.

3. In the next step, you apply a Normalize Spline modifier to spread the vertices of the shape more evenly. To get a better idea of what's happening, select and right-click Landscape and choose Properties in the Quad menu. In the Properties dialog, Display Properties area, check the Vertex Ticks option (see Figure 5.7). Click OK to close the dialog. This enables you to see the vertices of objects without going to sub-object Vertex level. The vertices are not evenly spaced, but occur as you picked them during tracing.

warning

It is very important to follow the next step carefully. The Normalize Spline modifier has a default setting of 20 units (inches). If applied directly to this large contour set, the computer resources could be used up, requiring you to reboot and start this exercise again.

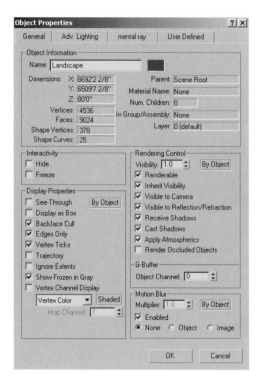

FIGURE 5.7   *In the Object Properties dialog for Landscape, check the Vertex Ticks option to show vertices in the viewports.*

4. Now, apply a Normalize Spline modifier to assign vertices at regular intervals along each spline. However, you first apply the Normalize Spline modifier to a simple line to set a spacing that will not degrade the performance of your computer. In the Perspective viewport, create a line in any clear area of the display. In the Modify panel, Modifier List, choose Normalize Spl. In the Parameters rollout, enter 1920 in the Seg Length field and press Enter (see Figure 5.8). Press Delete on the keyboard to delete the line. 3ds max remembers that setting the next time you apply the modifier.

FIGURE 5.8
Apply the Normalize Spline modifier to a short line and set the Seg Length to 1920. This number was determined to be a good balance between accurate contours and surface detail through trial and error.

5. In the Perspective viewport, select the Landscape object. In the Modify panel, Modifier List, choose Normalize Spl. You now have regularly spaced vertices on splines that still fit the map contours (see Figure 5.9). In the Perspective viewport, right-click Landscape, choose Properties from the Quad menu, and clear the Vertex Ticks in Display Properties. Click OK to close the dialog.

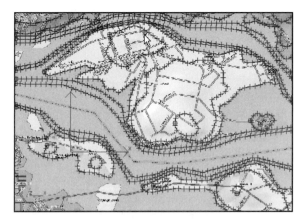

FIGURE 5.9   *With Normalize Spline at 1920-inch intervals, the contours have regularly spaced vertices and still match the map contours.*

6. In the Create panel, Geometry panel, click Standard Primitives and choose Compound Objects from the list. In the Object Type rollout, click the Terrain

button and your contours become surfaced with faces. The corners of the new mesh are truncated because there the terrain object can interpolate only where there are contour lines. Otherwise, the edge is determined in a straight line to the next known point (see Figure 5.10).

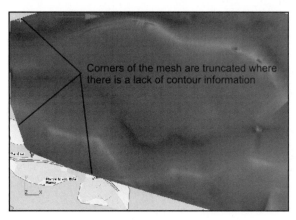

Corners of the mesh are truncated where there is a lack of contour information

Figure 5.10   *Lack of contour information causes the corners of the mesh to truncate in a straight line to known points. Always trace contours outside the map areas you consider important.*

7. Now, create a water plane and position it. Right-click in the Top viewport to activate it. Right-click the viewport label, and clear Show Background in the menu. Click Zoom Extents All in the lower right of the display. In the Create panel, Geometry panel, select Standard Primitives in the list under Compound Objects. Click the Plane button and drag out a plane in the Top viewport that is slightly larger than the landscape. Rename it Water. On the main toolbar, click the Select and Move button and, on the status bar, enter –3 in the Z-axis field. This moves the water down as if the tide were out some to give a clearer view of the islands (see Figure 5.11).

8. Save the file; it should already be called Ch05_Terrain03.max.

> **note**
>
> The Perspective viewport might look strange and blotchy. This is because with objects as large as this viewed from a distance, the graphics card has trouble deciding which surface to display and tries to show both simultaneously. The final rendered images will be fine.

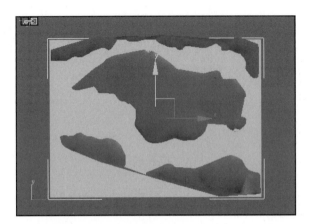

FIGURE 5.11   *Create a water plane and move it down three feet for a clearer view of the islands.*

Creating a Skydome

In Exercise 5.4, you learn to place a camera in your scene to give you a more natural view of the scene. You already have your landscape and your water, but what about a sky? You learn to turn a hemisphere inside out—that is, flip the face normals—so that it is visible when viewed from the center outward. This surface then serves as your sky in the background. You also remove unnecessary faces for a more efficient model, but do it in a manner that would enable you to get the deleted faces back if you were to change your mind.

Exercise 5.4   Creating a Skydome Surrounding the Landscape

1. Open the file called Ch05_Terrain03.max on the CD-ROM or from the preceding exercise. From the File pull-down menu, choose Save As, point to an appropriate subdirectory on your hard drive, and use the plus sign button to save a new file with the name incremented to Ch05_Terrain04.max.

2. You first place a camera in the scene that will give you a view from the river looking toward Seavey Island, the larger land mass in the middle of the scene. Right-click in the Top viewport to activate it. In the Create panel, Cameras panel, click the Target button. In the Top viewport, click and drag from the middle of the river to a point about midway through the center of the left side of the island (see Figure 5.12).

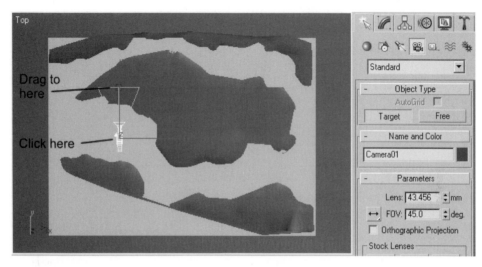

Figure 5.12   *Click and drag a target camera from the middle of the river straight up to the middle of the island.*

3. Right-click in the Perspective viewport and press C to switch from a Perspective viewport to a Camera viewport. The camera and its target are both on the World coordinate plane. Make sure Camera01 is still selected and, on the main toolbar, click the Select and Move button. On the status bar, enter 200 in the Z-axis Absolute Transform Type-In field and press Enter to move the camera up for a bird's eye view of the river and island (see Figure 5.13).

4. Activate the Top viewport. In the Create panel, Geometry panel, click the GeoSphere button. In the Top viewport, pick in the center of the water plane and drag right to the far edge of the water plane. The appears in the Front and Left viewports, but not at all in the Camera01 viewport (see Figure 5.14). This visibility issue is caused by the direction of the face normals of the geosphere. They point outward from the center, making the geosphere invisible when viewed from the inside out. Rename the object Skydome.

tip

Generally speaking, a target camera is usually pointed toward a specific position with limited range of motion. A free camera is one that is animated along a path like a moving camera or viewpoint riding in a vehicle.

note

The geosphere is only partially visible in the Top viewport, but this is a process called *viewport clipping*, which is based on the size of objects and distance from the viewer. It's not solely a result of the direction of face normals.

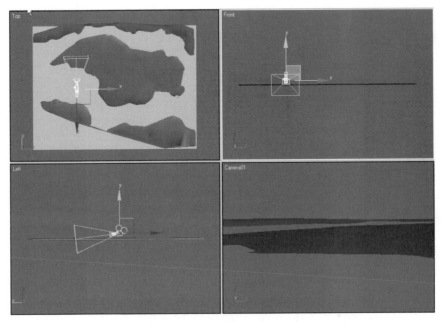

FIGURE 5.13   *Using the Select and Move and Absolute Transform Type-In, move Camera01 200 feet higher. The camera's target remains on the World coordinate plane, resulting in a bird's eye view of the island.*

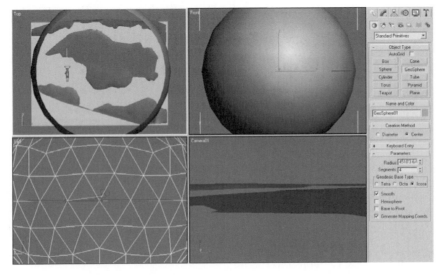

FIGURE 5.14   *Pick and drag a geosphere from the center to the outer right edge of the water plane. Face normals cause the geosphere to be visible or partially visible in some viewports, but not in others.*

5. Make sure the geosphere is still selected and, in the Modify panel, Parameters roll-out, click the Hemisphere option to remove half the sphere and to cap the base with faces. On the main toolbar, click the Select and Move button and, in the Left or Front viewport, move Skydome downward in the negative Y-axis to be slightly below the Terrain01 and Water objects.

6. In the Modify panel, Modifier List, choose the Normal modifier. This flips the face normals to make them visible to the camera. The faces that cap the bottom of the Skydome are unnecessary overhead and you will delete them. But, you do so with a modifier so that you have the option to undelete if you should need to do so. Right-click the selected Skydome and choose Convert To, Convert to Editable Mesh from the Quad menu. In the Modify panel, Stack view, expand Editable Mesh and highlight Polygon sub-object level. On the main toolbar, click the Select Object button and toggle from crossing mode to window mode. In the Left viewport, drag a selection window around only the bottom edge of the hemisphere to select the bottom cap polygons (see Figure 5.15).

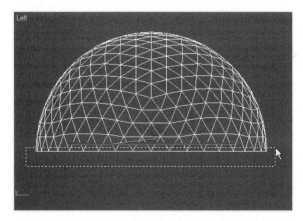

FIGURE 5.15   *Use window selection mode to select the bottom cap polygons of the Skydome.*

7. In the Modify panel, Modifier List, choose DeleteMesh. In the Modify panel, Modifier List, choose Mesh Select to return control to the entire object. The faces are now gone from the Skydome, making it more efficient, but you have the option of removing or disabling (the light bulb symbol left of the modifier in Stack view) the DeleteMesh modifier at anytime to get the faces back, leaving you with greater flexibility.

8. Save the file. It is already named Ch05_Terrain04.max.

Later in this chapter, you reopen this file and reference in objects from other scenes to assemble your boatyard on the island.

Creating Low-Polygon Trees

note

This chapter covers the modeling of these trees, and they will look rather unconvincing. In Chapter 7, "Introduction to Materials and Mapping," you add materials that turn them into much more pleasing objects in the rendered image.

As mentioned at the beginning of this chapter, 3ds max 6 enables you to create trees in many ways, varying from tree images mapped to flat planes to complex, botanically correct forests. All the methods have pluses and minuses that you must weigh for your production needs, keeping in mind that you can mix tree types in a scene to strike a balance that works for you.

In this section, you learn to create two types of generic, efficient trees that, when viewed from a distance, can be sufficient for many scenes. You create an evergreen tree and a deciduous tree that have a low polygon count, cast decent shadows, and can be viewed from any angle.

Once again, I stress the theme of much of the modeling in this book: efficiency. Too many times, schedules and budgets are not met because of scenes that have unnecessary detail in the modeling. This is especially true in large outdoor scenes with shadow-casting sunlight.

An Efficient Evergreen Tree Using Array

In creating an efficient evergreen tree, you learn to use the Array tool to position the boughs of the tree around the trunk. With low-polygon count as a goal, the modeling is kept extremely simple, starting with a Plane and a Cone primitive object. Exercise 5.5 walks you through the steps.

Exercise 5.5   Creating a Low-Polygon Evergreen Tree

caution

For the vertices to be welded you must release within four pixels of the target vertex. Zooming in or maximizing the viewport can help. You can check by selecting all the vertices and seeing that you have five selected as reported in the Modify panel, Selection rollout.

1. Open the file called Ch05_Evergreen01.max on the CD-ROM. From the File pull-down menu, choose Save As, point to an appropriate subdirectory on your hard drive, and use the plus sign button to save a new file with the name incremented to Ch05_Evergreen02.max. The scene contains a Cone and Plane primitive. The Cone has been set to 1 height segment and 5 sides in the Modify panel for a face count of 20, down from a default of 288 faces.

2. In the Top viewport, select Bough01, the flat plane in the scene. You edit this into a rough shape of a fir or spruce bough. Right-click Bough01 and, from the Quad menu, choose Convert To, Convert to Editable Mesh. In the Modify panel, Stack view, expand Editable Mesh and highlight Vertex sub-object level. In the Modify panel, Edit Geometry rollout, click the Target button in the Weld area (see Figure 5.16). In the Top viewport, pick and drag the upper-left vertex and release when over the middle left vertex. Repeat the process for the lower-left vertex and, again for the right-side vertices. The result should look like Figure 5.17.

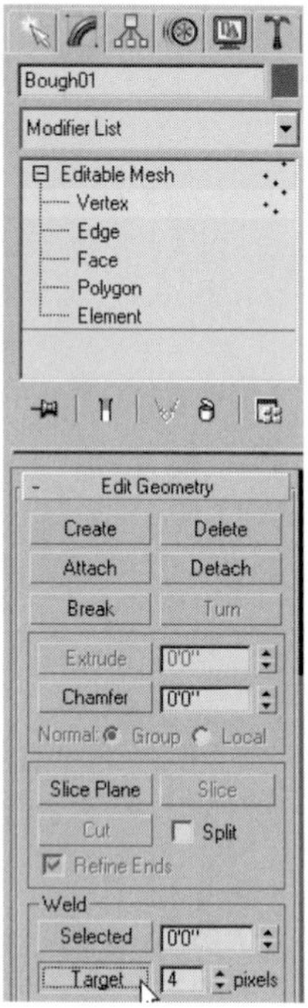

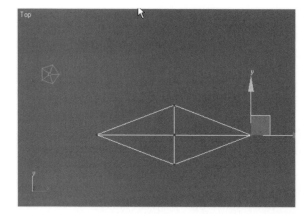

FIGURE 5.16
In Vertex sub-object mode, click the Target button in the Edit Geometry rollout, Weld area.

FIGURE 5.17   *Pick and drag the left-corner vertices to weld to the left middle vertex, and then repeat the process for the right side of the Bough01. The result is a diamond made of four faces.*

3. Now, move vertices to create a bough shape. In the Top viewport, drag a selection window around the three vertical middle vertices. Click Select and Move and move them, using the Transform gizmo, right to about ¼ of the way to the end (see Figure 5.18).

4. In the Front viewport, move the vertex on the left up 4 feet in the Y-axis (use the Offset Mode Transform Type-In) and move the right vertex up 2 feet. It looks like Figure 5.19.

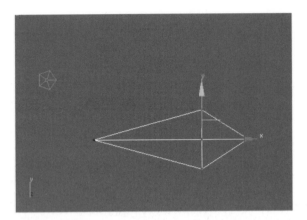

FIGURE 5.18 *Move the three vertical middle vertices right to about ¼ of the way to the end.*

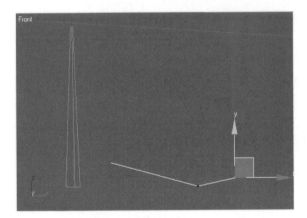

FIGURE 5.19 *As seen in the Front viewport, move the left vertex up 4 feet in the positive Y-axis and move the right vertex up 3 feet.*

5. In the Perspective viewport, select the vertex in the middle of the object and, using Transform Type-In, move it up 2 feet in the positive Z-axis. The bough now looks like Figure 5.20. In the Stack view, click Editable Mesh to exit sub-object mode.

6. Now, align Bough01 to Trunk01 so that it is centered on the right side as seen from the Top viewport. Activate the Top viewport and make sure Bough01 is selected. On the main toolbar, click the Align button and pick Trunk01. In the Align Selection dialog, check Y Position and make sure Center is checked for both Current and Target Objects. Click the Apply button to set the alignment and clear

the positions. Check X Position and check Minimum in the Current Object column and Maximum in the Target Object. The alignment should look like Figure 5.21. Click OK to exit the dialog.

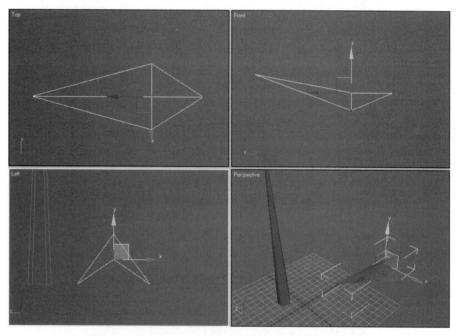

FIGURE 5.20   *In the Perspective viewport, select the vertex in the middle of the plane and move it 3 feet in the positive Z-axis.*

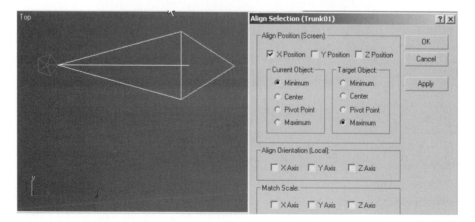

FIGURE 5.21   *In a two-step alignment, position Bough01 to the right center of Trunk01.*

7. The Array command is used to make a radial array of boughs around the base of the trunk. The radial array is about the pivot point of the object, which, in the case of Bough01, is in the geometric center of the object. You move the pivot point of Bough01 to the pivot point of Trunk01. In the Hierarchy panel, Adjust Pivot rollout, click the Affect Pivot Only button (see Figure 5.22). You align it—not the whole bough—to the trunk.

8. On the main toolbar, click the Align button. In the Top viewport, pick Trunk01. In the Align Selection dialog, check X Position, and then check Pivot Point in the Current and Target columns. The pivot tripod of Bough01 moves to the pivot of Trunk01 (see Figure 5.23). Click OK to exit the Align Selection dialog. In the Hierarchy panel, Adjust Pivot rollout, click Affect Pivot Only to exit that mode.

FIGURE 5.22
To align the pivot point of an object, you must be in Hierarchy, Affect Pivot Only mode.

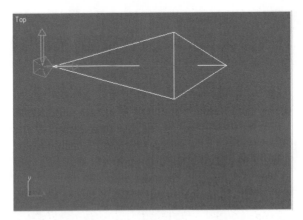

FIGURE 5.23   *In the Align selection dialog, check X Position and Pivot Point in both columns to move the pivot of the Bough01 to the pivot of Trunk01.*

9. In the Tools pull-down menu, choose Array. This can be a pretty intimidating dialog, but it is quite simple and very powerful. You create a radial array with a total of 12 boughs each 30 degrees offset from the other in the Z-axis. In the Array dialog, enter 30 in the Incremental Z-axis Rotate field. In the Type of Object area,

check the Copy radio button (you attach all boughs to a single object later) and, in the Array Dimensions area, enter 12 in the 1D Count field (see Figure 5.24). Click OK, and the result looks like Figure 5.25.

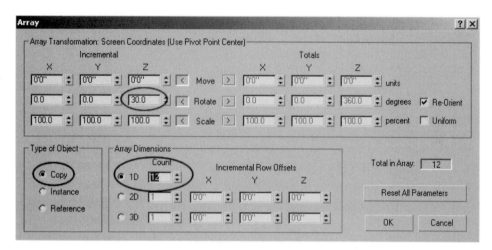

FIGURE 5.24 *In the Array dialog, enter 30 in the Z-axis Rotate field, check the Copy radio button, and enter 12 in the 1D Count field.*

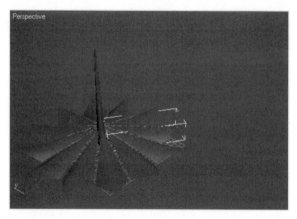

FIGURE 5.25 *The one-dimensional array of 12 boughs will be equally spaced around the base of the trunk.*

10. In the Modify panel, Edit Geometry rollout, click the Attach List button. In the Attach List dialog, highlight all bough objects, everything but Trunk01 in the list. Click the Attach button, and they become one object called Bough12.

11. In the next step, you perform another array, but this will include Rotate, Move, and Scale settings to create a cone of boughs winding up the trunk, each level getting smaller toward the top. Click the Zoom Extents All button to fill the viewports with all objects. Right-click in the Top viewport to activate it. In the Tools pull-down menu, choose Array. In the Array dialog, enter 1'10" in the Incremental Z-axis Move field, and enter 15 in the Incremental Z-axis Rotate field. In the Incremental Scale fields, enter 80 in the X and Y axes, and 95 in the Z-axis. Enter 10 in the 1D Count field (see Figure 5.26). Click the OK button. For the end result, see Figure 5.27.

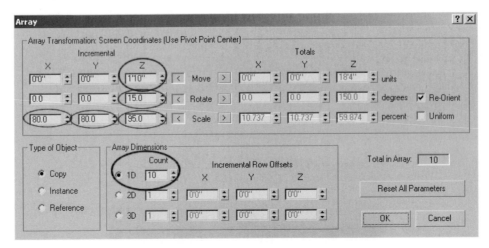

FIGURE 5.26   *This array will move, rotate, and scale each level of boughs to form a cone-shaped tree.*

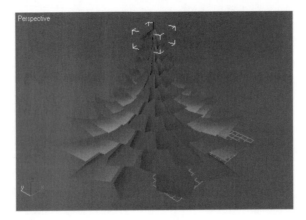

FIGURE 5.27   *The resulting one-dimensional array of attached boughs will be 10 levels high, each level rotated by 15 degrees, and each slightly smaller in all three axes.*

12. With the topmost bough still selected, in the Modify panel, Edit Geometry rollout, click Attach List, highlight all boughs in the list, and click Attach to make the boughs all one object. In the File pull-down menu, choose Summary Info and you see that the scene—that is, the evergreen tree—only contains a total of 500 faces.

13. Save the file. It should already be named Ch05_Evergreen02.max.

note

A default Scotch Pine created with the Foliage tools in AEC extended objects has around 60,000 faces, whereas a Blue Spruce often has more than 20,000 faces. The exact face count is randomly assigned for each tree you create. The detail level of both trees is much higher than this evergreen, but you should use higher-density mesh objects only when the viewer is close enough to need the detail.

An Efficient Deciduous Tree Using Scatter Compound Object

In Exercise 5.6, you create a low-polygon deciduous tree using a new tool called the *scatter compound object*. It enables you to create a single leaf and scatter it randomly over the surface of a distribution object—in this case, a tree canopy. As in the case of the evergreen tree, you apply materials to this object in Chapter 7 that result in a more convincing tree when rendered.

Exercise 5.6   Creating a Low-Polygon Deciduous Tree

1. Open the file called Ch05_Deciduous01.max on the CD-ROM. From the File pull-down menu, choose Save As, point to an appropriate subdirectory on your hard drive, and use the plus sign button to save a new file with the name incremented to Ch05_Deciduous02.max. The file contains a trunk created by beveling, moving, and rotating the polygons of an editable poly object and a leaf object that is just a 2D shape in the form of a triangle.

2. First, you learn editable poly tools that will enable you to smooth Trunk01 for a more organic form. In the Perspective viewport, select Trunk01. In the Modify panel, Subdivision Surface rollout, check the Use NURMS Subdivision option. Enter 1 in the Iterations field in the Display area (see Figure 5.28). Right-click Trunk01 and choose Properties in the Quad menu to see that the smoothed trunk has 370 faces (more than you need for a low polygon tree).

tip

3ds max 6 has a new display type called Isoline Display to simplify the object in the viewport. You can disable this to see the entire mesh in the Subdivision Surface rollout.

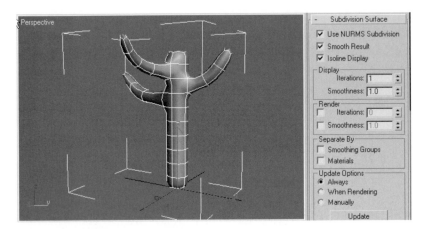

FIGURE 5.28   *In the Modify panel, Subdivision Surface rollout, check the Use NURMS Subdivision check box and set Iterations to 1.*

3. Right-click Trunk01 and, in the Quad menu, choose Convert To, Convert to Editable Mesh. Right-click and choose Properties again and you see that the editable mesh now has 740 faces. The editable mesh polygon count is the one that is accurate when calculating the efficiency of objects. In the Modify panel, Modifier List, choose Optimize. Optimize reduces the face count by combining faces that have an angle of 4 degrees or less at a shared edge. In the Modify panel, Parameters rollout, enter 12 in the Face Thresh field of the Optimize area. This reduces the face count to 354, which is still is acceptable as a tree trunk (see Figure 5.29).

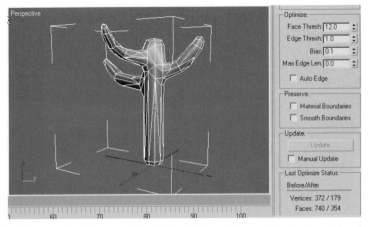

FIGURE 5.29   *Applying an Optimize modifier to Trunk01 and increasing the Face Threshold to 12 degrees reduces the face count to less than half while retaining a reasonable appearance.*

4. Right-click Trunk01 and convert it to an editable mesh through the Quad menu. This removes the overhead of the Optimize modifier, but preserves the resulting face count by collapsing the modifier stack and "baking" the results (see Figure 5.30).

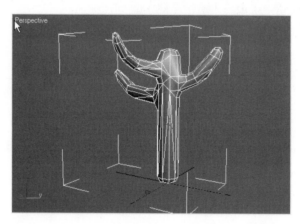

FIGURE 5.30   *Converting Trunk01 with the Optimize modifier to an editable mesh reduces the overhead of math of optimizing and bakes-in the result for an efficient mesh object.*

5. Save the file. It is already called Ch05_Decidious02.max.

Creating the Leaf Canopy

You have a trunk but still need a canopy of leaves. In Exercise 5.7, you create three geospheres, attach them together, and randomize the surface with a Noise modifier. The resulting object serves as a distribution object over which you scatter leaves in Exercise 5.8.

Exercise 5.7   Creating a Canopy Distribution Object for Leaves

1. Open the file called Ch05_Deciduous02.max on the CD-ROM or from the preceding exercise. From the File pull-down menu, choose Save As, point to an appropriate subdirectory on your hard drive, and use the plus sign button to save a new file with the name incremented to Ch05_Deciduous03.max.

2. In the Top viewport, create three geospheres and then resize them and move them into position in the other viewports, approximately as in Figure 5.31.

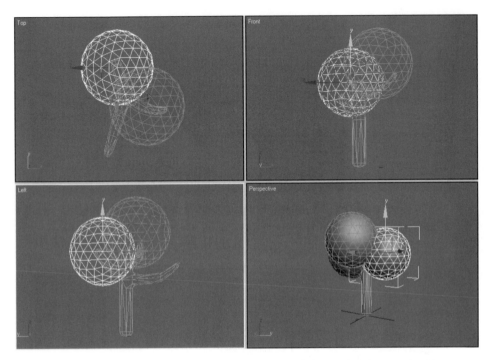

FIGURE 5.31   *Create three geospheres in the Top viewport, and then resize them and position them using Select and Move in the other viewports.*

3. Right-click any geosphere and, in the Quad menu, convert it to an editable mesh. Right-click again and choose Attach from the Quad menu. Pick each of the other two geospheres to attach them into a single object. In the Modify panel, Edit Geometry rollout, click the Attach button to exit that mode.

4. With the new geosphere object selected, go to the Modify panel, Modifier List, and choose Noise. In the Parameters rollout, enter 30 in the Scale field and 5 in the X, Y, and Z Strength fields. This randomly displaces vertices of the object by a maximum of 2.5 in the three positive or negative axis directions (see Figure 5.32). Right-click the object and convert to an editable mesh.

caution

Be careful not to attach Trunk01 to the geospheres. If you do accidentally attach it, use the Undo button to back out and try again to attach only the three geospheres together.

Also, get into the habit of clicking the Attach button in the Modify panel to exit Attach mode as soon as you are finished attaching objects to avoid adding unwanted objects.

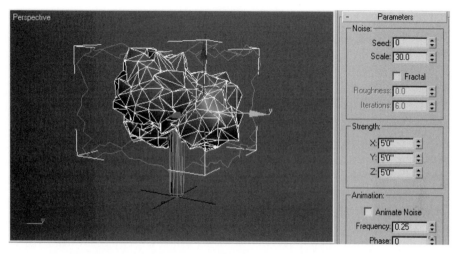

FIGURE 5.32 *Applying a Noise modifier and increasing the Strength amounts randomly displaces vertices of the object by a maximum of 2.5 feet in any direction. The Scale factor adjusts the effect for the density of the mesh object.*

5. Save the file; it should already be called Ch05_Decidious03.max.

Creating and Scattering Leaves

You have a tree trunk and you have a solid canopy, but what you need is individual leaves that allow light to pass through and cast convincing shadows.

You have a 2D triangle in the scene that you will convert to a single 3D face; it will have no thickness but will be a visible surface.

You then take the single face and scatter it over the surface of the distribution object you created in Exercise 5.7. The scatter compound object creates a new object over your distribution object and scatters the leaf over it as a target. You hide this new object and delete the original distribution object to have leaves suspended in space.

Exercise 5.8   Using the Scatter Compound Object to Duplicate a Leaf in Space

1. Open the file called Ch05_Deciduous03.max on the CD-ROM or from the preceding exercise. From the File pull-down menu, choose Save As, point to an appropriate subdirectory on your hard drive, and use the plus sign button to save a new file with the name incremented to Ch05_Deciduous04.max.

2. In the Perspective viewport, select the 2D NGon primitive shape called Leaf01. Right-click and, in the Quad menu, choose Convert To, Convert to Editable Mesh.

3. With Leaf01 selected, go to the Create panel, Geometry panel, pick on Standard Primitives, and choose Compound Objects from the list. Click Scatter in the Object Type rollout. In the Pick Distribution Object rollout, pick the Pick Distribution Object button (see Figure 5.33).

4. In the Perspective viewport, pick the distorted geosphere canopy. It appears to change color, and Leaf01 moves from its original position. Actually, you are seeing a new object that is a copy of the original distribution object, and Leaf01 has become part of this new object.

5. At the bottom of the Modify panel, expand the Display rollout and check Hide Distribution Object (see Figure 5.34). The copy of the distribution object is hidden and you see your leaf near the top of the original canopy.

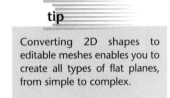

tip

Converting 2D shapes to editable meshes enables you to create all types of flat planes, from simple to complex.

FIGURE 5.33

In the Create panel, Geometry panel, pick on Standard Primitives, and choose Compound Objects from the list. Click Scatter in the Object Type rollout. In the Pick Distribution Object rollout, pick the Pick Distribution Object button.

FIGURE 5.34　*At the bottom of the Modify panel, in the Display rollout, check the Hide Distribution Object option to hide the new copy of the canopy.*

6. In the main toolbar, click the Select Objects button to exit Scatter creation mode. In the Perspective viewport, select the canopy object and press Delete to delete it. You now have a trunk and one leaf in space (see Figure 5.35). Your leaf might appear 2D because of face normals.

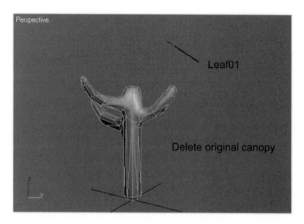

Figure 5.35   *Delete the original canopy object and you are left with Leaf01 suspended in space. You might not see your leaf correctly because of face normals pointing away from you.*

7. Select Leaf01; you might have to use Select by Name because objects with face normals pointing way from you cannot be selected in the viewports. In the Modify panel, Scatter Objects rollout, enter 2000 in the Duplicates field of Source Object Parameters area and press Enter (see Figure 5.36). You now have 2,000 leaves (faces) scattered randomly over the hidden distribution surface.

Figure 5.36   *In the Modify panel, Scatter Objects rollout, enter 2000 in the Duplicates field for a canopy of leaves.*

8. In the Scatter Objects rollout, enter 15 in the Vertex Chaos field and press Enter. This randomly moves vertices of the leaves to fill out the canopy and produce different-sized leaves.

note

Again, you will not see all 2000 leaves because of face normals. You remedy this in Chapter 7 by applying a double-sided material to the leaves.

9. Right-click the leaves and convert to an editable mesh in the Quad menu. The math behind an editable scatter object takes up a fair amount of computer resources and converting, once you have finished all edits, reduces overhead. Rename the object Leaves (it is a single object).

10. Save the file. It is already called Ch05_Deciduous04.max.

Building a Scene in a Collaborative Environment

In this section, you use the ShapeMerge compound object to cut new edges of a boat ramp into the terrain you created in the beginning of the chapter.

You also learn some of the options available to you when working with others in a collaborative environment where different members or teams are producing different parts of the scene that must be combined into a single scene for final production. You also learn about new capabilities with alignment tools. You learn to use Merge and XRef from the File pull-down menu.

You also learn to use a scatter compound object that provides random duplicates within a restricted area that you specify.

Cutting a Boat Ramp into Terrain

In Exercise 5.9, you use ShapeMerge to cut a 2D shape into the terrain that will become a boat ramp for your shipyard scene. Again, ShapeMerge projects the 2D shape into a 3D surface to define new edges and faces. The new faces can then be selected and edited.

Exercise 5.9   Using ShapeMerge to Cut a Boat Ramp into the Terrain

1. Open the file called Ch05_BoatRamp01.max on the CD-ROM. From the File pull-down menu, choose Save As, point to an appropriate subdirectory on your hard drive, and use the plus sign button to save a new file with the name incremented to Ch05_BoatRamp02.max. This file is similar to the Ch05_Terrain04.max file you

created earlier in the chapter and contains sky-dome, landscape, and water objects. A 2D shape has been added to the scene called ramp_shape that will define a boat ramp cut into the terrain.

2. In the Top viewport, select Landscape. It is the terrain compound object created from contour lines. Right-click it and, from the Quad menu, choose Convert To, Convert to Editable Mesh. This reduces the complexity of the object, making the following steps more reliable.

tip

ShapeMerge can be made more reliable if you first modify the shape by lowering the Interpolation settings from the default 6. Interpolation is the number of intermediate steps between vertices of shapes that define curvature.

3. In the Create panel, Geometry panel, click Standard Primitives and choose Compound Objects from the list if it is not still the active panel. In the Object Type rollout, click the ShapeMerge button.

4. In the Create panel, Pick Operand rollout, click the Pick Shape button. In the Top viewport, pick the ramp_shape rectangle. The shape appears to turn white, but you are actually seeing the new edges that are being projected into the landscape object (see Figure 5.37). On the main toolbar, click the Select Obj button to exit ShapeMerge mode.

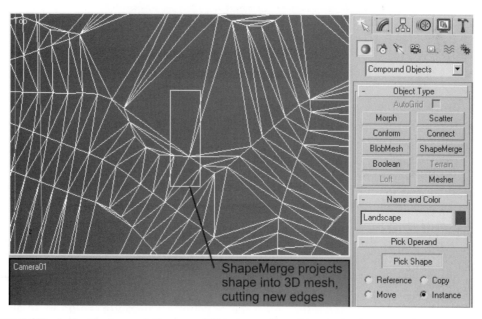

FIGURE 5.37   *In the Create panel, Compound Objects, use ShapeMerge to project ramp_shape into the Landscape mesh to cut new edges and define new faces.*

5. Right-click Landscape and convert to an editable mesh again. It became a ShapeMerge object in step 4. In the Modify panel, Stack view, expand Editable Mesh and highlight Polygon sub-object mode. The new polygons created by ShapeMerge are automatically selected. On the main toolbar, enter BoatRamp in the Named Selection Sets field and press Enter.

Creating a named selection set at this point is an important step because after you deselect the polygons, it can be difficult to reselect them.

6. In the Modify panel, Edit Geometry rollout, enter –4 in the Extrude numeric field. This extrudes the selected faces downward and creates new side faces for a boat ramp depressed into the landscape. In the Modify panel, Stack view, highlight Editable Mesh to exit sub-object mode (see Figure 5.38).

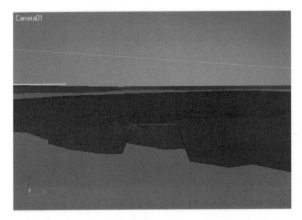

FIGURE 5.38 *Extruding the newly selected polygons with a negative amount produces a depressed boat ramp in the landscape.*

7. Save the file; it is already called Ch05_BoatRamp02.max.

XRef and Merge: Bringing Objects from Other Scenes

You have created other scenes in previous chapters that contain buildings and boats that you want to use in your current scene. In this section, you learn to use XRef objects to import objects from other scenes with a one-way link to the original file. If you open, edit, and save the original objects in the original file, they automatically update when you open the new scene or perform a reload operation in an already open file. This enables you to place the objects that others might be building in your scene for reference and keeps them up-to-date as they change them or add detail to the mesh.

XRef objects have a smaller memory footprint in your scene than in the original and enable you to display simple proxy objects as placeholders for complex objects for more viewport efficiency. The full object, not the proxy, always renders by default, however.

Merging objects into the scene simply imports the objects as copies of the original with no connection to the original.

XRef objects can be "bound" to become merged objects, thereby breaking the connection to the original.

In Exercise 5.10, you XRef some buildings and merge others from previous files to learn the fundamental process and to begin to populate your shipyard scene.

caution

Although it would seem that XRef objects would always be preferred, quirks do crop up, especially on more complex scenes. If you start to have issues with XRef objects, it is wise to bind them into the scene.

Exercise 5.10   XRef and Merge: Working Collaboratively

1. Open the file called Ch05_BoatRamp02.max on the CD-ROM or from the preceding exercise. From the File pull-down menu, choose Save As, point to an appropriate subdirectory on your hard drive, and use the plus sign button to save a new file with the name incremented to Ch05_BoatRamp03.max.

2. In the File pull-down menu, choose XRef Objects. In the XRef Objects dialog, click the Add button in the Add/Set area. On the CD-ROM, find Ch03_Skylight04.max and double-click it in the list. This brings up the XRef Merge dialog with a list of any objects in the file. Highlight the object called Floor in the list (see Figure 5.39). Click OK. The file path and name will be entered in the XRef Files pane (upper) and the object will be listed in the XRef Objects pane (lower). Click the Close button to close the XRef Objects dialog. The object is in your scene, but you might not see it because it comes in at its created coordinate point, which might be far from your viewports.

3. To position the object near the boat ramp, click the Align button on the main toolbar. Press H and double-click ramp_shape in the Pick Object dialog. In the Align Selection dialog, check X, Y, and Z Position to align the building with the shape, center to center. Click OK.

tip

The XRef'ed objects are selected as they come into the new file. If you are XRef'ing multiple objects, it is wise to use named selection sets to make later selection easier. With just one object, however, it doesn't matter.

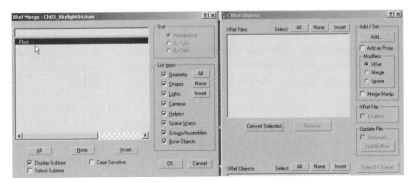

FIGURE 5.39 *XRef objects enable you to open an existing file and select objects from that file to be used in the current file. An XRef object also retains a connection to the original.*

4. Click and hold on the Zoom Extent All button and choose the Zoom Extents All Selected button from the flyouts. It has a white box in the button (See Figure 5.40) and zooms in all viewports to the selected object(s). Rename the object Big_Shed01.

5. Move Big_Shed01 to just behind the boat ramp. You might have to use several viewports to get it in place, and you can use the white bounding box corners in the shaded Camera viewport to make sure it is not floating above the landscape (see Figure 5.41).

FIGURE 5.40
Use the Zoom Extents All Selected to zoom in all viewports on the selected object or objects. Note that a Camera viewport will never be affected by zooming commands.

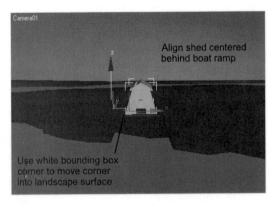

FIGURE 5.41 *Move the Shed01 centered behind the boat ramp and use the white bounding box corner to determine when the left-front corner of the shed is below the surface of the landscape.*

6. In the File pull-down menu, choose Merge. On the CD-ROM find Ch03_Outbuilding04.max. In the Merge dialog, highlight all three objects and click OK. On the main toolbar, enter Outbuildings in the Named Selection Sets window and press Enter. Use Align to align the new buildings to Big_Shed01 using a common center. Move each of the three buildings off to the left of the shed and use the bounding boxes to make sure that are not floating above the landscape. You can activate the Camera01 viewport and press P to change to a Perspective viewport where you can zoom and pan for a better view.

7. Select Out_building01. In the Modify panel, highlight Rectangle in the Stack view and change the size to a 50-foot width. Highlight Bevel in the Stack view and change Level 1: Height to 20 feet. The merged objects retain their original editing capabilities. Activate the Perspective viewport if you created one and press C to return to the Camera01 viewport. The scene should look similar to Figure 5.42. The merged objects can be edited in this scene. To edit the XRef object, you must save this file, open the original file for the building and edit it there, and then reopen this file to see the changes.

8. Save the file. It is already named Ch05_BoatRamp03.max.

> **note**
>
> This might seem a cumbersome process. Take time to practice moving and aligning objects in various viewports and it quickly becomes second nature to you.

> **tip**
>
> Although you cannot change the parameters of the XRef object in this scene, you can apply new modifiers and edit the object with the modifiers. The changes in this file are never passed back to the original, however.

FIGURE 5.42 *Center the three new buildings on Big_Shed01 and move them into place along the left of the shed. Switch from a Camera to Perspective viewport and use the white corners of the bounding box for alignment to the surface. Edit Out_building01 to change the size.*

> **tip**
>
> In the File pull-down menu, there is also a Replace tool. This enables you to open any file and replace an object in the current scene with an object that has exactly the same name from the opened file.

New Alignment Tools

In this section, you merge a few new objects into the scene and learn a feature of the Align tool that will rotate objects so their axes are in alignment. An example use might be a light fixture that you have in your scene that is rotated at some unknown angles and you need to align a 3ds max light to it. With the Align tool, you have the option of aligning objects based on their local reference coordinate systems. After the axes are aligned, aligning, moving, or rotating the objects can be done using those local coordinates.

In Exercise 5.11, you first merge a boat ramp, and then merge in a completed boat. The boat has a parent object called a dummy, which is what you align to the ramp so that the boat sits correctly.

Exercise 5.11   Aligning Based on Local Axes

1. Open the file called Ch05_BoatRamp03.max on the CD-ROM or from the preceding exercise. From the File pull-down menu, choose Save As, point to an appropriate subdirectory on your hard drive, and use the plus sign button to save a new file with the name incremented to Ch05_BoatRamp04.max.

2. In the File pull-down menu, choose Merge, and find the file called Ramp.max in the Chapter 5 folder on the CD-ROM. Highlight Boat_ramp in the Merge dialog and click OK. The ramp has been prepositioned in front of the shed.

3. From the File menu, Merge, find USSAgamenticus.max, also in the Chapter 5 folders. In the Merge dialog, in the List types area to the right, clear Lights and Cameras. This hides these object types in the list. Pick the All button at the bottom of the dialog to highlight all objects in the list (see Figure 5.43). Click OK.

4. On the main toolbar, enter Boat in the Named Selection Sets field and press Enter. It makes selecting the objects easier next time. You do not want to align the selected objects to the ramp because the center of each object will occupy the same position and the boat will be a mess. The boat parts have all been linked to each other with hierarchical linking, a system of child, parent, and ancestors that you learn more about in Chapter 14, "Set Key Animation." Right now, you only need to know that the top "ancestor" is a helper dummy object named Dummy_Master. On the main toolbar, click Select by Name button. In the Select Objects dialog, check Display Subtree at the bottom. Highlight Dummy_Master near the top of the list, and you see that all its "child" objects are indented (see Figure 5.44). Click the Select button.

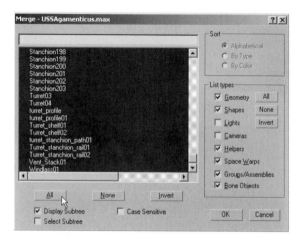

FIGURE 5.43   *In the Merge dialog, you can hide objects in the list by object type to make selections easier. Click OK to merge the objects.*

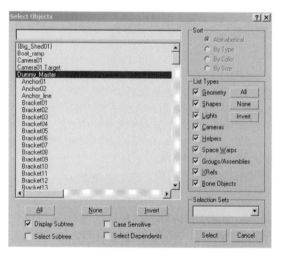

FIGURE 5.44   *Hierarchical linking is indicated in name lists when Display Subtree is checked. Child objects are indented to parent objects.*

5. On the main toolbar, click Align, press H, and double-click Boat_ramp in the list. In the Align Selection dialog, check the X, Y, and Z Position and make sure both columns are set to Center. Click OK. Zoom in on the Boat_ramp and you see that the boat sits sideways to the ramp.

note

The concept of child-parent linking is simple: Where the parent goes, the child must go with it; however, the child can have its own actions.

6. Activate the Top viewport. On the main toolbar, click the Select and Rotate button, and then click the Angle Snap Toggle to turn it on. Use the Transform gizmo to rotate the boat 90 degrees in the Z-axis so that the bow points toward the shed (see Figure 5.45). Zoom in to view the entire boat in the Top, Front, and Left viewports.

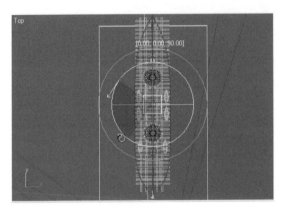

Figure 5.45   *With Angle Snap toggled on, rotate the Dummy_Master 90 degrees in the Top viewport so that the bow points toward the shed.*

7. The boat is now centered over the ramp and the bow is pointing forward, but the ramp tilts uphill while the boat is horizontal. With Dummy_Master selected, click the Align button and pick the Boat_ramp in the Top viewport. In the Align Selection dialog, check the Z-Axis check box in the Align Orientation (Local) area. The dummy and its children tip in the Left viewport to align with the angle of the ramp (see Figure 5.46). Click OK.

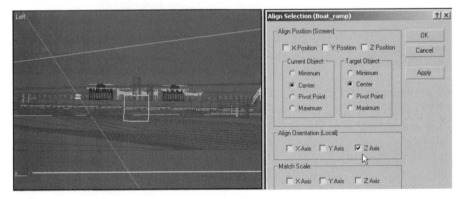

Figure 5.46   *Use the Align Orientation (Local) options to tip the boat angle (actually, the parent dummy) to match the ramp. Everything is based on the local axis.*

8. To move the boat up onto the ramp, click Select and Move, and then pick View to the right of the Transform buttons on the main toolbar, and choose Local in the list. In the Left viewport, move the Dummy_Master by its local Z-axis until the bottom of the boat appears to rest on the ramp.

9. Save the file. It is already called Ch05_BoatRamp04.max.

Scatter: With More Control

In Exercise 5.12, you learn to use scatter to place trees randomly within controlled areas in the scene.

Exercise 5.12   Scatter on Selected Faces Only

1. Open the file called Ch05_BoatRamp04.max on the CD-ROM or from the preceding exercise. From the File pull-down menu, choose Save As, point to an appropriate subdirectory on your hard drive, and use the plus sign button to save a new file with the name incremented to Ch05_BoatRamp05.max.

2. In the Top viewport, select Landscape. In the Modify panel, Stack view, highlight Polygon sub-object. In the Top viewport, select the two triangles shown in Figure 5.47. In the Stack view, highlight Editable Mesh to exit sub-object mode.

FIGURE 5.47   *In sub-object Polygon mode, select the two faces shown at either side of the shed. Use the Ctrl key to add to a selection set.*

3. In the File pull-down menu, choose Merge. Find the file on the CD-ROM called Tree.max. In the Merge dialog, highlight Evergreen01 in the list and click OK. One evergreen tree, which is a single object with the boughs and trunk attached, is merged into the scene. You might not be able to see it.

4. In the Create panel, Object Type rollout, click Scatter. In the Pick Distribution Object rollout, click the Pick Distribution Object button and, in the Top viewport pick Landscape. The Landscape object should appear to change color in the shaded Camera viewport. In the Display rollout, check Hide Distribution Object. In the Scatter Objects rollout, enter 50 in the Duplicates field and press Enter. This scatters 50 trees over the landscape, so you might see some of them show up in your viewports. There can also be some unexpected rotation, as shown in Figure 5.48.

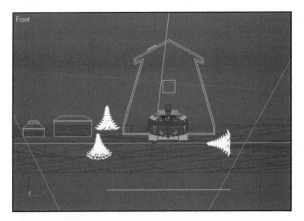

FIGURE 5.48 *Scattering 50 evergreen trees over the large landscape makes for a sparse forest, and some of the trees have odd rotations.*

5. In the Scatter Objects rollout, Distribution Object Parameters area, clear the Perpendicular check box. This ensures that all trees are vertical and not perpendicular to the face they are on. In the Distribution Object Parameters area, check the Use Selected Faces Only option (see Figure 5.49). This scatters the 50 trees over the last selection set rather than the entire object.

6. In the Transforms rollout, Scaling area, enter 50 in the Z field and press Enter. This randomly scales the trees a maximum of 25 percent higher or lower (see Figure 5.50).

7. Right-click the trees and convert to an editable mesh to reduce overhead. Do this only when you know that you have finished with scatter editing.

8. Save the file; it should already be called Ch05_BoatRamp05.max.

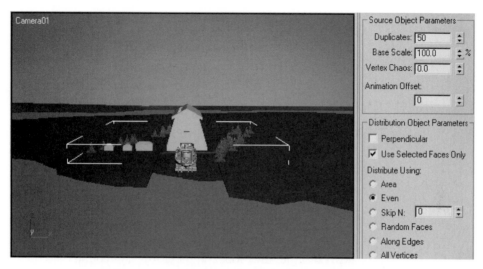

FIGURE 5.49   *In the Distribution Object Parameters area, clearing Perpendicular rights the trees and checking Use Selected Faces Only scatters the duplicates only on the last selection set of faces.*

FIGURE 5.50   *Entering 50 in the Scaling Z-axis field randomly applies scaling between plus 25 percent and minus 25 percent of the original height.*

Summary

Creating relatively accurate terrains does not have to be difficult. In this chapter, you learned a method in which you traced the contour lines of a topographical map that was used in max as a background image. You learned to control the aspect ratio of the map to avoid distortions as the viewports changed and to determine the size of a map feature that could be matched with an object in the scene to set a scaling factor.

You learned to move the contour lines to the proper elevation based on a naming scheme and to smooth the shapes with the Normalize Spline modifier. Using the terrain compound object results in a surface that is easily recognizable as the topographical map terrain.

You then created and adjusted a skydome object and learned to XRef and merge objects from other files. The ShapeMerge command enabled you to cut areas in surfaces that could be edited—in this example, a boat ramp—and you learned to place objects in space with both the Array tool and the scatter compound object.

The result is a shipyard, complete with ironclad boat, on the banks of Seavey Island, in the Piscataqua River, on the coast of Maine and New Hampshire.

Some of the topics covered in this chapter included the following:

- **Setting a scale from background maps**—You learned to trace a background map and retain the scale for relatively accurate terrain modeling.
- **Terrain compound object**—Exercises showed you how to convert contour lines into landscape meshes.
- **Normalize Spline**—You learned how to use this modifier to control vertex placement on 2D shapes.
- **Skydome**—You learned to create a hemisphere that accepts maps to simulate the sky in outdoor scenes.
- **ShapeMerge**—You learned to cut new edges into mesh objects with 2D shapes to define new modeling or material boundaries.
- **Scatter compound object**—You learned to make efficient, low-polygon trees and distribute them in large-scale landscape scenes.
- **XRef objects**—As you learned in this chapter, cross-referencing objects from other files merges the object into the current scene with a one-way editing connection from the original to the reference.

CHAPTER 6

Fundamental Outdoor Lighting with Standard Lights

In This Chapter

In this chapter, you learn to light the shipyard scene that you constructed in Chapter 5, "Creating Convincing Terrain," to simulate bright sunlight. You will use the standard lights lighting type in conjunction with the default Scanline renderer of 3ds max 6.

Standard lights are fast, with a minimum of mathematical overhead to process. However, unlike photometric lights that you will learn about in Chapter 12, "Photometric Lighting: Bounced Light Calculation," there is no bounced light from the surface of objects as there is in the real world.

Instead of approaching lighting with standard lights as a physical phenomena, it might be better to think of it as "painting with light." You are an artist who wants to paint your surfaces with light to obtain the brightness values that result in a convincing image. This is how a movie set is lit, too. Instead of relying on natural light, engineers place lights in the scene—the position, intensity, and color have nothing to do with the real world, but evoke emotions from the viewers based on artistic principles.

Some of the tools and processes you learn about in this chapter include the following:

- **Sunlight System**—Consisting of a compass rose and a directional light, the Sunlight System can be adjusted accurately for the date, time, and position of the sun for any location on earth.

- **Exclude/Include**—This is a feature of 3ds max 6 lights that enables you to determine which objects in the scene the light affects for better lighting control. This, of course, is not possible in the real world.

- **Fill lights**—You learn to place lights in the outdoor scene to simulate the effect of natural light that bounces in the atmosphere and from surfaces.

- **Shadows**—You learn to adjust the shadows being cast by objects onto other objects. This is very important to give weight to objects in the scene.

- **Skydome lighting**—You learn to light the skydome independently from other objects in the scene for a more convincing effect.

Key Terms

- **Raytrace**—In this case, raytrace refers to the shadows calculated by shooting sample rays at objects from light sources to determine the edges of shadows.

- **Hotspot/beam**—An area of light from a source that has full illumination based on the intensity at the source.

- **Falloff/field**—An area of light laterally outside the hotspot where the light diminishes in strength. Outside the falloff, there is no light.

- **Overshoot**—The ability of a directional light (light cast within a cylinder) or spotlight (light cast within a cone) to simulate the effect of an omni light (all directions).

- **Angle of incidence**—The angle that a light strikes a surface determines its intensity on the surface. Light striking a surface perpendicularly is full intensity.

- **Attenuation**—The amount a light diminishes in strength as a function of the distance from the source.

The Sunlight System

As mentioned earlier, the Sunlight System consists of a compass rose for positioning and a directional light that acts as the sun source.

A directional light in 3ds max 6 casts light from the source within two cylinders: the hotspot and falloff cylinders. The inner hotspot cylinder has full-intensity light. The light within the area between the hotspot and outer falloff cylinders diminishes in a linear manner. There is no light outside the falloff cylinder. There are also no shadows calculated outside the falloff cylinder.

There is, however, an option that is checked for directional lights in the Sunlight System called *overshoot*, which causes light to emanate from the source of the light in all directions. For efficiency, overshoot proves useful to control the area that casts shadows while still having some light in outlying areas.

The advantage of lighting outdoor scenes with a Sunlight System is speed in rendering. The setup time can be a bit longer than the alternative (Daylight System with radiosity rendering), but the render times tend to be much faster.

Placing a Sunlight System in an Outdoor Scene

In Exercise 6.1, you learn to place the Sunlight System in your scene and adjust it for the appropriate date, time, and location. You learn about some important adjustments to the default settings of the Sunlight System that can make its use very confusing to new users.

Exercise 6.1   The Sunlight System

1. Open the file called Ch06_Sunlight01.max on the CD-ROM. From the File pull-down menu, choose Save As, point to an appropriate subdirectory on your hard drive, and use the plus sign button to save a new file with the name incremented to Ch06_Sunlight02.max. The scene is basically the one you created in Chapter 5 with the island, river, and shipyard; the camera angle has changed to a lower, closer view; and the objects have been given a gray color. There is default lighting in the viewports that will turn off when you add your own lights.

2. Right-click in the Top viewport to activate it. You can see the cyan rectangle in front of the camera. In the Create panel, Systems panel, Object Type rollout, click the Sunlight button (see Figure 6.1).

caution

Do not click the Daylight System in the Object Type rollout. Daylight uses photometric lights that do not function with the default Scanline renderer. You will learn more about photometric lights in Chapter 12.

FIGURE 6.1   *The Sunlight System is found in the Create panel, Systems panel.*

3. In the Top viewport, click and drag slightly from the middle of the big shed near the upper end of the rectangle until you see a compass rose appear. The size of the compass rose is not so important and, because of the size of this scene, it might disappear outside the viewport rather quickly. Release the mouse button and push the mouse forward on the mouse pad to push the Sun01 object away from the center of the Compass01 until it is about two-thirds of the way to the outside of the skydome object, as seen in the Left viewport. Click to set the position of the Sun01 object (see Figure 6.2). The Sun01 object has Ray Traced Shadows enabled by default.

warning

The default background for 3ds max 6 is a middle gray color (as are the objects in this scene). The compass rose is also gray, which makes it difficult to see. It is the position of the center of the compass rose, called Compass01, that is most important; you can select Compass01 and modify the size of the rose later, if you want to see it completely in the viewport.

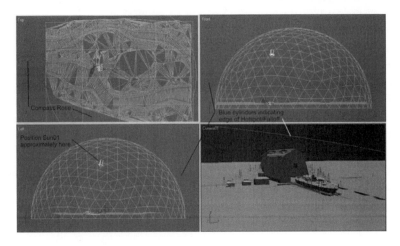

FIGURE 6.2   *Viewports showing the selected Compass01 centered roughly on the large shed in the Top viewport and the position of Sun01 in the Left viewport.*

4. Select Sun01 in the Top viewport. You see a thin
    light blue cylinder from the light source to the
    compass center. This is actually two cylinders, a
    light blue hotspot and a darker blue falloff cylin-
    der. In the Modify panel, Directional Parameters
    rollout, clear the Overshoot check box. In the
    Hotspot/Beam field, enter 3000, and in the Falloff/
    Field field, enter 3200 (see Figure 6.3). This is large
    enough to light the visible areas of your scene.

caution

Raytraced shadows can take
considerable time to calculate
and render, depending of
things such as the density of
the mesh in the scene and
particular light adjustments. If
you have a slow machine, this
file could take a while for test
renders. With a dual 650MHz
P3 with 384MB of RAM, for
example, the Camera view-
port renders in just more than
25 minutes.

You might want to avoid any
test rendering until some
adjustments have been made.

FIGURE 6.3   *Clearing the Overshoot check box in the Directional
Parameters rollout enables you to adjust the hotspot
and falloff cylinders to cover the area of your scene you
need to have lit by direct sunlight.*

5. Right-click in the Camera01 viewport to activate it
    and, on the main toolbar, click the Quick Render
    (Production) button at the far right to render the
    viewport. The sun hits the ground and casts shad-
    ows, but leaves many areas, the sky included, very
    dark to black. This is a function of the angle of
    incidence with which the light strikes the surface
    (see Figure 6.4). Close the Rendered Frame
    Window.

6. Save the file. It should already be called
    Ch06_Sunlight02.max.

note

Changing the hotspot and
falloff sizes to cover too much
of the scene can have a detri-
mental effect on render times.
Use sizes that cover the necessary areas of your scene only
and do not have a small
hotspot with a large falloff.
The distance between the two
affects the softness at the edge
of the lit area.

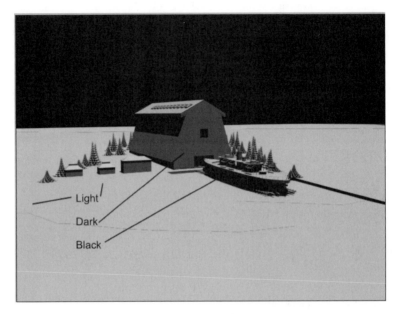

FIGURE 6.4   *A test render shows brightly lit ground, dark buildings, and a black sky and shadow areas. This is because of the angle of incidence of the light to the surface. The ground surface is almost perpendicular to the light, and therefore is the brightest.*

The Exclude Feature—Higher Levels of Control

In Exercise 6.2, you learn to use a feature that enables you to exclude objects in the scene from the effect of the light. This provides a level of lighting control that goes beyond anything in the real world.

First, think about what it is you see when you go outdoors on a cloudless day. The sky that you "see" is not a dome with the sun shining on it; rather, it is the sunlight being bounced around in the dust and water droplets in our atmosphere. As mentioned before, standard lights and scanline rendering do not calculate the effects of the bounced light. Instead, you want to make the skydome appear to have its own light source and not be affected by Sun01 at all.

You also learn to adjust the position of the light for a specific time of day, date, and location, and then exclude the skydome from the sun. If you try to select the sun and move it, nothing will happen. It is positioned by a special animation controller that calculates the position using accurate input. You will change the position of the sun in the Motion panel.

Exercise 6.2   Position the Sun and Exclude the Sky

1. Open the file called Ch06_Sunlight02.max on the CD-ROM or from the preceding exercise. From the File pull-down menu, choose Save As, point to an appropriate subdirectory on your hard drive, and use the plus sign button to save a new file with the name incremented to Ch06_Sunlight03.max.

2. In the Left viewport, select Sun01. In the Motion panel, Control Parameters rollout, enter 10 in Hours, 0 in Mins, and 0 in Secs in the numeric fields for a 10 a.m. time. Set the date to 2 in Month, 28 in Day, 2003 in Year. Click the Get Location button and choose Portsmouth NH from the list (see Figure 6.5). Click OK. The sun will be coming over your right shoulder as seen in the Camera01 viewport, and you can see that the sky-dome behind the shed is now lit.

tip

For larger cities, you can pick directly on the map of the United States to set the location. There are also maps of the other continents. For more exact work for locations with no listings, you can enter the latitude and longitude directly in the Motion panel.

You also can use a setting called North Direction, which enables you to adjust to the actual north direction of your scene.

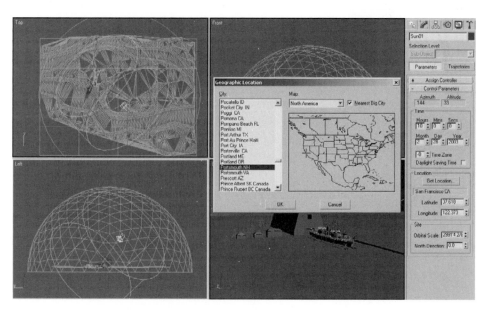

FIGURE 6.5   *With Sun01 selected, in the Motion panel set the time for 10 a.m. and the date to 28 February 2003. Click the Get Location button and choose Portsmouth NH from the list.*

3. With Sun01 selected, go to the Modify panel. In the General Parameters rollout, click the Exclude button. In the Exclude/Include dialog, highlight Skydome in the left column and click the double right-arrow button between the columns to push the skydome into the right side column (see Figure 6.6). The Sun01 object no longer affects illumination or shadows from the skydome object. Click OK.

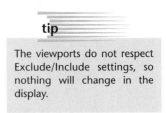

tip

The viewports do not respect Exclude/Include settings, so nothing will change in the display.

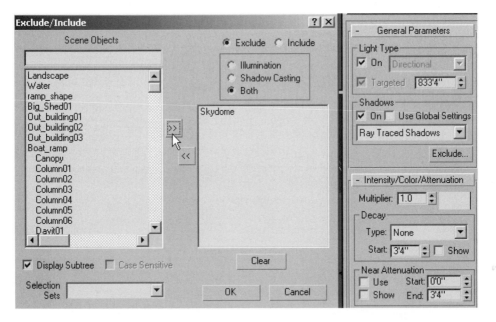

FIGURE 6.6   *In the Modify panel for Sun01, click the Exclude button. In the Exclude/Include dialog, highlight Skydome in the left column and push it into the right column.*

4. Activate the Camera01 viewport and click Quick Render on the main toolbar. You will see the sky is absolutely black (see Figure 6.7).

5. Save the file; it is already called Ch06_Sunlight03.max.

FIGURE 6.7   *With the skydome object excluded from Sun01, there can be no light on it in the rendered image. Note the longer shadows caused by the lower angle of Sun01, also.*

Adding Fill Lights to Simulate Bounced Light

All the light in this scene is coming from one source: the Sun01 directional light. The shaded side of objects is pure black. In reality, light would bounce off surrounding surfaces and elements in the atmosphere and "fill" the shaded area with a softer, weaker light.

In 3ds max 6, using Standard lights, you have to simulate that effect by adding fill lights and adjusting the intensity for the values you deem appropriate for your artistic view.

In film and photography, fill lights and reflectors are used extensively to balance the light and dark areas. Traditional painters often will do a "value sketch," a black-and-white base painting to set the brightness levels for the balance they want.

In this short, but important, section of this chapter, you add lights for balance.

Fill Lights: Adjusting the Balance of Light Values

In Exercise 6.3, you learn to place and adjust two fill lights and to exclude the sky-dome from them. In a more complex scene, you might have many fill lights to achieve the correct levels of contrast and balance, but that is an artistic decision, not a technical one, and is beyond the scope of this book.

Exercise 6.3   Adding and Adjusting Fill Lights

1. Open the file called Ch06_Sunlight03.max on the CD-ROM or from the preceding exercise. From the File pull-down menu, choose Save As, point to an appropriate subdirectory on your hard drive, and use the plus sign button to save a new file with the name incremented to Ch06_Sunlight04.max.

2. Activate the Top viewport and zoom out to see space around your entire scene. In the Create panel, Lights panel, click the Omni button in Object Type rollout. Click in the Top viewport outside the skydome on the left (the edge can be seen as a large gray circle), about 90 degrees from the angle of Sun01 (see Figure 6.8).

> **tip**
>
> Fill lights for an outdoor scene should be placed a fair distance away from the object they are lighting to minimize any effects from the angle of incidence. If the lights are too close, you will get brighter light on surfaces that are perpendicular to the source and this could cause a shading effect across your scene.

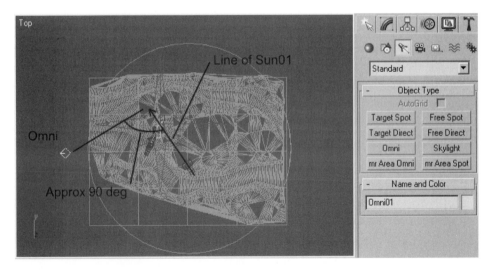

FIGURE 6.8   *Place an omni light outside your scene and perpendicular to the line of the Sun01 object.*

3. In the Modify panel, Intensity/Color/Attenuation rollout, enter 0.6 in the Multiplier field (see Figure 6.9). This reduces the intensity of the fill light to 60 percent of that of the Sun01 object.

4. In the General Parameters rollout, click the Exclude button and exclude skydome from this light. It also is important that you do not have Shadows checked on for fill lights in outdoor scenes.

tip

Shadow-casting omni lights can be very expensive in computer resources. An omni light is actually six spotlights with an algorithm to clean up overlapping areas. Omni lights take six times longer to calculate shadows.

FIGURE 6.9   *Set the Multiplier value of Omni01 to 0.6 and the intensity is 60 percent of the Sun01 on surfaces at the same angle of incidence.*

5. Click the Select and Move button on the main toolbar, hold the Shift key, and clone the light as a Copy beyond the skydome and in alignment with direction of the Sun01 (see Figure 6.10). In the Modify panel, Intensity/Color/Attenuation rollout, set the Multiplier to 0.4. This light is sometimes known as a backlight, and the multiplier value can be increased to set objects off from a dark background. The skydome is already excluded in the clone.

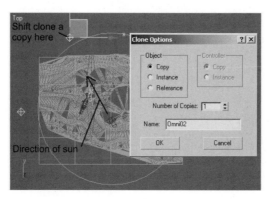

FIGURE 6.10   *Move Omni01 with the Shift key to make a Copy clone in line with the direction of Sun01 and set the intensity to 0.4. This light is sometimes known as a backlight.*

6. Activate the Camera01 viewport and click Quick Render on the main toolbar. The scene has a much more balanced light that is especially noticeable on the boat, shed, and trees. The landscape and water are barely affected by these lights because of the extremely low angle of incidence (see Figure 6.11).

FIGURE 6.11   *Adding fill lights give the scene a more balanced look that simulates the effect of bounced light from surfaces and in the atmosphere.*

7. Save the file; it is already called Ch06_Sunlight04.max.

Shadow Optimization

You have carefully crafted your model for efficiency, but adding shadow-casting lights has increased rendering times considerably. You also can make adjustments to optimize the calculations performed by Sun01 shadows. The default type of shadows for the Sunlight System is raytraced shadows. A sampling of rays are fired from the light to surfaces to calculate where the edges of shadows should fall.

In this section, you adjust a setting that is almost guaranteed to cut rendering times noticeably, and then you switch to a new type of shadow calculation.

Max Quadtree Depth and Advanced Ray Traced Shadows

In the process of firing rays from the light source to surfaces in a raytraced shadow light, 3ds max 6 uses a Max Quadtree Depth setting to determine where rays should be fired for the best effectiveness. You can change that setting for a courser or finer refinement of the process. In Exercise 6.4, you learn to adjust the number to speed rendering. This is never a set number, but varies depending on the density of

note

I have personally never found or heard of anyone benefiting from a Max Quadtree Depth of less than 7.

mesh objects and the overall size of the scene itself, and you must experiment by adjusting up from the default setting of 7. The maximum setting is 10, but you must also try 8 and 9 to see which works best for any given scene.

You also learn to change the shadow type used by Sun01 for further optimization.

Exercise 6.4   Max Quadtree Depth and Advanced Ray Traced Shadows

1. Open the file called Ch06_Sunlight04.max on the CD-ROM or from the preceding exercise. From the File pull-down menu, choose Save As, point to an appropriate subdirectory on your hard drive, and use the plus sign button to save a new file with the name incremented to Ch06_Sunlight05.max.

2. Right-click in the Camera01 viewport to activate it, if it isn't already, and click the Quick Render button on the main toolbar. When the scene is rendered, note the rendering time listed in the status bar (see Figure 6.12).

FIGURE 6.12   *After rendering the Camera01 viewport, note the rendering time shown in the status bar.*

3. In the Left viewport, select Sun01. In the Modify panel, Ray Traced Shadow Params rollout, enter 10 in the Max Quadtree Depth field. Render the Camera01 viewport again and note the new rendering time. For my machine, it dropped from 3m26s to 16s—an astonishing time savings.

note

I have done the testing for you and found that 10 is the fastest for this particular scene. In your own scenes, you must compare 8 and 9, as well.

4. In the Rendering pull-down menu, choose RAM Player at the bottom of the menu. In the RAM Player dialog, click the teapot button on the left called Open Last Rendered Image in Channel A (see Figure 6.13) and accept the default settings by clicking OK in the RAM Player Configuration dialog. This loads the last rendered image for viewing. Do not close the RAM Player.

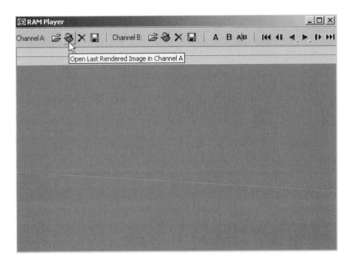

FIGURE 6.13   *Load the last rendered image into Channel A of the RAM Player for viewing.*

5. In the General Parameters rollout of the Modify panel, click Ray Traced Shadows and choose Adv. Ray Traced from the list (see Figure 6.14). This uses a different formula to calculate the ray firing.

6. Activate the Camera01 viewport and click Quick Render. The render time increased to 28s for my machine, but the quality of the shadows has increased. Some edges of shadows are noticeably less jaggy.

7. Activate the RAM Player dialog that is still open in your display and click the Open Last Rendered Image in Channel B button to the right side of the Channel A buttons. Click OK to accept the default configuration. You now have two images side by side in the RAM Player.

FIGURE 6.14
In the Modify panel, General Parameters rollout, change the shadow type for Sun01 to Adv. Ray Traced.

8. Click and hold the mouse button any place on the image and drag the mouse back and forth. Arrows at the top and bottom of the display will follow the cursor movements. You will compare the changes in shadow quality of the Ray Traced shadows on the left side of your cursor location and the Adv. Ray Traced shadows on the right, especially in the trees and small buildings and the edge of landscape and water.

9. Close all dialogs and save the file. It is already called Ch06_Sunlight05.max.

> **note**
>
> Ray Traced Shadows and Adv. Ray Traced shadows are generally the best options for outdoor scenes with shadows being cast by a sun where the shadows will have crisp edges.
>
> Advanced Ray Traced shadows can be adjusted for a softer edge as you would see in slightly cloudier sky simulations.

Lighting the Skydome

The scene is looking reasonably good as far as lighting is concerned except for the black sky in the rendered images. Remember that all the lights in the scene are set to exclude the skydome.

In this scene, you learn to place a light that is specifically lighting only the skydome. To be convincing, the light must be evenly distributed over the surface because in reality, light comes from the sky in the form of bounced light; it is not lit from a source.

Positioning and Adjusting a Light for the Sky

One omni light placed at the bottom center of the hemisphere will cast light evenly because the angle of incidence is the same for all faces.

However, that light shinning upward would appear strange on the undersides of the boat, roof eaves, and trees. In Exercise 6.5, you learn to use the Include feature of lights to simplify Exclude operations.

Exercise 6.5   Lighting the Sky

1. Open the file called Ch06_Sunlight05.max on the CD-ROM or from the preceding exercise. From the File pull-down menu, choose Save As, point to an appropriate subdirectory on your hard drive, and use the plus sign button to save a new file with the name incremented to Ch06_Sunlight06.max.

2. In the Create panel, Lights panel, click the Omni button in the Object Type rollout. In the Top viewport, click right in the center of the skydome to place the light on the World coordinate grid so its angle of incidence is the same for all faces of the skydome.

3. In the Modify panel, General Parameters rollout, click the Exclude button. In the Exclude/Include dialog, highlight Skydome in the left column and push it to the right column with the double right-arrow button. In the Exclude/Include dialog, check the Include radio button at the top right (see Figure 6.15). Click OK. This light is only going to light the skydome. You could use Exclude and push everything but the skydome into the right column, but you would have to remember to exclude each new object you created or merged into the scene.

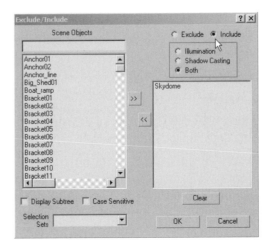

FIGURE 6.15 *Using the Include option of the Exclude feature is a simpler way to dedicate lights to specific objects. You do not have to remember to exclude new objects in the scene with this method.*

4. In the Camera01 viewport, select the skydome. Right-click the skydome and choose Properties from the Quad menu. In the Object Properties dialog, Rendering Control area, clear both Receive Shadows and Cast Shadows (see Figure 6.16). Click OK. This ensures that you will never cast shadows with the skydome or that objects will never cast shadows onto the skydome.

5. Render the Camera01 viewport and you see an evenly lit skydome as a backdrop for your scene, and now you are ready to apply some materials in the next chapter to begin making a more convincing image (see Figure 6.17).

6. Close all dialogs and save the file. It is already called Ch06_Sunlight06.max.

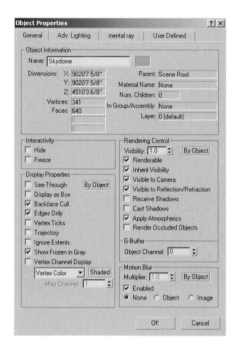

FIGURE 6.16 *In the Object Properties dialog, you can clear Receive Shadows and Cast Shadows to ensure the object can do neither.*

FIGURE 6.17 *Rendering the Camera01 viewport shows an evenly lit skydome.*

Summary

In this chapter, you took a scene with default lighting that seemed to come from no meaningful direction and added lights of your own to make the scene more convincing to the viewer. The objects now have shadows that "anchor" them to the ground and give them apparent weight (instead of them seeming to float in space).

You also adjusted the balance of light with fill lights to simulate the bounced light in the real world from surrounding objects and from the moisture and dust in the atmosphere.

Shadows can be accurately calculated for time, date, and location for anywhere in the world, and you learned ways to optimize the overhead involved in shadow calculations.

Some of the highlights of this chapter include the following:

- **Sunlight System**—You learned to place a compass rose and a directional light, the Sunlight System, and to adjust for the date, time, and position of the sun for accurate shadows.

- **Exclude/Include**—You learned to use this feature to determine which objects in the scene the light affects for better lighting control. This, of course, is not possible in the real world.

- **Fill lights**—You learned to place lights in the outdoor scene to simulate the effect of natural light that bounces in the atmosphere and from surfaces.

- **Shadows**—You learned to adjust the shadows being cast by objects onto other objects. This is very important to give weight to objects in the scene.

- **Skydome lighting**—You learned to light the skydome independently from other objects in the scene for a more convincing effect.

CHAPTER 7

Introduction to Materials and Mapping

In This Chapter

This chapter walks you through the process of creating and applying materials to objects in a scene to give them a more convincing appearance.

Materials alone do not make a good final image; they must be adjusted to work in conjunction with the lighting in the scene. This chapter focuses primarily on learning to create basic materials and make them fit the objects in the scene so that the patterns in the materials make sense to the viewer.

Some of the topics you learn about in this chapter include the following:

- **Material Editor**—You create all your materials by combining maps and attributes in the Material Editor before assigning the material to objects in the scene. This is a creation and preview space that you learn to navigate.

- **Applying maps in materials**—You learn to apply maps to various attributes of material to generate patterns and effects.

- **Simulate geometry**—Learning to simulate geometry (for example, raised patterns on a flat surface or holes through a surface) is one of the most important aspects of materials you learn in this chapter.

- **Mapping coordinates**—Some patterns require specific orientation information to fit objects correctly. You learn to apply these coordinates.

- **Material libraries**—You learn to create and save material libraries to store your materials.

You primarily learn to work with what are known as *procedural maps* to form patterns in your materials in this chapter. Procedural maps are, usually, random patterns that are mathematically generated at render time.

You also learn about creating material libraries to store and recall materials from other scenes. Management of material libraries is an important part of working efficiently with 3ds max 6, especially in a collaborative environment.

note

I tend not to use the words *realism* or *photorealistic* when speaking about computer renderings. What you want to achieve is a level of "convincibility" that evokes the emotional response from the viewers that you intend.

Reality is too complex and too cluttered with elements that our perception of the scene filters out. In 3ds max 6, those same elements can come across as "wrong." An example is triple-pane windows I observed in an airport. If I ever presented such complex and distorted reflections to a client, I would be off the project in a flash.

Again, you must develop the eye of an artist and decide what the viewer needs to see and focus the viewer's attention on those attributes.

Key Terms

- **Material**—Materials are applied to objects to control attributes such as color, shininess, opacity, and bumpiness, for example. Several different material types are available in 3ds max 6.

- **Maps**—Maps are patterns used within the attributes of materials. These can be procedural or a variety of image formats. Many different map types are available.

- **Material library**—Material libraries act as storage areas for materials and maps so that they can be accessed from any scene.

- **Luminance value**—This is the brightness values of individual pixels of maps that 3ds max 6 uses to create illusions such as bumps or opacity in a material.

- **Specular highlights**—Specular highlights refer to light scattered from a surface. This is one of the most important attributes of materials.

The Material Editor

This section provides a brief tour of the important features of the Material Editor that you will need to work through this chapter.

The Material Editor is a powerful tool, and you should take the time to investigate the capabilities of it with the tutorials that ship with 3ds max and the built-in Help files. Here, you learn to navigate the areas you will need for this book and to make sense out of some of the options.

Materials are made of layers of information that interact with light in your scenes to produce the illusion of specific real or imagined materials. For example, wood, steel, skin, or water are all made convincing through material adjustments.

An analogy might be a traditional painter's palette of colors that must be artfully mixed to satisfy the viewer's curiosity.

Open 3ds max 6 and click the Material Editor button on the main toolbar or press M for the shortcut key (see Figure 7.1).

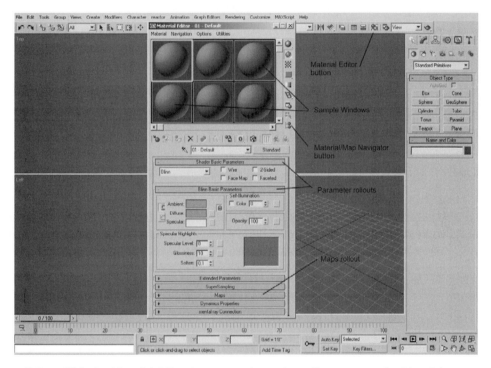

FIGURE 7.1   *Click the Material Editor button on the main toolbar to open the Material Editor.*

The areas important to use for this chapter are as follows:

- **Sample windows**—Materials are created and previewed here.
- **Parameters rollouts**—Basic color and shininess components are controlled here.

- **Maps rollout**—Maps or patterns can be applied to the various components.

- **Material/Map Navigator**—A hierarchical display of the structure of the material for easier navigation when editing.

In this section, you learn the essentials of what these areas of the Material Editor control—again, to familiarize you with the components that you will be using in the chapter exercises.

Sample Windows—Your Mixing Palettes

Again, to borrow from painters, the sample windows enable you to test components of materials and to preview the results before assigning the material to objects in your scene. Once applied, however, changes made in the sample windows automatically update in the scene. By default, you can see six sample windows available, but that does not mean you can have only six materials. The sample windows can be expanded to 24 materials seen at any one time, but you can have as many materials as you want in the scene or stored in material libraries.

The white border around the sample window identifies the currently active material.

Parameters Rollouts

These two rollouts—Shader Basic Parameters and Blinn Basic Parameters—enable you to adjust the basic color, opacity, and self-illumination components of materials, plus the more important components of the color, size, and shape of the specular highlights or scattered light from materials. You learn more about specular highlights in Exercise 7.2.

Maps Rollout

Maps can be applied to many components of materials for the purpose of creating patterns. The maps can be mathematically generated or still and animated images. They can be combined and layered for much complexity and control. Figure 7.2 shows the Maps rollout of a standard material type.

tip

Most components of the Blinn Basic Parameters rollout have a gray box to the right of them that is a map shortcut button. This enables you to access the Maps rollout options more directly.

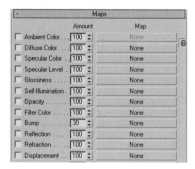

FIGURE 7.2   *You can apply maps as patterns to various components of a standard material in the Maps rollout and change the amount of influence within the material.*

Material/Map Browser

By clicking the button on the left of the row of buttons below the sample windows, you can see a hierarchical display of materials and maps to quickly select and view complex materials while editing. Figure 7.3 shows a view of the hierarchy of some materials in a library called Nature.mat. The spheres indicate materials, whereas the parallelograms indicate map levels.

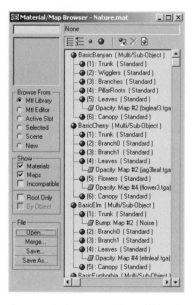

FIGURE 7.3   *The Material/Map Browser is important for efficiently moving through the hierarchy of materials and maps in the Material Editor or scene.*

Although this chapter focuses mostly on fundamental aspects of materials, the discussion will still get complex in places. Read the chapter over first to get an idea of the direction, and then go back and perform the exercises step by step. Keep your focus on the concepts being presented and the processes involved in creating materials rather than the individual steps, and you will have an easier time developing your materials for your scenes.

caution

3ds max 6 comes with a wide array of different materials and maps that are included as examples. Use them as examples only to see how a particular effect is achieved. You are the artist here, and you must develop your own style and signature to distinguish your work from others.

The default max maps and materials are identifiable in images, and you will get more respect in the industry with all custom materials.

Materials with Procedural Maps as Patterns

In this section, you learn to create and assign a material to the landscape, water, and skydome objects in your shipyard scene. The land will be mostly open grassy areas with random patches of dirt, whereas the water will be sparkling and reflective, and the sky will fade from rich color above to hazy white at the horizon.

You learn the important feature of simulating geometry with materials. This technique uses the Luminance value, or brightness, of pixels in a map to create the illusion of added geometry detail. White pixels cause the effect to happen at maximum strength, black pixels do nothing, and gray pixels function somewhere at 256 levels in between. You can judge the Luminance values within grayscale maps much easier than by guessing the luminance values of color maps. In this particular example, you use bump maps to make the landscape look rough in areas. This technique is much more efficient than actually creating small geometry for roughness.

These examples of fundamental techniques are not necessarily simple at first glance. Again, think about what you are doing in the exercises and what the end result is.

Creating the Illusion of a Grassy Landscape

Exercise 7.1 teaches you about assigning a material to the landscape object in your scene and adding patterns to components of the materials to change both the color and the apparent bumpiness of the landscape.

Exercise 7.1   Procedural Maps as Color and Bumps Within a Material

1. Open the file called Ch07_Intro_Mat01.max on the CD-ROM. From the File pull-down menu, choose Save As, point to an appropriate subdirectory on your hard drive, and use the plus sign button to save a new file with the name incremented to Ch07_Intro_Mat02.max. This is the outdoor shipyard scene with the sunlight that you will bring to life with materials.

The triangles in the corner of sample windows that indicate a hot" material are white if an object with that material is selected in the scene and gray if no objects with that material are selected.

2. On the main toolbar, click the Material Editor button or press M to bring up the Material Editor. It is a floating dialog that you can resize vertically and move around your display. The upper-left sample window is active as indicated by the white border, and all visible sample windows have the default gray material, none of which is assigned to any of the objects in the scene. In the Camera01 viewport, pick Landscape or use Select by Name and choose it in the list. In the Material Editor, click the Assign Material to Selection button below and left of the sample windows. The landscape should turn a slightly darker shade of gray and the sample window will have triangles in the corner to indicate it is a "hot" material, one assigned to an object in the scene (see Figure 7.4).

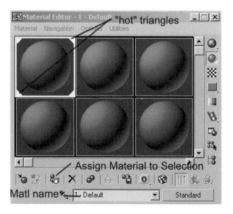

FIGURE 7.4   *Assigning a material to a selected object in the scene displays triangles in the corners of the sample window to indicate a "hot" material. Editing the sample window updates in the scene.*

3. In the Blinn Basic Parameters rollout, click the Diffuse color swatch, the large gray rectangle just to the right of Diffuse. In the Color Selector, adjust the diffuse color to a middle green (see Figure 7.5). The Ambient color swatch changes as they are locked together, and the landscape in the shaded Perspective viewport also turns green to match. This homogenous color is often fine for materials such as plastic or paint, but such a large expanse of consistent color is not appropriate for the rough ground of your shipyard. Close the Color Selector dialog.

note

The diffuse color is the color of a material in direct light, whereas the ambient color is the color in the shaded areas. These should remain locked together for consistency in rendering with the advanced lighting system in 3ds max 6.

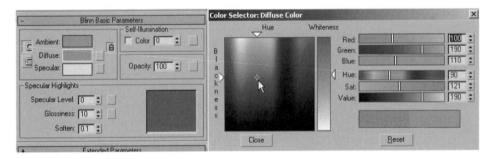

FIGURE 7.5   *Click the Diffuse color swatch and adjust it to a middle green. This exact color is not important for this exercise.*

4. In this step, you learn to apply a map to the color component that will completely override the green you just set in the Diffuse slot. In the Blinn Basic Parameters rollout, click the small gray square to the right of the Diffuse color swatch. This is the map shortcut for Diffuse. Double-click Noise in the Material/Map Browser (see Figure 7.6) to load Noise into the Diffuse slot. The sphere in the sample window turns to a blotchy gray.

note

Noise is a procedural map of randomly generated black and white areas. The map cannot be accurately seen in the viewports because it is generated at render time.

5. Activate the Camera01 viewport and click the Quick Render button on the main toolbar. The landscape appears to have a small blotchy pattern (see Figure 7.7). The pattern is too small, and the gray colors do not make the scene more convincing, however.

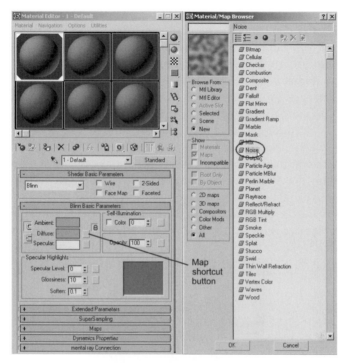

FIGURE 7.6   *Click the map shortcut button to the right of the Diffuse color swatch and double-click Noise in the browser. It now determines the color of the sample window sphere.*

FIGURE 7.7   *In the rendered image of the Camera01 viewport, the noise map in the Diffuse color map slot of the material makes the landscape appear to have a small blotchy pattern.*

6. Procedural maps have various adjustments for size, contrast, and color among other attributes. You adjust the size and the edge contrast to better place your pattern in the scene. The pattern needs to be somewhat larger. In the Material Editor, Noise Parameters rollout, enter 0.5 in the High Noise Threshold field and 0.49 in the Low field. Enter 100 in the Size field and press Enter (see Figure 7.8). The Noise Threshold settings adjust the contrast at the edges of the two colors, in this case black and white, and the Size setting makes the pattern larger or smaller. The sphere in the sample window now looks like the box of a well-known computer brand. The closer the threshold numbers are, the harder the edge; the higher the numbers are, the more of Color 1 (black). The size is the relative scale of the pattern. Render the Camera01 viewport.

tip

I find it easier to position the initial patterns by setting the adjustments to extreme settings. When I get the pattern adjusted in the scene, I back off to a more convincing look.

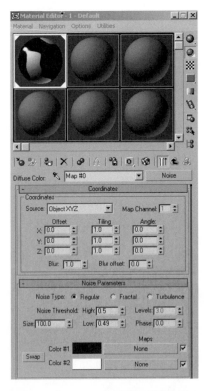

FIGURE 7.8   *In the Noise Parameters rollout, set the High Noise Threshold to 0.5 and the Low to 0.49 for a very hard edge between the two colors and an equal balance of black and white. Set the Size to 100 for a larger pattern.*

7. The pattern is an appropriate size for the scene, but the colors are certainly not landscape colors. In the Noise Parameters rollout, click the Color #1 swatch and, in the Color Selector, set Red=60, Green=100, and Blue=60 for a grayish-green color. Click on Color #2 and set it to Red=75, Green=60, and Blue=40 for a moderate brown color. Set the High Noise Threshold to 0.75 to apply more of Color #1 to the mix and to soften the edges somewhat. Render the Camera01 viewport, and you see mostly green with brown patches distributed evenly, but randomly throughout.

8. Now, add "texture" to the landscape in the form of bump mapping. Remember, it is white pixels of a map that will have the most effect, whereas black pixels do nothing. You want the brown dirt areas to have a different texture from the grassy areas, so you will learn to assign a map to each portion. The pattern is already set with this noise map, so you clone it from the Diffuse Color slot to the Bump slot and make it a copy. Then, instead of just changing Colors #1 and #2, you apply a map to Color 1. This is where the Material/Map Navigator proves useful. In the Material Editor, click the Material/Map Navigator button. In the Navigator list, highlight 1 – Default to return to the top level of the material (see Figure 7.9).

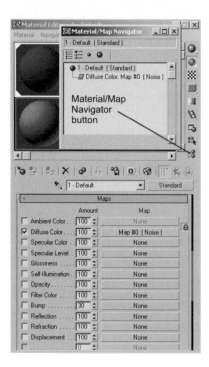

FIGURE 7.9   *Click the Material/Map Navigator button in Material Editor, and then high-light 1 – Default to return to the top level of this material.*

9. While you are at the top level of this material, rename it Landscape. It is always good practice to name materials as soon as you create them. In the Maps rollout, click and hold on the Map#(Noise) button in the Map column, Diffuse Color slot. Drag the map to the Bump None button and release when you see the cursor change to an arrow/rectangle combination (see Figure 7.10). In the Copy(Instance)Map dialog, make sure the Copy radio button is checked and click OK. You now have two maps, exactly the same in different slots.

> **note**
>
> Each time you load a map in 3ds max 6, it is randomly assigned a number—for example, Map#0(Noise). The number might differ on every machine.

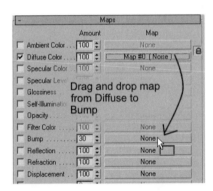

FIGURE 7.10 In the Maps rollout, drag and drop the noise map from the Diffuse Color slot to the Bump slot, choose Copy in the Copy(Instance)Map dialog, and click OK. To clone the map, you must see the arrow/rectangle cursor, not the international NO/rectangle cursor.

10. In the Material Editor, click the Material/Map Navigator button if the Navigator is not still open. In the Navigator list, highlight Bump:Map(Noise) level to edit that map. In the Noise Parameters rollout, you see the same green/brown colors you set. In the Color 1 slot, Maps column, click the None button and double-click Speckle in the list (see Figure 7.11). The speckle map now overrides the color swatch setting. The sample window sphere has a very rough look to it. You are simulating geometry with a bump map.

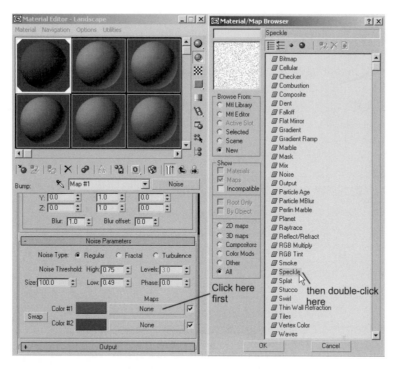

FIGURE 7.11 *Click the None button for Color #1 in the Maps column and double-click Speckle in the Material/Map Browser list.*

11. Render the Camera01 viewport and the landscape looks too rough. Use the Material/Map Navigator to go to the top level of the Landscape material. In the Maps rollout, set the Amount for the Bump slot to 5 (see Figure 7.12). This mitigates the bump amount to a more convincing effect. The bump is appearing only in the grassy areas because Color 2 is still a very dark value (brown) and has little effect in those areas of the landscape.

12. Close all windows and dialogs. Save the file; it should already be called Ch07_Intro_Mat02.max.

note

In the rendered image, viewing distance and angle and lighting can have a profound affect on how bump maps appear. You will often need to make adjustments to each for the final results.

tip

FIGURE 7.12 *At the top level of the Landscape material, Maps roll-out, set the Bump amount from 30 to 5 to reduce the effect of the bump in the material.*

Specular highlights are light scattered from a surface. They are your prime indicator of how "hard" the material is. Hardness is defined by the closeness of the molecules; the harder materials have dense molecules, while softer materials have spacing between the molecules.

When light strikes the surface, it either scatters off or is absorbed by the molecules. Metals, therefore, have bright specular highlights with sharp edges, whereas rubber has a broad and dull specular highlight.

Surface conditions such as oiliness or scratches can also affect the quality of the specular highlights.

Make a point of studying specular highlights in the world around you. Until you can see them and recognize them, you will not be able to reproduce them in 3ds max 6.

Creating and Assigning a Water Material

In Exercise 7.2, you create a water material that has color and bump patterns; you also learn to adjust the all-important specular highlights and to add reflections to the material for added depth when rendered.

Exercise 7.2   Creating a Water Material

1. Open the file called Ch07_Intro_Mat02.max on the CD-ROM or from the preceding exercise. From the File pull-down menu, choose Save As, point to an appropriate subdirectory on your hard drive, and use the plus sign button to save a new file with the name incremented to Ch07_Intro_Mat03.max.

2. On the main toolbar, click the Material Editor button to open it. Click the second sample window from the left in the top row. Change the name to Water. In the Blinn Basic Parameters rollout, click the Diffuse color swatch and, in the Color Selector, set Red=50, Green=50, and Blue=80 for a dark, grayish blue.

3. This time, click and drag the sample window in the Material Editor to the Water object in the Camera01 viewport. You see a tooltip with the name of the object when your cursor is properly positioned (see Figure 7.13). Drop the material onto the Water object.

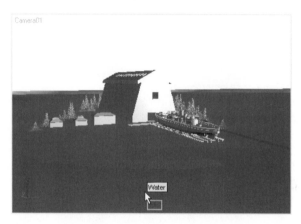

FIGURE 7.13   *You can drag and drop from the sample window to an object in the scene to assign a material to a single object. A tooltip appears to show which object will be assigned the material when you drop it.*

4. For the bump map in the Water material, you use a cellular map that looks like cells growing in a laboratory petri dish, but with some adjustments, it can be made to simulate wind wavelets on water. In the Material Editor, Maps rollout, click the None button in the Bump slot and double-click Cellular in the list. In the Cellular Parameters rollout, enter 50 in the Size field (see Figure 7.14) and press Enter. The slight bumps visible on the sample sphere and on the rendered Camera01 viewport look more like rough concrete than water.

5. In the Cellular Parameters rollout, click and drag the black color swatch at the bottom of the Division Colors area onto the gray swatch above (see Figure 7.15) and click Copy in the Copy or Swap Colors dialog. Again, you must have the arrow/rectangle cursor on the gray swatch before dropping.

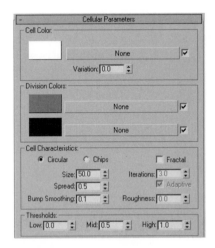

FIGURE 7.14   *In the Cellular Parameters rollout, enter 50 in the Size field and press Enter. The sphere in the sample window looks more like rough concrete.*

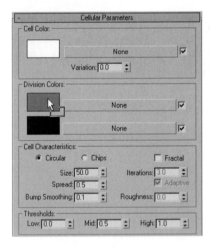

FIGURE 7.15   *Click and drag the black swatch in the Division Colors area to the gray swatch above and copy it. You now have two black swatches as division colors.*

    6. Use the Material/Map Navigator to go to the top level of the Water material. In the Maps rollout, enter –30 in the Bump Amount field and press Enter. The sample window and rendered Camera01 viewport now "ridges" rather than "bubbles," but still does not look like water.

7. Now, adjust the specular highlights by adjusting Specular Level (brightness) and Glossiness (size) of the highlights. In the Blinn Basic Parameters rollout, enter 100 in the Specular Level field for a very bright highlight. The sample window shows the bright, broad specular highlight. In the Glossiness field, enter 30 and press Enter to make the highlight smaller on the surface of the sample sphere. Render the Camera01 viewport and not much will have changed there (see Figure 7.16). Remember that lighting and materials work together. Also, a material can look much different on a curved surface (Sample Sphere) than on a flat surface (Water).

FIGURE 7.16   *Setting the Specular Level to 100 makes the highlight brighter and setting the Glossiness to 30 makes it smaller, but the changes do not appear the same on the sample window and the Water object in a rendered image.*

8. Now, apply a reflection map to Water material. In the top level of Water material, Maps rollout, click the Reflection slot None button and double-click Raytrace in the list of maps. Render the Camera01 viewport to see a very reflective surface reflecting mostly the gray skydome (see Figure 7.17). Close the windows and dialogs.

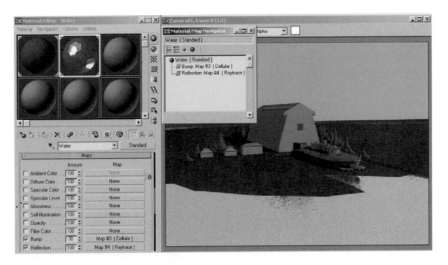

FIGURE 7.17 *Assign a raytrace map in the Reflection slot for a very reflective Water material in the rendered image.*

9. Now, create an omni light in the scene to increase the specular highlights on the water surface without adding to the overall lighting. In the scene, create a new omni light and position it as shown in Figure 7.18.

caution

Do not accidentally assign the raytrace map to the Refraction map slot.

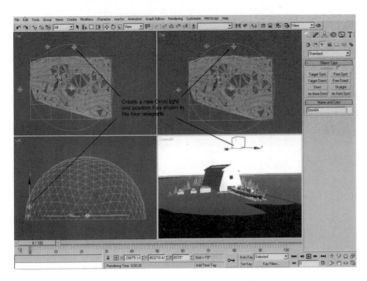

FIGURE 7.18 *Create a new omni light and position it as shown.*

tip

Raytrace reflection maps take a bit longer to render, but give accurate reflections on both curved and flat surfaces, and therefore make a good all-round reflection map choice.

10. In the Modify panel, Advanced Effects rollout, clear the Diffuse option (see Figure 7.19). The new omni light does not add any light to surfaces other than specular highlights and is positioned beyond the objects at a low angle as seen from the viewer to the water surface.

FIGURE 7.19
In the Modify panel, Advanced Effects rollout of the new omni light, clear the Diffuse check box so that the light only contributes to the specular highlights of objects in the scene.

11. In the Modify panel, General Parameters rollout, click the Exclude button. In the Exclude/Include dialog, push Water from the left column to the right column and check the Include radio button at the top right of the dialog. Click OK. The light now only affects the specular highlights of the water object. In the Material Editor, Maps rollout, enter 35 in the Reflection Amount field to reduce the reflections of the water. Render the Camera01 viewport. The water should now be less reflective and have bright specular highlights for a more convincing look (see Figure 7.20).

FIGURE 7.20   *Modifying the new omni light to include only the water object and reducing the reflection amount in the Material Editor, Maps rollout gives good specular highlights on the water surface and adds no light to the rest of the scene.*

12. Close all windows and dialogs and save the file. It should already be called Ch07_Intro_Mat03.max.

Creating a Tree Material

In Exercise 7.3, you learn to create a new material type that will be applied to the trees in your scene. Remember that the tree boughs were created from flat planes, which cannot be seen when the face normals are pointed away from the viewer. This would make portions of the boughs invisible.

You learn to apply a Double Sided material type to the trees. This material is made up of two materials: one that can be seen on the side of faces with normals; and another that can be seen on the backside of faces, that side with normals pointing away from the viewer. The two materials are similar, but the back materials are darker to represent the underside of thick boughs. You also use an extreme bump map amount to make the boughs appear more random.

Exercise 7.3   Double Sided Materials for Trees

1. Open the file called Ch07_Intro_Mat03.max on the CD-ROM or from the preceding exercise. From the File pull-down menu, choose Save As, point to an appropriate subdirectory on your hard drive, and use the plus sign button to save a new file with the name incremented to Ch07_Intro_Mat04.max.

2. Open the Material Editor and click in the far-right sample window in the top row to activate it. Rename the material Evergreen. To the right of the Name field, click the Standard button. The Material/Map Browser now only shows available material types (blue sphere icon), not available map types (see Figure 7.21). Double-click Double Sided in the list. Click OK to keep old material as sub-material in the Replace Material dialog.

3. Use the Material/Map Navigator to go to the Facing level and rename this material to Evergreen_top. In the Blinn Basic Parameters rollout, set the Diffuse color swatch to Red=95, Green=145, and Blue=75 for a light green.

tip

To see the effect of working on a map in isolation, and not the complete material, drag the "Noise" map type button and drop it on an empty Sample Slot. Select Instance from the dialog. Remember to re-select the Material sample slot to continue working on the material.

4. In the Maps rollout, set the Bump Amount from 30 to 300. This causes a severe bump effect that cuts down on the regular appearance of the simple geometry that makes the boughs. Click the None button for Bump and double-click Noise in the Material/Map Browser list. In the Noise Parameters rollout, enter 0.7 in High Noise Threshold, 0.4 in Low Noise Threshold, and 5 in the Size field. This is a small, contrasty, grayscale map.

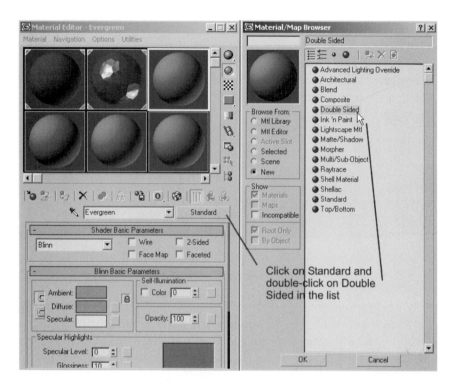

FIGURE 7.21   *Click the Standard button and double-click Double Sided in the list. Click OK in the Replace Material dialog to keep the old material in the upper slot called Facing Material of Double Sided material.*

5. In the Material/Map Navigator, go to the top-level material. In the Double Sided Basic Parameters rollout, drag and drop Evergreen_top (Standard) from the Facing Material slot to the Back Material slot. Choose Copy in the Instance (Copy) Material dialog, and click OK.

6. Click the Back Material button to go to that Material level and change the green Diffuse swatch to a much darker green. Rename the material at that level to Evergreen_bottom.

7. Click the Select By Name button in the main toolbar and select Evergreen01. In the Material Editor, click the Assign Material to Selection button.

8. Click the Select by Name button on the main toolbar and select Camera01. In the Modify panel, Parameters rollout, click the 135mm button to zoom in on your scene in the Camera01 viewport (see Figure 7.22). This enables you to see the trees better.

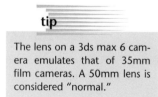

tip

The lens on a 3ds max 6 camera emulates that of 35mm film cameras. A 50mm lens is considered "normal."

FIGURE 7.22   *Select Camera01 and change it to a focal length of 135mm, a light telephoto lens.*

9. Activate the Camera01 viewport and click Quick Render on the main toolbar. The evergreen trees behind to boat do not have a clearly recognizable triangular shape to the boughs because of the severe bump mapping (see Figure 7.23).

FIGURE 7.23   *The double-sided material on the evergreen boughs has a severe bump map that reduces the regular pattern of the low-polygon model.*

10. Close all windows and dialogs and save the file. It should already be called Ch07_Intro_Mat04.max.

Creating and Mapping a Sky Material

So far in this chapter, you have been creating materials with patterns of procedural maps, noise, and cellular specifically. These maps are mathematically generated at render time and are random patterns. If you look at Figure 7.24, you see that the maps have typically been applied to the objects based on the Object XYZ coordinate system as seen in the Coordinates rollout of the Landscape material's Diffuse Color level.

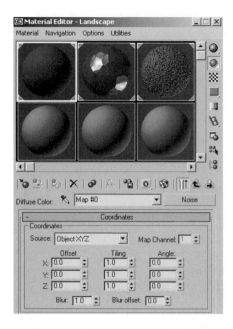

FIGURE 7.24   *The Coordinates rollout for the noise map in the Diffuse Color slot of the Landscape material shows that the pattern was fit to the object based on the Object XYZ coordinates.*

If the landscape object were rotated in space, the material color and bump patterns would stay fixed to the surface in a predictable manner and rotate with the object. However, you have limited control over exactly how the patterns fit and what real size they are.

You can apply a modifier called UVW Map to objects for more accurate control over the fit and placement of maps that are set to use the modifier.

In this section, you learn to apply and adjust the UVW Map modifier to resize and place a new type of map pattern to make the sky more convincing in your scene.

In Exercise 7.4, you create a sky material using a map type called gradient ramp, a grayscale ramp with parameters that can be adjusted for great control. The sky will be dark blue toward the zenith and white at the horizon. This lends the scene some depth by simulating the increasing amount of atmosphere you are viewing at low angles. The water vapor and dust in the sky are also denser closer to the surface.

You apply the pattern to the skydome and adjust the position and projection with a UVW Map modifier. It is distributed over the entire hemisphere, and no butt joints—where the dark and light areas of the map meet—are visible in the Camera01 viewport.

tip

You will see UVW often in relation to materials. It represents XYZ axes using the previous three letters in the alphabet and has no other meaning. The choice of letters has more to do with programming code management than anything else.

A handy "formula" to remember in 3ds max 6 is RGB= XYZ=UVW. You might have noticed that the Transform gizmos are color coded. Red= X-axis, green=Y-axis, and blue= Z-axis throughout the software.

Exercise 7.4   Creating and Mapping a Sky

1. Open the file called Ch07_Intro_Mat04.max on the CD-ROM or from the preceding exercise. From the File pull-down menu, choose Save As, point to an appropriate subdirectory on your hard drive, and use the plus sign button to save a new file with the name incremented to Ch07_Intro_Mat05.max.

2. On the main toolbar, click the Select by Name button and double-click Camera01 in the list. In the Modify panel, Parameters rollout, click the 50mm button to return to a wider-angle view.

3. Open the Material Editor from the main toolbar and click in the lower-left sample window to activate it. Rename this material Sky. Drag and drop the sample window onto the skydome in the Camera01 viewport.

4. In the Material Editor, Blinn Basic Parameters rollout, click the small gray square map shortcut button to the right of the Diffuse color swatch. Double-click Gradient Ramp in the Material/Map Browser list (see Figure 7.25). The map is a black-to-white gradient from left to right. You can see the gradient on the sample window sphere and in the Gradient Ramp Parameters rollout.

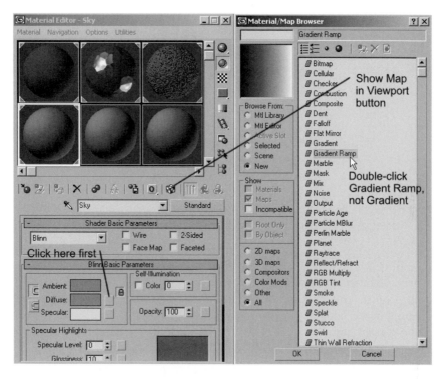

FIGURE 7.25 *The Gradient Ramp map is black to white and is applied horizontally around the sample window sphere.*

5. In the Material Editor, just below the sample windows, click the Show Map in Viewport button. The skydome in the Camera01 viewport becomes slightly darker gray. You are seeing a small portion of the middle of the gradient in your view with black being to your left and white to your right.

6. In the Gradient Ramp Parameters rollout, right-click the small green flag (arrow) at the lower left of the color ramp and choose Edit Properties in the menu (see Figure 7.26). In the Flag Properties dialog, click the color swatch and set it to Red=25, Green=25, and Blue=110 for a dark saturated blue. This is the zenith color.

7. Click, and then right-click, if the Edit Properties dialog is not open, the center flag in the ramp and set it to Red=100, Green=100, and Blue=230, for a lighter blue. The right flag remains white, and your skydome in the Camera01 viewport should be a light blue color. One problem now is that the gradient runs left to right and you want the dark blue at the top of your sky and white at the horizon. Close the Color Selector and Flag Properties dialog.

FIGURE 7.26   *Right-click the green flag at the lower left of the ramp and choose Edit Properties in the menu to set the color for that flag.*

8. In the Coordinates rollout for the gradient ramp map, you see that the coordinates are using Explicit Map Channel 1 and that the Angle settings are all set to 0.0. In the W field, enter 90 and press Enter. Your Camera01 sky is darker and the gradient ramp on the sample window sphere is showing dark blue at the top and white at the bottom now.

9. Select skydome in the Camera01 viewport. In the Modify panel, Modifier List, apply a UVW Map modifier. This acts as a "projector" for your map. By default, it is planar mapping in the Z-axis of the skydome (that is, projected from above). You see a Mapping gizmo around the skydome in the Top viewport (see Figure 7.27).

10. In the Modify panel, Parameters rollout, select the Spherical Mapping radio button. This projects from the center of a sphere outward in all directions. The UVW Map gizmo in the viewports now looks spherical. In the Modify panel, Stack view, expand UVW Mapping and highlight the Gizmo sub-object level. The gizmo in the viewport turns yellow and green. The green line represents where the map edges butt—in this case, dark blue and white of the Gradient Ramp map, which would be obvious in the rendered image. You do not want this seam to show in the Camera01 viewport. In the Front viewport, move the gizmo down in the negative Y-axis so that the horizon is at the skydome horizon and, in the Top viewport, rotate the gizmo in the Z-axis to place the green line behind the camera (see Figure 7.28). In the Modify panel, Stack view, click UVW Mapping to exit sub-object mode.

11. Close all windows and dialogs. Save the file; it should already be called Ch07_Intro_Mat05.max.

tip

The UVW Map modifier is also set to use Map Channel 1, the same map channel the map itself is using.

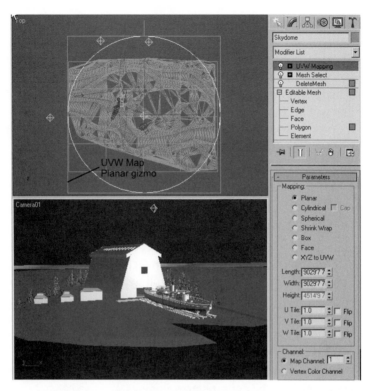

FIGURE 7.27 *The default setting for the UVW Map modifier uses planar mapping to project the map in the Z-axis of the skydome.*

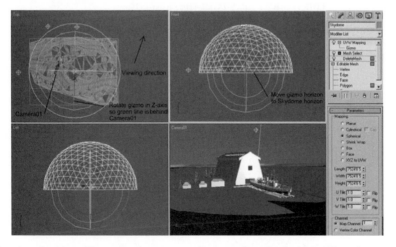

FIGURE 7.28 *At sub-object Gizmo mode, move and rotate the spherical Mapping gizmo so that the map in centered vertically on the skydome and the map edge is behind the camera (so the butt joint will not be visible in the Camera01 viewport).*

Fitting the Gradient Ramp to the View

The gradient ramp map is now being projected from the center of a spherical Mapping gizmo in all directions. However, you are viewing a small portion of a hemisphere and are only seeing a small part of the gradient. In Exercise 7.5, you learn to make adjustment to the coordinates of the gradient ramp map so that the whole gradient is filling the area of the Camera01 viewport. This is accomplished by adjusting parameters called Tiling and Offset for the map. You use these settings to compress and shift the gradient ramp into position.

Exercise 7.5   Using Tiling to Compress and Shift the Gradient Ramp to Fit the Viewport

1. Open the file called Ch07_Intro_Mat05.max on the CD-ROM or from the preceding exercise. From the File pull-down menu, choose Save As, point to an appropriate subdirectory on your hard drive, and use the plus sign button to save a new file with the name incremented to Ch07_Intro_Mat06.max.

2. Open the Material Editor and use Material/Map Navigator to get to the Diffuse Color map level, Coordinates rollout, of the Sky material (see Figure 7.29).

3. In the Coordinates rollout, clear the check boxes for U: Tile option. This keeps the map from repeating vertically when you adjust the size for easier viewing. In the U: Tiling field, enter 8 and press Enter. This reduces the size of the gradient ramp coverage to about 1/8 of the sample window sphere. You should also see the upper edge of the map in the Camera01 viewport (see Figure 7.30).

caution

U and V axes can get a little confusing in this example because you rotated the gradient map itself 90 degrees in the W: Angle of the Coordinates rollout, so vertical and horizontal are flipped.

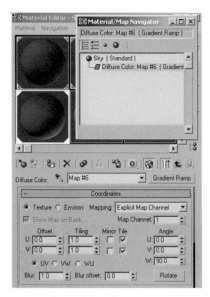

FIGURE 7.29   *In the Material Editor, go to the Gradient Ramp Coordinates rollout, for the Diffuse Color map of Sky material.*

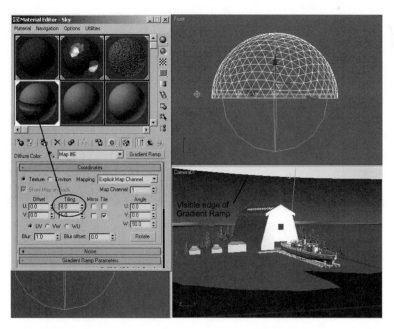

FIGURE 7.30   *Adjusting the Tiling settings in the Coordinates rollout changes the size of the map. In this case, you made it 1/8 its original size, compressing it into a smaller space.*

4. In the V: Offset field, enter 0.05. This offsets the gradient ramp upward so that the top edge moves upward in the Camera01 viewport. You should now see a soft gradient in the Camera01 viewport from blue at the top to white near the horizon (see Figure 7.31).

tip

Keep in mind that if you want different camera views or you will animate the camera in the scene, you want to allow for that in the sizing and placement of the gradient in the skydome.

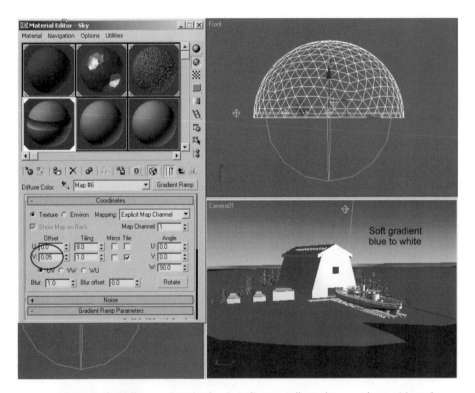

FIGURE 7.31 *Adjusting the Offset settings in the Coordinates rollout changes the position of the map. In this case, you move it up so that the edge does not show in the Camera01 viewport.*

5. In the Material Editor, Gradient Ramp Parameters rollout, enter 0.1 in the Noise Amount field and select the Fractal radio button. This adds random noise to the boundary of the gradient colors, giving the illusion of some clouds in the sky (see Figure 7.32).

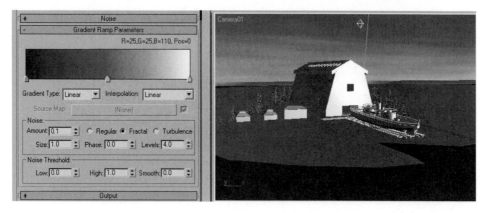

FIGURE 7.32   *In the Gradient Ramp Parameters rollout, enter 0.1 in the Noise Amount field and select the Fractal radio button for a cloudy look.*

6. Render the Camera01 viewport and you should have a decent-looking background sky that enables you to turn the camera about 250 degrees without seeing any seams in the bitmap.

7. If you modify Camera01 to be a 35mm lens showing more of the image, however, you see a default gray patch at the top of the image and you see that the water is reflecting this gray from overhead. It is because the diffuse color is still default gray and you have sized the bitmap with Tile turned off. The diffuse color should be the same as the dark blue of the gradient ramp (see Figure 7.33). You learn to use the Color Clipboard utility to fix the problem.

8. In the Utilities panel, click the Color Clipboard button (see Figure 7.34). Use the Material/Map Navigator to go to the Gradient Ramp level of Sky if you are not still there. Right-click the leftmost flag and choose Edit Properties. Drag and drop a copy of the color to a Clipboard swatch (see Figure 7.35).

Gray from default
Diffuse color showing
and reflecting

FIGURE 7.33   *When Camera01 is set to a wider-angle lens, the default diffuse color shows above the compressed map size and is reflected in the water.*

FIGURE 7.34   *In the Utilities panel, Utilities rollout, click the Color Clipboard button to open it.*

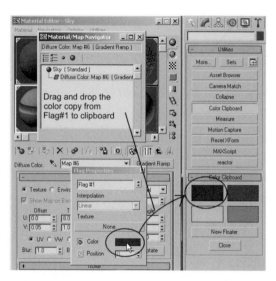

FIGURE 7.35   *Drag and drop a copy of the color swatch from Flag #1 Edit Properties dialog to a swatch in the Color Clipboard.*

9. Using the Material/Map Navigator, go to the top level of the Sky material and drag a drop a copy of the dark blue color swatch from the Color Clipboard to the Diffuse color swatch in the Blinn Basic Parameters rollout (see Figure 7.36). The sphere is now the same color as the top of the gradient ramp used as sky color.

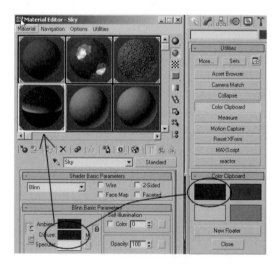

FIGURE 7.36   *You can now drag and drop a copy the color swatch from the Color Clipboard to the Diffuse swatch in the Blinn Basic Parameters so that the top of the gradient ramp and the color of the sphere match exactly.*

10. Close all windows and dialogs and save the file. It should already be called Ch07_Intro_Mat06.max.

Material Libraries to Store Materials

Essentially, you can store materials in three places in 3ds max 6:

- **Material Editor**—Materials can be kept in the 24 Material Editor sample windows.
- **Scene**—Materials can be applied to, and retrieved from, objects in the scene.
- **Material library**—Materials can be stored in a separate file with the .mat file extension.

Material Editor

Very often, you will be creating your materials from scratch in the Material Editor; as a matter of fact, I tend to recommend it, even though the learning curve seems steep at first.

Use the materials that ship with the software and materials that you might get from other sources as guides to creating your own materials. The materials in your scene will be the primary component of visualization that defines your style and acts as your signature to distinguish your work from others. Take the time to learn the ins and outs of the Material Editor and how the materials you create interact with light to make your images stand out. Nothing is more discouraging than to go into a presentation or job interview and have your scenes looking similar to the last applicant because all the materials are "out of the box."

When you open the Material Editor, you are presented with six sample windows with spheres that show a representation of the materials you are creating. I say representation because of the lighting and the fact that it is a sample sphere by default. Scene lighting profoundly affects the look of your material. You will often get a great-looking material on the sample sphere that is just plain embarrassing when rendered. Two things are the cause of this: the lighting and the shape of the surface. The shape of surfaces is especially important for materials with reflections and specular highlights, because each plays very differently over a flat or curved surface.

When you create a material in the Material Editor and save the file, the material remains in the editor and is there when you open the file again. If you create a material in the Material Editor and quit or reset without saving the material, however, the material is lost forever.

Scene Materials: A Better Choice

When you create materials in the Material Editor and assign them to objects in the scene, the materials are, of course, saved with the file. Even if you clear the Material Editor, as long as a material is assigned to an object, it is not deleted from the scene.

note

If you replace a material in a sample window that hasn't been assigned to an object in the scene, you lose that material.

Suppose, for example, that you created one material and assigned it to an object in the scene. By the way, you can tell that a material has been assigned to an object in the scene by the triangles in the corners of the sample window. These triangles indicate a "hot" material; when you change the material in the Material Editor, it automatically updates in the scene.

For whatever reason, you then drag one of the default sample windows on top of your hot material sample window. Your material disappears along with the triangles in the sample window. The material is still on the object in the scene even though it is not in the Material Editor any longer.

tip

If you double-click a sample window, you can magnify the window for better viewing. You also can rotate the sample by holding the mouse wheel down and moving the cursor over the original sample window (not the magnified one) or you can right-click the sample window and use Drag/Rotate.

But, you were not really finished editing that material, and now it's gone and you can't make any changes! No, that's not the case at all. You can retrieve materials from objects in the scene and place them back in the Material Editor by using the eyedropper button (Pick Material from Object), which is just to the left of the material name field, and picking the object in any viewport.

Material Libraries

The best way to deal with materials is to use material libraries. These are specific files with the .mat extension that store the descriptions of your materials. The biggest advantage of storing materials in libraries is that the materials are available from any scene and by all users in your company. It is a good habit to put your material in a library as soon as you create it.

tip

If you have Microsoft Access on your machine when you install max or VIZ, the Windows file association may be set to .mat files from Access. Changing the Windows file association to max or VIZ will enable you to use the library files while not harming Access in any way.

Material libraries can be opened from any scene, and the material can be dragged from the library to any sample window in Material Editor or directly onto objects in the scene.

Set your material libraries up in logical groupings that make sense for your production environment. The material descriptions do no take up much disk space and can be duplicated in many different libraries. For example, you should have a material library that contains all the materials for each project, but you also can have libraries that contain all stone materials or sky materials, or a library that contains high-resolution materials. Each of those libraries might contain some of the same material descriptions.

Accessing Materials in a Scene

You now know that materials can be stored in a scene, but there are several areas of a scene from which you can view those materials by choosing from the Browse From options of the Material/Map Browser. You can browse from the following:

- **Mtl Library**—An open library file.
- **Mtl Editor**—The 24 material sample windows.
- **Active slot**—Only the selected sample window in the Material Editor.
- **Selected**—Materials on the selected objects in the scene.
- **Scene**—All materials assigned to objects in the scene.
- **New**—The default listing of all material and map types used to create new materials.

The Material/Map Browser also has an option in the File area to merge material libraries into the current library when the Mtl Library option is selected. This would enable you to make all wood materials available in the current project file, for example.

Saving Materials to a Library: The Process

In Exercise 7.6, you learn to create a new material library and store your scene materials in it so that they can be accessed from other scenes.

Exercise 7.6   Creating and Saving a Material Library

1. Open the file called Ch07_Intro_Mat06.max on the CD-ROM or from the preceding exercise. From the File pull-down menu, choose Save As, point to an appropriate subdirectory on your hard drive, and use the plus sign button to save a new file with the name incremented to Ch07_Intro_Mat07.max.

2. Open the Material Editor. Click the Get Material button at the bottom left of the sample windows. In the Material/Map Browser, select the Browse From: Mtl Library button. You see a list of current maps and materials from the current default library called 3dsmax.mat (see Figure 7.37).

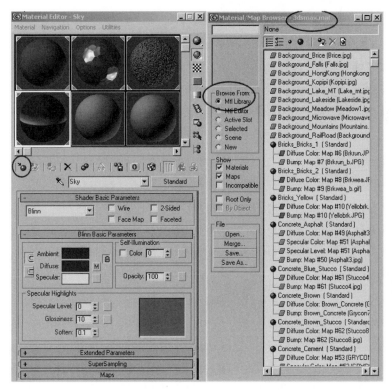

FIGURE 7.37   *Click the Get Materials button in Material Editor and check Mtl Library in the Browse From area for a list of current maps and materials in 3dsmax.mat library file.*

3. In the Material/Map Browser, at the top of the list, click the rightmost button called Clear Material Library. Answer Yes when prompted as to whether you want to delete all the materials. This does *not* delete anything from 3dsmax.mat. It just clears the list and clears the filename.

4. In the Material/Map Browser, File area, click the Save As button, choose a folder on your hard drive, and name the file Shipyard. It automatically gets the .mat file extension.

5. Drag and drop the Material Editor sample windows onto the Material/Map
   Browser blank list area to copy your four materials to the library (see Figure 7.38).

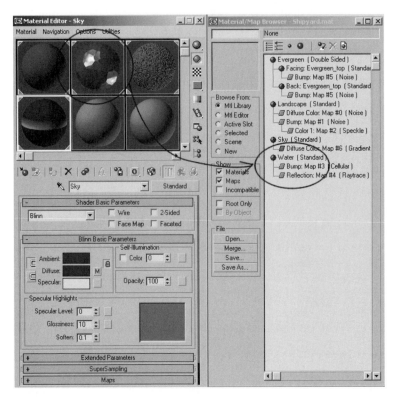

FIGURE 7.38 *Drag and drop the sample windows from your scene onto the list in the
Material/Map Browser and the materials and maps are saved in your new
library called Shipyard.mat that is on the hard drive.*

6. Close all windows and dialogs and save the file. It should already be called
   Ch07_Intro_Mat07.max.

Summary

Some of the topics you learned about in this chapter include the following:

- **Material Editor**—You created all your materials by combining maps and attributes in the Material Editor before assigning the material to objects in the scene. The Material Editor is a creation and preview space that you will learn to navigate.

- **Applying maps in materials**—You learned to apply maps to various attributes of material to generate patterns and effects.

- **Simulate geometry**—Learning to simulate geometry (for example, raised patterns on a flat surface or holes through a surface) is one of the most important aspects of materials you learned in this chapter.

- **Mapping coordinates**—Some patterns require specific orientation information to fit objects correctly. You learned to apply these coordinates to make the map fit the object the way you wanted it.

- **Material libraries**—You learned to create and save material libraries to store your materials that can then be opened from any other scene for reuse.

CHAPTER 8

The Fundamentals of Scanline Rendering

In This Chapter

Working with 3ds max 6 is all about producing images, either still images or animations. Images are created by rendering the 3D scenes you have created.

In this chapter, you learn about creating rendered images using the tried-and-true Scanline render engine that has been the standard renderer in 3ds max since version 1.

The main advantage of using the Scanline renderer is speed. It calculates the rendering through a top-down pass of rows of pixels, and through careful use of lighting and materials, you can create stunning images in a cost-effective manner:

- **The rendering process**—You learn to set up a scene to animate a still image and an animation sequence using the default Scanline renderer.

- **Render engines**—You learn about the different render engines or renderers in 3ds max 6.

- **Image resolution**—You learn to set image resolution for different scenarios.

- **File types**—You learn about some of the commonly used file types in 3ds max 6.

- **Network rendering**—You learn about the process involved in rendering a scene with multiple computers.

Key Terms

- **Renderer**—In 3ds max 6, you have several renderers available that process the modeling, lighting, materials, and effects into 2D images. They are Scanline, Radiosity, Light Tracer, and mental ray.

- **Resolution**—Images rendered from 3ds max 6 must be sized appropriately for their intended use. The resolution is the image size as measured horizontally and vertically by the number of pixels or points of color of an image.

- **Scanline**—The default Scanline renderer processes information in the scene and creates a 2D image one line at a time, progressing from top to bottom. It is known for its rendering speed.

- **Rendered Frame Window (RFW)**—When you render an image in 3ds max 6, the image is displayed in the viewports with the Rendered Frame Window. This is independent of any image you might save as a separate file.

- **Delta compression**—This is a typical method of creating animation sequences where a frame is calculated completely and stored, and then the subsequent frames are compared against the stored frame and only the changed pixels are stored. This makes smaller file sizes and faster playback possible.

- **Codec**—A codec is computer code that tells 3ds max 6 how to process and store a particular file format when rendered. Both the creator and the client viewing the files must have the same codec installed.

- **Network rendering**—This enables you to use multiple computers to calculate still images or animation sequences.

The Renderers

As mentioned in the introduction to this chapter, 3ds max 6 offers you several renderers or rendering engines, and each processes objects, materials, lights, and effects in a different manner. Each has its advantages and disadvantages, but having a wide choice of industry-accepted renderers makes you, the user, more productive and marketable.

The renderers available to you in 3ds max 6 are as follows:

- **Scanline**—This is the default renderer that processes the scene in horizontal lines from top to bottom. The Scanline render is one of the fastest in the industry, and the output can be used in a wide range of output needs.

- **Advanced lighting with Scanline**—Although not a standalone renderer, the Advanced Lighting options within the Scanline renderer—Radiosity and Light Tracer—add the calculation of bounced light and physically based lighting control to your scene. The scenes have a richer look because of the bounced light, but can take much longer to render.

- **Mental ray**—The mental ray rendering extensions built in to 3ds max 6 offer raytracing options that are an industry standard in the feature film world. Mental ray can work with an 3ds max 6 material and light, but also have special lights and shaders (materials) for specific effects such as caustics, or the effect of light diffused through glass or water, which are impossible with the other renderers. Setup time and rendering can be much longer with mental ray.

note

Other third-party renderers are available on the market that can be integrated into 3ds max 6 and offer different levels of quality and control and special effects such as flat cartoon-type rendering.

A search on the Internet and the 3ds max newsgroups will turn up more up-to-date specific information.

The Rendering Process

In Chapter 7, "Introduction to Materials and Mapping," you learned to use the Quick Render button to see a rendering of your scene in the Rendered Frame Window (RFW) on the screen. This did not save any image that you can access to the hard drive, although you have a Show Last Rendering option in the Rendering pull-down menu, which allows you to view the last rendered image of the current work session.

In this chapter, you perform exercises to render a scene in 3ds max 6 for a high-resolution still image and for two animation sequences, one a delta compression animation file and the other a series of numbered still images.

The basic process is simple enough: You activate the viewport you want to render, usually a Camera viewport, and then choose the image resolution you need, the file type you want, and choose a folder on the hard drive to store it. The software and computer handle the rest of the work for you.

The Render Scene dialog is called by going to the Rendering pull-down menu and choosing Render (see Figure 8.1). You also can use the F10 function key as a keyboard shortcut or the Render Scene teapot button in the main toolbar.

FIGURE 8.1   *Choosing Render from the Rendering pull-down menu or pressing the F10 function key opens the Render Scene dialog.*

The Render Scene dialog has five tabs with a variety of settings:

- **Common**—The Common tab enables you to set parameters such as the number of frames you want to render, the resolution, and the file type and locations to save the files. Within this tab, you also can assign which renderer will be used.

- **Renderer**—In the Renderer tab, you can set specific parameters of the currently active renderer, such as filtering and motion blurring.

- **Render Elements**—The Render Elements tab enables you to break out various components of a rendered image (for example, the lighting, reflections, or shadows) to separate files for post-processing with other software.

- **Raytracer**—You can adjust speed and quality parameters globally for raytracing in materials in this tab.

- **Advanced Lighting**—This tab has settings to choose and adjust the advanced Radiosity and Light Tracer rendering options.

In this chapter, you learn about the parameters in the Common tab for setting up the initial rendering process. You learn to set the resolution for printing and video output and to choose file types appropriate for those uses by rendering an outdoor animated scene.

Setting the Output Parameters for Print

One of your first decisions when rendering is the size, or resolution, of the rendered image that you will be saving to the hard drive. The resolution is the number of points in the mosaic that, viewed as a whole, create the image. You need sufficient resolution to contain the detail, but you must not use higher resolution than is efficient for your needs.

More resolution means larger file sizes and less efficiency, especially when playing back animations.

In Exercise 8.1, you learn to set up a scene for printing resolution and to save the settings as a preset for later retrieval.

Exercise 8.1   Setting Rendering Resolution and Presets for Print

1. Open the file called Ch08_Iceberg01.max on the CD-ROM. From the File pull-down menu, choose Save As, point to an appropriate subdirectory on your hard drive, and use the plus sign button to save a new file with the name incremented to Ch08_Iceberg02.max. This is the outdoor scene with the ship that has a few materials applied and has been animated to move across the camera view in an arctic scene (see Figure 8.2).

FIGURE 8.2   *The* Ironclad *glides silently past massive ice flows.*

2. From the Rendering pull-down menu, choose Render or press F10. In the Common tab, you will see, in the Time Output area, rendering is set to a Single frame. This is the frame that the Time slider below the viewports is set on. Drag the Time slider to frame 19 for a full view of the ship in the Camera01 viewport.

3. In the Output Size area, enter 3000 in the Width field and 2400 in the Height field. This is the resolution of the image that will be saved to the hard drive. The Pixel Aspect should be set to 1.0 for most printed images (see Figure 8.3). This means that there will be 3000 square pixels horizontally and 2400 square pixels vertically in the final image that is written to disk.

4. Scroll the Common Parameters rollout up and in the Render Output area click the Files button. In the Render Output File dialog, click the Save As Type: All Formats list and choose .jpg in the list (see Figure 8.4). This defines the file type that will be saved in the folder you choose. In the File Name field, enter Iceberg_still_print. Click the Save button. In the .jpg Image Control dialog, drag the Quality slider to the right for 100 and click OK.

5. At the bottom of the Render Scene dialog, click the window to the right of Preset and choose Save Preset. In the Render Presets Save dialog, enter print_test as the filename. In the Select Preset Categories dialog, highlight Common and press the Save button. The settings you have just made in the Common tab are now saved with a name, so you can quickly retrieve the settings at any time. This allows consistent renderings, especially in collaborative work.

tip

Much of this scene was created with techniques you learned in Chapter 7. There are, however, a few new things that you might investigate that are not covered as exercises in this book.

One aid to learning 3ds max 6 is to dissect other artists' scenes to try and discover what they used to create it. One hint is to select the dummy in the middle of the large iceberg on the left and go to the Motion panel. There has been an Attachment controller that uses the animated surface of the water for its position. The iceberg is linked to the dummy and tips and rolls as the wave passes through it.

The other object is an Atmospheric Apparatus Helper object with Volume fog to create looming clouds over the horizon and layered fog to create a hazy water surface in the background.

Use the online Help file in the pull-down menus to investigate these features.

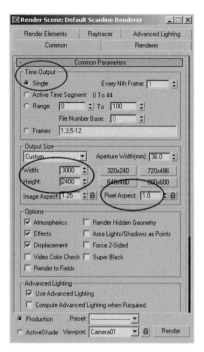

FIGURE 8.3   *To set the output size of the rendered image for printing, enter the Width and Height in pixels and make sure Pixel Aspect is set to 1.0.*

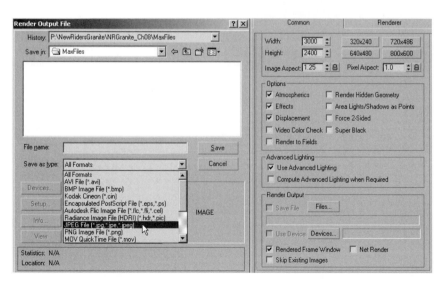

FIGURE 8.4   *Set the file as a .jpg file type and enter Iceberg_still_print as the name with the .jpg quality set to 100.*

6. Always check that you are rendering the correct viewport in the window to the left of the Render button. In the Render Scene dialog, click the Render button at the lower-right corner. Have patience; the scene will take a while to render because of the higher resolution. As you increase the resolution, the file sizes can grow exponentially. For example, a 320×240 image only contains 25 percent of a 640×480 image.

7. In the Rendering pull-down menu, choose Print Size Wizard. You must know two pieces of information: the paper size (if the default setting is metric, switch to inches, if necessary) and the printer's DPI (dots per inch) setting. Enter those in the appropriate fields of the Print Size Wizard dialog, and then choose a file type and location to render to. In this case, you are rendering to 10-inch by 8-inch paper in landscape format on a printer set to 300 dpi (see Figure 8.5). You do not need to render this image again.

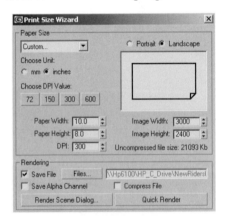

FIGURE 8.5   *Click the Rendering pull-down menu and choose Print Size Wizard to determine the necessary resolution for paper size and printer dpi settings.*

8. Close all windows and dialogs and save the file. It should already be called Ch08_Iceberg02.max.

---

tip

The images in the RFW might not be the same resolution as you have set because it is limited by the graphics card and monitor size. It is only intended as a preview.

---

note

What, you might ask, is the reasoning behind choosing a resolution of 3000×2400 for print? It was random in this case, but in production, it will depend mostly on the printer and the size of the intended print. The entire decision process can be a source of conflict and theory. However, 3ds max 6 has a tool that helps you make the decision: the Print Size Wizard.

---

tip

This is to be used as a rule-of-thumb starting point. Printing is a complex blend of art and science, and you must experiment with various printer settings, paper and ink combinations, and resolution settings before committing to a final image. Always render at the lowest resolution you need for the quality you want.

Setting the Output Parameters for Video

In Exercise 8.2, you determine basic presets for rendering for typical video playback. Here, the device that will record the images onto videotape determines the resolution. Each device is different, so you have to check the manufacturer's data for the device you use. This hardware resizing must be compensated for in the rendered image. The pixel aspect must also match this resizing so that the spheres in the scene do not render as ovals.

Exercise 8.2   Rendering for Videotape

1. Open the file called Ch08_Iceberg02.max on the CD-ROM or from the preceding exercise. From the File pull-down menu, choose Save As, point to an appropriate subdirectory on your hard drive, and use the plus sign button to save a new file with the name incremented to Ch08_Iceberg03.max.

2. From the Rendering pull-down menu, choose Render. In the Common tab of the Render Scene dialog, check the radio button in the Time Output area called Active Time Segment: 0 to 44. In the Output Size area, click the Custom window and choose NTSC D-1(video) option in the list. This is a typical video format setting. Notice it is 720×486 resolution with a pixel aspect of 0.9 (see Figure 8.6). Again, always check your equipment before entering this information.

3. Click the field to the right of Preset at the bottom of the dialog and choose Save Presets. Name this new file video_test, and choose the Common option in the dialog list.

4. At the bottom of the Common Parameters rollout, click the Files button in Render Output area, change the filename to Iceberg_video, and choose .avi in the list of file types in the Render Output File dialog (see Figure 8.7). Click the Save button in the .avi File Compression Setup dialog, and click OK to accept the default Cinepack codec. In the Render Scene dialog, click the Render button.

FIGURE 8.6
You can set the rendering to the Active Time Segment and choose from a list of typical output sizes that might match your equipment.

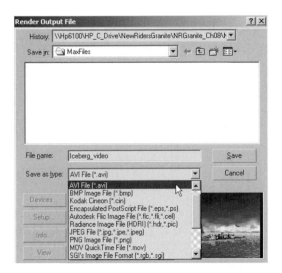

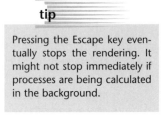

tip

Pressing the Escape key eventually stops the rendering. It might not stop immediately if processes are being calculated in the background.

tip

You can play the .avi animation back by finding it with Windows Explorer and double-clicking the filename or, in the Rendering pull-down menu, choose RAM Player and open the file from there.

You can also go to the File pull-down menu and choose View Image File to view images or animations.

FIGURE 8.7   *In the Render Output File dialog, you find a list of available file types in the Save As Type list. Choose .avi from the list.*

5. The first frame renders, and the second frame (of 45 total frames, 0 to 44) starts. The Rendering progress dialog gives you the Last Frame Time and the best-guess time remaining and continues the process until all frames are finished.

6. Close all windows and dialogs and save the file. It should already be called Ch08_Iceberg03.max.

Choosing File Types for Stills and Animations

So far in this chapter, you have rendered both a still image and an animation. For the still image, you chose a .jpg file type with highest quality as the rendering output and, for the animation, you chose an .avi file with a Cinepak codec.

Those were random choices for both the still and animation because you do not have a specific use in mind for the end results. In production situations, the choice of output file type can be a critical balance of quality, compression, and usability in post-processing or client viewing.

In this section, you learn some of the more common file types in use and some of the reasons why you might choose one or the other.

- For still images, the commonly used file types tend to be .jpg, .png, .tga, .tif, and .rpf.

- For animations, the commonly used file types tend to be .avi, .mov, and image sequence files.

A discussion of the various file types wouldn't be complete without a basic understanding of something called alpha channel.

Most images today are created at a color level of 24 bits. A *bit* is two pieces of computer information that define colors. The number of colors possible is calculated by 2 to the power of 24 or a maximum of 16.7 million colors in your palette.

The human eye can detect differences for only about 65,000 colors, so a large palette means that a complex image with lots of color gradients from dark to light will not show signs of banding because of lack of available colors.

Computer monitors are made of points of light. If a display shows a diagonal line across those points, a certain amount of stair-stepping effect is introduced. Computers use antialiasing to blend the diagonal boundary colors (see Figure 8.8).

FIGURE 8.8   *In a close-up of the upper-left edge of the iceberg, where it meets the sky, you can see the effects of antialiasing to smooth the stair-stepping effect of the pixels in a diagonal line.*

The computer is mixing the white of the iceberg and the blue of the sky to smooth the edge with varying bluish-white pixels. If you were to lift this iceberg from the blue background and place it on a red background, the edge would look terrible because of all the bluish pixels.

Some image types can be 32-bit images (.tga, .tif, and .png from the preceding list, for example). They have the same number of colors, but have an additional 8 bits of transparency information called alpha channel. Instead of mixing the edge colors, alpha channel uses transparency to smooth the boundary. When you place this information on a new background color, it matches perfectly.

Alpha channel files are used in 3ds max 6 specifically for masking and compositing in the materials and when rendering images that will be processed with new background images in compositing software such as Discreet combustion. In the animation file types previously listed, only the image sequence files—which would be still images of .png or .tga, for example—can have alpha channel.

Here, you learn a little about each file type and some of the pros and cons of using them.

Still Images File Types

Although these are not the only file types available for rendering still images, they are the more commonly used and will usually be accessible by your coworkers and clients:

- **.jpg**—These files were some of the first compressed files available for rendering still images, which accounts for their popularity. Everyone can access them, and all software can read and write them. The compression, however, is called "lossy," which means information is discarded to make the file smaller. This leads to a degradation of the image that can show as blocky areas of color, especially in sky areas or others with large expanses of similar colored pixels. There is no alpha channel.

- **.tga**—.tga files are not highly compressed and do not degrade in quality. The file sizes can be quite large as the resolution increases, but they are commonly used. .tga can have an alpha channel or not.

- **.tif**—These exhibit similar quality and size to .tga, but are often preferred by commercial printers. They may or may not have alpha channel.

- **.png**—A relative newcomer to the scene, .png files have a quality as high as 48-bit color with optional alpha channel, but are compressed to a size similar to .jpg. Unlike .jpg, the compression is lossless with no degrading of quality. Most programs today read and right .png files.

■ **.rpf**—This file type is not so commonly used but merits mentioning because of its integration with the Discreet Combustion compositing software. It allows the storage of extra information that allows a 2D image to appear to be 3D when imported into Combustion. The files can be very large.

The file type you choose for your work depends on many factors relating to how it will be used and by whom, and you might find that other file types might be better for you. In any case, the important common element to study further is alpha channel and how it can work for you.

Animation Image File Types

Not only do you have to be concerned with the file type itself in animation rendering, you also must carefully choose one of the many codecs or compressors available within the file type.

Some of the criteria you need to include in your decision are compression amounts, color quality, playback speed, resolution, and compatibility with the viewer's computer.

The decision of which file type to use is further complicated by the fact that the codecs are being modified and developed almost on a daily basis.

The codecs are known as delta compressors. They save the first frame completely, and then render and save only the changed pixels of the following frames, hence the compression. This makes it difficult to edit the animations after rendering, and it is impossible to take advantage of 3ds max 6 built-in network rendering because it can't piece the changed pixel files together in the correct order.

In any case, it is highly recommended that you do not render directly to an animation codec. Always render to a series of sequential .png or .tga files and convert those to animation files later by using the RAM Player in 3ds max 6 or some other available software.

When you choose to render a series of frames in 3ds max 6 and choose a still image file type, max automatically saves each frame with sequential names (for example, Test0001.png, Test0002.png, and so on).

This allows for more flexible post-processing in other software and makes it easier for you to rerender any number of frames for areas that need to be fixed or changed. Converting to animation files is always quicker than rerendering scenes.

Network Rendering

One of the absolute best features of 3ds max has always been the free built-in network rendering capability. This enables you to distribute individual frames of an animation or, now in 3ds max 6, portions of a still image over any number of computers to be compiled back on a single machine.

The rendering machines, called servers, do not need to be licensed copies of 3ds max 6, but only need a core of the program installed on the machine, and each machine needs to be on a TCP/IP network.

Network rendering is called by 3ds max 6, but the rendering management is handled by backburner, which is included on the CD-ROM that max 6 ships on.

The server computers that do the rendering must have a system component called Server started, and the rendering machine must have a component called Manager started.

After the manager and server components have started, you need to specify a range of frames in the renderer, save to a still image format, and check the Net Render option in Common Parameters rollout (see Figure 8.9).

caution

Make sure you have a clean network with the proper permissions so that each machine can access the machine that is managing the rendering. You need administrator access for the initial setup.

tip

The rendering machine can be used both as manager and server by starting each component. After the manager process is complete, the server process can be used in the backburner network rendering.

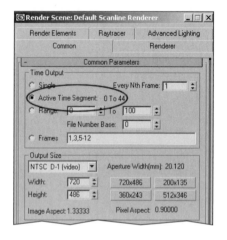

FIGURE 8.9   *Network rendering must be to still image file types, and you must check the Net Render option in the Render Scene dialog. Backburner must be installed, and the manager and server components must be running on the appropriate machines.*

By opening the Queue Monitor component included in backburner, you can manage which jobs are sent to which machines on the network and you can view the progress of the rendering (see Figure 8.10).

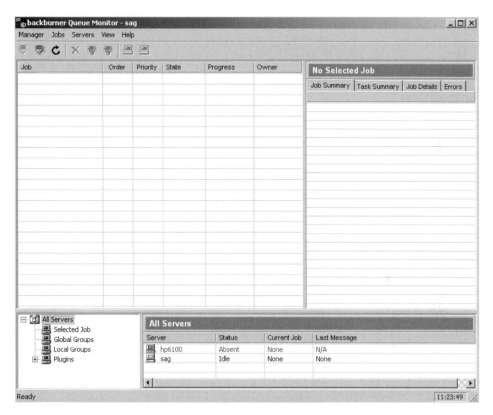

FIGURE 8.10   *When rendering begins, you can use backburner Queue Monitor to assign jobs to machines and track the progress of the rendering.*

To distribute the rendering of parts of a still image over the network, you need to choose Single in the Render Scene dialog and choose the Split Scan Lines option presented when you click the Render button, then pick the Define button. In the Strips Setup dialog, you choose the number of strips based on the resolution and number of machines available on the network, and the image file will be reassembled on completion.

caution

Network rendering does not directly support the mental ray renderer in 3ds max 6. You must have licenses for each machine on the network you want to use.

Use the online Help file in 3ds max 6 for a complete guide to setting up and using the network rendering capabilities, but be sure you are using it to increase production where applicable.

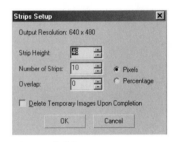

FIGURE 8.11
When you net render a single frame with Split Scan Lines turned on, you can set the distribution based on the image resolution and number of available machines.

Summary

In this chapter, you learned the fundamentals of rendering output. Although many variables will factor into the approach you take to rendering, the process is simple and will become a normal part of your routine. Some of the things you have learned include the following:

- **The rendering process**—You learned to set up a scene to animate a still image and an animation sequence using the default Scanline renderer.

- **Render engines**—You learned about the different render engines or renderers in 3ds max 6.

- **Image resolution**—You learned to set image resolution for different scenarios, still and animated scenes.

- **File types**—You learned about some of the commonly used file types in 3ds max 6 and some of the pros and cons of each type.

- **Network rendering**—You learned about the process involved in rendering a scene with multiple computers, be it an animation or a distributed still image.

PART III

Interior of Ship's Bridge

CHAPTER 9

Diving Deeper into Modeling Techniques

In This Chapter

You have worked on an outdoor scene throughout this book so far, and now it's time to bring the focus to some interior exercises that will give you a little practice with techniques you have already learned and to introduce you to some powerful new modeling methods.

You might not have realized it, but the old boat from the mid-1800s that you created in Chapter 4, "Shipbuilding 101: The Making of a Boat," is operated from a high-tech command center located in the bow. This advanced center is made of reinforced honeycomb walls to resist the stress of battle and to protect from collisions with the ice of the artic.

Your task is to build these walls and some of the command and support systems that are the heart of the boat. In the process of constructing this scene, you learn new modeling techniques that offer options that give you more control than others you have already learned. Again, there is no right way or wrong way to model in 3ds max 6. What you need to do is learn many of the possibilities and choose the method that works best for you in any given situation.

Sometimes, one modeling method works best to a certain point, but then you need to modify it in a way that the original technique does not allow. The interior walls of the boat will be such an example, where box modeling works fine for the basic object, but you will then learn about a method that enables you to deform that wall system into many more forms. You will accomplish this with a World-space PathDeform modifier.

You then need some equipment in the command center that allows for changes later in the design process. Lofting is the answer to that challenge and enables you to closely control the density (that is, number of faces) in the mesh you build. You use lofting to create a control console and some air-handling ductwork.

Finally, you learn ways to create smooth surfaces while still retaining an efficient mesh. Anyone can build rounded edges and smooth surfaces that enhance the lighting and materials in the scene, but only a master modeler can do it with efficiency and productivity in mind.

Some of the techniques covered in this chapter include the following:

- **Box modeling**—You learn to use box modeling techniques to create a complex honeycomb wall system.

- **PathDeform**—PathDeform is a powerful tool that enables you to deform 3D mesh objects along a complex path.

- **Lofting**—You learn to use one of the most powerful and flexible modeling methods that converts simple 2D shape to complex 3D objects.

- **Smoothing**—You learn the methods of smoothing surfaces to control the "roundness" at shared edges of polygons.

Key Terms

- **World-space modifier**—World-space modifiers are based on the fixed World coordinate system. As modified objects are transformed through World space, they "pass through" the modifications.

- **Object-space modifier**—Modifiers that function in Object space use the object's own coordinate system to define the changes. As the object transforms through space, the modifications travel with it.

- **Lofting**—Lofting is the method of extruding one or more 2D shapes along a single 2D path.

- **Path**—The extrusion path in lofting.

- **Shape**—A 2D shape that defines a cross-section in lofting.

- **Path and shape steps**—These are intermediate steps between vertices of shapes that define curvature.

- **Smoothing**—This describes whether a shared edge between two faces appears sharp or smoothed.

Command Center Honeycomb Walls

Your ironclad boat is sailing in dangerous waters and needs a secure, high-tech command center from which to control and protect it from harsh environments.

Your task is to construct strong walls that conform to the shape of the bow of the boat, always keeping in mind that the scope of the project might change at any minute and that keeping the face count to a minimum is of paramount importance.

In this section, you review the technique of box modeling to build the initial honeycomb walls. Your project director specifies that you will be viewing objects at a close enough distance in the scene to require the detail that you can only get with modeling.

You then deform the honeycomb walls to fit a rough V-shape of the bow of the boat and add curvature from the floor to the ceiling. You accomplish this task with the World-space PathDeform modifier.

Constructing the Honeycomb Wall

In Exercise 9.1, you use box modeling to edit a Box primitive that is converted to an editable poly. Editable poly objects, you will remember, have some unique editing functions (such as Connect and Inset) that are not available in other forms of 3ds max 6 modeling. Each honeycomb panel will be about 2 feet by 2 feet square and 5 inches deep with a slight bevel at the edges. The beveled edges add more faces to the object, but the way those bevels will interact with lighting is well worth the extra geometry.

Remember, too, that although this exercise creates walls, you can apply the methods you learn here to other objects, such as paneled doors, concrete floor systems, waffled surfaces, or perhaps even a golf ball.

Exercise 9.1   Creating Honeycomb Objects

1. Open the file called Ch09_interior01.max on the CD-ROM. From the File pull-down menu, choose Save As, point to an appropriate subdirectory on your hard drive, and use the plus sign button to save a new file with the name incremented to Ch09_interior02.max. This is a simple scene with a floor, ceiling, storage box, and several 2D shapes that you use to construct 3D geometry. A camera is in the scene, too.

2. Right-click in the Top viewport to activate it and select the triangular 2D shape called wall_path. This shape defines the honeycomb wall around the control room and to build the wall the right size you need to know the length of the path. In the Utilities panel, click the Measure button. In the Shapes area of the Measure rollout, you see that the Length of this object is 159 feet 10 3/8 inches (see Figure 9.1). For your purposes in this exercise, rounding to 160 feet is fine. This becomes the length of the wall.

3. In the Create panel, Geometry panel, click Box in the Standard Primitives, Object Type rollout and drag a box of any size in the Top viewport. In the Modify panel, enter 10 in the Length field, 160 in Width, and 1 in the Height field. In Length Segs, enter 5, and in Width Segs, enter 80. This creates 2 foot by 2 foot polygons. Name the object Wall01.

4. Right-click the Camera01 viewport label and choose Edge Faces from the menu. From the Tools pull-down menu, choose Isolate Selection. Right-click in the Camera01 viewport and press P to switch to a Perspective viewport. Then, press U on the keyboard to switch to a User viewport, which is nonorthographic but has no perspective. Use the Arc Rotate tool in the User viewport to view the wall from the upper left and click the Zoom Extents All button at the lower right of the display to see the entire box in all viewports. It should look similar to Figure 9.2.

5. Right-click the Wall01 and choose Convert To, Convert to Editable Poly in the Quad menu. In the Modify panel, Stack view, highlight Polygon sub-object mode. On the main toolbar, make sure you are in Window selection mode. In the Left viewport, drag a selection window around the top of the Wall01 to select only the top polygons. In the Edit Polygons rollout, click the Settings button for Inset. This insets 1 inch around the perimeter of the selection set. In the Inset

FIGURE 9.1

Use the Measure tool in the Utilities panel to measure the length of the wall_path shape. Round up to the nearest foot and make note of the number; in this case, 160 feet.

tip

On slower machines, clicking OK could result in a few seconds pause while the settings are calculated and applied. Have patience.

Polygons dialog, select the By Polygon radio button to inset each polygon individually. Enter 3" in the Inset Amount field and press Enter. This creates a space between each selected polygon (see Figure 9.3). Click OK. Zoom the User viewport to see the results.

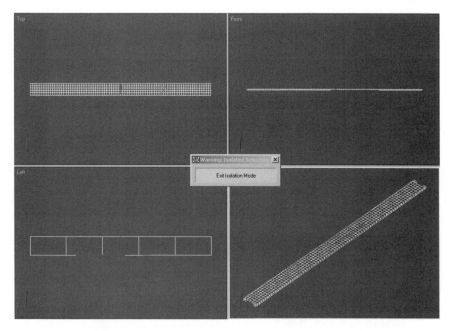

FIGURE 9.2   *Switch the Camera01 viewport to a Perspective viewport by pressing P, then to a User viewport by pressing U, and Zoom and Arc Rotate to see the Wall01 object that is in Isolation mode.*

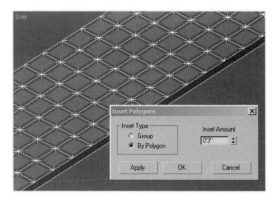

FIGURE 9.3   *Using Inset in By Polygon mode insets each polygon individually.*

6. In the Edit Polygons rollout, click the Settings button for Bevel. Enter –1 in both the Height and the Outline Amount fields. The bevel type is not important now because all the polygons are separated by unselected polygons through which the effect cannot pass. Click OK. This puts a 45-degree chamfer at all edges of the panels.

7. In the Edit Polygons rollout, click the Settings button for Extrude. Enter –4 in the Extrusion Height field, and press Enter for a deeper-set panel. Click OK. (See Figure 9.4). On the main toolbar, Named Selection Sets window, enter panels and press Enter. This makes it easier to reselect the panels if you need them later.

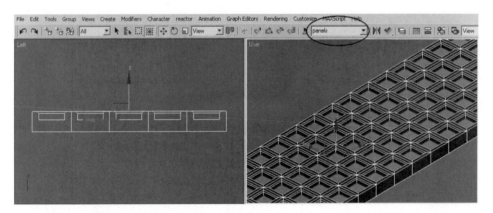

FIGURE 9.4   *Extrude the selection by minus 4 inches and create a named selection set of the polygons for later use.*

8. In the Modify panel, Stack view, highlight Editable Poly at the top of the list to exit sub-object mode. In the viewports, click the Exit Isolation Mode button to return all objects to the scene.

9. Close all windows and dialogs and save the file. It should already be called Ch09_interior02.max.

Bend It, Shape It...Deforming the Wall

You now have a particularly long wall lying flat on the floor, but you want it to be a futuristic curved wall that fits the shape of the boat's bow.

In Exercise 9.2, you learn to use the World-Space PathDeform modifier to use the triangular shape with the rounded corners as the base of the wall. You also bend the wall so that it turns inward as it reaches the ceiling.

The important thing about PathDeform is that the object being deformed has enough segments along the path to accept the deformation.

Exercise 9.2   Deforming a Bent Object Along a Path

1. Open the file called Ch09-interior02.max on the CD-ROM or from the preceding exercise. From the File pull-down menu, choose Save As, point to an appropriate subdirectory on your hard drive, and use the plus sign button to save a new file with the name incremented to Ch09_interior03.max.

tip

The correct axes to use have been predetermined through some trial and error to make this exercise flow more smoothly. The actual settings depend on which viewports the objects were created in and what reference coordinate systems are in effect; so, the settings might differ if you re-create this exercise on your own.

2. First, move the pivot point of Wall01 to align it with what will become the bottom of your wall. Remember that the Bend modifier uses the pivot of an object as the default center of bending. With Wall01 selected, in the Hierarchy panel, Adjust Pivot rollout, click the Affect Pivot Only button. On the main toolbar, click the Align button. In the Top viewport, pick Wall01. In the Align Selection dialog, check Y Position, Pivot Point in the Current Object column, and Maximum in the Target Object column (see Figure 9.5). Click OK. In Hierarchy panel, click Affect Pivot Only to exit that mode.

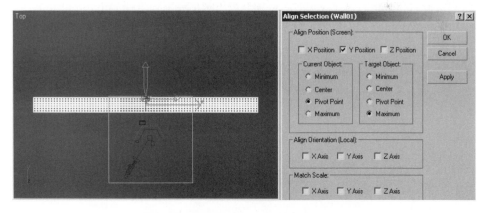

FIGURE 9.5   *In the Align Selection dialog, check Y Position and choose Pivot Point in Current Object column and Maximum in Target Object column. Click OK.*

3. In the Modify panel, Modifier List, choose the Bend modifier. In the Parameters rollout, enter 25 in the Angle field, 90 in the Direction field, and check the Y radio button in the Bend Axis area. Your wall goes through distortions with each new data entry, but in the end, it looks like Figure 9.6.

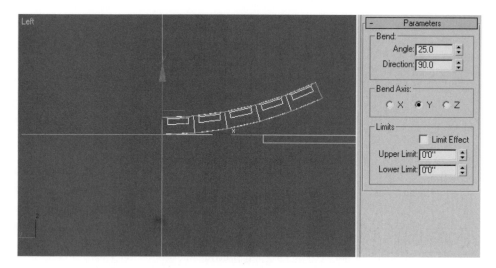

FIGURE 9.6   *In Affect Pivot Only mode, use Align to align the pivot point to the maximum side of the Y-axis of the Top viewport.*

4. Now, deform the bent wall around the path. With Wall01 selected, go to Modify panel, Modifier List, and choose the PathDeform (WSM) modifier in the World-Space modifiers list (see Figure 9.7).

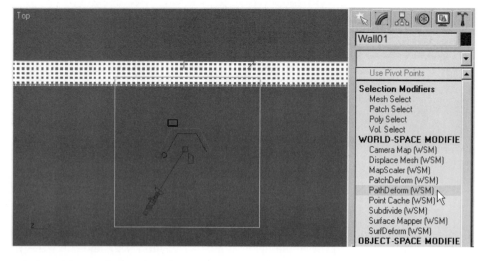

FIGURE 9.7   *Select Wall01 and apply the PathDeform (WSM) World-space modifier.*

5. In the Parameters rollout, click the Pick Path button and, in the Top viewport, pick wall_path. Wall01 deforms very oddly. In the Parameters rollout, click the Move to Path button. Enter 90 in the Rotation field and check the X PathDeform Axis radio button. This orients the wall correctly on the path (see Figure 9.8).

caution

Do not choose the Patch-Deform (WSM) object or the PathDeform further down in the Modifier List under Object-space modifiers.

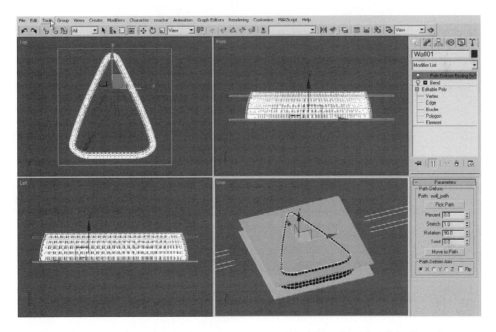

FIGURE 9.8   *In PathDeform (WSM) Parameters rollout, click Pick Path and pick wall_path, click Move to Path, enter 90 in Rotation, and check the X PathDeform Axis radio button.*

6. Right-click in the User viewport and press C to switch to the Camera01 viewport. Right-click the Camera01 viewport label and clear the Edged Faces option. The viewport should look like Figure 9.9. The bevel on the panel edges catch the light to enhance the look.

7. Close all windows and dialogs and save the file. It should already be called Ch09_interior03.max.

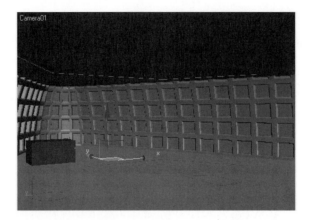

FIGURE 9.9   *Switch the User viewport to the Camera01 viewport by pressing C and turn off Edged Faces by right-clicking the viewport label and clearing it in the menu.*

A Modeling Technique Called Lofting

The term *lofting* comes from shipbuilding. The ribs of a ship are drawn out full size on the floor of a loft at the boatyard. The ribs are then cut and positioned along the keel of the ship, and the skin is applied to create the hull.

In 3ds max 6, you determine a 2D path (keel) and 2D cross-section shapes. 3ds max 6 then applies the skin for you, making a 3D surface.

The biggest advantage of lofting is that simple 2D shapes can generate complex 3D objects with flexible editing and control of face density.

There can only be one path along which any number of shapes can be placed. The path and shape objects can be open or closed shapes. The only real restrictions are that each shape along the path must have the same number of splines and a path can have only one spline. For example, you cannot loft a Circle primitive and a Donut primitive on the same loft path, nor can you loft a shape along a Donut primitive. The Circle primitive has one spline, and the Donut primitive has two.

In this section, you create two objects with lofting: a command console and an air-handling duct. The console will be a single shape along the path, and the duct will be two shapes on the path. This creates a transition from a circular to rectangular cross-section.

One particularly important aspect of lofting is the relative position of the first vertex of each shape along the path. The loft mesh surface is created by first stitching vertices and shape steps to form the segments of the skin. You learn more about these terms as you go along in the exercises.

Another important thing to know is that the pivot point of a shape determines where it attaches to the start (first vertex) of the path. Transforming the pivot point of the shape affects the orientation on the path.

Finally, the Local reference coordinate system axes of the shape and path affect the orientation of a shape on the path. The positive local Z-axis of the shape aligns along the path.

A lack of understanding of the first vertex and the default orientation keeps many users from taking advantage of the power of lofting. The important fundamentals in this chapter enables you to take full advantage of the tool.

You also learn the power of mesh optimization that lofting has to make your models more efficient or more detailed as you might require.

Lofting Fundamentals

In Exercise 9.3, you learn to loft a single shape along a path to build a command console for the control instruments for your boat. The console could be created with other techniques, such as box modeling, but you would not have the ease of editing or the ability to optimize the mesh.

Exercise 9.3   Lofting 2D Shapes Along a 2D Path

1. Open the file called Ch09_interior03.max on the CD-ROM or from the preceding exercise. From the File pull-down menu, choose Save As, point to an appropriate subdirectory on your hard drive, and use the plus sign button to save a new file with the name incremented to Ch09_interior04.max.

2. In the Camera01 viewport, using Select by Name, select console_shape, a closed parallelogram, and console_path, an open inverted U shape. In the Tools pull-down menu, choose Isolate Selection (Alt+Q) to hide the other objects. Click the Zoom Extents All button. In the Camera01 viewport, press P to switch to a Perspective view and Arc Rotate so that the viewport looks similar to Figure 9.10.

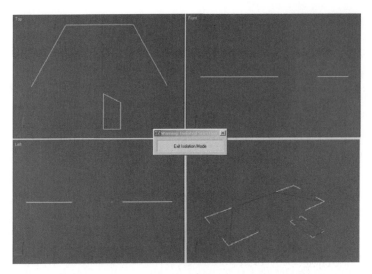

FIGURE 9.10   *Select console_shape and console_path and isolate the selection. Zoom Extents All and switch the Camera01 viewport to the Perspective viewport and Arc Rotate to be viewing from upper left.*

3. In the Perspective viewport, select console_path. In the Create panel, Geometry panel, click Standard Primitives, and choose Compound Objects from the list. In the Object Type rollout, click the Loft button (see Figure 9.11).

4. In the Creation Method rollout, click the Get Shape button and, in the Perspective viewport, pick console_shape. Your first lofted object looks like Figure 9.12. A nice object, but not the right console for your boat. The object would not sit on the floor, but would drop below it.

5. Remember that the shape's pivot point attaches itself to the path's first vertex, and the shape's pivot point location is in the geometric center of the shape. You move the pivot point to the lower-left corner of the console_shape, which modifies the loft object. On the main toolbar, click the Select Object button. In the Top viewport, select console_shape. You see the pivot tripod axis in the center of the modified rectangle shape. In the Hierarchy panel, click the Affect Pivot Only

FIGURE 9.11

In the Create panel, Geometry panel, Compound Objects panel, check the Loft button in the Object Type rollout.

button. On the main toolbar, click the Align button and then click the edge of console_shape in the Top viewport. In the Align Selection dialog, check X and Y Position, check Pivot Point in the Current Object column and Minimum in the Target Object column. The pivot point aligns to the lower-left corner of the shape as seen in the Top viewport (see Figure 9.13). Click OK. In the Hierarchy panel, click Affect Pivot Only to exit that mode.

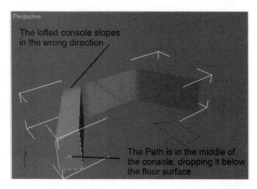

tip

Generally, you select the path and then use Get Shape to attach a clone (instance) of the shape to the path.

If the shape is already positioned correctly in the scene, however, you may use the Get Path option to clone the path to the shape's location.

FIGURE 9.12   *In the Creation Method rollout, click Get Shape, and pick the console_shape object in the Perspective viewport. The shape is lofted along the path. However, the console is backward and too low in relation to the floor surface.*

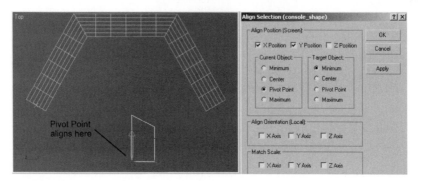

FIGURE 9.13   *In the Hierarchy panel, Affect Pivot Only mode, use Align to position the pivot point at the minimum axes of both X and Y position.*

6. In the Perspective viewport, select the Loft01 object. In the Modify panel, rename it Console01. In the Creation Method panel, click the Get Shape button and pick the console_shape in the viewport. The Console01 jumps up and the path is now defining the inside-bottom corner. The console still slopes in the wrong direction, however.

7. While you are still in Get Shape mode, hold the Ctrl key and pick the console_shape in the Perspective viewport again. Holding the Ctrl key while performing a Get Shape action flips the shape clone 180 degrees around its pivot point. The negative local Z-axis of the shape orients down the path (see Figure 9.14).

caution

It is important that you are in the Modify panel when you pick Get Shape and pick the console_shape. Otherwise, you would be creating a completely new loft object.

tip

The shape is cloned to the path as an instance to create the object. Any modifications to the original shape are passed to the clone to edit the loft object. However, moving the pivot point is not a modification, but a transformation, and you must use Get Shape to update the changes on the loft object.

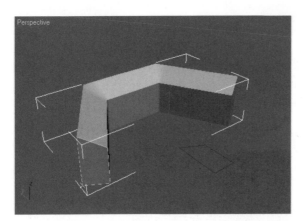

FIGURE 9.14   *Holding the Ctrl key while performing a Get Shape operation in the Modify panel flips the shape 180 degrees and replaces the current shape on the first vertex of the path.*

8. Close all windows and dialogs and save the file. It should already be called Ch09_interior04.max.

Modifying the Shapes to Change the Loft

In Exercise 9.4, you learn to modify the original 2D loft shape to make relatively complex changes to the 3D loft object. You are taking advantage of the fact that the cloned shape on the path is an instance of the original, a powerful option.

You add a kick space to the front of the console and round the sharp edge along the top back of the sloped surface.

Exercise 9.4   Modifying the Original Shape to Change the Instance Clone on the Path

1. Open the file called Ch09-interior04.max on the CD-ROM or from the preceding exercise. From the File pull-down menu, choose Save As, point to an appropriate subdirectory on your hard drive, and use the plus sign button to save a new file with the name incremented to Ch09_interior05.max.

2. On the main toolbar, click the Select Object button. In the Top viewport, select console_shape. In the Modify panel, Stack view, expand Editable Spline and highlight Segment sub-object level. Select the shorter vertical segment on the right side of the shape. In the Modify panel, near the bottom of the Geometry rollout, enter 2 in the Divide field and click the Divide button. This adds two new vertices to the segment (see Figure 9.15).

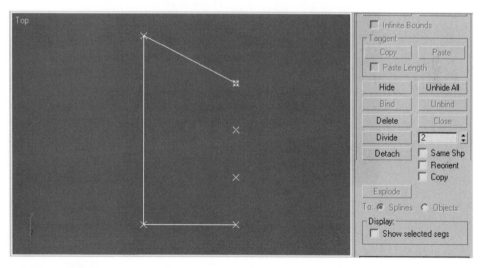

FIGURE 9.15   *In sub-object Segment mode, select the short vertical segment of console_shape. Enter 2 in the Divide field of the Geometry rollout, and click Divide to add two new vertices to the segment.*

3. In the Modify panel, Stack view, highlight Vertex sub-object level. On the main toolbar, click the Select and Move button. In the Top viewport, move the three vertices on the right side to look similar to Figure 9.16. You notice in the other viewports that the changes are being reflected in the Console01 object (see Figure 9.17).

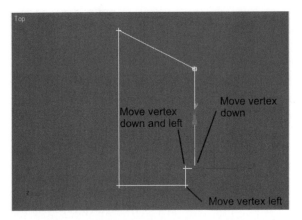

FIGURE 9.16   *Move three vertices down and/or left to define a kick space at the bottom right of the 2D shape. Use the Transform gizmo, but just guess at the size for this example.*

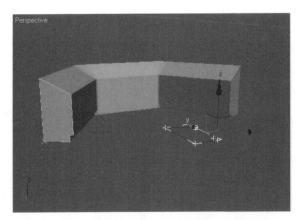

FIGURE 9.17   *A kick space is being created at the inside bottom of Console01 as you modify the 2D shape.*

4. While in Vertex sub-object mode, select the top two vertices of console_shape. In the Modify panel, Geometry rollout, enter 4 in the Fillet field and press Enter. This rounds the top edges of the console for the entire length (see Figure 9.18). In Stack view, highlight Editable Spline to exit sub-object mode.

caution

Do not click the Fillet button during this operation. There are two ways to use Fillet: by entering numbers in the field and pressing Enter or by clicking the Fillet button, and then interactively dragging the fillet in the viewport.

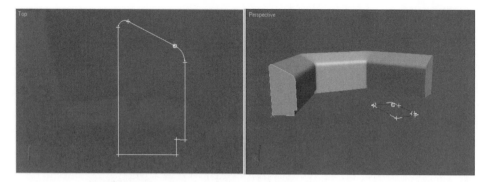

FIGURE 9.18   *In Vertex sub-object mode, select the top two vertices of the shape and enter 4 in the Fillet field. Press Enter to see the results on the shape and the loft object.*

5. Close all windows and dialogs and save the file. It should already be called Ch09_interior05.max.

Loft Optimizations

You have created a loft object, but is it as efficient as it could be? The face count of lofted objects with curves can get out of control quickly, so it is important to be vigilant.

In Exercise 9.5, you check the face count of the object, and then use path and shape step controls to adjust the density of the mesh so that it retains the look, but is substantially more efficient.

Exercise 9.5   Using Path and Shape Steps to Optimize Loft Objects

1. Open the file called Ch09_interior05.max on the CD-ROM or from the preceding exercise. From the File pull-down menu, choose Save As, point to an appropriate subdirectory on your hard drive, and use the plus sign button to save a new file with the name incremented to Ch09_interior06.max.

2. In the Perspective viewport, select Console01. Right-click the Perspective label and check Edged Faces in the menu. Right-click Console01, and choose Properties in the Quad menu. You see that the object has 1,820 faces. Click OK. In the Perspective viewport, you can see segmentation cause by vertices, path steps, and shape steps (see Figure 9.19).

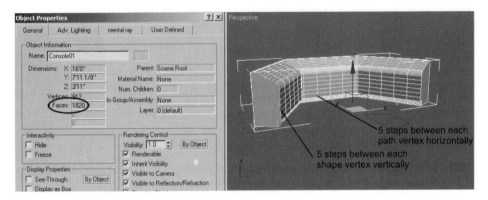

FIGURE 9.19   *There are, by default, five path steps and five shape steps between each vertex to define curvature. The segmentation shows this when Edged Faces is on
or when in Wireframe mode.*

3. In the Modify panel, Skin Parameters rollout, decrement the Path Steps by 1 until you get to 0. Watch the Console01 in Perspective as you change each amount. When you get to 0, you will only have horizontal segments, except where the path vertices are. There is no curvature in the path, so the object does not change. Right-click Console01 and choose Properties. You see that there are only 380 faces. Click OK to close the dialog.

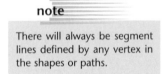

note

There will always be segment lines defined by any vertex in the shapes or paths.

4. Decrement the Shape Steps field by 1 until you get to 0. The Console01 now only has 60 faces, but the curvature is completely gone from the object and it looks terrible (see Figure 9.20).

5. The Path Steps and Shape Steps settings adjust the number of steps between each vertex equally, so just adding shape steps increases the face count in places where the extra detail is not needed. To repeat the definition of path and shape steps, there are points between vertices that define curvature. The path has no curvature, so 0 Path Steps is fine. The shape has curvature only at the filleted areas. Instead of adjusting steps at this point, you would be better off adding vertices to the curved segments of the original 2D shape. In the Top viewport, select console_shape. In the Modify panel, Stack view, highlight Segment and select the two curved segments at the upper corners. In the Geometry rollout, enter 3 in the Divide field and click the Divide button. This adds three new vertices to define the curvature (see Figure 9.21). Exit sub-object mode.

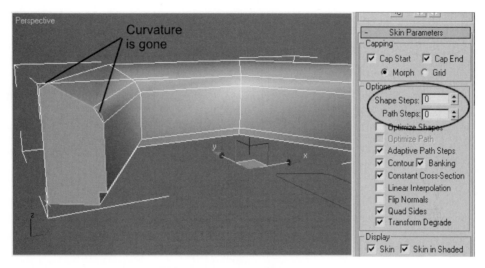

FIGURE 9.20   *With Path Steps and Shape Steps set to 0, the object is only 60 faces but is no longer acceptable visually.*

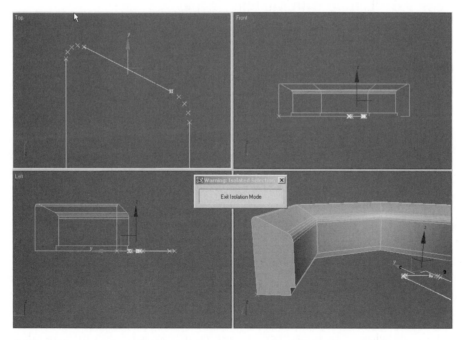

FIGURE 9.21   *Using Divide to add three new vertices to each curved segment of the original shape adds segments to the mesh only where needed.*

6. Select Console01, right-click it, and choose Properties to see that the object looks like it did originally (but instead of 1820 faces, it now has only 108). Click the Exit Isolation Mode button to return all objects.

7. Save the file. It should already be called Ch09_interior06.max.

Lofting Multiple Shapes on a Single Path

warning

Knowing this simple lofting process of adjusting path and shape steps is critical to fast, flexible modeling in 3ds max 6. Make sure you understand this exercise before proceeding. Otherwise, it is much too easy to overwhelm even the most powerful computers with lofted objects.

In Exercise 9.6, you learn to loft two shapes on the same path for a more complex object. The important thing learned here is the effect of the first vertex on a lofted object. With a single shape, the first vertex has no noticeable effect because it is constant along the path. If the first vertices of multiple shapes are not in the same relative position, however, twisting occurs along the loft object. You learn to correct that.

Exercise 9.6   Lofting with Multiple Shapes

1. Open the file called Ch09_interior06.max on the CD-ROM or from the preceding exercise. From the File pull-down menu, choose Save As, point to an appropriate subdirectory on your hard drive, and use the plus sign button to save a new file with the name incremented to Ch09_interior07.max.

2. Using Select by Name, select duct_path, duct_shape01, and duct_shape02. Isolate the selection. This is another inverted U that will be used as the path, and a square and a circle, respectively, that will be shapes. Click Zoom Extents All to view all objects. With the shapes all selected, right-click in the Top viewport and choose Properties in the Quad menu. In the Object Properties dialog, Display Properties area, check Vertex Ticks (see Figure 9.22). This enables you to see the vertices of the selected shapes without being in sub-object mode.

3. You notice a white box around each first vertex on each spline of each shape. (They are all simple shapes.) The first vertex of the square and circle are out of relative position by 45 degrees. In the Top viewport, select duct_path. In the Create panel, Geometry panel, Compound Objects panel, click the Loft button. In the Creation Method rollout, click the Get Shape button. In the Top viewport, pick duct_shape01 (square). You now have a simple square duct in the scene. The Path Steps and Shape Steps settings are remembered from the preceding exercise. In the Modify panel, Skin Parameters rollout, enter 5 in both the Path Steps and Shape Steps fields. Rename the object Duct01. You will optimize later (see Figure 9.23). In the Skin Parameters rollout, clear the Transform Degrade check box so the changes you make later will be visible in the viewport.

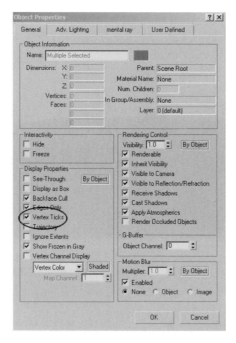

FIGURE 9.22   *By turning Vertex Ticks on in the Object Properties dialog, you can see vertex ticks in the viewports without being in sub-object mode.*

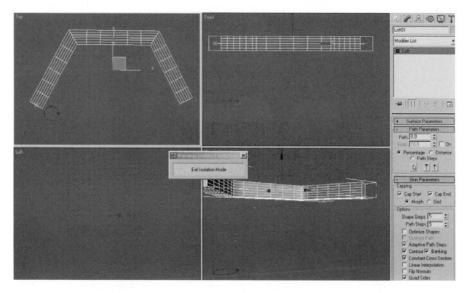

FIGURE 9.23   *A square shape lofted along a Path with both the Path Steps and Shape Steps fields set to 5.*

4. In the Modify panel, Path Parameters rollout, enter 100 in the Path field and press Enter (see Figure 9.24). This puts the active Get Shape level at 100 percent along the path—that is, at the other end as indicated by the yellow tick at the end of the path.

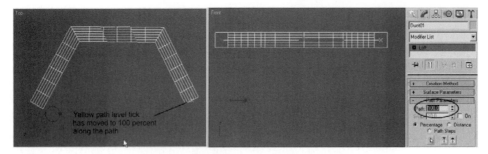

FIGURE 9.24   *Setting Path to 100 moves the active Get Shape level from the start of the path to the end of the path as indicated by the yellow tick. Otherwise, when you get the next shape, it would just replace the one at 0 percent along the path.*

5. In the Creation Method rollout, click the Get Shape button to turn it on and pick duct_shape02 (circle) in the Top viewport. The Duct01 now starts as a square cross-section on the left and ends as a round cross-section on the right with a 45 degree twist along the way (see Figure 9.25).

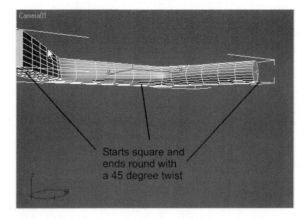

FIGURE 9.25   *With a square shape at the start and a round shape at the end, the Duct01 changes form, but has an unwanted twist along the length.*

6. Not only is there a twist, the duct should also not transition from square to circle over the entire length. You first get the transition in a smaller area halfway along the path. In the Modify panel, Path Parameters rollout, enter 45 in the Path field and press Enter. The active Get Shape level is now just before the halfway point on the path. Click the Get Shape button, if it is not still active, and pick the duct_shape01 (square) in the Top viewport. Now, the Loft starts as a square cross-section, holds that form until 45 percent, and then changes from a square to a circle.

7. In the Path field, enter 60. With Get Shape on, pick the duct_shape02 again. Now, the transition takes place within 15 percent of the Path (between 45 and 60), but still has the twist.

8. Loft objects also have sub-object levels. In the Stack view, expand Loft and high-light Shape in the list. On the main toolbar, click the Select Object button. In the Front viewport, move the cursor over the loft object and pick when you are over the shape clone at 60 percent and see the small crosshair cursor (see Figure 9.26). The clone shape turns red when selected.

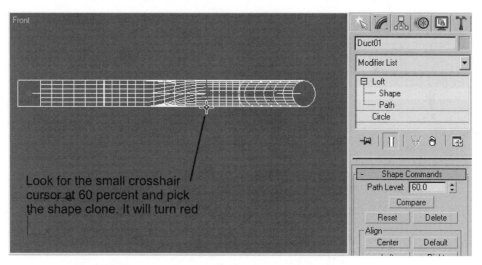

FIGURE 9.26 *In Shape sub-object mode, select the clone shape at 60 percent along the path. It turns red when selected.*

9. On the main toolbar, click the Select and Rotate button. Notice that the reference coordinate system is locked on Local for each shape. In the status bar at the bottom of the display, toggle to Offset Transform Type-In mode. In the Transform Type-In Z-axis field at the bottom center of the display, enter 45 and press Enter (see Figure 9.27). The twist is removed at that point.

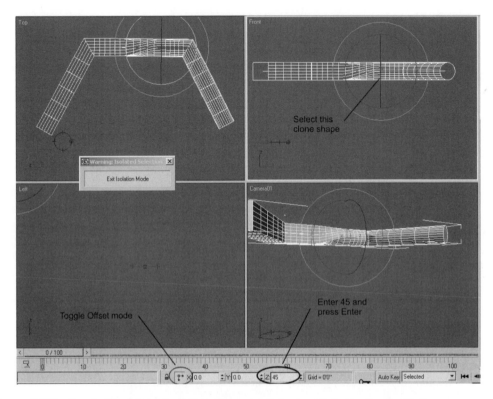

FIGURE 9.27   *Toggle Offset Transform Type-In mode and enter 45 in the Z-axis rotation.*
Press Enter. The twist is removed at that point.

10. Select the clone shape at 100 percent of the way
along the path and rotate it 45 degrees. The twist
is removed from the entire Loft object. In the
Stack view, highlight Loft level to exit sub-object
mode. In the Skin Parameters rollout, set the
Shape Steps to 3 and the Path Steps to 0 (see
Figure 9.28).

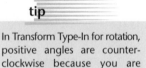

tip

In Transform Type-In for rotation,
positive angles are counter-
clockwise because you are
looking down the axis.

11. Exit Isolation mode. You now have an efficient console and duct, but there is
some strange shading (see Figure 9.29). You take care of that in Exercise 9.7.

12. Close all windows and dialogs and save the file. It should already be called
Ch09_interior07.max.

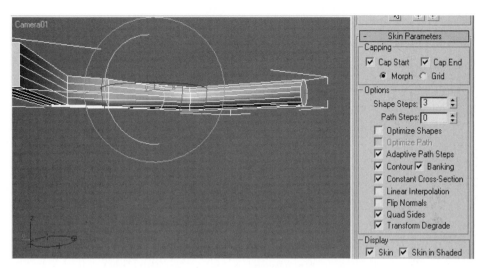

FIGURE 9.28   *Rotating both circle clone shapes 45 degrees removes any twist, and setting the Shape Steps field to 3 and the Path Steps field to 0 is a good compromise between efficiency and visual acceptance.*

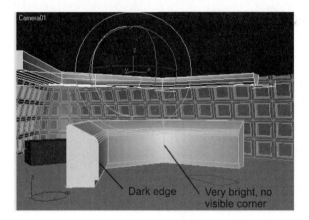

FIGURE 9.29   *The duct and the console are efficient, but have some strange shading on the surfaces.*

Smoothing Faceted Surfaces

Through the creation and editing of lofted objects, there has been a process going on that assigns numbers called smoothing group numbers to each face. The rule is that if two adjacent faces share a common number, the edge between them is smoothed;

otherwise, it is a hard edge. 3ds max 6 does a pretty good job at guessing, but is not always right, causing odd shading in some areas and noticeable facets in other areas. In Exercise 9.7, you apply a Smooth modifier that reapplies the smoothing group numbers based on the angle that faces meet. This makes your objects appear correct in the scene.

Exercise 9.7   Assigning Smoothing Groups with Smooth Modify

1. Open the file called Ch09_interior07.max on the CD-ROM or from the preceding exercise. From the File pull-down menu, choose Save As, point to an appropriate subdirectory on your hard drive, and use the plus sign button to save a new file with the name incremented to Ch09_interior08.max.

2. On the main toolbar, click the Select Object button and select the ceiling object. Click the Select and Move button and move the ceiling object up so that the duct shows in the room (see Figure 9.30).

FIGURE 9.30   *Move the Ceiling01 object up to reveal the entire duct.*

3. Activate the Camera01 viewport and, on the main toolbar, click the Quick Render button to render the scene. In the Rendering pull-down menu, choose RAM Player. In the RAM Player dialog, click the Open Last Rendered Image in Channel A button (teapot on the left). Click OK in the RAM Player Configuration dialog to accept the defaults. Close the Rendered Frame Window. Minimize (do not close) the RAM Player window.

4. Click the Select Object button and, in the Top viewport, select Console01. In the Modify panel, Modifier List, choose Smooth modifier. In the Parameters rollout, check the Auto Smooth check box. It is set for a threshold of 30 degrees. If two faces share a common edge at 30 degrees or less, the edge will be smoothed. Otherwise, it will be a hard edge. Render the Camera01 viewport and not much will have changed with the Console01. In the Threshold field, enter 15.8 and press Enter. Render the Camera101 viewport. There is now an acceptable level of smoothing to make the object look better.

5. Select the Duct01 and Wall01 objects and apply a single Smooth modifier to the two objects with Auto Smooth checked on and a threshold of 22.8 degrees. Render the Camera01 viewport. Maximize the RAM Player and click the Open Last Rendered Image in Channel B. Click OK. In the RAM Player, click and hold in the display area and move the cursor back and forth to compare the two images (see Figure 9.31).

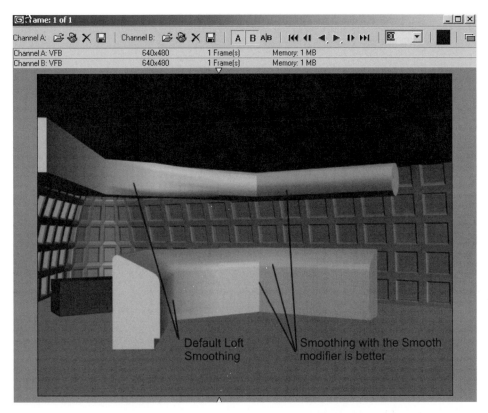

FIGURE 9.31 *Default loft smoothing is shown on the left in the RAM Player (Channel A), and smoothing with the Smooth modifier is shown on the right.*

6. Close all windows and dialogs and save the file. It should already be called Ch09_interior08.max.

Summary

In this chapter, you learned more about box modeling and about deforming 3D objects along a shape with PathDeform (WSM) modifier. Then, you learned the important steps that make lofting a productive, efficient tool in 3ds max 6. It enables you to create very complex 3D objects with simple 2D shapes that are editable to affect the mesh object.

Some of the techniques covered in this chapter included the following:

- **Box modeling**—You learned to use box modeling techniques to create a complex honeycomb wall system.
- **PathDeform**—PathDeform is a powerful tool that enables you to deform 3D mesh objects along a complex path. You learned to apply it to create a complex wall.
- **Lofting**—You learned to use one of the most powerful and flexible modeling methods that converts simple 2D shapes to complex 3D objects.
- **Smoothing**—You learned ways to smooth surfaces to control the "roundness" at shared edges of polygons.

CHAPTER 10

Modeling with Patch Surfaces

In This Chapter

So far in this book, you learned to create interesting 3D objects, some by starting with 2D shapes that, through various modifiers and construction methods such as lofting, end up as 3D objects. You also have started with 3D primitive objects and pushed and pulled at sub-object level until they resembled a boat, for example. In any case, all the objects you created are classified as polygon mesh objects, objects made up of triangular or quad sets of vertices, edges, and surfaces.

In this chapter, you learn a different form of modeling in which the final objects are made of patch surfaces. These smooth-flowing surfaces can be manipulated by adjusting Bézier handles at each vertex that influence the curvature of the surface between adjacent vertices in a weighted manner. Figure 10.1 shows a basic comparison between an editable mesh surface and an editable patch surface. In each, a vertex has been moved in the Z-axis. The editable mesh has a vertex at each visible intersection, whereas the editable patch has only nine total vertices. The white lines on this patch surface are for display only and are not all editable edges. There is a clear difference in the surfaces of the two objects.

This weighted relationship between vertices and the Bézier handles (similar to Bézier vertices in Shapes) enables you to create smooth surfaces more easily than with mesh objects.

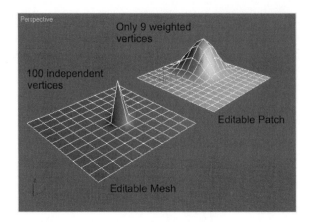

FIGURE 10.1 *An editable mesh on the left and editable patch on the right, each with a vertex moved in the Z-axis.*

You can create patch surfaces in three ways: You can use a Patch Grid primitive object, which is just a flat plane with patch attributes; you can convert other types of surfaces to an editable patch by right-clicking or applying an Edit Patch modifier; or you can create a spline cage and apply a Surface modifier to create a skin over the cage.

In this chapter, you learn the last method: skinning a cage of splines. The cage can be made of vertices and segments that form three- or four-sided areas to describe the surface. There must be one or more vertices at each intersection within a specific tolerance to define the tri or quad cage element.

Patch modeling from a spline cage is a technique used by modelers to create characters, soft furniture, or rolling landscapes and golf courses.

In this chapter, you create the smooth curves of a chair cushion, starting with the four individual splines that you can think of as cross-sections through the half a cushion.

Some of the techniques covered include the following:

- **Spline modeling**—You learn to create a spline cage that can be surfaced with a patch for organic modeling.

- **Patch surface**—You learn to surface a spline with a surface that has Bézier control of the curvature. These are effective for organic objects.

> **note**
>
> At render time, all objects are converted to polygon mesh triangles for the purpose of calculating the rendered image.

- **Symmetry modifier**—You learn to apply this modifier again to turn a half model into a symmetrical surface quickly and easily.

- **Cap Holes modifier**—You learn to add a Cap Holes modifier to close an open surface.

Key Terms

- **Spline cage**—A cage of 2D shapes that will accept a skin of patches to create a flowing surface.

- **Patch**—A mathematical surface definition that can be edited with Bézier controls for smooth surfaces.

- **Show End Result**—This toggle in 3ds max 6 enables you to work at a lower modifier level while still seeing the end result of the entire stack.

Organic Modeling with Spline Cages and Patch Surfaces

An office-chair cushion serves as the example in this chapter as you learn the fundamentals of modeling with spline cages and patches. You learn to attach the 2D shapes that describe the cushion surface into a compound shape, to modify them to add cross-sections to build the cage, and then add a surface to the cage. You will further adjust this surface with Bézier handles, and finally, you will mirror the half cushion and clean it up for a complete cushion.

Learn the process, and then try some objects on your own that would benefit from an organic appearance—you might try automobile parts, faces, or a computer mouse, for example.

The process itself is simple enough, but you must learn to see in 3D to manipulate the Bézier control handles in 3D space. With a little practice, you will find this a handy modeling tool.

Building a 2D Spline Cage

The first step is to build the cage that will be skinned with the patch surface. The cage must be constructed with three- or four-sided components with vertices at each of the corners of each component connected by segments.

2D splines cannot have more than two segments at each vertex; so, to construct the four-sided cage components, you must have two vertices at each corner that are within a specified tolerance of each other.

The order in which you attach the shapes into a compound shape is very important. The surface skin follows the order; so, if you attach the third to the first, and then attach the second, and finally the forth shape, the surface overlaps itself.

Exercise 10.1   Constructing a Spline Cage

1. Open the file called Ch10_Cushion01.max on the CD-ROM. From the File pull-down menu, choose Save As, point to an appropriate subdirectory on your hard drive, and use the plus sign button to save a new file with the name incremented to Ch10_Cushion02.max. This file contains four individual splines that describe the top surface of half an office chair cushion. The longer spline is the center of the cushion.

2. The individual shapes need to be attached into a single compound shape. Again, you must do this must in order. In the Perspective viewport, select Shape01, the longer shape on the upper-left side. Right-click in the viewport and choose Attach in the Quad menu. Then, pick the other three shapes in order (see Figure 10.2). You see a new cursor with four circles to indicate valid shapes to attach, and each shape turns the color of Shape01 as it is successfully attached. Click the Attach button to exit that mode.

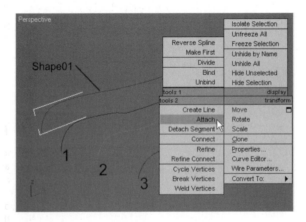

FIGURE 10.2   *Select Shape01 and right-click to access the Attach feature in the Quad menu. Pick the other three shapes in order.*

3. You must now construct the cage, again with three- or four-sided components. Each spline has the same number of vertices, so it will be easy to create a four-sided cage. 3ds max 6 even has a new tool that simplifies the task called Cross Section. In the Modify panel, Geometry rollout, select the Bézier radio button in New Vertex Type area and click the Cross Section button. In the Perspective viewport, pick the long spline when you see the new cursor (see Figure 10.3).

> **caution**
>
> Do not use the Modify panel, Attach Multiple button to attach the shapes because you have no control over the order. The Attach button in the Modify panel and individual picks is the same as using Attach from the Quad menu, however.

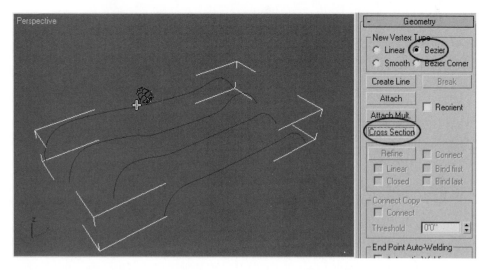

FIGURE 10.3 *Set New Vertex Type to Bézier, click the Cross Section button, and pick each spline in order starting at the upper left of the Perspective viewport.*

4. As you pick the splines, you see the cross-section segments forming the four-sided cage elements along the vertices of each spline and a dotted rubber-band line shows where you are. After picking the last spline (see Figure 10.4), right-click to finish the action. Click the Cross Section button in the Modify panel to exit that mode. Name the object Cushion01.

> **tip**
>
> If you go to Vertex sub-object mode and drag a selection window around one of the interior intersections of the cage, you see in the Selection rollout that there are two vertices at the intersection where four segments meet.

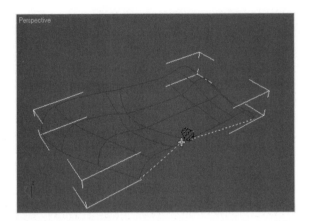

FIGURE 10.4 *Click the Cross Section button, then pick the splines in order. Right-click to finish the action after picking the last spline.*

5. Now, modify the Bézier handles at corners of the cage nearest you to round the cushion into a more organic form (see Figure 10.5). In the Edit pull-down menu, choose Hold to save the scene in a buffer file in case you make mistakes and want to use Fetch to return to this point in editing. In the Perspective viewport, zoom in to the corner of the cage nearest you. In the Modify panel, Stack view, highlight Vertex sub-object level. In the Perspective viewport, drag a selection window around the two vertices at the corner closest to you. Zoom in very close. On the main toolbar, click the Select and Move button. Press X on the keyboard to turn off the Transform gizmo to allow free movement of the cursor. There are actually four handles total on the two vertices selected, but two are right at the vertex. Carefully move those two handles away from the vertex. You will need them later (see Figure 10.6). Repeat for the corner at the other end of the spline.

note

Take a deep breath. Steps 5 to 7 take a little patience to accomplish because they require some very careful picking. You will be on your own. Look ahead in the exercise to visualize where you are going and take your time. These steps illustrate a very common occurrence that can frustrate new users, keeping you from taking advantage of the tool. Take your time and think about what you are doing and why. If you absolutely make a mess, a finished example is waiting for you in Exercise 10.2.

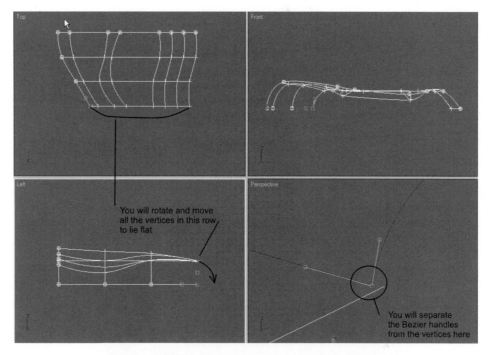

FIGURE 10.5   *Adjust vertices and Bézier handles to round the end into a more organic form.*

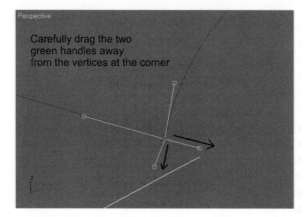

FIGURE 10.6   *Carefully move the two green handles away from the vertex. It will be easier to grab the green box at the end of the Bézier handle by approaching from the corner with the cursor.*

6. Now, rotate all the vertices along that edge about a common pivot point and move them to lie in a plane with the bottom of the cushion. In the Left viewport, select all the vertices at the right edge of the cushion. On the main toolbar, click Select and Rotate button, click and hold on the Use Pivot Point Center button to the right of the Reference Coordinate System field, and choose the Use Selection Center flyout button (see Figure 10.7). Press A to turn on Angle Snap. In the Left viewport, use the Transform gizmo to rotate the selected vertices -90 degrees about the Z-axis. Press A to turn off Angle Snap. Click Select and Move on the main toolbar and move them down (negative Y-axis) until they are at the bottom level of the cushion (see Figure 10.8).

tip

You need to move the Select and Move cursor close to the green handle at the vertex to get hold of it. If you are on the vertices, you move them instead. If you move the vertices by mistake, you can right-click to cancel the action while you are still holding the left mouse button down. Otherwise, you have to use the Undo button to put the vertices back into position.

Sometimes, approaching the handles from a different direction can make selection easier, too.

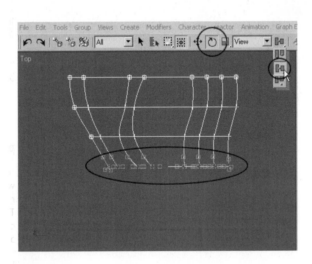

Figure 10.7 *Click Select and Rotate and set to Use Selection Center mode.*

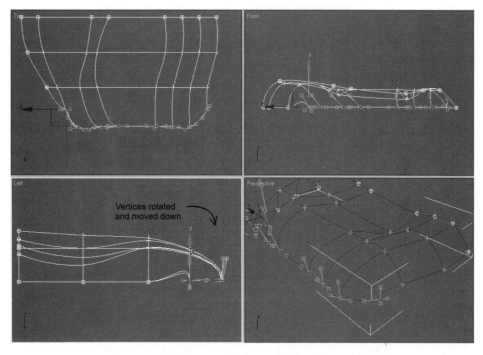

FIGURE 10.8   *With Use Selection Center mode and in the Left viewport, rotate the vertices as a group by -90 degrees. Then move them down flush with the bottom of the cushion.*

7. To clean up the corners and edge of the cushion, select pairs of vertices and adjust the handles until the edge of the cushion looks similar to Figure 10.9. You have to work a little in each viewport to see where you are in space and exactly which handle you are manipulating.

8. Close all windows and dialogs and save the file. It should already be called Ch10_Cushion02.max.

tip

If your cursor movement is somehow restricted to either the X- or Y-axis, press X to toggle the Transform gizmo back on and click in the yellow box when your cursor is near the apex of the restrict arrows. This will set you to move in both X and Y axes freely. Press X to toggle the gizmo off.

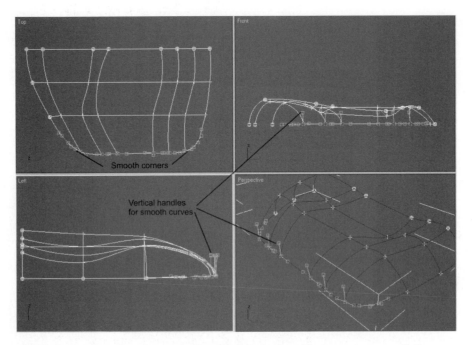

FIGURE 10.9   *Select pairs of vertices and adjust the handles in each viewport to smooth the edge of the cushion.*

Skinning the Cage

Whew, Exercise 10.1 might just have taken its toll on your nerves, but be assured that it just takes a little practice to get a feel for working in 3D space. It is wise to start with simple objects instead of waiting until you have a complex job hanging over you with a tight deadline.

If you are not happy with the results you got, you will be able to open a finished cage in Exercise 10.2 so that you can continue.

In this exercise, you learn to use a Surface modifier to create a patch surface over the cage.

Exercise 10.2   Creating a Patch Surface over the Cage

1. Open the file called Ch10_Cushion02.max on the CD-ROM or from the preceding exercise. From the File pull-down menu, choose Save As, point to an appropriate subdirectory on your hard drive, and use the plus sign button to save a new file with the name incremented to Ch10_Cushion03.max.

2. In the Perspective viewport, select Cushion01. In the Modify panel, Modifier List, choose Surface. The cushion should mostly disappear in the Perspective viewport except for small areas. This is normal behavior (see Figure 10.10). This is because of face normals pointing mostly away from you. In the Modify panel, Parameters rollout, check the Flip Normals check box. Right-click the Perspective label and choose Edged Faces in the menu. You should see a smooth surface and the edges of the cage (see Figure 10.11).

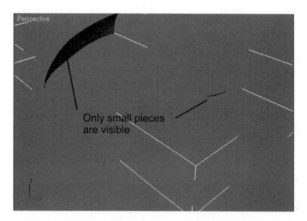

FIGURE 10.10   *Apply a Surface modifier to the spline cage, and the cushion should mostly disappear in the Perspective viewport.*

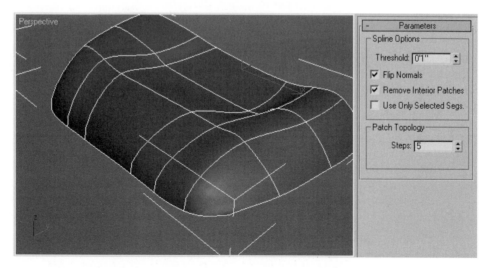

FIGURE 10.11   *Check Flip Normals in the Parameters rollout and choose Edged Faces in the Perspective label right-click menu to see the entire smooth surface with cage lines showing.*

3. In the Modify panel, Stack view, highlight Vertex level under Editable Spline. The viewports show a wireframe cage again.

4. Click the Show End Result On/Off Toggle button just below Stack view (see Figure 10.12). It is the second from the left. This enables you to work at sub-object level to adjust the cage while seeing the end result of all modifiers, in this case the Surface modifier, for ease of editing.

5. In the Stack view, first highlight Editable Spline, and then highlight Surface to make sure you are out of sub-object mode and back to the top of the stack.

6. Close all windows and dialogs. Save the file; it should already be called Ch10_Cushion03.max.

Figure 10.12

Go to sub-object Vertex level and toggle the Show End Result On/Off Toggle button to see both the cage and sub-object selections while viewing the surface, too.

Editing the Patch Surface

After you apply the Surface modifier to a spline cage to create a patch surface, you must go through some editing processes to turn it into a complete cushion. First and most noticeably, it is still a half cushion. You use the Symmetry modifier to mirror, slice, and weld two halves together in one operation. If you Arc Rotate in the Perspective viewport, you notice there is no bottom surface on the half cushion (see Figure 10.13), nor will there be when it is a whole cushion. You learn to apply a Cap Holes modifier to create faces as a cushion bottom.

Symmetry Modifier and More Editing

In Exercise 10.3, you apply a Symmetry modifier to mirror, slice, and weld two halves into a whole cushion only to discover that it would be very uncomfortable to sit on. This requires you to edge along the mirror edge. You also learn about the nature of some modifiers and the effect on future editing of patch surfaces.

caution

It is important that you exit sub-object mode when necessary before going to the top of the modifier stack. Otherwise the modifier may only be operating on the last selection and not the whole object.

There are, of course, exceptions, such as with Mesh Select modifiers, when you will want to remain in sub-object mode so that the modifier above that point is only operating on the selection set defined by that Mesh Select modifier.

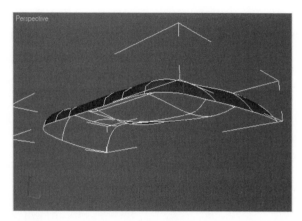

FIGURE 10.13   *If you Arc Rotate in the Perspective viewport, you will see there is no bottom to the half cushion and face normals cause most of the surface to disappear.*

Exercise 10.3   The Symmetry Modifier and More Editing

1. Open the file called Ch10_Cushion03.max on the CD-ROM or from the preceding exercise. From the File pull-down menu, choose Save As, point to an appropriate subdirectory on your hard drive, and use the plus sign button to save a new file with the name incremented to Ch10_Cushion04.max.

2. Select Cushion01 in the Perspective viewport. In the Modify panel, Modifier List, choose Symmetry. The object is mirrored, but in the wrong axis. In the Parameters rollout, select the Z radio button in the Mirror Axis area. You magically have a whole cushion now, but a very sharp seam runs down the middle where the two halves meet. In the Modify panel, Stack view, highlight sub-object Vertex. In the Top viewport, select the four center vertices at the middle seam to determine where the problem is (see Figure 10.14). Selecting pairs at a time, adjust the Bézier handles and move the pairs to look similar to Figure 10.15. Take your time and remember to use the X key to control Axis Constraints.

3. In the Modifier panel, Stack view, exit sub-object mode then return to the top of the stack.

4. Close all windows and dialogs and save the file. It should already be called Ch10_Cushion04.max.

tip

You can only manipulate vertices on the original side. The side created by Symmetry modifier automatically adjusts accordingly.

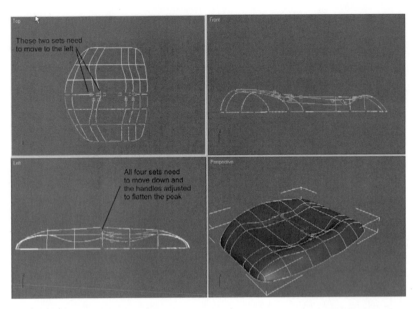

FIGURE 10.14   *Selecting the four middle vertex sets in the middle of the seat reveals a sharp ridge and strange curvature.*

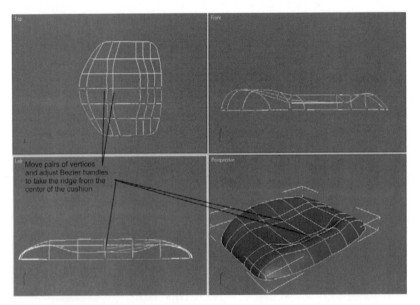

FIGURE 10.15   *Slowly move pairs of vertices and adjust Bézier handles to remove the sharp edge at the middle of the object.*

Capping the Bottom to Close the Object

In Exercise 10.4, you add a Cap Holes modifier to put a surface across the bottom of the cushion, making it a closed object. The Cap Holes modifier looks for open edges in a surface and does its best to determine how best to close it. If this were an object that was an open surface with missing faces, the Cap Holes modifier would just close those holes and not cap the bottom.

Exercise 10.4   Cap Holes Modifier

1. Open the file called Ch10_Cushion04.max on the CD-ROM or from the preceding exercise. From the File pull-down menu, choose Save As, point to an appropriate subdirectory on your hard drive, and use the plus sign button to save a new file with the name incremented to Ch10_Cushion05.max.

2. In the Perspective viewport, select Cushion01. In the Modify panel, Stack view, highlight the Surface modifier, and, in Parameters rollout, set the Patch Topology Steps to 1. This reduces the complexity of the Cushion01. Highlight Symmetry in the Stack view to return to the top level. Right-click on Cushion01 and choose Convert to Editable Patch in the Quad menu. This is necessary because the Cap Holes modifier will conflict with the Symmetry modifier and create a faceted cushion.

3. In the Modify panel, Modifier List, choose Cap Holes. You might notice a slight change in the curvature of the surface caused by the Cap Holes modifier because new tangency information must be added to flatten the new surface.

4. Arc Rotate in the Perspective viewport to view the cushion from below and you will see the solid surface (see Figure 10.16).

5. Save the file. It should already be called Ch10_Cushion05.max.

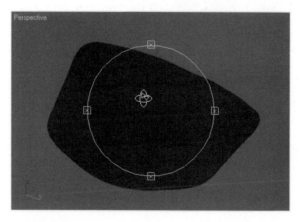

Figure 10.16   *By using Arc Rotate to view the underside of Cushion01, you will see that Cap Holes modifier has created a new surface to close the cushion.*

Summary

Patch surfaces enable you to create a smooth-flowing surface that might otherwise be difficult to construct and edit while keeping the smooth surface.

It is often best practice to keep the object as a true patch object until all editing is complete before adding modifiers that will convert the patch to a mesh object.

Some of the techniques covered in this chapter include the following:

- **Spline modeling**—You learned to create a spline cage that can be surfaced with a patch for organic modeling.
- **Patch surface**—You learned to surface a spline with a surface that has Bézier control of the curvature. These are effective for organic objects.
- **Symmetry modifier**—You learned to apply this modifier again to turn a half model into a symmetrical surface quickly and easily.
- **Cap Holes modifier**—You learned to add a Cap Holes modifier to close an open surface.

CHAPTER 11

Materials and Mapping: A Different Approach

In This Chapter

In Chapter 7, "Introduction to Materials and Mapping," you learned to create and apply fundamental materials to objects in the scene for a more convincing look. For the most part, the materials had patterns derived from types of maps called *procedural maps*—random patterns generated mathematically at render time. You adjusted the size of those patterns until they looked "right" in the scene. However, the patterns never had any basis on anything in the real world other than what you thought was appropriate for the scale of the scene.

More often in production, you will want materials to have patterns that specifically match what you would see as you look around your environment. In this chapter, you learn to analyze maps to determine their real-world coverage and apply mapping coordinates corresponding to that in your scene.

You also learn more about using bump mapping to simulate geometry in your scene to reduce the overhead of complex geometry.

So far, you have been applying one material per object. If you drag and drop a new sample window onto an object that has a material assigned, it will just replace the existing material. Objects are not always made up of one material, however, and you will learn to use the concept of multi/sub-object materials and material ID numbers to control which faces of an object get the submaterials of this special material.

Metals and cloth are two very different materials, and in this chapter, you learn to adjust reflections and specular highlights appropriately for each to make them more convincing when rendered.

Often, you will want to position a company logo or other image on top of another material. You learn to use decaling techniques in this chapter to allow that in any material.

Many objects such as light bulbs, computer monitors, and TV screens are affected little by lights in a room because they give off light that counters any shading on the objects. You learn to simulate that effect with self-illuminated materials in 3ds max 6.

You also learn about using sequentially numbered files as animated maps in your materials and about a new feature in 3ds max 6 that enables you to select objects in a scene based on their material assignment. This might not sound like a big deal to new users, but it is a very handy new tool.

Some of the techniques covered in this chapter include the following:

- **Specific mapping coordinates**—You learn to apply map patterns in a material to match real-world sizes (for example, bricks that are 8 inches by 3 inches to simulate standard brick sizes).

- **Bump maps**—You learn new options to use bump maps to simulate geometry more effectively.

- **More than one material per object**—You learn to apply several materials to a single object with multi/sub-object material type and material ID numbers.

- **Metallic materials**—You learn some of the fundamentals of simulating the hard look of metal through materials.

- **Cloth materials**—You learn other material shader options to make materials appear soft like cloth.

- **Decal materials**—You learn to apply decals that allow the basic material to show as a background.

- **Self-illumination**—You learn to create materials that appear to glow from within.

- **Animated materials**—You learn to apply animated maps to create materials that change over time.

- **Select by Material**—You learn a feature in 3ds max 6 that enables you to select objects based on the assigned materials.

Key Terms

- **UVW Map**—A modifier that enables you to apply mapping coordinates to specific sizes.

- **Multi/sub-object material**—A material type composed of any number of submaterials to a limit of 1,000. This must be used in conjunction with material ID numbers.

- **Material ID number**—A number assigned to individual faces that determine which material of a multi/sub-object material is applied.

- **Shader**—A material attribute that describes the shape of specular highlights in a material.

- **Decal**—A map with a transparent background used within a material to reveal the underlying color (much like the stick-on decals of model airplanes and so on).

- **Self-illumination**—A material attribute that overrides the shaded ambient portion of a material and makes it appear to glow from within.

- **IFL files**—Image File List; a sequentially numbered list of still images that function as an animated file in 3ds max 6.

Real-World Mapping Coordinates

In this section, you learn to analyze a map that will be used in both the color and bump slots of a floor tile material to determine how many real-world units the pattern would cover.

After you calculate the units' coverage of a single repeat of the map, you set a UVW Map modifier gizmo to that size, and the pattern will be the right size over the entire surface.

Creating and Adjusting an Accurate Floor Tile Material

In Exercise 11.1, you use a map to define both the color and bump pattern within a floor tile material. The focus of the exercise is for you to learn how to obtain correct sizes of patterns, but you also learn more about specular highlights and reflections in a material.

> **note**
>
> Maps in 3ds max 6 are referred to as "tiling" maps—that is, they are placed once in the material and repeated over and over in all directions.
>
> Some maps—for example, a photo—are considered "non-tileable" and show a distinct repeating pattern with noticeable edges. In contrast, tileable maps have matching edges—the left matches the right and the top matches the bottom—and will repeat without a distinct repeating edge.

You must first determine from the map how much area one repeat would cover in the real world. This requires that you know the size of each tile. Floor tiles could be anywhere from 2 feet by 2 feet down to 2 inches by 2 inches and any combination of sizes in between.

Your floor will be made up of individual tiles that measure 1 foot on each side.

Exercise 11.1   Creating a Floor Tile Material

1. Open the file called Ch11_interior01.max on the CD-ROM. From the File pull-down menu, choose Save As, point to an appropriate subdirectory on your hard drive, and use the plus sign button to save a new file with the name incremented to Ch11_interior02.max. This file contains the interior scene from Chapter 9, "Diving Deeper into Modeling Techniques," with a little more detail. The duct has been rounded at one end with an option in lofting called Scale Deformation, the chair cushion has been turned into a chair, and a few objects have been added to the control panel along with a toolbox, some lamps, and a large screen.

2. In the Camera01 viewport, select the object called Floor. In the Tools pull-down, choose Isolate Selection or press Alt+Q. On the main toolbar, click the Material Editor button or press M. In the Material Editor, highlight the first sample window, rename it Tile_floor, and drag and drop it onto the floor in the Camera01 viewport.

3. You will set the color of the material with a tile map pattern. In the Material Editor, click the small gray shortcut square next to the Diffuse color swatch. In the Materials/Map Browser, double-click Tiles in the list (see Figure 11.1). This applies a gray-and-black pattern to the diffuse color of the material. In the Material Editor, click the Show Map in Viewport button, just below the sample windows to display the map on the floor in the Camera01 viewport.

4. In the Material Editor, Tiles map, Diffuse Color level, click the Advanced Controls rollout to expand it. Click the Texture: color swatch in the Tiles Setup area, and, in the Color Selector, set the color to dark blue, red = 45, green = 40, and blue = 110. Click the Grout Setup, Texture color swatch and set it to a light gray, red = 170, green = 170, and blue = 170. The colors in the Camera01 change accordingly (see Figure 11.2). Close the Color Selector.

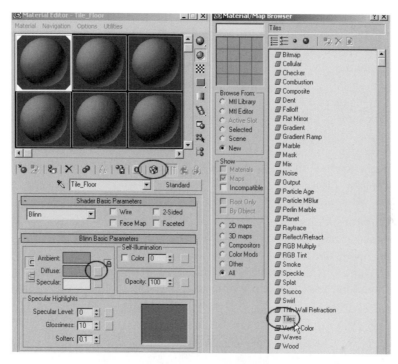

FIGURE 11.1   *Assign a tiles map in the Diffuse Color slot. Toggle Show Map in Viewport on Material Editor to see the map on the Floor surface in the shaded Camera01 viewport.*

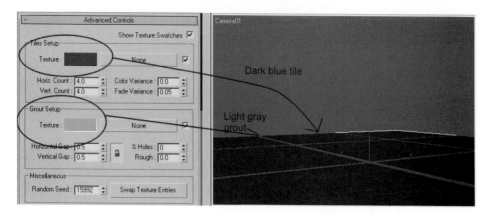

FIGURE 11.2   *In the Advanced Controls rollout of tiles map, set the tiles color to dark blue and the grout color to light gray.*

5. Right-click in the Top viewport to activate it and right-click the label, and then choose Smooth + Highlights from the menu to see the map as it appears on the floor. The size of the floor is 60 feet by 60 feet with only 4 tiles by 4 tiles over the entire floor. Very large tiles, indeed. For the proper size, you first analyze the pattern. In the Advanced Controls rollout, Tiles Setup area, you see that the pattern is made up of a 4 Horiz Count and 4 Vert Count and the reflection of what you see over the floor in the Top viewport. You predetermined, however, that you would be using tiles that were 1 foot by 1 foot each. The 4 tiles across at 1 foot each cover an area of 4 feet. The 4 tiles down at 1 foot each cover an area of 4 feet. Therefore, the real-world coverage of one repetition of your pattern covers 4 feet by 4 feet.

6. You use UVW Map modifier to adjust the size of one repetition. With Floor selected, go to the Modify panel, Modifier List, and choose UVW Map. UVW Map defaults to planar mapping and fits the bounding box of the object from the Z-axis. Therefore, nothing has changed except you can see an orange edge of the UVW Map gizmo at the edge of the floor. In the Modify panel, Parameters rollout, enter 4 in the Length and Width fields. Press Enter. The result is a pattern of 4 stretched over the entire floor (see Figure 11.3).

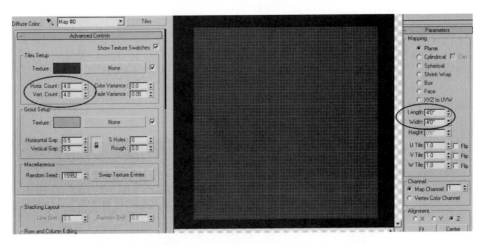

FIGURE 11.3   *If you want accurate tiles that are 1 foot by 1 foot, center of grout to center of grout, multiply the size of each tile by the horizontal and vertical counts, and enter that as the size of the UVW Map gizmo.*

7. Floor tiles should appear hard and have some shininess to them, so you set the specular high-lights accordingly. In the Material Editor, click the Material/Map Navigator button at the lower right of the sample windows. Highlight the top level of Tile_floor material in the list. In the Material Editor, Blinn Basic Parameters rollout, enter 30 in the Specular Level field. This is the brightness of scattered light from a surface. The Glossiness is fine at 10. This is the size of the specular high-light. The sample window appears to have a broad shine to it.

8. The tiles should appear raised above the level of the grout. You do this with a copy of the Diffuse Color Tiles map in the Bump slot. In the Material Editor, click the Maps rollout to expand it. In the Maps rollout, click and drag the tiles map in the Diffuse Color slot to the None button to the right of Bump. When you see the cursor with the box and arrow, drop the map. In the Copy (Instance) Map dialog, make sure the Copy radio button is selected and click OK. You now have the same map in each slot (see Figure 11.4).

note

When zoomed out in the Top viewport to see the entire floor, the graphics card might not be able to display the pattern cor-rectly. Using Quick Render in the Top viewport should show the proper results.

tip

If the map looks skewed or dis-torted in the viewports, right-click the viewport label and choose Texture Correction in the menu.

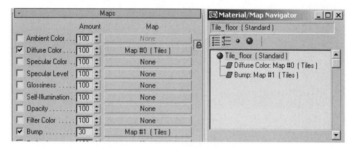

FIGURE 11.4 *Drag and drop a copy of the Diffuse Color Tiles map to the Bump slot in the Maps rollout.*

9. In the Material/Map Navigator, highlight Bump [Tiles] to go to that level. In the Advanced Controls rollout, Tiles Setup, Texture color change the color swatch from dark blue to pure white. In Grout Setup, Texture, change the color swatch from light gray to pure black. Remember that bump works on the luminance values of colors: White bumps, black does nothing, and shades of gray are somewhere in between. Click the Exit Isolation Mode button in the viewports to bring back the other objects.

10. In the Material/Map Navigator, highlight the top level. This floor needs reflections. In the Maps rollout, enter 30 in the Reflection Amount field. Click the None button to the right of Reflection and double-click Raytrace in the Material/ Map Browser list. A raytrace reflection map gives accurate reflections and functions on both flat or curved surfaces.

11. Right-click in the Camera01 viewport and, on the main toolbar, click the Quick Render button. The floor should be very reflective so that you can see the whole wall in the reflections (see Figure 11.5). There is too much reflection. Reflections are light rays and should obey the rules of physics that cause light to attenuate over distance. You use a different form of attenuation that offers more control.

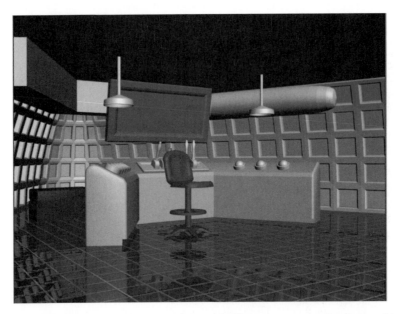

Figure 11.5   *On the main toolbar, click the Quick Render button to render the Camera01 viewport. You see very distinct reflections, including the entire wall to the ceiling.*

12. At the Reflection level of the material, click the Attenuation rollout to expand it. In the Falloff Type list, choose Exponential. In the Ranges, enter 250 in the End field. This means the reflections will go from the surface to 250 inches maximum with a moderately rapid falloff exponent, 2.0 (see Figure 11.6). Higher exponent numbers clip the reflections more quickly. Render the Camera01 viewport and you see that the reflections look more natural.

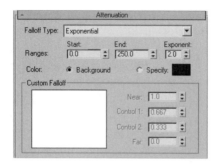

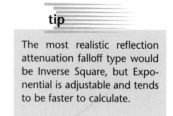

tip

The most realistic reflection attenuation falloff type would be Inverse Square, but Exponential is adjustable and tends to be faster to calculate.

FIGURE 11.6 *In the Attenuation rollout, enable Exponential Falloff Type and set the End Range to 250 for a more convincing reflection.*

13. Right-click on the Top viewport label and choose Wireframe in the menu. Close all windows and dialogs. Save the file; it should already be called Ch11_interior02.max.

Ceiling Panels Using Maps Within Maps for Bumps

In Exercise 11.2, you also use the Tiles map as a basis for a paneled ceiling that is similar to the walls and inset panels that are 2 feet by 2 feet each. However, to reduce face counts, you simulate the geometry using maps in the Bump slot. The primary map be Tiles again to lay out the 2-foot by 2-foot spacing. Each "tile" will be a gradient ramp map that will be set to a box pattern configuration with grayscale colors. Remember that white bumps, black doesn't, and shades of gray are somewhere in between.

Exercise 11.2   Gradient Ramp Map Within Tiles Map for the Ceiling

1. Open the file called Ch11_interior02.max on the CD-ROM or from the preceding exercise. From the File pull-down menu, choose Save As, point to an appropriate subdirectory on your hard drive, and use the plus sign button to save a new file with the name incremented to Ch11_interior03.max.

2. In the Camera01 viewport, select the ceiling object. Open the Material Editor, select the second sample window in the top row and name the material Ceiling_panel. Drag and drop the sample window onto the ceiling in the Camera01 viewport.

3. In the Material Editor, Blinn Basic Parameters rollout, enter 20 in the Specular Level field for some shininess. Click the Maps rollout to expand it. Enter 100 in the Bump Amount field, click the None button in the Bump map slot, and double-click Tiles in the Material/Map Browser list.

4. In the Modify panel, Modifier List, click UVW Map and, in the Parameters roll-out, enter 8 in both the Length and Width fields. Following the logic of the preceding exercise, this makes 4 horizontal by 4 vertical tiles over an 8-foot by 8-foot area. Each tile, or ceiling panel in this case, will be 2 feet by 2 feet. On the main toolbar, click the Quick Render button to render the Camera01 viewport. The ceiling is black because the scene is using the default lighting, which is above the ceiling and not striking the visible surface.

5. Right-click in the Top viewport to activate it. In the Create panel, Lights panel, Object Type rollout, click the Omni button and pick below the chair as seen from the Top viewport. This sets the omni on the floor. On the main toolbar, click the Select and Move button. In the Left viewport, use the Y-axis restrict Transform gizmo arrow to move the light to about the seat cushion level (see Figure 11.7). The rendered Camera01 viewport should look like Figure 11.8.

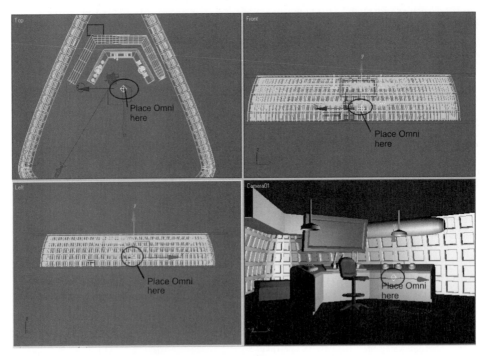

FIGURE 11.7   *Place an omni light in the Top viewport, and then move it up to about the level of the seat cushion.*

FIGURE 11.8   *In the rendered Camera01 viewport, the ceiling bump is visible with the new omni light.*

6. In the Material Editor, expand the Advanced Controls rollout for the Tiles map level. Instead of setting a solid color for the Tiles Setup Texture, use a gradient ramp map. Click the None button to the right of the Tiles Setup Texture color swatch and double-click Gradient Ramp in the Material/Map Browser list. In the Gradient Ramp Parameters rollout, click the Gradient Type Linear field and choose Box from the list (see Figure 11.9). This puts one box gradient ramp pattern over the 4-by-4 pattern of tiles. You fix that with the Tiling parameters of the pattern, and then shift it into alignment with the Offset parameters.

7. In the Coordinates rollout for Gradient Ramp, enter 4 in the U and V Tiling fields to repeat this map to match the number of tiles. The sample window now shows the proper repeat, but the pattern does not fit each tile, yet. In both the Offset U and V fields, enter 0.125. This shifts the map one-eighth of a map and centers it in each tile (see Figure 11.10).

tip

You can make the sample window a larger floating window by double-clicking it and dragging the corners to change the size. Note, however, that an expanded sample window can slow performance, especially with animated materials. Use the feature only when necessary for clarity.

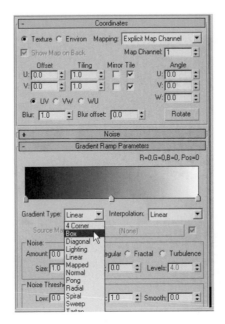

Figure 11.9 *Change the pattern of the gradient ramp from linear to box in the Gradient Ramp Parameters rollout, Gradient Type list.*

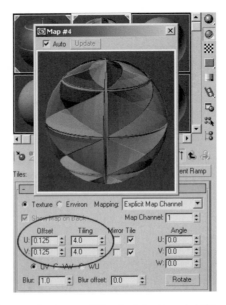

Figure 11.10 *Setting the box gradient ramp Tiling to 4 by 4 and shifting in each direction by 0.125 map size centers the box gradient in each of the 4-by-4 tiles.*

8. Now, change the gradient ramp flags to change the ramp. In the Gradient Ramp Parameters rollout, click the middle flag, right-click it, and choose Edit Properties. In the Flag Properties dialog, click the color swatch and set it to pure black (see Figure 11.11).

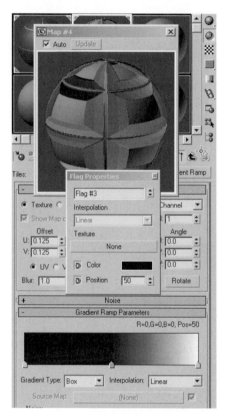

FIGURE 11.11   *Click the middle flag to turn it green, and then right-click and choose Edit Properties from the menu. Click the color swatch and set it to black in the Color Selector.*

9. Click in the white ramp area just above the flag at the far right to clone that color. Click and drag the new flag left until the Pos (position) reads 75 (see Figure 11.12). You can also enter 75 in the Position field of Flag Properties to move the flag.

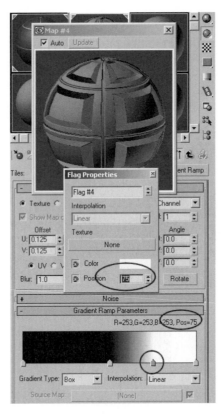

FIGURE 11.12   *Click at the far right of the ramp to clone a new white flag and drag it left to position 75. You can also enter 75 in the Position field of Flag Properties to move the flag.*

10. Activate the Camera01 viewport and use Quick Render to see the results (see Figure 11.13). The panels appear similar to the walls, but with a more gradual slope because of the ramp configuration. This is all an illusion, however, because you have added no actual geometry to the original box that makes up the ceiling.

11. Close all windows and dialogs and save the file. It should already be called Ch11_interior03.max.

note

You have to be the final judge as to whether you need geometry or a bump map will be enough to convince the viewer of your intentions. Just be aware of the option and use it when it makes sense.

Figure 11.13   *The gradient ramp map within a tiles map in a bump slot gives the illusion of panels without adding geometry, thus reducing overhead.*

Multiple Materials on Single Objects

So far, all your material assignments have been one material per object. Essentially, that is all that is allowed. If you drag the Ceiling_panel material sample window onto the Floor object, for example, the Tile_floor material assigned now will be replaced. You will not have two different materials on the floor.

Many times, however, two materials on the same object would be convenient. It makes managing objects much easier if you're dealing with a single object rather than a collection of objects grouped together or included in a named selection set.

There is a special material type called multi/sub-object material. It is one material with up to 1,000 available submaterials. Object's faces are assigned a material ID number that corresponds to the sub-object material. Some objects, such as the Box primitive, already have different material ID numbers assigned by default, one number for each pair of triangles per side of the box.

Each submaterial can be any type of material with all the options and attributes available.

You create and assign multi/sub-object materials to the light fixtures so that there is one color inside and one outside, and to the walls for a material on the structure and another in the infill areas.

Apply Two Materials to a Single Light Fixture

Light fixtures are often a "fashion" color on the outside and a bright white reflective color inside for better efficiency. In Exercise 11.3, you learn to create and apply a multi/sub-object material of green and white enamel to your fixtures.

The light fixtures were created with the Lathe modifier on a 2D shape. The fixture was then given a thickness with the Shell modifier. The Shell modifier enables you to change the material ID numbers on the surfaces it has created.

Exercise 11.3   Multi/Sub-Object Material and Material ID Numbers

1. Open the file called Ch11_interior03.max on the CD-ROM or from the preceding exercise. From the File pull-down menu, choose Save As, point to an appropriate subdirectory on your hard drive, and use the plus sign button to save a new file with the name incremented to Ch11_interior04.max.

2. In the Camera01 viewport, select Light_fixture01 on the right side. From the Tools pull-down menu, choose Isolate Selection. Activate the Camera01 viewport and press P to switch to Perspective view. Zoom and Arc Rotate to view the fixture from below (see Figure 11.14).

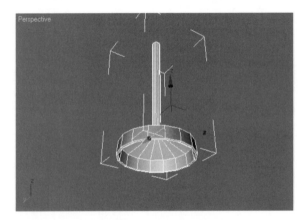

Figure 11.14   *Switch the Camera01 viewport to Perspective and zoom and Arc Rotate to view the fixture from below.*

3. In the Material Editor, activate the upper-right sample window. It is a standard material type. Click the Standard button below and right of the sample windows and double-click Multi/Sub-object in the Material/Map Browser list (see Figure 11.15). In the Replace Material dialog, click OK to accept Keep Old Material as Sub-Material. Name this main material Light_fixture. Drag and drop the sample window onto Light_fixture01 in the Perspective viewport. The multi/sub-object material is made up of 10 materials by default, but you can change that at any time.

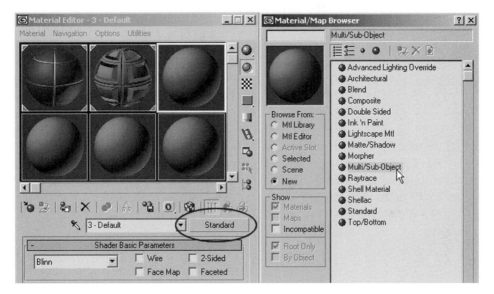

FIGURE 11.15   *In the Material Editor, click the Standard button and double-click Multi/Sub-Object in the Material/Map Browser list to change to a new material type. In the Material/Map Browser, the blue sphere icon represents material types, whereas a red or green parallelogram represents map types.*

4. You only need two materials for the fixture so, in the Multi/Sub-Object Basic Parameters rollout, click the Set Number button. In the Set Number of Materials dialog, enter 2 (see Figure 11.16). Click OK.

5. Using the Material/Map Navigator, highlight the first submaterial. Name it Enamel_Green. Click the Diffuse color swatch and, in the Color Selector, set it to dark green, red = 40, green = 75, and blue = 40. The entire fixture turns green in the Perspective viewport.

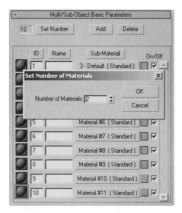

FIGURE 11.16   *In the Multi/Sub-Object Basic Parameters rollout, click the Set Number button and set to 2 submaterials.*

6. Highlight the second submaterial in the Material/Map Navigator and name it Enamel_white. Set the Diffuse color swatch to pure white and drag and drop the Diffuse swatch onto the Specular swatch and click Copy in the dialog to copy the color. Nothing changes in the Perspective viewport because all the faces of the fixture have material ID 1 assigned to them.

7. With the Light_fixture01 selected, go to the Modify panel, Parameters rollout for the Shell modifier. Check the Override Outer Mat ID option and set the Outer Mat ID field to 2. The inside of the fixture should turn white (see Figure 11.17).

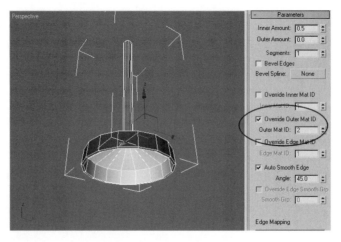

FIGURE 11.17   *By changing the material ID numbers of the fixture faces, you can assign two materials to the lamp. The material ID numbers correspond to the submaterials in the multi/sub-object material type.*

8. In the Blinn Basic Parameters rollout of each sub-material, set the Specular Level to 80 and the Glossiness to 35 to make the material quite shiny.

9. In the viewports, click the Exit Isolation Mode button to return the other objects in the scene and select Light_fixture02 in the Camera01 viewport. It is an instance clone of the other fixture. From the Material Editor, click the Assign Material to Selection button at the bottom of the sample windows. Activate the Camera01 viewport, if it is not still active, and click Quick Render on the main toolbar; you should see that both fixtures are green outside and white inside.

10. Close all windows and dialogs and save the file. It should already be called Ch11_interior04.max.

Set Material ID Numbers Manually

In Exercise 11.4, you learn to set the material ID numbers of faces manually. It's a simple process in which you first select by face, polygon, or element, and then change the material ID in the Modify panel. This way, you control explicitly where submaterials of a multi/sub-object material are assigned.

Here, you apply a multi/sub-object material to the walls of your command center and set a different material for the infill areas of the panels. If you remember, you created a named selection set for those polygons when you created the wall in Chapter 9. This aids in reselection if you should deselect them.

Exercise 11.4   Modifying Explicit Material ID Numbers

1. Open the file called Ch11_interior04.max on the CD-ROM or from the preceding exercise. From the File pull-down menu, choose Save As, point to an appropriate subdirectory on your hard drive, and use the plus sign button to save a new file with the name incremented to Ch11_interior05.max.

caution

In the Shell modifier, the terms "inner" and "outer" are relative terms and don't necessarily correspond to what you might perceive on the object. The viewport the original 2D shape was created in and the position of the first vertex of the original shape can affect the terminology. If it doesn't work as expected, try something else.

note

Instance clones only transfer modifications between objects in a two-way link. Transformations and material assignments are not part of the instancing.

tip

If you accidentally deselect the panels while in Polygon sub-object mode, you can choose panels from the Named Selection Sets field on the main toolbar to reselect them.

2. In the Camera01 viewport, select Wall01. In the
Modify panel, Stack view, highlight the Polygon
sub-object mode under Editable Poly. The wall lies
flat and you should still see the infill polygons
shaded in red to indicate that they are selected. In
the Modify panel, Polygon Properties rollout, enter
2 in the Set ID field and press Enter. This assigns
material ID 2 to the selected polygons only (see
Figure 11.18).

3. In Stack view, highlight Editable Poly to exit sub-
object mode, and then highlight Path Deform
Binding to return to the top of the stack.

4. Open the Material Editor and click the lower-left
sample window to activate it. Click the Standard
button and double-click Multi/Sub-Object in the
Material/ Map Browser list. Click OK in the
Replace Material dialog to Keep Old Material as
Sub-Material box. Name the material Wall_panel
and use the Set Number button to set the number
of submaterials to 2.

5. Using the Material/Map Navigator, highlight the
first submaterial. In the Material Editor, rename it
Framing and set the diffuse color to dark yellow:
red = 155, green = 145, and blue = 60—a nice mil-
itary color. In the Blinn Basic Parameters rollout,
enter 40 in the Specular Level field and 25 in the
Glossiness field.

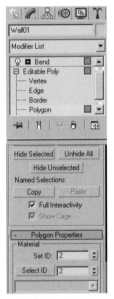

FIGURE 11.18

*In the Modify panel, Stack
view for Wall01, highlight
Polygon sub-object mode.
There should already be a
selection set of the infill panels.
In the Polygon Parameters rollout, enter 2 in the Set ID field
and press Enter.*

6. In the Material/Map Navigator, highlight the second submaterial. In the Material
Editor, rename it Panels. This will be the same green color as the enamel on the
outside of your light fixtures. In the Material Editor, click the Get Material button,
just below the sample windows on the far left. In the Material/Map Browser, select
the Mtl Editor radio button in the Browse From field. Clear the Root Only check
box in the Show area. In the Browser, drag and drop (1) Enamel_Green [Standard]
to the Standard button in Material Editor (see Figure 11.19). Make sure the Instance
radio button is selected in the dialog and click OK. Changing either material now
affects the other because of the two-way instance link. Check New in the Browse
From area of the Material/Map Browser and close it.

7. In the Material/Map Navigator, highlight the top level. Drag and drop the sample
window onto the Wall01 object in the Camera01 viewport, and you see the framing
shift color and the panels turn green.

FIGURE 11.19 *You can drag and drop materials from the Material/Map Browser into the Standard button in the Material Editor and make them either copy or instance clones.*

8. Right-click in the Camera01 viewport and click Quick Render on the main toolbar. The scene is starting to take shape with the multicolored walls (see Figure 11.20).

FIGURE 11.20 *The multicolored walls with the other materials are starting to make the scene more convincing.*

tip

Assigning material ID numbers can be done with a series of modifiers to keep a history of changes for easier editing in complex situations.

You can apply a Mesh Select modifier, select the faces you want, and then apply a Material modifier and set the ID, apply another Mesh Select/Material combination on top of that, and so on. Each combo could also have a UVW Map modifier at the top for different mapping of the sub-materials.

Experiment with it on a simple object that you create in a new scene and you will quickly see the advantages.

9. Close all windows and dialogs and save the file. It should already be called Ch11_interior05.max.

Working with Shaders to Control Specular Highlights

You have been increasing the specular level to control the brightness of specular highlights and the glossiness value to control the size of the specular highlights to have the materials appear harder and shinier.

However, the materials you have been making in this chapter have been enamel coatings or cast floor tiles, materials with a regular molecular makeup. The round specular highlights created by the default Blinn shader work fine for this type of material as well as for most plastics or paint.

You create two new materials in this section that will be more convincing with differently shaped specular highlights.

Metals tend to have elongated specular highlights because extruded or rolled metals develop a molecular grain similar to that of wood, scattering the light along the direction of the grain.

On the other end of the spectrum, fabrics and other soft porous materials tend to absorb and scatter the light widely from the surface.

You complete two exercises that focus on changing the shape of the specular highlights by using the Anisotropic shader for metal and the Oren-Nayar-Blinn shader for fabric.

Metallic Materials and Shaders

In Exercise 11.5, you create a stainless steel type of material for the command console in the scene. The material type will be a raytrace material, which has the reflections built in so that they are affected by the other material attributes, instead of being applied on top of the material as with standard and raytrace maps.

The material will use an Anisotropic shader to simulate scattered light from the surface being elongated by the grain of the metal.

Exercise 11.5   Metallic Material

1. Open the file called Ch11_interior05.max on the CD-ROM or from the preceding exercise. From the File pull-down menu, choose Save As, point to an appropriate subdirectory on your hard drive, and use the plus sign button to save a new file with the name incremented to Ch11_interior06.max.

2. In the Camera01 viewport, select Console01. In the Modify panel, Modifier List, choose UVW Map. In the Parameters rollout, Mapping area, select the Face radio button. This applies the maps to each face individually.

3. Open the Material Editor and choose the middle sample window in the bottom row. Click the Standard button to change material type and double-click Raytrace material type in the Material/Map Browser list. Rename this material Stainless.

> **caution**
>
> If you don't see Raytrace in the list, you might not have selected the New radio button in the Browse From area of the Material/Map Browser dialog as directed at the end of the preceding exercise.

4. The raytrace material has a different layout and controls than standard materials that you have been using so far. In the Raytrace Basic Parameters rollout, set the diffuse color to light gray, enter 190 in the Red, Green, and Blue fields.

5. In the Shading field, click Phong and choose Anisotropic from the list. This is a new shader in the raytrace material and opens new fields in the Specular Highlight area for more control over shape and angle (see Figure 11.21). You see the specular highlight on the sample window is elongated rather than round as in the other sample windows.

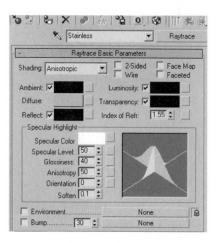

FIGURE 11.21   *By switching to the new Anisotropic shader for raytrace material, you open new controls for specular highlight shape.*

6. To increase the brightness, set the Specular Level to 100; for a smaller highlight, set the Glossiness to 60; and to change the angle of scattering, enter 45 in the Orientation field; then, press Enter.

7. Stainless steel usually has a scratched surface that you will simulate with a bump map. In the Material Editor, click the Maps rollout to expand it. In the Maps rollout, click None to the right of Bump and double-click Noise in the Material/Map Browser list.

tip

You can adjust the grayscale in the Color Selector by dragging in the Value ramp or entering a number in the numeric field.

8. The noise pattern should be much smaller and tighter with an elongated shape. In the Noise Parameters rollout, enter 0.6 in the High Noise Threshold field and 0.4 in the Low field to increase the contrast at the edges. In the Size field, enter 0.03 for a very small pattern. To elongate the pattern and to use the UVW Map coordinates, go to the Coordinates rollout and set Source to Explicit Map Channel and enter 4 in the V Tiling field (see Figure 11.22).

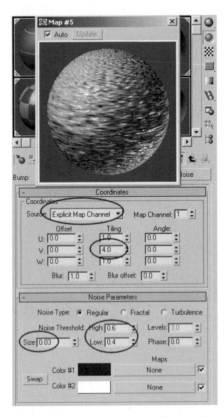

FIGURE 11.22   *A small, elongated noise map simulates scratches on the surface of stainless steel.*

9. The Bump Amount is set to the default 30, which is too extreme, but can make it easier to adjust in the sample window. Use the Material/Map Navigator to go up one level of the material and set the Bump Amount to 1. Click the Assign Material to Selection button below the sample windows to put the material onto Console01.

10. Raytrace reflections are built in to this material but must be adjusted to show. In the Raytrace Basic Parameters rollout, click the color swatch for Reflect and set the red, green, and blue to 60 each. Black is no reflection, white is pure reflection.

11. Select Duct01 and assign the Stainless material to it. Activate the Camera01 viewport and click the Quick Render button on the main toolbar. The scene should look even more convincing (see Figure 11.23).

> **note**
>
> As you are developing materials, keep in mind that they work hand in hand with lighting. You only have one omni light in your scene, so the materials might need adjustment when you place the final lighting in Chapter 12, "Photometric Lighting: Bounced Light Calculation."

FIGURE 11.23 *Assign the Stainless material to Console01 and Duct01 for an even more convincing look.*

12. Close all windows and dialogs. Save the file; it should already be called Ch11_interior06.max.

Fabric Material with Oren-Nayar-Blinn Shader

In Exercise 11.6, you learn to use another shader called Oren-Nayar-Blinn to create soft, broad specular highlight to represent porous materials such as cloth or vinyl on chair cushions. You make this new material a multi/sub-object and clone the Stainless for the chair stand.

Exercise 11.6   Soft Specular Highlights with the Oren-Nayar-Blinn Shader

1. Open the file called Ch11_interior06.max on the CD-ROM or from the preceding exercise. From the File pull-down menu, choose Save As, point to an appropriate subdirectory on your hard drive, and use the plus sign button to save a new file with the name incremented to Ch11_interior07.max.

2. In the Camera01 viewport, select Chair01. It is one object made of cushion and stand elements that will get materials. Open the Material Editor and activate the lower-right sample window. Change it from standard material type to multi/sub-object by clicking the Standard button and double-clicking Multi/Sub-Object in the Material/Map Browser. You can Keep Old Material as Sub-material and set the number of submaterials to 2. Rename the material to Chair and drag and drop the sample window onto the Chair01 in the Camera01 viewport.

3. Click and drag the Stainless sample window and drop it onto the first material button in the Multi/Sub-Object Basic Parameters rollout. Choose Instance in the dialog (see Figure 11.24).

FIGURE 11.24   *Click and drag the Stainless sample window and drop it on the first material button for Chair. Clone it as an instance.*

4. Using the Material/Map Navigator, highlight the second material in the multi/sub-object. Rename it Cushion. In the Shader Basic Parameters rollout, click Blinn and choose Oren-Nayar-Blinn in the list. Click the Diffuse color swatch and, in the Color Selector, set it to maroon: red = 115, green = 15, and blue = 15.

5. In the Oren-Nayar-Blinn Basic Parameters rollout, Specular Highlights area, enter 25 in Specular Level and leave the default 10 in Glossiness and press Enter. The result is a broad, soft specular highlight that darkens between the highlight and the edge of the sample sphere (see Figure 11.25).

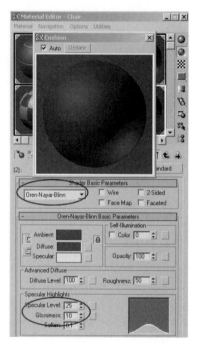

FIGURE 11.25 *Using the Oren-Nayar-Blinn shader with fairly low Specular Level and Glossiness settings results in a soft, porous look to the specular highlights.*

6. With Chair01 selected, go to Modify panel, Stack view, and expand Editable Mesh. Highlight Element sub-object mode and the two cushions should shade red in the Camera01 viewport. If not, select them in the Camera01 viewport. In the Surface Properties rollout, Material area, enter 2 in the Set ID field and press Enter. In Stack view, exit sub-object mode. Render the Camera01 viewport and you should see dull highlights on the chair cushions as you would see with soft cloth or vinyl (see Figure 11.26).

note

My interpretation of material settings might not convince you in the least. Materials and lighting are a subjective topic, so feel free to experiment with settings to find your own style using these lessons as guides.

FIGURE 11.26   *The new material on the cushions has a softer look with broad, dull specular highlights.*

7. Close all dialogs and windows. Save the file. It should already be called Ch11_interior07.max.

Other Productive Material Attributes

In this section, you learn a few useful material attributes that enable you to apply decal images to surfaces, create self-illuminating effects, apply animated maps, and finally, a new feature that enables you to select objects by their materials.

Decal materials are similar to the stick-on decals for model planes or cars or like the lick-and-stick tattoos you see around. A very important component is the alpha channel transparency information that allows the background material to show behind the decal.

Light bulbs and computer screens give off light and are therefore not affected by most lights or shadows in the scene. You learn to simulate this effect. However, the material does not actually add light to the scene in this example.

You also learn to use animated or sequential images in materials that will play back in your scene. For example, you apply a series of images to the large screen in the scene that will advance frame by frame as you move the Time slider or render an animation.

A new feature that has been on the wish list for a while is the ability to select objects by their material assignment. Although it sounds like a simple enough tool, it can prove very productive on most projects.

Decal Materials

You want to place a logo on the toolbox in the scene. The logo is white text on a black background. Normally, if this were used as a diffuse map, the result would be a black material with white text. However, the image is a PNG file with alpha channel information and the black will be treated as transparency, allowing the underlying color of the material to show through every place but where it is white. You will then learn to disable the tiling of the map and resize and position it on the toolbox.

Exercise 11.7   Decal Maps and Alpha Channel

1. Open the file called Ch11_interior07.max on the CD-ROM or from the preceding exercise. From the File pull-down menu, choose Save As, point to an appropriate subdirectory on your hard drive, and use the plus sign button to save a new file with the name incremented to Ch11_interior08.max.

2. In the Camera01 viewport, select Storage_Box01 to the left of the console. Click Tools on the main toolbar and choose Isolate Selection. Press P to switch Camera01 to a Perspective viewport and zoom in on the box. Use Arc Rotate to view the box from the top left (see Figure 11.27).

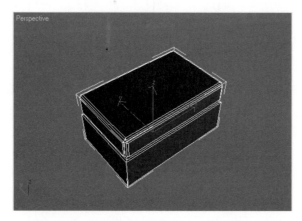

Figure 11.27   *Select and isolate the Storage_Box01, switch from Camera01 to Perspective, and Arc Rotate to view from upper left.*

3. In the Material Editor, place the cursor between sample windows and click and drag left when you see the hand cursor to reveal unused sample windows. There are 24 sample windows, but you are set to look at only 6 at a time. Highlight the next available sample window.

4. Click the Diffuse color swatch and set it to a bright orange-red: red = 210, green = 45, and blue = 30. Click the gray square map shortcut to the right of the Diffuse color swatch and double-click Bitmap in the Material/Map Browser list. In the Select Bitmap Image File dialog, set the File As Type field to All Formats and locate Toolbox_Text.png on the CD-ROM and double-click it in the list to load it (see Figure 11.28). This black image with white text would normally override the Diffuse color setting and turn the sample window black, except for the white text.

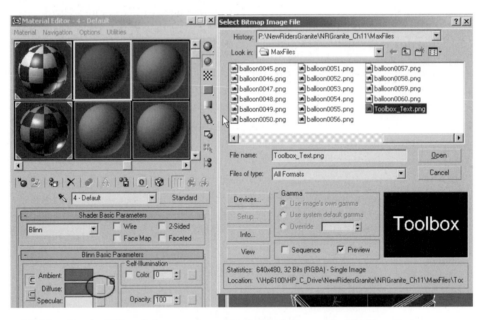

FIGURE 11.28   *Use the Diffuse Color map shortcut to load a bitmap called Toolbox_Text.png into the Diffuse Color map slot.*

5. In the Bitmap Parameters rollout, Alpha Source area, you see the Image Alpha radio button is selected. Because this PNG image was created with alpha channel, it is automatically applied and the black of the image turns transparent, allowing the base diffuse color to show through. Click the View Image button in the Cropping/Placement area to see the bitmap (see Figure 11.29). Close the Specify Cropping/Placement dialog.

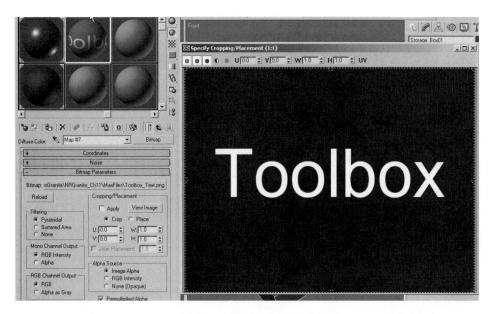

FIGURE 11.29   *Click the View Image dialog in the Cropping/Placement area. The image is transparent where the Alpha channel is black and opaque where the Alpha channel is white.*

6. In the Material Editor, click the Show Map in Viewport button just below the sample windows. Drag and drop the sample window onto the box in the Perspective viewport. In the Modify panel, Modifier List, choose UVW Map. In the Parameters rollout, Alignment area, select the Y-axis radio button. Click the Fit button to resize the gizmo. The text shows on the front of the toolbox (see Figure 11.30).

7. The text is too large and should be positioned on the front of the lid. In the Material Editor, Coordinates rollout, set the U and V Tiling to 2 and the V Offset to 0.3. The makes the text smaller and moves it up, but the map is tiling and repeating over the entire box. Clear the U and V Tile check boxes and you are left with only the original image as a decal on your base material. Render the Perspective viewport to see the resulting material on the box (see Figure 11.31). Go to the top level of the material and rename it Toolbox. Close all dialogs and windows.

The image file was created in 3ds max 6. It was 2D text converted to an editable mesh with a pure white, fully self-illuminated material applied. The image was rendered and saved as a PNG file type with the Alpha channel option checked.

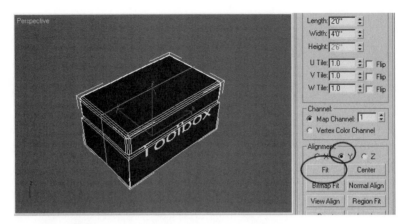

FIGURE 11.30 *Apply a UVW Map modifier to the box and use Y-axis alignment. Click Fit to resize the gizmo.*

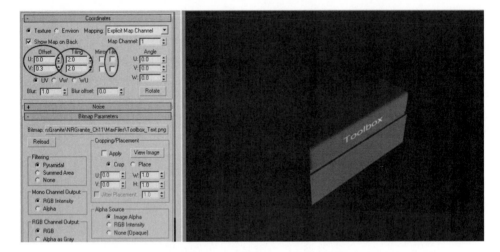

FIGURE 11.31 *Set Tiling to 2 in each axis to make the image smaller, enter 0.3 in the V Offset to move it up, and clear the Tile check boxes to keep it from repeating over the entire box.*

8. Click the Exit Isolation Mode button to return the other objects in the scene and render the Camera01 viewport to see the new toolbox in the scene.

9. Save the file; it should already be called Ch11_interior08.max.

Self-Illuminated Materials

Again, self-illuminated materials do not actually cast light in the scene by default, but have their ambient color areas overridden so that they appear to glow from within and are not affected by light and shadow in the scene.

In Exercise 11.8, you create a multi/sub-object material for the lights on the console by copying the Chair material and changing the Self-Illumination levels of one of the submaterials.

Exercise 11.8   Creating Self-Illuminated Material

1. Open the file called Ch11_interior08.max on the CD-ROM or from the preceding exercise. From the File pull-down menu, choose Save As, point to an appropriate subdirectory on your hard drive, and use the plus sign button to save a new file with the name incremented to Ch11_interior09.max.

2. In the Camera01 viewport, select FlashingLight01. Isolate the selection, switch to Perspective viewport, and zoom in on the object.

3. Open the Material Editor, right-click on the active sample window and choose 5x3 Sample Windows in the menu. This enables you to see 15 smaller sample windows of the 24. Drag and drop the Chair material sample window onto the sample window at the upper right and rename the new copy Flashing Light (see Figure 11.32). If you get the Instance (Copy) Material dialog, choose Copy so the new material can be changed without affecting the original.

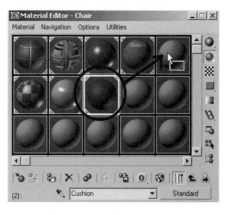

Figure 11.32 *Drag and drop the Chair material to the upper-right sample window. Rename it Flashing Light.*

4. In the Flashing Light sample window, use the Material/Map Navigator to high-light Cushion and rename it Light Bulb. Change the diffuse color to bright red and set the shader type to Blinn from Oren-Nayar-Blinn. The sample window shows lit and shaded areas.

5. In the Blinn Basic Parameters rollout, Self-Illumination area, check the Color check box. Drag the Diffuse color swatch to the Self-Illumination color swatch and choose Copy in the dialog (see Figure 11.33). The sample window appears to glow.

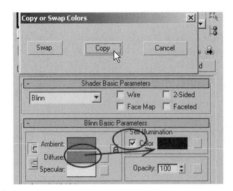

FIGURE 11.33   *Switching Self-Illumination to the Color option and dragging the Diffuse color swatch to the Self-Illumination color swatch as a copy makes the material appear to glow red.*

6. In the Material/Map Navigator, go to the top level of the material in the list. Drag and drop the Sample Windows onto the light object in the scene. The appropriate material ID numbers have already been assigned to the elements. Exit isolation mode.

7. Drag and drop the sample window onto the remaining two flashing light objects on the console and render the Camera01 viewport to see the illusion of glowing from within on the bulbs.

8. Close all windows and dialogs and save the file. It should already be called Ch11_interior09.max.

Animated Maps in Materials

In Exercise 11.9, you learn to apply a series of still images of a balloon flying across a landscape to the screen of the large monitor above the console. Again, it is a multi/sub-object material. The screen itself is animated and self-illuminated for a convincing look of a plasma screen.

Exercise 11.9   Animated and Self-Illuminated Material

1. Open the file called Ch11_interior09.max on the CD-ROM or from the preceding exercise. From the File pull-down menu, choose Save As, point to an appropriate subdirectory on your hard drive, and use the plus sign button to save a new file with the name incremented to Ch11_interior10.max.

2. In the Camera01 viewport, select Plasma_display01 and isolate the object. Open the Material Editor. Drag the Flashing Light sample window down to the slot just below it and rename the new material Plasma Display.

3. Drag and drop the sample window onto the object in the Camera01 viewport. In the Modify panel, Stack view, go to Polygon sub-object level and pick on the screen surface to select it if it is not already highlighted red. In the Polygon Properties rollout, enter 2 in the Set ID field. Exit sub-object mode in Stack view. The screen in the viewport now appears red and the frame is silver.

4. In the Material Editor, use the Material/Map Navigator to go to the Light Bulb material level and rename it Plasma screen. Click the gray square to the right of Self-Illumination color swatch in the Blinn Basic Parameters rollout, and double-click Bitmap in the Material/Map Browser list. In the Select Bitmap Image File dialog, go to the CD-ROM and highlight balloon0010.png in the list. Check the Sequence check box at the bottom left of the dialog (see Figure 11.34).

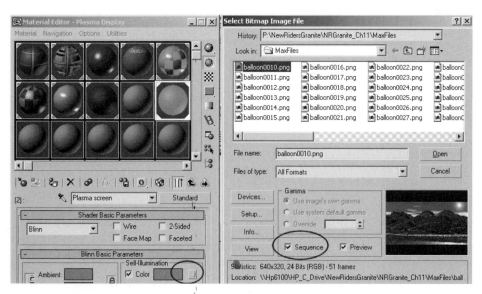

FIGURE 11.34 *Click the map shortcut button to the right of the Self-Illumination color swatch. Highlight balloon0010.png on the CD-ROM and check the Sequence option.*

5. Click the Open button in the dialog, and then click OK in the Image File List Control dialog to load all the images in sequence and generate a new file called balloon0037.ifl (the number might be different) and place it in the Self-Illumination slot. This file is an ASCII file that can be edited with any text editor and just lists all the images in the sequence in order. When the scene is rendered, it will use one image per frame of animation. This file is only 50 images long, so repeat twice if you render all 100 current frames.

The uppercase M in the shortcut button indicates a map that is active. A lowercase m indicates a map that is inactive.

6. In the Material/Map Navigator, come up one level to Plasma screen. Drag the shortcut button with the M from the Self-Illumination to the Diffuse Color shortcut button (see Figure 11.35), choose Instance, and click OK.

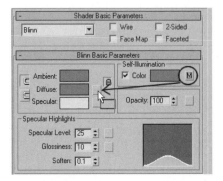

FIGURE 11.35   *Drag and drop the shortcut button with the map from Self-Illumination as an instance onto the shortcut for Diffuse Color.*

7. Exit isolation mode. In the Camera01 viewport, use Quick Render to render frame 0, then frame 25, and then frame 45 by setting the Time slider to the appropriate frame and clicking the Quick Render button for each of the three frames. You see the balloon progress across the screen for each frame (see Figure 11.36).

8. Close all windows and dialogs. Save the file; it should already be called Ch11_interior10.max.

Notice that the Color option is checked to the left of the Self-Illumination color swatch. This causes the actual colors of the map to tint the Self-Illumination, as well as using the luminance values of pixels for Self-Illumination intensity. If you clear the Color check box, the effect is more subdued and less convincing.

FIGURE 11.36 *Rendering a few different frames of your scene shows that the balloon is animated across the image on the big screen.*

Selecting Objects by Material

As mentioned, as far as features go, the ability to select objects by the material assigned to them might not seem all that exciting, but it helps you get your work done more quickly, and that's the main point of this whole book.

In Exercise 11.10, you apply the Stainless material to the other objects in the scene that have no materials. You then learn to use the Select by Material option in Material Editor to find them again.

Exercise 11.10   Select by Material

1. Open the file called Ch11_interior10.max on the CD-ROM or from the preceding exercise. From the File pull-down menu, choose Save As, point to an appropriate subdirectory on your hard drive, and use the plus sign button to save a new file with the name incremented to Ch11_interior11.max.

2. In the Top viewport, select the objects that have not yet been assigned materials: five gauges, four handles, and a frame on the console. You can use Select by Name to select Gauge01-Gauge05, Handle01-Handle04, and Instrument_panel01.

3. Open the Material Editor and highlight the Stainless sample window. Click the Assign Material to Selection button at the bottom of the sample windows. In the Top viewport, click in empty space to deselect all objects.

4. At the top of the Material Editor, click the Utilities pull-down menu and choose Select Object by Material (see Figure 11.37). All the objects that have the Stainless material assigned are selected when you click Select in the dialog.

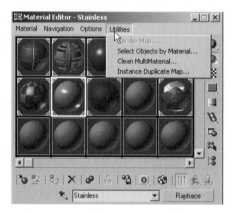

FIGURE 11.37 *Using the new Select by Material utility in the Material Editor enables you to select all objects that have the currently active material assigned.*

5. Close all windows and dialogs and save the file. It should already be called Ch11_interior11.max.

Summary

Materials are one of the most important aspects of 3ds max 6 for you to master to quickly and efficiently create scenes that you can sell to your client or represent as your artwork.

Some of the fundamental material techniques covered in this chapter included the following:

■ **Specific mapping coordinates**—You learned to apply map patterns in a material to match real-world sizes (for example, bricks are 8 inches by 3 inches to simulate standard brick sizes).

■ **Bump maps**—You learned new options to use bump maps to simulate geometry more effectively, thus reducing the scene overhead.

- **More than one material per object**—You learned to apply several materials to a single object with the multi/sub-object material type and material ID numbers.

- **Metallic materials**—You learned some of the fundamentals of simulating the hard look of metal through materials.

- **Cloth materials**—Making materials appear soft like cloth required you to learn other material shader options.

- **Decal materials**—Applying decals that allow the basic material to show as a background were the topic of Exercise 11.7.

- **Self-illumination**—Learning to create materials that appear to glow from within is a useful lesson you learned, both with a light and a plasma display screen.

- **Animated materials**—You learned to apply animated maps to create materials that change over time.

- **Select by Material**—You learned a feature in 3ds max 6 that enables you to select objects based on the assigned materials.

CHAPTER 12

Photometric Lighting: Bounced Light Calculation

In This Chapter

In Chapter 6, "Fundamental Outdoor Lighting with Standard Lights," you learned about lighting an outdoor scene with standard light types, specifically sunlight and omni lights. The omni lights were needed because standard lights rendered with the default Scanline renderer do not calculate the effect of light bouncing off surfaces. Therefore, the omni lights acted as fill lights to keep the shaded areas in the scene from being completely black. The advantage of using standard lights in any scene is that it can render quickly.

Figure 12.1 shows the interior of the command center with two standard omni lights in the overhead fixtures. The shadows have been turned on, and the scene was rendered with the default Scanline renderer. By default, the standard lights do not attenuate or diminish in strength over distance, so the scene is quite bright.

The brightness of the light falling on any surface is a function of the light strength and the angle of incidence of the light to the surface. Surfaces that are parallel to the direction of the light beam are black, as are the areas in the shadows cast by the two lights.

Figure 12.1   *Interior of command center rendered with the Scanline renderer. Two standard omni lights are in the overhead fixtures with Shadow Casting turned on.*

In this chapter, you learn to use photometric lights in conjunction with the
Radiosity renderer.

Photometric lights are based on real physics and conform to the laws that govern the
behavior of real lights, including attenuation. Attenuation is based on the inverse
square law, which states that light strength diminishes by the formula one over the
distance from the source squared. For example, if a light measures 100 lux at the
source, at 4 feet away, it is 1 over 4 squared or 1/16th the strength.

In this chapter, you learn some of the differences in light quality from the four basic
photometric lights—Point, Linear, Area, and Daylight—and learn about some of the
options you have to control light distribution from the light sources to simulate real-
world lighting.

The prime advantage of photometric light and the Radiosity renderer is the way they
function with materials to calculate light bounced off the surfaces of objects back

into the space. This can aid tremendously in convincing your clients that you are a master of 3ds max 6.

Two factors weight heavily on the quality and cost-effectiveness of radiosity rendering: meshing and materials.

All lighting information is stored in the vertices and faces of your model, and if the integrity of the model is not sufficient—that is, if adjacent objects do not have vertices that are close to one another—the lighting must be interpolated over large areas and the quality will suffer. A process called *meshing* is necessary for radiosity rendering; meshing creates copies of your objects with vertices spaced on a distance you specify. Generally, the closer the vertices, the better the quality; but the more vertices, the slower the calculation and rendering performance.

You also learn in this chapter to control meshing at both global and local levels, and you learn modeling techniques that will enable you to use less meshing for optimized performance.

The quality of radiosity rendering also is affected by Exposure Control settings. The process is much like photography: If the film receives too much light, it is overexposed; and if it receives too little, it is too dark. You must adjust Exposure Control in 3ds max 6 photometric lighting much as you would have to change the f-stop on a camera to control the amount of light that reaches the film.

Some of the topics covered in this chapter include the following:

- **Photometric lighting**—Photometric lighting uses lights based on the laws of physics to calculate direct and bounced light within the Radiosity renderer.

- **Meshing for photometrics**—You learn about meshing, which enables you to add vertices and faces to a radiosity mesh that is a clone of your scene for the storage and interpolation of the radiosity solution. Smaller meshes give better results, but at a cost of lost efficiency.

- **Modeling for photometrics**—The relative location of vertices on adjacent objects can significantly affect the efficiency of the radiosity solution. You learn some modeling techniques that will increase productivity.

- **Specular highlight issues**—You learn that radiosity solutions do not create bold specular highlights because of the nature of bounced light. Some notes will give you options to correct that.

Key Terms

- **Photometric**—Physically correct light sources that interact with surfaces in radiosity rendering.

- **IES file**—A mathematical pattern of light from a source. IES stands for Illuminating Engineering Society, the group that defines lighting standards.

- **Meshing**—Adding vertices and faces to your model to specifically store photometric lighting information.

- **Scanline renderer**—Scanline rendering uses standard lights.

- **Radiosity renderer**—Radiosity rendering uses photometric lights.

Photometric Lights

In this section, you learn about the fundamental types of photometric lights in 3ds max 6:

- **Point**—Point lights cast light in all directions by default, but can have their distribution pattern changed to make them act as spotlights.

- **Linear**—Linear lights are similar to a fluorescent light fixture with multiple bulbs. The light is focus downward and to the sides of the fixture.

- **Area**—Area lights are similar to square or rectangular fixtures with multiple bulbs. The reflectors and diffusers focus the light downward and to the sides and soften the light.

Point Lights and Radiosity Renderer

In Exercise 12.1, you learn to set up a scene that is lit by two photometric point lights inside the hanging fixtures in the command center scene.

You learn about changing the renderer from the default Scanline renderer to the Radiosity renderer required to calculate the bounced light from photometric lights and to use fundamental Exposure Control. You learn to adjust the brightness of the lights and to recalculate the radiosity solution so that it can be rerendered correctly.

Exercise 12.1   Using Point Lights in a Scene

1. Open the file called Ch12_Photometric01.max on the CD-ROM. From the File pull-down menu, choose Save As, point to an appropriate subdirectory on your hard drive, and use the plus sign button to save a new file with the name incremented to Ch12_Photometric02.max.

2. Activate and render the Camera01 viewport with Quick Render on the main tool-bar. The image looks similar to Figure 12.2. If anything, the scene is much darker than the standard omni lights and Scanline renderer shown in the introduction to this chapter. The only difference is that omni lights, which cast light in all direc-tions, are replace by point lights, which also cast light in all directions. The scene is darker, however, because the photometric point lights obey the laws of physics and attenuate, or lose strength, based on the inverse square law. However, photo-metric lights must use the Radiosity renderer to be effective.

Figure 12.2 *Interior of command center rendered with the Scanline renderer. Two photo-metric point lights are in the overhead fixtures with Shadow Casting turned on.*

3. In the Rendering pull-down menu, choose Advanced Lighting, Radiosity from the menus (see Figure 12.3). You see a Radiosity dialog, which asks whether you want to use Camera Exposure Control, always answer Yes.

4. If you render the Camera01 viewport, you see an increase in light in your scene, but it still is not very convincing (see Figure 12.4). Radiosity rendering requires that you calculate the effect of bounced light before rendering.

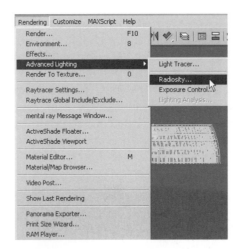

FIGURE 12.3   *You can use the Radiosity renderer by going to the Rendering pull-down, Advanced Lighting, Radiosity.*

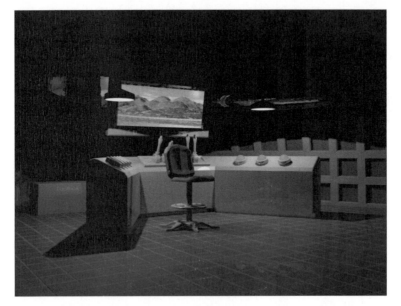

FIGURE 12.4   *Activating the Radiosity renderer and enabling Camera Exposure Control results in a better image, but no bounced light has been calculated.*

5. In the Render Scene dialog, Advanced Lighting tab, Radiosity Processing Parameters, enter 35 in the Initial Quality field, and then click the Start button to start the processing (see Figure 12.5). The initial quality refers to the percentage of calculations of a full radiosity solution will be done before you can see some results of bounced light. Reducing the number results in faster rendering, with lower quality, but a lower quality is fine for test rendering.

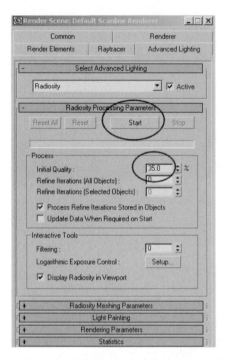

FIGURE 12.5   *Enter 35 in the Initial Quality field for faster calculations with lower quality and click the Start button to start the process.*

6. Render the Camera01 viewport and you will see the effects of bounced light on the walls and in the detail that is starting to show in the ceiling. The extra brightness of the light on the console and floor results from the light bouncing on the bright white interior of the light fixtures. Remember, point lights cast light in all directions. However, you will also see artifacts, especially on the chair cushions and in the corner of the wall behind the console (see Figure 12.6).

FIGURE 12.6   *After you calculate the radiosity process and render the image, you can see that the bounced light fills in the shadows and even begins to light up the ceiling.*

7. On the main toolbar, use Select by Name to select the FPoint01 photometric point light. In the Modify panel, Intensity/Color/Distribution rollout, Intensity area, enter 3000 in the numeric field. This is in candelas, a standard U.S. measurement of light intensity. Both point lights in the scene are instance clones, so changing one affects the other. In the Render Scene, Advanced Lighting dialog, you see a notice under the Reset All button that the current radiosity solution is invalid (see Figure 12.7). You have changed the intensity of the lights, but the information stored in the mesh vertices contains the old settings. Click the Reset All button and answer Yes to the warning dialog to remove the old information, and then click Start to process the new light intensities and store that information. Render the Camera01 viewport to see that the scene is much brighter all over, but the artifacts remain.

8. Close all windows and dialogs. Save the file; it should already be called Ch12_Photometric02.max.

note

The file will take a little longer to save and is a larger file. It must save the new mesh that is created to store radiosity calculations in the vertices and faces.

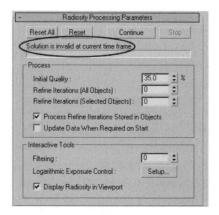

FIGURE 12.7 *Changing the light intensity in the scene has made the current radiosity calculations stored in the mesh vertices invalid. You must reset and start the calculations to see the new results in the next rendering.*

Light Distribution Patterns

As mentioned, point lights cast light in all directions by default. In Exercise 12.2, you change the distribution pattern to spotlight, and then to that specified by an IES file.

Each lighting manufacturer scientifically determines the light distribution patterns of their bulbs and fixtures and makes files available that can be loaded into the photometric lights in 3ds max 6 to more accurately simulate the specific fixture.

These lighting distribution patterns are especially important to photographers and cinematographers for proper lighting. This is, of course, important to architects and lighting designers, but it is also useful for those of you not particularly interested in the physics of it all but who want a more convincing look to your renderings.

Exercise 12.2   Changing Light Distribution Patterns

1. Open the file called Ch12_Photometric02.max on the CD-ROM or from the preceding exercise. From the File pull-down menu, choose Save As, point to an appropriate subdirectory on your hard drive, and use the plus sign button to save a new file with the name incremented to Ch12_Photometric03.max.

2. The default point lights in the fixtures are radiating light in all directions and the light is bouncing from the bright white insides of the fixtures to flood the floor with light. Sometimes, however, you want more control over the direction and coverage of the light source. In 3ds max 6, you can change the distribution pattern

of point lights to be spotlights, light cast in a cone pattern. Select FPoint01 in the scene. In the Modify panel, Intensity/Color/Distribution rollout, click the Distribution: Isotropic field and choose Spotlight from the list (see Figure 12.8). Notice the shape of the light icon changed in the viewport, and you have two blue cones showing the coverage of the selected light.

FIGURE 12.8
With FPoint01 selected in the scene, you can change the distribution pattern in the Modify panel, Intensity/Color/ Distribution rollout, to spotlight.

3. Press 9 to call the Render Scene dialog and, in the Radiosity Processing Parameters rollout, click the Reset All button, check the option in the warning box not to show the warning again, if you are continuing from Exercise 12.1, and then click the Start button to process and store the new solution in the mesh. When the solution is finished, activate the Camera01 viewport, and click Quick Render on the main toolbar. The amount of light in the scene is greatly diminished, even though the lights are still the same intensity. Because the light is focused in two narrow cones onto the console and floor, much less light is bounced in the scene.

FIGURE 12.9
The hotspot/beam cone is full-intensity light. The light strength diminishes laterally in a linear fashion from Hotspot/ Beam to falloff/field, creating a hard or soft edge to the light. Outside the falloff cone, there is no light.

4. In the Spotlight Parameters rollout, enter 100 in the Hotspot/Beam field and 130 in the Falloff/Field field (see Figure 12.9). In the Render Scene dialog, click Reset All, and then click Start. Use Quick Render to see the changes. Notice the two cones are larger on the selected light in the viewport. The hotspot is the cone of full-intensity light, whereas the falloff is the area in which the light dies out to nothing. The closer the cones are in diameter to each other, the harder the edge of the light in the scene. There is now considerably more light in the scene, both in terms of direct light within the larger cones and the resulting extra bounced light.

5. Another option to the distribution pattern of lights is the use of web distribution files. These are mathematical calculations from lighting manufacturers that simulate the patterns from specific lighting fixtures. In the Intensity/Color/Distribution rollout, click Distribution: Spotlight window and choose Web in the list. In the

Web Parameters rollout, click the Web File: None button (see Figure 12.10). In the Open a Photometric Web dialog, go to the CD-ROM and double-click the file ERCO_81628.023+T4_75W-120V_MINI_CAN.ies. Notice the shape of the light in the fixture in the shaded viewport. In the Render Scene dialog, reset and restart the radiosity solution, and then render the Camera01 viewport. Try the same with ERCO_22138.023+CFM_42W_GX24Q.ies for a different distribution pattern. The IES files also affect the intensity and color of the light to match the real fixture.

FIGURE 12.10
After setting Distribution to Web, in the Web Parameters rollout, click the Web File: None button to open a manufacturer's IES file.

6. In the Intensity/Color/Distribution rollout, click the Distribution: Web window and choose Isotropic and, in the Intensity field, enter 3000 to return the lights to their original state.

7. Close all windows and dialogs and save the file. It should already be called Ch12_Photometric03.max.

note

These two IES files are from the German lighting company ERCO and are available for download at http://www.erco.com in the Download area.

The entire 3D light fixture can be downloaded into the scene from ERCO and other manufacturers, too.

Linear Lights and Area Lights

Light emanating from a point source, whether it is in all directions or focused, is not going to cover all of your lighting needs. Two of the more commonly found light sources are either long narrow fixtures or rectangular fixtures that have one or more bulbs in them.

Linear light types in 3ds max 6 are intended to simulate the light that would be cast by a fluorescent fixture with one or two bulbs. They are usually 3 to 4 feet long. The light from the bulbs is focused by the reflector downward and out to the sides.

Area lights, on the other hand, tend to be rectangular fixtures with two to four bulbs and a plastic diffusing cover on the fixture. These fixtures cast light downward and out in a more diffuse manner with a soft-edged effect on the scene.

caution

Downloading and using 3D objects might not be as cost-effective as it first seems. Many objects from manufacturers—lights, furniture, mechanical equipment, and so on—are translated directly from engineering files to 3ds max 6 format and can be terribly inefficient.

In Exercise 12.3, you change the light types in the fixtures to linear and area lights to see the effect the changes have on the scene. Both types also can have appropriate IES files assigned to simulate real fixtures.

Exercise 12.3   Changing from Point to Linear and Area Light Types

1. Open the file called Ch12_Photometric03.max on the CD-ROM or from the preceding exercise. From the File pull-down menu, choose Save As, point to an appropriate subdirectory on your hard drive, and use the plus sign button to save a new file with the name incremented to Ch12_Photometric04.max.

2. Press 9 and, in the Render Scene dialog, Advanced Lighting tab, click the Reset button if you are continuing from Exercise 12.2, and then click Start to recalculate the radiosity with the original point lights. Use Quick Render to render the Camera01 viewport. This will be a baseline image for seeing the changes made next.

3. Select FPoint01 in the Camera01 viewport. In the Modify panel, General Parameters rollout, Light Type area, click Point and choose Linear in the list (see Figure 12.11). The icon in the viewports changes to a symbol with a line through it to indicate the direction and length of the light source.

FIGURE 12.11
In the Modify panel, General Parameters rollout, click Point and choose Linear in the list. The icon in the viewport changes to indicate the length and direction of the light source.

4. In the Render Scene dialog, Advanced Lighting tab, click Reset, and then click Start. Render the Camera01 viewport. The linear light source casts much different lighting and shadows. Because it does not fit the shape of the light fixture, you also see some new green areas of bounced light that come from the outside of the fixture. The light projects downward and outward and casts little light up into the white areas of the fixture.

5. In the Modify panel, General Parameters rollout, Light Type area, switch from the Linear to Area light type. In Render Scene, Advanced Lighting tab, click Reset, and then click Start and render Camera01 viewport when the calculations are finished. Area lights are projected from a default 1 meter–by–1 meter square source and, like the linear lights, very little light projects upward.

caution

The default length for a linear light is 3'3 2/8" (or 1 meter). Avoid the temptation to change that number by more than 18" or so either way; otherwise, you might introduce distortion. If you need a string of lights, use multiple lights placed end to end.

6. Shadows are important when calculating lights, and real area light fixtures tend to have softer shadows. In the General Parameters rollout, Shadows area, click Shadow Map and choose the Adv. Ray Traced shadow type in the list. You can render the Camera01 viewport without resetting and starting the radiosity to see the changes. This shadow type is much softer, but takes about five times longer to render for this scene (see Figure 12.12).

tip

To better compare the new lighting with the previously rendered image, you could use RAM Player from the Rendering pull-down menu. Load the point light rendering in Channel A and, when you render it, place the linear light in Channel B.

Figure 12.12   *A soft convincing light and shadow effect result from area lights combined with advanced raytraced shadows.*

7. In the Modify panel, General Parameters rollout, set the shadow type back to Shadow Map and the light type back to Point.

8. Close all windows and dialogs. Save the file; it should already be called Ch12_Photometric04.max.

caution

When trying combinations of light types and shadow types, avoid using area lights with area shadows. The rendering times are not productive for the quality of output.

Meshing Parameters for a Better Radiosity Solution

Radiosity calculations are stored in the vertices and faces of a special mesh object that is basically an exact replica of your mesh so far during the radiosity rendering in this book.

However, that is seldom enough to get a good solution for the calculations. For example, the console sits on a floor that was created from a Box primitive. The only vertices of the floor are the eight in the far corners. The vertices are nowhere near the vertices at the bottom corners of the console, so no good lighting information can be calculated between the two objects.

Meshing parameters enable you to adjust the radiosity mesh density by specifying a maximum distance between vertices of objects.

There are essentially two ways to set the meshing parameters: globally and locally. In this section, you adjust the parameters using both methods and compare quality and processing time for the rendered images.

Global Meshing Parameters

With global meshing parameters, you can set a mesh size for every object in the scene. This is primarily useful when all objects are roughly the same size and contribute equally to the radiosity solution.

If you have a room with four walls, a floor, and ceiling, for example, global meshing might be perfect. However, if you add a few desks and chairs, the overhead of meshing these smaller objects at a small enough size to make a difference in the scene, your productivity might drop greatly.

In Exercise 12.4, you use global meshing parameters settings to refine the radiosity solution for your scene. You also learn about refine iterations and filtering used in conjunction with a higher initial quality (you set it low for speed in Exercise 12.1 to further increase the quality of the rendering).

Exercise 12.4   Global Meshing Parameter Settings

1. Open the file called Ch12_Photometric04.max on the CD-ROM or from the preceding exercise. From the File pull-down menu, choose Save As, point to an appropriate subdirectory on your hard drive, and use the plus sign button to save a new file with the name incremented to Ch12_Photometric05.max. This scene should have the Point lights with Shadow Map shadows.

2. Press 9 and, in the Render Scene dialog, Advanced Lighting tab, click the Reset All button if you are continuing from Exercise 12.3, and then click the Start button. Use Quick Render from the Main toolbar to render the Camera01 viewport. At the bottom center of the status line, note the rendering time. The number can also be found in the File pull-down menu, Summary Info dialog. In the Rendering pull-down, choose RAM Player. In the RAM Player dialog, click Open Last Rendered Image in Channel A, and click OK to accept the default settings. Minimize the RAM Player, but do not close it. On my test machine, the render time was 54 seconds, and the radiosity calculations were 51 seconds, as seen in the Statistics rollout of the Advanced Lighting tab.

3. In the Render Scene dialog, Advanced Lighting tab, expand the Radiosity Meshing Parameters rollout, and check Enabled in the Global Subdivision Settings area. By default, it is set to 3'3 2/8" (see Figure 12.13). Reset All and click Start, and then render the Camera01 viewport. Maximize the RAM Player and load this image in Channel B. It is much brighter overall and has some extremely bright faces scattered throughout the scene. This is because there are more vertices to store lighting information.

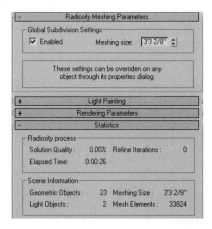

FIGURE 12.13   *In the Render Scene dialog, Advanced Lighting tab, check Enabled in the Radiosity Meshing Parameters rollout.*

4. Right-click the Camera01 viewport label and choose Edged Faces in the menu. This shows the new meshing in the viewport. No vertex is farther than 1 meter from any other (see Figure 12.14). The render time is 1:01, and calculations took 0.50 seconds.

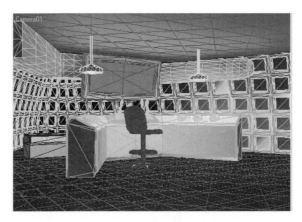

FIGURE 12.14   *Turning on Edged Faces in the shaded viewport shows the new meshing object.*

5. In the Radiosity Meshing Parameters rollout, enter 1 in the Global Subdivision Settings Meshing Size field and press Enter. Reset the solution with Reset All and click Start. Render the Camera01 viewport when finished. Notice that when you click Reset All, the previous meshing solution is discarded and the mesh looks like the original again. The mesh is dense and took 1:27 to calculate and 1:11 to render. The scene is much brighter, but still plagued with bright spots around the scene (see Figure 12.15). You learn to fix those as you progress through the exercises.

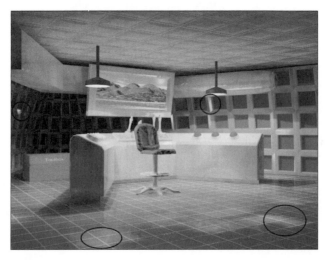

FIGURE 12.15   *With small global meshing sizes, the radiosity solution takes longer but the scene is brighter because of the extra vertices and faces for storing information.*

6. Close all windows and dialogs. Save the file; it should already be called Ch12_Photometric05.max.

Local Meshing Parameters

In Exercise 12.5, you learn a generally more efficient way to mesh objects that is especially appropriate when the objects in your scene vary in size and the amount they contribute to the radiosity solution.

In the example mentioned in the introduction to Exercise 12.4, a room with a few desks and chairs, the desks and chairs might not influence the overall radiosity effect enough to warrant being meshed. If a desk were bright red, for example, it might influence the ceiling enough to show a red cast, but if the desk is neutral gray, the effect would not be noticeable.

You learn how to activate and adjust local meshing on a per-object basis by changing the object's properties.

Exercise 12.5   Local Meshing Parameter Settings

1. Do not continue from the previous exercise, but open the file called Ch12_Photometric05.max on the CD-ROM. From the File pull-down menu, choose Save As, point to an appropriate subdirectory on your hard drive, and use the plus sign button to save a new file with the name incremented to Ch12_Photometric06.max. This file is the same file saved in the preceding exercise, but with Reset All performed to discard the previous radiosity solution.

2. Press 9 to open the Render Scene dialog, and in Advanced Lighting tab, Radiosity Meshing Parameters rollout, clear the Enabled check box in the Global Subdivision Settings area.

3. In the Camera01 viewport or from the Select by Name list, select Floor, Ceiling, and Wall01 in the scene. Enter small mesh in the Named Selection Sets field on the main toolbar and press Enter. Right-click in the viewport and choose Properties in the Quad menu. In the Object Properties dialog, Adv. Lighting tab, Radiosity-Only Properties area, clear Use Global Subdivision Settings check box to turn it off and enter 1 in the Meshing Size field (see Figure 12.16). Click OK.

tip

When you archive files or send files to clients or coworkers who have a compatible copy of 3ds max, it can prove useful to Reset All and save the file to significantly reduce the file size.

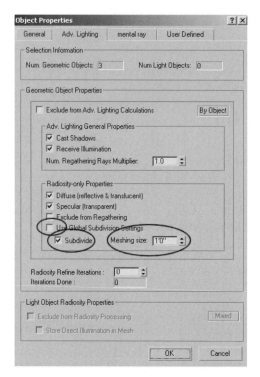

FIGURE 12.16   *By selecting objects and right-clicking in the viewport, you can use the Object Properties dialog, Adv. Lighting tab to disable Use Global Subdivision Settings and set Local Meshing Size for the selected objects only.*

4. In the Render Scene dialog, Advanced Lighting tab, Radiosity Processing Parameters rollout, click the Start button. When the calculations are finished, use Quick Render on the main toolbar to render the Camera01 viewport. The radiosity processing time is 1:09 on the test machine, and the rendering time is 1:01. This is roughly 10 percent faster than when global meshing was set to 1 foot in the preceding exercise.

5. In the Camera01 viewport, select Console01 and Duct01, create a named selection set called med mesh, and press Enter. Right-click in the viewport and choose Properties in the Quad menu. In the Object Properties dialog, Adv. Lighting tab, Radiosity-Only Properties area, Clear Use Global Subdivision Settings check box and enter 2 in the Meshing Size field.

> **note**
>
> While time savings of a few seconds might seem inconsequential, keep in mind that this is a very small scene with few objects. It's the percent of savings that is important, and a few percentage points in a typical scene could be the difference of getting a project done on time and budget or not.

6. In the Render Scene dialog, Advanced Lighting tab, Radiosity Processing Parameters rollout, click the Reset All button, then the Start button. When the calculations are finished, use Quick Render on the main toolbar to render the Camera01 viewport. The radiosity processing time is 1:15 on the test machine, and the rendering time is 1:09.

7. Close all windows and dialogs and save the file. It should already be called Ch12_Photometric06.max.

tip

Objects can be placed on layers in 3ds max 6 and properties of objects, including meshing parameters, can be adjusted on a per-layer basis. The results would be the same as on a per-object setting; it's just another option of management that you might investigate on your own.

Fine-Tuning the Radiosity Results

You are probably disappointed with the results you have seen with radiosity rendering so far. The images have been too bright, washed out, blotchy, and inconsistent. In Exercise 12.6, you perform several steps that refine your scene for more convincing renderings.

The first thing is Exposure Control. You might remember that when you switched from the Scanline renderer to the Radiosity renderer, the Camera Exposure Control was turned on. It acts like the aperture of a camera to control how much light strikes the film or, in this case, the renderer.

In the following exercise, you adjust Refine Iterations. This re-analyzes the radiosity solution to refine the transfer of lighting information from vertex to vertex across faces of the solution mesh.

Then, you use filtering to smooth out the final rough edges to the solution. This is essentially a blurring function where there is contrasting pixel information in the rendered image. Because of this, you must be careful not to set filtering so high that it blurs your small shadow areas.

Exercise 12.6   Exposure Control, Refine Iterations, Filtering, and Light Painting

1. Open the file called Ch12_Photometric06.max on the CD-ROM. From the File pull-down menu, choose Save As, point to an appropriate subdirectory on your hard drive, and use the plus sign button to save a new file with the name incremented to Ch12_Photometric07.max. This file is the same file saved in the preceding exercise, but with Reset All performed to discard the previous radiosity solution.

2. Press 9 to open the Render Scene dialog, and in Advanced Lighting tab, Radiosity Processing Parameters rollout, enter 85 in the Initial Quality field. You had reduced this number to speed processing at a cost to quality, but you are ready now to increase the quality of the rendering. Click the Start button to process the radiosity, and then render the Camera01 viewport. Save this image in Channel A of the RAM Player. The elapsed time for processing as seen in the Statistics rollout is much higher, but the rendering time remains the same.

tip

Logarithmic Exposure Control tends to be the best for still images because it adjusts the scene differently in the low-tone, mid-tone, and high-tone areas, and enables you to control contrast more easily.

3. In the Radiosity Processing Parameters rollout, Interactive Tools area, click the Setup button for the Logarithmic Exposure Control (see Figure 12.17). Enter 55 in the Brightness field and render the Camera01 viewport. This is a post process, so you do not need to recalculate radiosity. The result is a less "overexposed" image. You may load this rendering into Channel B of the RAM Player for comparison.

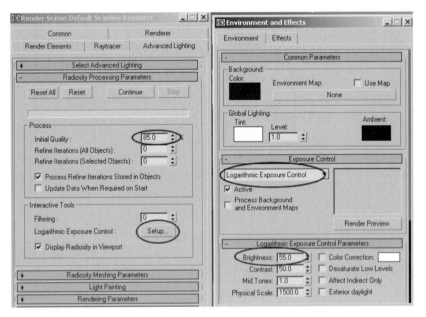

FIGURE 12.17 *By going to the Environment and Effects dialog and lowering the Brightness in the Logarithmic Exposure Control Parameters rollout, you are reducing the amount of light that reaches the renderer, making a more pleasing image.*

4. The next setting you will change, Refine Iterations, uses the initial quality solution and performs a number of refinement passes to clean up what it perceives as discrepancies in the solution. In the Render Scene dialog, Radiosity Processing Parameters rollout, Process area, enter 10 in the Refine Iterations (All Objects) field (see Figure 12.18). Click Reset All, and then click Start before rendering the Camera01 viewport. You should see better-defined blotches, primarily in the walls and floor.

note

Refine Iterations are usually set from 3 to 20 or so. Increase the initial quality by a few percentage points instead of going higher in Refine Iterations.

tip

Refine Iterations might be set to operate only on currently selected objects in the scene or on a per-object basis in the Object Properties dialog.

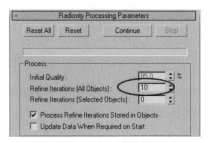

FIGURE 12.18   *In the Radiosity Processing Parameters rollout, enter 10 in the Refine Iterations (All Object) field. This makes 10 refinement passes to refine the amount of information passed between vertices. You must recalculate the radiosity solution to see the results in a new rendering.*

5. The scene still has bright and dark areas, especially in the walls and floor. In the Radiosity Processing Parameters rollout, Interactive Tools area, enter 2 in the Filtering field. This is a post process, so it requires no recalculation. Render the Camera01 viewport. Load this image into Channel B of the RAM Player to compare it with the image from step 2 (see Figure 12.19). You have learned the fundamental tools you will work with to achieve the quality of renderings you require. You must strike a compromise between the increased settings and the processing and render times. Each scene will be different, and lighting and material changes will affect the outcome of any solution.

note

These steps will suffice for much of your radiosity needs; however, there are more advanced tools for radiosity processing—such as a process known as *regathering*, and light-painting tools to touch up the final image by lightening or darkening vertices.

FIGURE 12.19   *In the RAM Player, compare the results of the images from step 2 and from step 5. The floor, ceiling, and walls are cleaner and the radiosity more evenly distributed. Step 5 took considerably longer to process the radiosity, but about the same time to render.*

6. Some stubborn areas of the radiosity solution are still causing brighter and darker areas in the scene. You could increase meshing, refining, or filtering in those objects until you get rid of the problem areas. You also can use light painting. In the Camera01 viewport, select Wall01. Right-click the viewport label and clear the Edged Faces option. Right-click the label again, and choose Configure in the menu. In the Viewport Configuration dialog, Rendering Options area, clear Display Selected with Edged Faces (see Figure 12.20). Click OK.

7. In the Render Scene dialog, Advanced Lighting tab, expand the Light Painting rollout. It is important that the object you want to paint is selected. You first lighten an area that is too dark. In the Intensity field, enter 1000, and enter 50 in the

> **caution**
>
> Painting on vertices is progressive. If you go over the same vertices, the effect adds to or subtracts from the previous pass, based on the Intensity and Pressure settings.
>
> A Clear button removes all current light painting from the scene.

Pressure field. Click the Add Illumination to a Surface button. In the Camera01 viewport, move the point of the paint cursor to the corner vertices of the dark green panel, just to the right of the bottom of the Console01 and click and hold the left mouse button and move it to paint over existing pixels (see Figure 12.21). Click the Subtract Illumination from a Surface button and paint the vertices of some light areas on the wall behind and left of the Console01.

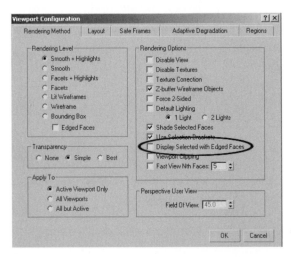

FIGURE 12.20   *Right-click the viewport label and disable Edged Faces for all objects, and then right-click the label again and choose Configure. Clear the Display Selected with Edged Faces option in the dialog.*

FIGURE 12.21   *"Spray" paint the vertices at the corners of the darker green panel at the lower right of Console01 to lighten the panel to match neighboring panels.*

8. Close all windows and dialogs and save the file. It should already be called Ch12_Photometric07.max.

Modeling Issues with Radiosity Renderings

Modeling specifically with radiosity rendering in mind can make the process more efficient. You perform global or local meshing to ensure that vertices are close enough together to pass sufficient information for the quality of rendering you require.

It is most always worth a little extra time in modeling to make sure that you have vertices in adjacent objects that are in close proximity to their neighboring objects' vertices to reduce the need for small meshing sizes.

Also, objects that are open—for example, a flat plane as opposed to a box—are not good at calculating radiosity solutions.

Figure 12.22 shows a simple bathroom that is lit only by sunlight streaming through a small window. Practically all the light in the room is bounced light from the floor and walls. The rendered image shows several problem areas, even though the meshing for the major object is set to 1 foot and Refine Iterations and Filtering are turned on.

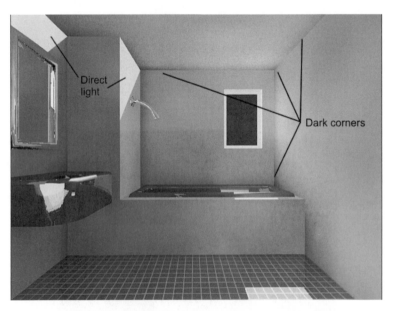

FIGURE 12.22   *A small bathroom lit by sunlight through a window. Local meshing for walls, floor, and ceiling is set to 1 foot and the Refine Iterations are at 5 and Filtering at 2. However, bright and dark areas still need to be addressed.*

In this section, you adjust the vertex positions of objects in the model to make them closer to each other on adjacent objects and you convert the floor and ceiling from flat planes to see the effect of open versus closed objects in the radiosity solution.

Vertex Placement for Efficient Radiosity Solutions

In Exercise 12.7, you adjust the object's vertex placement in the bathroom scene to affect the radiosity solution of the bounced light from sunlight through a small window.

It is easier to get into the habit of modeling with vertex placements that will enhance the process than it is to edit the model later. Meshing parameters are intended to bridge the gap in areas where efficient modeling for radiosity just does not make sense and should not be used to "hammer" the model into submission.

Exercise 12.7   Modeling for Radiosity

1. Open the file called Ch12_Modeling01.max on the CD-ROM. From the File pull-down menu, choose Save As, point to an appropriate subdirectory on your hard drive, and use the plus sign button to save a new file with the name incremented to Ch12_Modeling02.max. This scene is a small bathroom with light coming through the window in the far wall and bouncing off the floor and walls to light the room. The walls are boxes that run by each other at the corners, and the floor and ceiling are flat planes with corners at the outer corners of the walls (as illustrated in a wireframe User view in Figure 12.23).

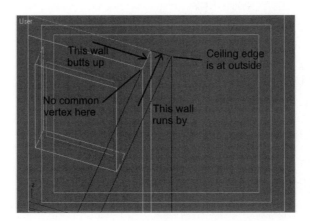

Figure 12.23   *At a typical corner, one wall runs by the other, and the floor and ceiling extend to the outside edge.*

2. Press 9 to open the Render Scene dialog. In the Radiosity Processing Parameters rollout, click Start. When the calculations are finished, render the Camera01 viewport. Open the RAM Player and Open the Last Rendered Image in Channel A.

note

Your rendered results might not be exactly the same as the images shown, and fixing problems in one area changes the results in other areas of the scene.

3. Select Wall_right from the Select by Name list. In the Modify panel, Parameters rollout, enter 11 in the Width field. This shortens the two long walls (instance clones) of the room by 6 inches in either direction, making them match the inside corner of the 6-inch-thick end walls.

4. Select Ceiling in the Select by Name list and, in the Modify panel, Parameters rollout, enter 11 in the Length and 9 in the Width fields. The corner of the ceiling now matches the vertices of the walls.

5. In the Advanced Lighting tab, Radiosity Processing Parameters rollout, click the Reset All button, and then click Start. Render the Camera01 viewport when the processing is finished. The quality in the corners where the vertices now meet is greatly improved (see Figure 12.24). The scene is also a bit brighter because of more accurate bounce light. Open this image in Channel B of the RAM Player to see the difference this simple editing change can make.

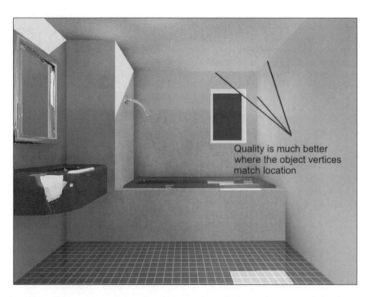

Quality is much better where the object vertices match location

FIGURE 12.24 *Just by editing the walls and ceiling so that their vertices match in the upper corner of the room, you greatly improve the radiosity solution, all else being equal.*

6. Close all windows and dialogs. Save the file; it should already be called Ch12_Modeling02.max.

Open Mesh Objects Versus Closed Mesh Objects

The most notable problem with an open mesh in the bathroom scene is that, because of face normals, the ceiling plane does not block the sunlight—that is, it does not cast a shadow. The bright light at the top left of the bathroom is wrong and is contributing heavily to the radiosity solution.

In Exercise 12.8, you edit the ceiling plane to turn it into a box-like object. You then compare the rendered scene that results from the closed ceiling object.

Exercise 12.8   Using Closed Objects in Radiosity Solutions

1. Open the file called Ch12_Modeling02.max on the CD-ROM or from the preceding exercise. From the File pull-down menu, choose Save As, point to an appropriate subdirectory on your hard drive, and use the plus sign button to save a new file with the name incremented to Ch12_Modeling03.max.

2. In the Camera01 viewport, select Ceiling from the Select by Name list and press Delete to delete the object. In the Display panel, Hide rollout, click Unhide by Name. Double-click Box_Ceiling in the Unhide Objects dialog (see Figure 12.25). This is a box the size of the ceiling opening with a material assigned and meshing set to 6 inches in the Object Properties dialog.

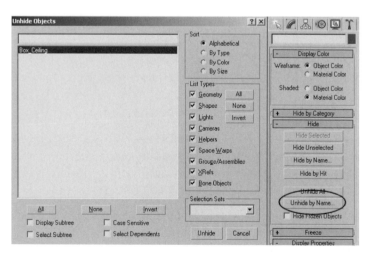

FIGURE 12.25   *Select Box_Ceiling and click the Unhide by Name button in the Display panel, Hide rollout.*

3. In the Render Scene dialog, Advanced Lighting tab, click Reset All if you are continuing from Exercise 12.7, and then click Start to run the radiosity solution. Render the Camera01 viewport. The bright areas to the upper left are gone as is the resulting reflection from the corner of the sink, and the edges at the wall and ceiling are cleaner (see Figure 12.26).

FIGURE 12.26   *A closed ceiling object results in a better solution at the edges of the walls and ceiling and blocks the direct light at the upper left and the resulting reflection on the sink.*

4. Close all windows and dialogs. Save the file; it should already be called Ch12_Modeling03.max.

Reduced Specular Highlights Discussion

You need to be aware of an issue with radiosity processing and the reduction of specular highlights in materials. It is this author's belief that specular highlights are important to the material's capacity to convince the viewer that it is hard or soft.

Because of the nature of light that bounces in all directions in a radiosity scene, the specular highlights are overpowered and washed out.

One solution is to add powerful lights to the scene that contribute only to the specular component of lighting. They do not light the diffuse or direct lighting, nor do they contribute to the radiosity solution.

You also should include only specific objects, so that the specular highlights are added only to those objects that you want to bring to the viewer's attention.

The Specular Only switch is found in the Modify panel, Advanced Effects rollout. You must clear the Diffuse component check box (see Figure 12.27).

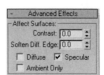

Figure 12.27
You can set lights in Modify panel, Advanced Effects rollout, to affect only the specular highlights.

By right-clicking a light in the scene and opening Object Properties, Light Object Radiosity Properties area, you can Exclude from Radiosity Processing so that the light is contributing only direct light to the scene (see Figure 12.28).

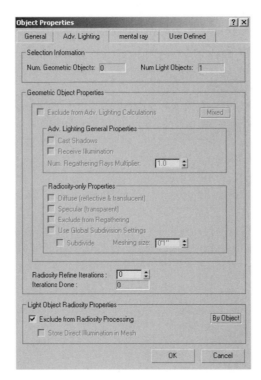

Figure 12.28   *You can disable the capability of a light to contribute to the radiosity processing in the Object Properties dialog, Adv. Lighting tab.*

You can include or exclude specific objects from all aspects of the light with the Exclude button found in the Modify panel, General Parameters rollout. The intensity, which is controlled by the Multiplier value of the light can be found in the Intensity/Color/Distribution rollout and can be set as high as you need to get the specular highlights you want in your scene.

This process is a "trick" and does not follow the laws of physics of the photometric lights; as with standard lights, however, you are usually not looking for realism, but the perception of realism, which is more important to a good image.

Summary

Radiosity rendering can make scenes much more convincing to the viewer. If you don't follow some fundamental rules about lighting, meshing, and modeling, however, the process can quickly become inefficient and cost you valuable production time.

Some of the topics covered in this chapter included the following:

- **Photometric lighting**—You learned that photometric lighting uses lights based on the laws of physics to calculate direct and bounced light within the Radiosity renderer.

- **Meshing for photometrics**—You learned that meshing enables you to add vertices and faces to a radiosity mesh that is a clone of your scene for the storage and interpolation of the radiosity solution. Smaller meshes give better results, but at a cost of lost efficiency.

- **Modeling for photometrics**—You learned how the relative location of vertices on adjacent objects can significantly affect the efficiency of the radiosity solution.

- **Specular highlight issues**—You learned that radiosity solutions do not create bold specular highlights, because of the nature of bounced light. Some notes helped you with options to correct that shortcoming.

CHAPTER 13

Radiosity Rendering: Material Control

In This Chapter

In this chapter, you learn about a new material type that enables you to manipulate your materials for better results when using radiosity rendering and to use some of the features of Exposure Control that can enhance your images as a postprocessing effect:

- **Advanced Lighting Override**—You learn to use this material type on top of existing materials for control of reflectance, color bleed, and some special effects.

- **Exposure Control**—You learn about processing your images after radiosity calculations for better contrast ranges.

Materials work just fine with radiosity in general. When a material has too much effect on a surrounding object, however, you can go into the color swatch and darken the color to cause less light to bounce from the material. In the case of materials that derive color from maps, you can go into the Output rollout or add an Output map type and adjust the Output amount. However, the materials in the Material Editor sample windows can become so dark, it is difficult to adjust the other parameters.

The Advanced Lighting Override material sits on top of your regular material and superimposes changes to the underlying base material. This enables you to change not only the amount of bounced light (reflectance), but also the color bleed and whether the material can actually contribute light to the scene as if it were a photometric light.

Key Terms

- **Reflectance**—The intensity of light bounced from material surfaces in radiosity rendering

- **Color bleed**—The amount of color transferred from one surface to another with bounced light in radiosity rendering

- **Luminance scale**—An Advanced Lighting Override material attribute that sets the intensity of self-illuminated materials that act as photometric lights in a radiosity rendering

Material Issues with Radiosity Rendering

The bathroom scene looks much better than when you started, but a couple of noticeable problems still remain. The overall brightness of the room is too high, and the blue floor and red fixtures have too much influence on the colors of the walls and ceiling.

In this section, you learn to control those aspects of materials used in radiosity called *reflectance* and *color bleed*. Reflectance is the intensity of the light bounced from materials, and color bleed is the amount of color that bounced light transfers to other objects.

Published ranges for many materials' reflectance vary widely, shown in the following small sample from the online Help file.

Material	Minimum	Maximum
Ceramic	20%	70%
Fabric	20%	70%
Masonry	20%	50%
Plastic	20%	80%
Wood	20%	50%

As you can see, the choice is fairly subjective, which allows for adjustment and enables you to obtain the look that you think is convincing.

There is a special material type called Advanced Lighting Override that you will learn to use to control both reflectance and color bleed.

Material Reflectance

3ds max 6 has photometric lighting that accurately follows the laws of physics. An element of subjectivity still exists, however, because of the wide variations in the reflectance values and color bleeding from surfaces (aspects of every lighting scenario).

Although manufacturers publish tables that list reflectance value ranges for different types of materials, the ranges are wide enough to offer you plenty of latitude as to what you think looks best.

In Exercise 13.1, you learn to enable the Reflectance and Color Bleed display in the Material Editor, and you learn to apply an Advanced Lighting Override material type to your existing materials to control the reflectance values to darken your bathroom scene.

Exercise 13.1   Applying the Advanced Lighting Override Material to Control Reflectance of a Material

1. Open the file called Ch13_ Materials01.max on the CD-ROM. From the File pull-down menu, choose Save As, point to an appropriate subdirectory on your hard drive, and use the plus sign button to save a new file with the name incremented to Ch13_Materials02.max.

2. In the Customize pull-down menu, choose Preferences. In the Preference Settings dialog, Radiosity tab, Material Editor area, check Display Reflectance & Transmittance Information (see Figure 13.1). Click OK. Open the Material Editor and you can see the values displayed below the sample windows (see Figure 13.2).

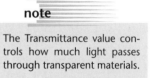

note

The Transmittance value controls how much light passes through transparent materials.

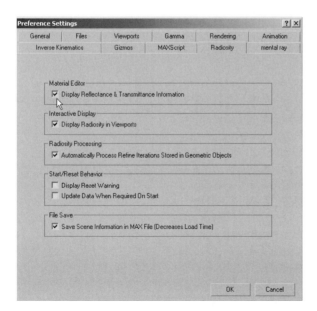

FIGURE 13.1   *In Customize, Preferences, Radiosity tab, check Display Reflectance & Transmittance Information.*

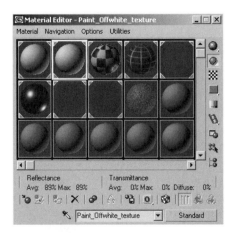

Figure 13.2 *The Reflectance & Transmittance Information now shows up just below the sample windows in the Material Editor.*

3. Activate the Tile_floor sample window and you see that the Average Reflectance is 41 percent and the lightest areas reflect a maximum of 83 percent of the light striking the surface. You assign a new material over the top of the tile floor material to give you control of the settings. In the Material Editor, click the Standard button next to the Tile_floor name field. In the Material/Map Browser, double-click Advanced Lighting Override material type. Choose Keep Old Material as Sub-Material, and click OK. This material is riding on top of Tile_floor, the base material (see Figure 13.3).

4. In the Render Scene dialog, Advanced Lighting tab, click the Start button. Render Camera01 and put the last rendered image into Channel A of the RAM Player.

5. In the Material Editor, Advanced Lighting Override Material rollout, Override Material Physical Properties area, enter 0.5 in the Reflectance Scale field and press Enter. Reset All and Start the radiosity calculations, render the Camera01 viewport, and load the new image into Channel B of the RAM Player. A comparison shows the new image to be noticeably darker (because the reflectance is half what it was before, but the lower walls have about the same amount of blue).

6. Close all windows and dialogs and save the file. It should already be called Ch13_Materials02.max.

note

You might notice random changes around the tub. They are the result of vertices of the tub unit that have no corresponding vertices in the walls, floor, or ceiling. You could adjust this with the mesh objects or by setting the meshing size to a smaller number.

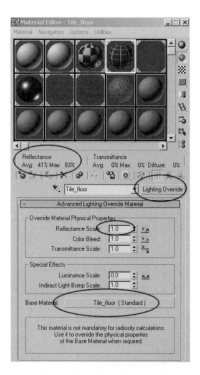

Figure 13.3 *The Advanced Lighting Override material sits on top of your base material to add extra control for reflectance, color bleed, and other attributes.*

Material Color Bleed

Color bleed refers to reflected light transmitting the color from a surface to surrounding surfaces. Too much color bleed looks artificial, whereas too little reduces the effectiveness of radiosity rendering to make a convincing scene. In Exercise 13.2, you learn to adjust the color bleed of materials.

Exercise 13.2   Adjusting Color Bleed with the Advanced Lighting Override Material

1. Open the file called Ch13_Materials02.max on the CD-ROM or from the preceding exercise. From the File pull-down menu, choose Save As, point to an appropriate subdirectory on your hard drive, and use the plus sign button to save a new file with the name incremented to Ch13_Materials03.max.

2. Reset any current radiosity solution and Start a new solution. Render the Camera01 viewport and load the image into Channel A of the RAM Player.

3. In the Material Editor, Advanced Lighting Override Material rollout, Override Material Physical Properties area, enter 0.5 in the Color Bleed field and press Enter. Reset All and Start the radiosity calculations, render the Camera01 viewport, and load the new image into Channel B of the RAM Player. The lower walls are considerably less tinted with blue, and the neutral colors are showing more appropriately.

4. In the Material Editor, activate the Paint_Tub sample window to the left of Tile_floor sample window. Use the Material/Map Navigator to go to the Tub material level. Click the Standard button and double-click Advanced Lighting Override in the Browser list. Keep the old material as a submaterial. In the Advanced Lighting Override Material rollout, enter 0.5 in the Color Bleed field and press Enter.

5. Drag the Lighting Override material type button from Paint_Tub onto the Tub sample window and choose Instance and click OK (see Figure 13.4). This puts the same material onto the sink with the Color Bleed set to 0.5.

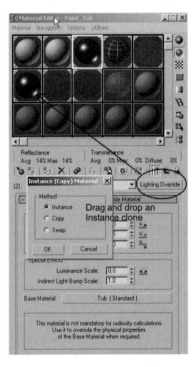

Figure 13.4 *Drag and drop the Advanced Lighting Override material to the Tub sample window as an instance clone. This keeps the tub and sink material the same.*

6. Reset All and Start the radiosity calculations and render the Camera01 viewport. Load the image into Channel B of the RAM Player. The reduced red color bleeding gives the image a more natural look.

7. Close all windows and dialogs. Save the file; it should already be called Ch13_Materials03.max.

Materials as Photometric Light Sources

In this section, you open a new file and learn to adjust the Advanced Lighting Override material to cause self-illuminated materials to actually emit light into a scene (much like adding a new photometric light).

In Chapter 12, "Photometric Lighting: Bounced Light Calculation," you learned to enable self-illumination in materials that cause the material to appear to glow from within by overpowering the ambient area of light—that is, the material in shaded or shadowed areas.

In Exercise 13.3, you open a new file that has a light fixture over the sink. It is the same fixture that sat on the console in the interior scene except the Self-Illumination color has been changed from red to yellow and an Advanced Lighting Override material has been added to the bulb material.

Exercise 13.3   Turning Self-Illuminated Materials into Photometric Light Sources

1. Open the file called Ch13_AdvLight01.max on the CD-ROM. From the File pull-down menu, choose Save As, point to an appropriate subdirectory on your hard drive, and use the plus sign button to save a new file with the name incremented to Ch13_AdvLight02.max.

2. Reset any current radiosity solution and start a new solution. Render the Camera01 viewport and load the image into Channel A of the RAM Player. The new light fixture near the mirror has a bulb that glows with self-illumination but does not affect the lighting in the scene (see Figure 13.5).

3. Open the Material Editor and use the Material/Map Navigator to go to the Light Bulb level of the Flashing Light material. In the Advanced Lighting Override Material rollout, enter 3500 in the Luminance Scale field and press Enter (see Figure 13.6). This makes the intensity of the material equal to a 3500 lux light in the scene.

FIGURE 13.5   *A new light fixture in the scene has a self-illuminated material that glows. There is also an Advanced Lighting Override material on the self-illuminated material.*

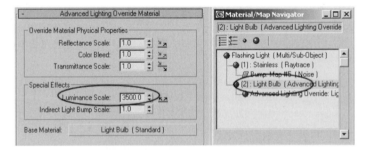

FIGURE 13.6   *Use the Material/Map Navigator to go to the Light Bulb level of the Flashing Light material and, in the Material Editor, Advanced Lighting Override Material rollout, Special Effects area, enter 3500 in the Luminance Scale field.*

4. In the Render Scene dialog, Advanced Lighting tab, click Reset All, and then click Start. When the calculations are finished, render the Camera01 viewport and load the image into Channel B of the RAM Player. You can see the extra light in the corner of the tub unit and on the wall and mirror.

5. Close all windows and dialogs and save the file. It should already be called Ch13_AdvLight02.max.

Exposure Control Options

You have used Exposure Control to change the overall brightness of a scene; to fine-tune the rendering for a more convincing image, however, it is sometimes useful to adjust the contrast.

Exposure Control offers two tools that can enhance the contrast of a scene: a Contrast setting and a Mid Tones setting.

The Contrast adjustment tends to lighten the light areas, darken the dark areas, and leave the mid-range of pixel brightness relatively the same.

With the Mid Tones setting, you can adjust the brightness of those areas while leaving the high- and low-light areas relatively untouched.

note

These adjustments are subjective. I happen to like scenes with a good range of contrast, from dark to light through a variety of grayscales.

This scene has no meshing on some of the objects and no good shadows to create dark areas. Learn the lessons here and apply them to your renderings to adjust them to your tastes and needs.

Contrast and Mid Tones Adjustment

In Exercise 13.4, you adjust the Contrast and Mid Tones of a rendering, first to extremes to see the differences, and then to a setting that might prove useful for this particular image.

Exercise 13.4   Adjusting Exposure Control Contrast and Mid Tones Settings

1. Open the file called Ch13_AdvLight02.max on the CD-ROM. From the File pull-down menu, choose Save As, point to an appropriate subdirectory on your hard drive, and use the plus sign button to save a new file with the name incremented to Ch13_AdvLight03.max.

2. Reset any current radiosity solution and start a new solution. Render the Camera01 viewport and load the image into Channel A of the RAM Player.

3. In the Render Scene dialog, Advanced Lighting tab, Radiosity Processing Parameters rollout, Interactive tools area, click the Setup button or press 8 to open the Environment and Effects dialog. In the Logarithmic Exposure Control Parameters rollout, enter 100 in the Contrast field and render the Camera01 viewport (see Figure 13.7).

note

Changes in Exposure Control occur during postprocessing and do not require a reset and recalculation of the radiosity solution.

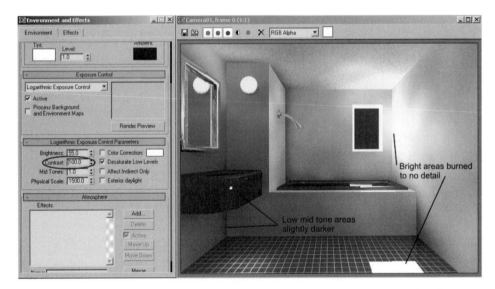

FIGURE 13.7 *Setting Contrast to 100 burns the detail from the bright areas while slightly darkening the lower tones of this scene.*

4. Set the Contrast to 10 and render the Camera01 viewport. The scene is flat and contains no detail. Enter 70 in the Contrast field and render again. The scene has some detail in the bright areas, which is especially noticeable in the floor tile.

5. In the Logarithmic Exposure Control Parameters rollout, enter 2 in the Mid Tones field and render the Camera01 viewport. Because this scene contains few dark areas, it seems as though everything is brighter. Notice the brightest areas still contain details, whereas the sink became much brighter. This is not the same as adjusting the Brightness amount, which changes all pixels equally.

6. Set Mid Tones to 0.1 and render the Camera01 viewport. Again, the detail in the bright floor is about the same, whereas the sink is much darker. Set Mid Tones to 0.8 and render the Camera01 viewport.

7. Load the last rendered image into Channel B of the RAM Player and compare the two images. The adjusted image has more apparent depth and sharpness than the original.

8. Close all windows and dialogs and save the file. It should already be named Ch13_AdvLight03.max.

Summary

Fine-tuning the Exposure Control settings of Contrast and Mid Tones can add extra punch and "3D-ness" to your scenes. Because the changes do not have to be recalculated as part of the radiosity solution, but are applied as a postprocess to rendering, you can make the changes relatively quickly and the changes almost always significantly enhance your image.

Topics you learned in this chapter include the following:

- **Advanced Lighting Override**—You learned to use this material type on top of existing materials for control of reflectance, color bleed, and some special effects.

- **Exposure Control**—You learned about processing your images after radiosity calculations for better contrast ranges.

The material covered in this chapter requires you to develop an artist's view of light and to develop in your mind what type of image will make the most impact with your client. Take the time to experiment.

PART IV

Setting Things in Motion

CHAPTER **14**

Set Key Animation

In This Chapter

You have modeled a couple of scenes, assigned materials, and placed lights; now, it's time to learn some fundamental animation techniques.

In this chapter, you learn some important methods of animation that you will use often in your projects to come:

- **Set Key animation**—With this animation method, you set keys in time that record the state of objects or actions you have performed.

- **Editing and cloning keys**—Animation keys that record events in time can be edited or cloned to change the state of your animation.

- **Dummy objects**—Helper objects, in the shape of a cube or cross-hair point, that aid in animation control and never render in the scene.

- **Hierarchical linking**—Hierarchical linking sets up parent-child relationships between objects for animation control.

3ds max 6 uses a form of animation widely referred to as *key frame animation*. The term derives from traditional cel animation used in hand-drawn cartoons. Suppose, for example, that a team is composed of a master animator and junior animators. The master animator draws the key poses of the action to set the story line. The junior animators then draw on film to set the intermediate steps between the key frames that bring the scene to life when played back at a certain speed.

In 3ds max 6, you are the master animator. You set keys at points in time when an action starts and finishes, and the program then acts as the junior animator to fill in the in-between frames.

The Set Key method of animation gives you the control to record only the part(s) that you need—for example, position or rotation changes—thus keeping the tracking and editing of the keys as simple as possible.

As animation keys are created in this chapter, they show up as rectangles on the track bar at the bottom of the display screen. The default track bar shows frames 0 to 100.

You can think of the track bar as sort of an appointment calendar. Each key represents an event that will happen in time. You can move the keys in time on the track bar to adjust the speed that events relate to each other; keys closer together represent faster action, and keys far apart are slower actions. In this chapter, you learn to adjust timing by moving and cloning keys.

In the exercises in this chapter, you work in a scene that represents the engine room of the boat from previous exercises. Although the boat is from the mid-1800s and the command room is from a more present day, the engine room might fall somewhere in between. There is water in the bilge that reflects light back into the room, casting eerie shadows from the engine itself and other equipment. Your job in this phase of the projects is to start the propeller shaft and gear rotating and get the engine to chug, and then to start a primitive pump system to keep the boat afloat.

Key Terms

- **Key**—An indicator used to record action in time.
- **Dummy**—A nonrenderable helper object to aid animation.
- **Hierarchical linking**—To set up a parent-child relationship between objects.

Set Key Animation for Rotation

In Exercise 14.1, you learn to animate the rotation of the propeller shaft of the boat using two forms of Set Key animation—one that works only with the transforms in 3ds max 6: Move, Rotate, and Scale. Another form uses a Set Keys button to create keys for various aspects of animation.

The shaft should not rotate right from the start of your animation; instead, it should be still until a few frames have passed, and then it should rotate 270 degrees over the rest of the time.

You will then adjust it to rotate a full 360 degrees over the same time by editing an individual key, and then you will change the speed of that rotation by moving keys in time.

The important thing with Set Key animation is that you are creating keys only when you need them.

Exercise 14.1   Setting and Adjusting Object Transform Animation Keys

1. Open the file called Ch14_SetKey01.max on the CD-ROM. From the File pull-down menu, choose Save As, point to an appropriate subdirectory on your hard drive, and use the plus sign button to save a new file with the name incremented to Ch14_SetKey02.max. You are in the engine room of your boat looking forward to the engine on the right and a pump system on the left. There are two overhead lights (standard omni lights) shining downward from fixtures. There is also a fill light behind the camera and to the left with a bluish color to give the engine a colder look. A light below the hull simulates light bouncing from the water in the bilge and casting shadows of the engine and grating onto the ceiling.

2. In the Camera01 viewport, select the Shaft_Gear object at the back of the engine that is nearest you in the scene. Your animation will be 100 frames long, but the shaft should not start rotating until frame 10 and should finish 270 degrees of rotation at frame 100. You first set a rotation key at frame 10 that records the current rotation of the shaft at frame 0 to frame 10—that is, no rotation. You use a method of Set Key animation to create the key. Make sure the Time slider is set to frame 0 (see Figure 14.1).

note

There is a form of animation called Auto Key. When you enable the Auto Key mode and are at any frame other than frame 0, most edits become animated whether you intend them to or not. Auto Key also tends to create keys of many aspects, regardless of whether they are animated, which results in some confusion in the management and editing of keys.

FIGURE 14.1   *Drag the Time slider to the left of the track bar to make sure it is at frame 0 of 100 frames.*

3. Right-click the Time slider. In the Create Key dialog, enter 10 in the Destination Time field and clear the Position and Scale check boxes (see Figure 14.2). Click OK. This reads the amount of rotation at frame 0 and copies that information to the new key at frame 10.

tip

If no key is created at frame 10 to record the rotation from frame 0, the next action automatically starts at frame 0. You want no rotation from frame 0 until frame 10.

FIGURE 14.2   *Right-click the Time slider and set Destination Time to 10. Clear the Position and Scale check boxes so that no unnecessary keys are recorded for those actions. This form of Set Key animation can record keys only for the transforms: Move, Rotate, and Scale.*

4. Drag the Time slider right to frame 100. You will now use another form of Set Key animation valid for many types of animation. On the status bar, click the Key Filters button and clear all but Rotation in the Set Key Filters dialog (see Figure 14.3). Close the dialog.

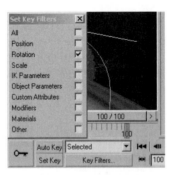

FIGURE 14.3   *On the status bar, click the Key Filters button and clear all but Rotation in the Set Key Filters dialog. You will only record rotation keys, not the other animation aspects.*

5. On the status bar, click the Set Key Mode toggle. It and the Time slider bar and active viewport frame turn red to indicate you are in Set Key mode. On the main toolbar, click the Select and Rotate button. On the main toolbar, click the Angle Snap Toggle to enable it. The default is a 5-degree rotation snap.

6. In the Camera01 viewport, pick and drag on the green Y-axis restrict circle of the Transform gizmo and rotate the Shaft_Gear 270 degrees. You see the angle of rotation on the status bar and on the Transform gizmo itself (see Figure 14.4). Click the large Set Keys button (with the key symbol) to set the animation key at frame 100. Click the Set Key Mode toggle to exit that mode.

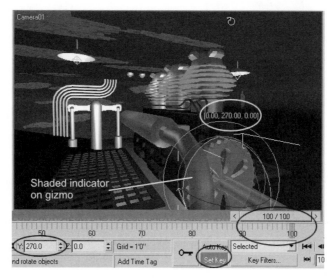

Figure 14.4   *With Angle Snap toggled on, at frame 100, rotate the Shaft_Gear 270 degrees in the Y-axis.*

7. Click the Play Animation button on the status bar to play the animation (see Figure 14.5). The shaft is still for 10 frames, and then rotates through the rest of the time. Stop the playback.

8. You realize that the shaft should have rotated a full 360 degrees (or any other number) from frame 10 to frame 100. There is no need to re-rotate the shaft. On the track bar, select the key at frame 100. It turns white. Right-click the selected key and highlight Shaft_Gear: Y Rotation in the menu (see Figure 14.6).

Figure 14.5

Click the Play Animation button on the status bar to play the animation in the active Camera01 viewport.

tip

As you play back, it might appear that the shaft is rotating in the wrong direction. This is the same strobe effect you see on wagon wheels in western movies, for example, which is based on the rotation speed and playback rate.

FIGURE 14.6 *Select the key at frame 100 to turn it white, and then right-click it and highlight Shaft_Gear: Y Rotation in the menu.*

9. In the Shaft_Gear: Y Rotation dialog, enter 360 in the Value field (see Figure 14.7) and press Enter. Close the dialog and play the Camera01 viewport animation; the shaft rotates 90 degrees more in the same amount of time.

10. You now realize you want the animation to wait until frame 30 before beginning. Pick and drag the key at frame 10 to frame 30 (see Figure 14.8). The rotation will be faster on playback as a result of the 360 degrees being completed in 70 frames rather than the 90 frames.

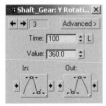

FIGURE 14.7

Enter 360 in the Value field of the Shaft_Gear: Y Rotation dialog to edit the number of degrees stored in the key at frame 100.

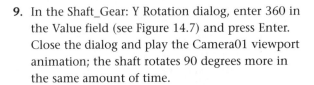
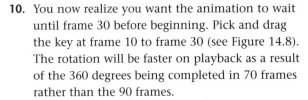

FIGURE 14.8 *Pick and drag the Y Rotation key at frame 10 to frame 30. The rotation angle is the same, but is now completed in 20 frames less; therefore, the rotation is faster.*

11. Close all windows and dialogs. Save the file; it is already called Ch14_SetKey02.max.

Set Key Animation for Modifiers

You will use Set Key animation in Exercise 14.2 to give a comic appearance to the finned cylinders at the top of the engine. The cylinders will seem to chug up and down over the animation—something they would never do, but it will add a comic element to your animation.

An XForm modifier has been added to one of the three cylinders and, because they are instance clones, the modifier will affect all three in the same manner. The sub-object Center of the XForm has been aligned to the bottom of the cylinder, and you will animate the scale of the gizmo in the World Z-axis over time.

You will then use a method of cloning keys to repeat action over the length of the animation to achieve this chugging or puffing effect.

Exercise 14.2   Using Set Key with Modifiers

1. Open the file called Ch14_SetKey02.max on the CD-ROM or from the preceding exercise. From the File pull-down menu, choose Save As, point to an appropriate subdirectory on your hard drive, and use the plus sign button to save a new file with the name incremented to Ch14_SetKey03.max.

2. The three cylinders at the top of the engine are instance clones of each other, so pick any one to affect all three. In the Modify panel, Stack view, expand the XForm modifier and highlight sub-object Gizmo. On the main toolbar, click and hold on the Select and Uniform Scale button and choose Select and Non-uniform Scale, the second from the bottom.

3. On the status bar, click the Key Filters button and clear all but Modifiers in the menu. Close the menu. Make sure the Time slider is at frame 0. On the status bar, click the Set Key Mode toggle to highlight it and the slider bar in red. Drag the Time slider to frame 20 and click the large Set Keys (with the key symbol) button. This creates a key at frame 20, recording the current state of the modifier.

4. In the main toolbar, toggle the Percent Snap button on. Drag the Time slider to frame 40. In the Camera01 viewport, pick and drag downward on the Z-axis restrict arrow of the Scale Transform gizmo until the Z-axis reads 80 on the status bar (see Figure 14.9). Click the large Set Keys button to record 80-percent scaling at frame 40. Click Set Key to toggle that mode off.

5. In the Modify panel, Stack view, highlight XForm to exit sub-object mode. Play the animation in the Camera01 viewport; the cylinders compress once between frames 20 and 40. You want it to happen more than once throughout the animation, however.

6. On the track bar, select the key at frame 20 to turn it white. Hold the Shift key and drag the key from frame 20 to frame 60. You can drag it right through the key at frame 40. Remember the key at frame 20 recorded the uncompressed state. Play the animation, and you now see the cylinder compress between frames 20 and 40 and uncompress between frames 40 and 60.

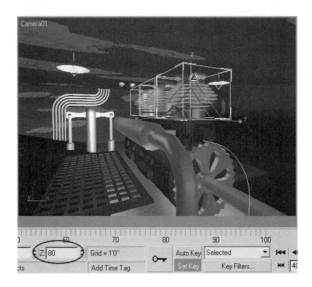

FIGURE 14.9 *Pick and drag the Z-axis scaling restrict arrow until it reads 80 on the status bar. Click Set Keys to record that scaling at frame 40.*

7. Clone the key with Shift-Move from frame 40 to frame 80 and the key from frame 20 to frame 100. The keys now represent uncompressed at frames 0, 20, 60, and 100, while you have compressed keys at frames 40 and 80. When you play back the Camera01 viewport now, it looks as if a bellows action from the cylinders is starting the rotation of the propeller shaft.

8. Close all windows and dialogs. Save the file; it is already called Ch14_SetKey03.max.

Hierarchical Linking and Dummy Objects

Other important topics covered in this chapter are hierarchical linking and dummy objects. With hierarchical linking, you set up an ancestry between objects. A child is linked to a parent, the parent to a grandparent, the grandparent to a great-grandparent, and so on. The basic principle is that the child must always follow its parent, but can have its own actions. An example might be a train with boxcars. All the boxcars follow the locomotive, but each boxcar bumps and rounds the curves on its own. Another example is a hand, forearm, and upper arm. The hand is doing its own thing, but never leaves the forearm, which is always attached to the upper arm.

Although objects can certainly be linked to one another, the use of dummy objects offers more flexibility and control. A dummy object is a nonrenderable cube that can function as a control handle or secondary pivot point within a hierarchy. An example of this might be a planet and moon system, where the moon is linked to a dummy at the center of the plant. As the dummy rotates, the moon orbits the planet, but the moon can have motion independent of the rotation that moves it closer to the planet at certain points in the orbit. Each action is completely independent of the other, and therefore more manageable.

The process of linking is simple: You click the Select and Link button, and then pick and drag from the child object to its parent object to establish the link.

Creating Dummy Objects

In Exercise 14.3, you open a file that is similar to the scene from the preceding exercise. The difference is that the pump arm to the left of the engine has been animated to rock back and forth.

You will add two dummy objects—one at the top of each of the Pump_piston objects—that will act as connector pins to the Pump_arm. You will then link them so that they animate with the pumping action.

In this exercise, you learn to make adjustments to the linking that will enable you to control which axis inherits the rotation, in this example, of its parent object.

Exercise 14.3   Adding and Linking Dummy Objects

1. Open the file called Ch14_Linking01.max on the CD-ROM. From the File pull-down menu, choose Save As, point to an appropriate subdirectory on your hard drive, and use the plus sign button to save a new file with the name incremented to Ch14_Linking02.max.

2. Make sure you are at frame 0 in the Time slider. In the Front viewport, select Pump_arm, the horizontal rocker of the pump, and use Zoom Extents Selected to fill the viewport with the object. You will create dummy helper objects and align them to the top of the two Pump_piston objects. In the Create panel, Helpers panel, Object Type rollout, click the Dummy button. In the Front viewport, pick and drag to create a dummy that looks similar to Figure 14.10.

tip

If you select the Pump_arm object and look at the track bar, you see 5 Y-axis rotation keys between frame 0 and frame 20; if you play the animation, however, the rocking action repeats throughout the 100-frame animation sequence.

Use the online Help file to look up Graph Editors, Dope Sheet, and Out-of-Range Types under Controllers to find how this was accomplished.

By reverse-engineering scenes, you can learn a lot about how 3ds max 6 functions.

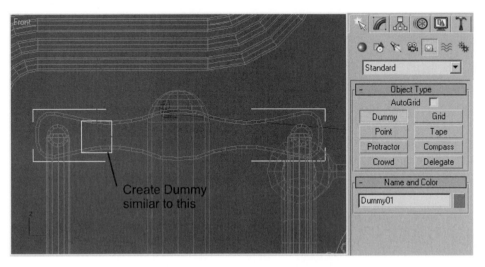

FIGURE 14.10   *In the Create panel, Helpers panel, Object Type rollout, click the Dummy button and click and drag a dummy near the left middle of Pump_arm.*

3. On the main toolbar, click the Align button and pick Pump_piston01, the vertical shaft at the left end of the Pump_arm. In the Align Selection dialog, check X Position and Z Position. Select the Center radio button in both the Current and Target Object columns. Click Apply to set the position and clear the check boxes. Check Y Position and check Center in the Current Object column and Maximum in the Target Object column. Click OK. This aligns the center of the dummy cube with the top center of the piston.

4. On the main toolbar, click Select and Move to toggle it on. Hold the Shift key and drag Dummy01 to the right by using the X-axis restrict arrow of the Transform gizmo. Choose Copy in the Clone Options dialog and click OK. On the main toolbar, click Align and pick Pump_piston02, the shaft on the right. In the Align Selection dialog, check X Position. In the Current and Target column, check the Center radio button. Click OK. The two dummies are aligned to the top center of the two pistons.

5. On the main toolbar, click the Select and Link button. In the Front viewport, click Dummy01 and drag to the left middle of Piston_arm. You see a dashed rubber-band line from the center of the Dummy01 and the link cursor when over an appropriate object (see Figure 14.11). Release when you see the cursor, and the Pump_arm flashes white briefly to indicate the link has been established.

tip

If you link a child to the wrong parent, select the child object and, on the main toolbar, click the Unlink Selection button.

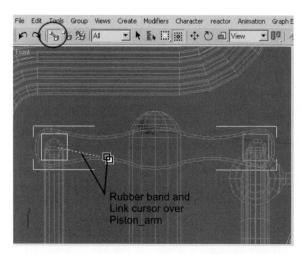

FIGURE 14.11   *On the main toolbar, click the Select and Link button. Click and drag from the child object (Dummy01) to the parent object (Piston_arm) and release the left mouse button. Piston_arm briefly flashes white.*

6. To confirm that the link has been made correctly, click the Select Object button to exit link mode, and then click the Select by Name button on the main toolbar. The child object is indented from its parent (see Figure 14.12). Click the Cancel button to dismiss the dialog.

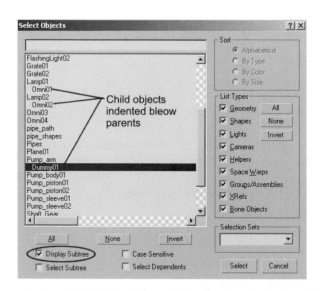

FIGURE 14.12   *In the Select Objects dialog, checking the Display Subtree option indents child objects below their parent objects.*

note

Notice the omni lights are already linked to the lamp objects. This makes it easier to make sure the lights stay with the lamps if they are moved.

7. On the main toolbar, click Select and Link and
   drag from the Dummy02 to the Piston_arm to
   link them, too. Check in the Select by Name
   dialog to make sure the link was made.

8. Drag the Time slider slowly and notice the
   dummy objects rotating with the Pump_arm.
   Notice especially the rotation of the dummies as
   they keep their orientation to the arm (see Figure
   14.13). Drag the Time slider to frame 0.

caution

You must remember to click
the Select Object button or
perform some other action that
gets you out of Select and Link
mode. Otherwise, you see the
Select Parent dialog and not
the Select by Name dialog.

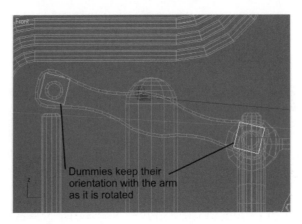

Dummies keep their
orientation with the arm
as it is rotated

FIGURE 14.13   *Drag the Time slider and notice the dummies keep their orientation as they
rotate with the arm.*

9. Close all windows and dialogs. Save the file; it should already be called
   Ch14_Linking02.max.

Controlling Link Inheritance

In Exercise 14.4, you link the pistons to the dummy objects and notice that the animation is not at all what you want. Because of the position of the piston pivot points
and, because the orientation of the dummy objects as they inherit the rotation of
their parent object, the pistons behave a bit strangely, correct for the setup perhaps,
but not as you want them to.

You will change the axis of rotation inheritance of the dummy objects for the correct
up-and-down action of the pistons.

Exercise 14.4   Editing Link Inheritance

1. Open the file called Ch14_Linking02.max on the CD-ROM or from the preceding exercise. From the File pull-down menu, choose Save As, point to an appropriate subdirectory on your hard drive, and use the plus sign button to save a new file with the name incremented to Ch14_Linking03.max.

2. In the Front viewport, select Pump_piston01 on the left side. You link this to Dummy01, but use Select Parent instead of dragging to make sure you get it right. On the main toolbar, click the Select and Link button. On the main toolbar, click the Select by Name button. In the Select Parent dialog, double-click Dummy01 (see Figure 14.14). Dummy01 flashes white.

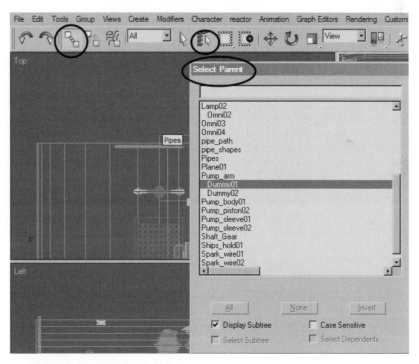

FIGURE 14.14   *On the main toolbar, click Select and pick Pump_piston01. Click Select and Link in the main toolbar. Click Select by Name and double-click Dummy01 in the Select Parent dialog.*

3. Repeat Step 2 for the Pump_piston02 to Dummy02 link. Drag the Time slider and you see that the pistons wave back and forth—because the pistons and their parents, the dummies, inherit all the rotation values of the grandparent Pump_arm. Drag the Time slider to frame 0.

4. You do want the pistons to rotate with the arm, but not in the World Y-axis in this example. You will tell the dummies not to inherit the Y-axis rotation of the parent. On the main toolbar, click the Select Object button. In the Front viewport, select Dummy01 on the left side. In the Hierarchy panel, click the Link Info button. In the Inherit rollout, clear the Rotate Y check box (see Figure 14.15).

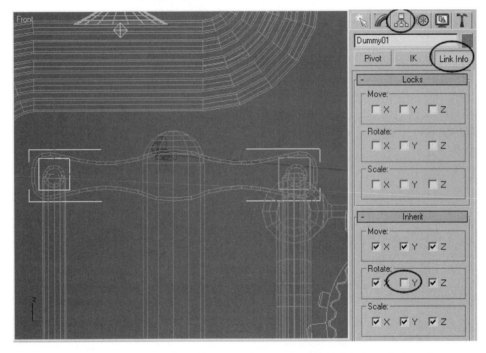

FIGURE 14.15   *Select Dummy01 and, in the Hierarchy panel, click Link Info and clear the Rotate Y check box.*

5. Drag the Time slider and notice the left piston acts as you would expect, because its Dummy01 no longer inherits the rotation in the World Y-axis of the arm.

6. Repeat step 5 for Dummy02. Drag the Time slider and the pistons both pump up and down with the action of the arm (see Figure 14.16).

7. Close all windows and dialogs and save the file. It should already be called Ch14_Linking03.max.

note

There is a little side-to-side motion because the rotation of the arm describes an arc at the centers of the dummies. That would be the case in a real situation such as this.

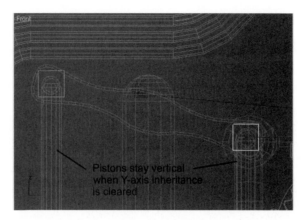

FIGURE 14.16   *When you clear the World Y-axis inheritance of the arm rotation for each dummy, the pistons do not rotate about that axis; instead, they hold their original orientation and keep the pistons vertical.*

Summary

In this chapter, you learned two important methods of Set Key animation that enable you to create keys for specific aspects of your scene, such as rotation or modifier parameters, as you need them. This keeps the number of generated keys to a manageable minimum.

Some of the topics covered in this chapter include the following:

- **Set Key animation**—With this animation method, you learned to set keys in time that record the state of objects or actions you have performed.

- **Editing and cloning keys**—You learned that animation keys that record events in time can be edited or cloned to change the state of your animation.

- **Dummy objects**—You learned that helper objects, in the shape of a cube or cross-hair point, that aid in animation control and never render in the scene can be created to make some animation easier.

- **Hierarchical linking**—You learned that hierarchical linking sets up parent-child relationships between objects for animation control.

CHAPTER 15

Controllers/Constraints

In This Chapter

In this chapter, you learn to change the type of animation controller or constraint that determines parameters of motion for objects:

- **Time Configuration**—With Time Configuration, you can change the number of frames to control the duration of the animation.

- **Animation controller**—All aspects of animation are handled by controllers assigned to object transforms or object parameters.

- **Animation constraints**—Animation constraints are similar to controllers except that they use other objects, such as splines in the case of a Path constraint to define motion.

- **Attachment constraint**—This constraint is used to control the motion of an object based on the position and orientation of a specific face of a mesh object.

- **LookAt controller**—This constraint is applied to the rotation of an object to control the direction in which the axes of the object point.

- **List controller**—Controllers and constraints can be stacked within a list controller for combinations of motion control.

The scenario for this chapter is an Artic environment with the ironclad boat. You assign new animation constraints and controllers to navigate the boat along a path around a large iceberg.

The water surface is already animated with a Wave modifier and a line object in the scene has the same Wave modifier applied to cause it to wave in coordination with the water. The line itself also has a Normalize

Spline modifier to place extra vertices along the line to give the line enough flexibility to follow the wave of the water.

You learn to determine and set the number of frames required to have the boat travel around the iceberg at a specific speed. The boat stays on the surface of the water because the line that you use as a path has the same wave frequency as the water, but you use other animation controllers to give the boat a secondary bobbing motion as it cuts through the waves.

You also add a controller to a dummy helper object that is the parent of the iceberg to cause it to be affected by the wave action.

Key Terms

- **NTSC**—National Television System Committee is the official body in the United States that determines the standards for television. Important to this chapter is that the animation rate used is 29.97 frames per second, commonly rounded to 30 frames per second.

- **Upnode**—This control element within a LookAt constraint defines which direction is defined as "up."

Time Configuration

One of the first steps to producing an animation is setting the timing of animated objects to represent realistic speeds and velocities as they move through the scene.

In this section, you learn to adjust the number of frames in the animation to simulate the ironclad boat moving at a constant 5 miles per hour as it rounds the iceberg.

For this exercise, speed and timing are based on the U.S. standards for television playback as set out by the governing body know as the National Television Systems Committee (NTSC). Early in the development of television in the United States, a playback rate of roughly 30 frames per second was chosen and remains the common rate for computer animation today. Japan uses the NTSC standard as well.

The default frame count for 3ds max 6 is 100 frames or 3.3 seconds of animation.

You must do a little math to determine the required number of frames for you to animate the boat at a specific speed using this formula: Speed=Distance ÷

note

Other parts of the world and industries use different standard animation playback rates. PAL, the standard in much of Europe, is 25 frame per second, whereas movie film is recorded at 24 frames per second.

Time. You then set the number of frames by multiplying 30 times the number of seconds.

The known factors in the equation are the speed of the boat at 5 miles per hour and the distance traveled, which you determine in Exercise 15.1 by selecting the path and using the Utilities, Measure tool.

First, you need to translate 15 miles per hour into feet per second. There are 5280 feet in 1 mile, so 15×5280 = 79,200 feet per hour. 79,200 ft/hr ÷ 60 min/hr ÷ 60 sec/min = 22 feet/second.

This information is used in the Time Configuration dialog to set the total number of frames for your animation.

Exercise 15.1   Time Configuration

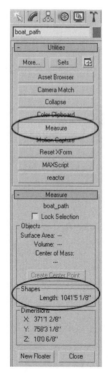

1. Open the file called Ch15_TimeConfig01.max on the CD-ROM. From the File pull-down menu, choose Save As, point to an appropriate subdirectory on your hard drive, and use the plus sign button to save a new file with the name incremented to Ch15_TimeConfig02.max. You have determined in the opening section of Chapter 15 that the boat will be traveling at 15 miles per hour or 22 feet per second. The total number of frames required for correct playback will be the distance traveled divided by the speed of the boat times 30.

2. To determine the length of a path, use the Measure tool in the Utilities panel. In the Top viewport, select the spline called boat_path. In the Utilities panel, Utilities rollout, click the Measure button. You can read in the Shapes area that the path is 1040 feet, as rounded to the nearest foot (see Figure 15.1). The 1040 feet divided by 22 feet per second equals roughly 48 seconds to cover the distance. At 30 frames per second time 48 seconds, the total number of frames must be 1440.

3. On the status bar, click the Time Configuration button, just to the left of the viewport navigation buttons at the lower right of the display (see Figure 15.2). This scene already has an animated

FIGURE 15.1
Select the boat_path shape and use Utilities, Measure to determine the length of the shape.

Wave modifier on the water surface. If you just lengthen the number of frames, the water stops animating at frame 100 as it currently does. You must adjust this existing animation to fit the new total number of frames. In the Time Configuration dialog, Animation area, click the Re-scale Time button. In the Re-scale Time dialog, enter 1440 in the Frame Count field (see Figure 15.3). Click OK, and then click OK again to see on the track bar

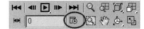

FIGURE 15.2
Clicking the Time Configuration button and entering the information in the dialog enables you to set the total number of frames of an animation.

and on the Time slider that the total number of frames has changed from 100 to 1439. The total number of frames is 1440, including frame 0.

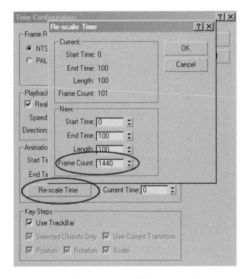

FIGURE 15.3   *In the Time Configuration dialog, Animation area, click the Re-scale Time button. Then, in the Re-scale Time dialog, enter 1440 in the Frame Count field.*

4. Save the file; it should already be called Ch15_TimeConfig02.max.

Animation Controllers and Constraints

Animation constraints or controllers that are assigned to the various aspects of objects and environments that can be animated determine animation parameters in 3ds max 6. By changing the type of constraint or controller, you can use a variety of animation parameters to adjust things such as transformations, color changes, and visibility of objects to name a few examples.

You can assign animation constraints and controllers in two places in 3ds max 6: the Motion panel and the graph editors. The Motion panel accepts constraints and controllers only for the transformation of objects, whereas the graph editors accept changes to all aspects of animation.

In Exercise 15.2, you change the default controller on the Dummy_Master object, called a Position XYZ controller, to a constraint called the Path Constraint. This enables you to use a shape in the scene to determine the travel of the Dummy_Master object that will pull the boat through the water.

Exercise 15.2   Assigning Animation Constraints or Controllers

1. Open the file called Ch15_Constraint01.max on the CD-ROM. From the File pull-down menu, choose Save As, point to an appropriate subdirectory on your hard drive, and use the plus sign button to save a new file with the name incremented to Ch15_Constraint02.max.

2. The individual boat parts are linked to a parent object called Dummy_Master. It is this Dummy helper object that you animate by assigning a new animation constraint. In turn, it pulls the boat along the path. In the Top viewport, select Dummy_Master. In the Motion panel, expand the Assign Controller rollout, and highlight Position: Position XYZ. Click the Assign Controller button to open the Assign Position Controller dialog and double-click Path Constraint in the list (see Figure 15.4).

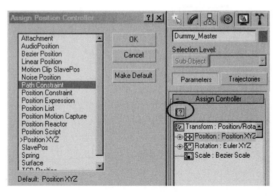

FIGURE 15.4   *In the Motion panel, highlight Position: Position XYZ and click Assign Controller. Double-click Path Constraint in the Assign Position Controller dialog.*

3. In the Motion panel, Path Parameters rollout, click the Add Path button. In the Top viewport, pick the boat_path shape (see Figure 15.5). The dummy object jumps to the first vertex of the path. Click the Add Path button to exit that mode. If you drag the

Time slider, you see the dummy pull the boat down
the path. The dummy and boat keep their original
orientation. Set the Time slider to frame 0.

tip

You can assign multiple paths
to a single Path constraint,
each with a weighting value.
The numbers don't mean anything but show a relative
weighting. Two paths with a
weight of 50 are the same as
with a weight of 1, and the
object will be equally spaced
between the paths.

note

When you assigned the Path
constraint to the position of
the dummy object, the default
Position XYZ controller was
removed and replaced by the
new controller. That process is
important to you in Exercise
15.3.

Figure 15.5 *In the Motion panel, Path Parameters rollout, click the
Add Path button and pick the boat_path in the Top
viewport. The boat_path appears in the Target list
with a weight of 50.*

4. You want the boat to travel forward down the path. In the Motion panel, Path
Parameters rollout, check Follow in the Path Options area. This aligns the dummy
and boat sideways to the path.

5. At the bottom of the Path Parameters rollout,
choose the Y-axis radio button. This points the
back of the boat down the path. Check the Flip
option to orient the boat with the front pointing
down the path (see Figure 15.6). Drag the Time
slider and you see the boat move along the curved
path, riding over the waves as it progresses. Set
the Time slider to frame 0.

6. Save the file; it should already be called
Ch15_Constraint02.max.

note

If you switch to Local reference
coordinate system in the main
toolbar, you see which axis of
Dummy_Master faces down
the path.

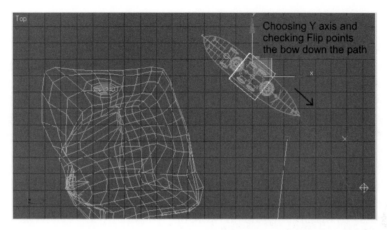

Choosing Y axis and checking Flip points the bow down the path

FIGURE 15.6 *By choosing the Y-axis radio button and checking the Flip option in the Path Parameters rollout, you can reorient the Dummy_Master on the path to cause the boat to move forward along the path.*

List Controllers

In Exercise 15.2, you exchanged the default Position XYZ controller on a Dummy helper object with a Path constraint that uses one or more splines to constrain the position of the object over time.

As noted in the exercise, when you assigned the Path constraint the original controller was replaced and its animation parameters were no longer available to you.

In many situations, you might want a combination of constraint or controller capabilities on a single object, but it is not possible just by assigning a new constraint or controller in place of another.

One of the most important animation controllers included with 3ds max 6 is the List controller. Think of it as a container that can hold any number of other constraints or controllers that are applied to the same animation parameter—Position, Rotation, Color, for example—to combine the effects that each offers.

In Exercise 15.3, you try an experiment to illustrate the effectiveness of a List controller by substituting a Path constraint with a Noise controller. This gives undesired results, so before you start, you will use the Hold option from the Edit pull-down menu to allow a safe recovery from the experiment. This is a good habit to get into for much of your work, especially while you are new to 3ds max 6.

When you see that the results are not what you want, you use the Fetch command to recover, and you apply the List controller to correct the situation.

Exercise 15.3   Assigning the List Controller

1. Open the file called Ch15_Constraint02.max on the CD-ROM or from the preceding exercise. From the File pull-down menu, choose Save As, point to an appropriate subdirectory on your hard drive, and use the plus sign button to save a new file with the name incremented to Ch15_Constraint03.max. The boat travels around the iceberg and rolls gently over the waves as it moves. You want to add a secondary up and down motion to the boat that would simulate the momentum of the boat bobbing from the wave action.

2. You will be adding a Noise controller to the Position transform of the Dummy_ Master that applies random position changes, but are not sure that this is exactly what you want. The first thing you will do is save the file as it is to the Hold buffer, so that if things do not work out, you can use the Fetch command to return to this state. In the Edit pull-down menu, choose Hold. A file is written to disk that contains your entire scene until overwritten with a new Hold action.

3. In the Top viewport, select Dummy_Master near the center of the boat, if it's not already selected. In the Motion panel Assign Controller rollout, you see that the dummy has the Path constraint that you assigned in Exercise 15.2. Expand the Assign Controller rollout, highlight Position: Path Constraint, and click the Assign Controller button. Double-click Noise Position in the Assign Position Controller list. The dummy and boat move to near the 0,0,0 World coordinate position and the Noise Controller dialog displays (see Figure 15.7).

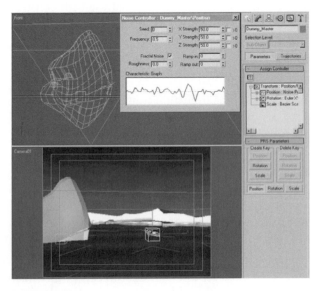

FIGURE 15.7 *Assigning a Noise Position controller to the Position of Dummy_Master replaces the Path constraint, causing the dummy to move near 0,0,0 World coordinate.*

4. Right-click in the Camera01 viewport to activate it and click the Play Animation button. The dummy and boat will appear to jitter rapidly in place and not travel along the path. You have replaced one constraint with another controller. In the Edit pull-down menu, choose Fetch. Click Yes in the About to Fetch, OK? dialog.

5. In the Top viewport, select Dummy_Master. In the Motion panel, Assign Controller rollout, highlight Position: Path Constraint. Click the Assign Controller button and double-click Position List in the list. Drag the Time slider and you will see that the dummy and boat still move along the path.

6. In the Assign Controller rollout, click the plus sign to the left of Position: Position List to expand it. The Position List controller contains the Path constraint and an Available slot (see Figure 15.8).

7. Save the file; it should already be called Ch15_Constraint03.max.

FIGURE 15.8
Assigning a position list to the Path constraint demotes the Path constraint in the list and creates a new Available slot within the Position List controller.

Adding the Noise Controller to the List Controller

You have now learned to add a new Position List controller to an existing Path constraint without replacing the Path constraint, but making it a subset of the Position List controller, retaining its animation parameters.

In Exercise 15.4, you add the Noise controller to the available slot in the Position List controller to begin stacking new animation parameters onto existing parameters.

However, you need to adjust the Noise controller from a random jittering motion in all three axes to a smoother random action affecting only the World Z-axis as the dummy and boat move down the path.

Exercise 15.4   Adding and Adjusting a Noise Controller

1. Open the file called Ch15_Constraint03.max on the CD-ROM or from the preceding exercise. From the File pull-down menu, choose Save As, point to an appropriate subdirectory on your hard drive, and use the plus sign button to save a new file with the name incremented to Ch15_Constraint04.max.

2. Select Dummy_Master in the Top viewport. In the Motion panel, Assign Controller rollout, highlight the Available slot in the Position List controller. Click the Assign Controller button and double-click Noise Position in the Assign Position Controller dialog. The Noise Position shows below Path Constraint and another Available slot appears below Noise Position. Drag the Time slider slowly and you see the random jitter occurs as the boat moves along the path. This is easier to see in the Camera01 viewport.

3. You only want random up and down motion, not side to side or front to back. In the Noise Controller dialog, right-click the spinners for X Strength and Y Strength to set them both to 0. The Strength amount determines the maximum value used in the random number generation. With the default strength of 50, random numbers are generated between –25 and +25 units (see Figure 15.9)—in this case, inches—moving the Dummy_Master above or below the path. For a boat this size, that is hardly noticeable.

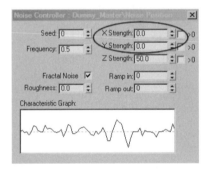

FIGURE 15.9   *In the Noise Controller dialog, right-click the spinners to the right of the X Strength and Y Strength numeric fields to set the amount to 0.*

4. In the Noise Controller dialog, enter 200 in the Z Strength field. Drag the Time slider and you see that the up and down motion of the boat significantly increases, but that it is too rough and quick to be effective. Clear the Fractal Noise check box to smooth the Characteristic Graph in the dialog and the resulting motion.

5. Enter 0.02 in the Frequency field to smooth the action to a more convincing secondary motion as the boat travels over the waves (see Figure 15.10). Close the Noise Controller dialog and play the Camera01 viewport animation. The boat rises and sinks slightly independent of the wave action.

6. Close all the dialogs and save the file. It should already be called Ch15_Constraint04.max.

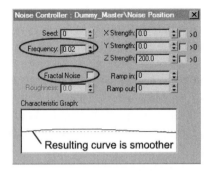

FIGURE 15.10 *A smaller Frequency setting in the Noise controller smoothes the action to make it more convincing.*

Attachment Constraint

When objects are animated, it is actually the pivot point that controls the animation. When using hierarchical linking, as you did to link the parts of the boat to the Dummy_Master object, it is the relative animation of each object's pivot point that causes the child object to mimic the motion of the parent object.

The surface of the water is animated using a Wave modifier that does not transform the pivot point, but only deforms the surface. If you want the iceberg to move according to the waving of the water, linking the iceberg would not be the solution because the parent's (water) pivot point does not move.

The Attachment constraint solves the problem by attaching the pivot point of one object to a face on another object independent of its pivot point.

The Iceberg01 object in the scene is linked as a child object to Iceberg_Dummy01. In Exercise 15.5, you assign an Attachment constraint to the Iceberg_Dummy01 and choose a face on the Water object to position the dummy and have it follow its motion. Iceberg01 will then rise, fall, and rotate to remain perpendicular to the chosen face as it moves.

Exercise 15.5   Using an Attachment Constraint to Control the Iceberg Motion

1. Open the file called Ch15_Constraint04.max on the CD-ROM or from the preceding exercise. From the File pull-down menu, choose Save As, point to an appropriate subdirectory on your hard drive, and use the plus sign button to save a new file with the name incremented to Ch15_Constraint05.max.

2. In the Top viewport, select Iceberg_Dummy01 near the center of Iceberg01. In the Motion panel, Assign Controller rollout, highlight Position: Bezier Position, the default controller type for dummy objects. Click the Assign Controller button and double-click Attachment in the Assign Position Controller dialog list. The Iceberg_Dummy01 and its child Iceberg01 move to World coordinate 0,0,0.

3. In the Motion panel, Attachment Parameters rollout, click the Pick Object button (see Figure 15.11). In the Top viewport, pick the Water object. Drag the Time slider and you see that nothing happens yet because you haven't specified a face on the water object to control the dummy. Set the Time slider to frame 0.

4. In the Motion panel, Attachment Parameters rollout, Position area, click the Set Position button. In the Top viewport, click and drag the cursor on the Water object to the left of the boat. You see a red tick on the Set Position triangle under the cursor, representing the position of the dummy's pivot point on the face (see Figure 15.12). The Iceberg01 might flip rather wildly as the Iceberg_Dummy01 reorients itself on the face. Click the Set Position button to exit that mode. Drag the Time slider to see that the Iceberg01 rocks and rolls with the wave motion. Set the Time slider to frame 0.

FIGURE 15.11
In the Motion panel, Attachment Parameters rollout, you must click the Pick Object button and pick the Water object in the scene as the controlling surface.

FIGURE 15.12
Click the Set Position button and click, hold, and move the cursor on the face you want to attach the object to.

5. The Iceberg_Dummy01 stays on, and perpendicular to, the face you chose, causing the Iceberg01 to rotate too much for such a heavy floating object. You add a LookAt constraint to the rotation of the Iceberg01 to cause its Upnode to stay aligned to the World Z-axis to stop the rotation. Select Iceberg01 and, in the Motion panel, Assign Controller rollout, highlight Rotation: Euler XYZ. Click the Assign Controller button and double-click LookAt Constraint in the Assign Rotation Controller dialog list.

6. Drag the Time slider, and you see the Iceberg01 move up and down with the waves, but no longer rotate with its parent, Iceberg_Dummy01. Notice in the LookAt Constraint rollout that the Upnode Control is set to Axis Alignment and the Source and Upnode are both set to the Z-axis, keeping the object vertical in the scene (see Figure 15.13).

7. Save the file; it should already be called Ch15_Constraint05.max.

Summary

In this chapter, you learned the following topics:

- **Time Configuration**—You learned to use Time Configuration to change the number of frames to control the duration of the animation.

- **Animation controller**—You learned that all aspects of animation are handled by controllers assigned to objects or object parameters.

- **Animation constraints**—You learned to assign Animation constraints that are similar to controllers except that they use other objects, such as splines in the case of a Path constraint, to define motion.

- **Attachment constraint**—You learned to use this constraint to control the motion of an object based on the position and orientation of a specific face of another mesh object.

- **LookAt constraint**—You learned to assign this constraint to the rotation of an object to control the direction in which axes of the object point.

- **List controller**—You learned about one of the most important constraints that allows other controllers and constraints to be stacked within a List controller for combinations of motion control.

tip

Assigning the Attachment constraint to the Iceberg_Dummy01 enables you to adjust the position or rotation of its child, Iceberg01, on the water surface.

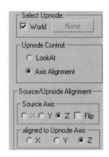

FIGURE 15.13

Assigning a LookAt constraint to Iceberg01 keeps its Z-axis aligned with the World Z-axis, whereas its parent Iceberg_Dummy01 still rotates to stay perpendicular to the face it is attached to.

CHAPTER 16

Graph Editors

In This Chapter

In this chapter, you learn to use graph editors, the Dope Sheet, and the Curve Editor in 3ds max 6 to fine-tune animations and to apply ease curves to influence existing animation:

- **Dope Sheet**—This graph editor presents the animation keys in a spreadsheet-like format, allowing you a broad view of animation relationships that can then be edited.

- **Curve Editor**—The Curve Editor displays animation with function curves shown on a graph to make editing easier to visualize.

- **Ease curves**—These function curves are superimposed on top of existing animation to fine-tune the motion. The ease curves can easily be removed, without affecting the underlying animation, if the changes are not what you want.

In the chapter, you return to the engine room of the boat to find that things are not going so well. The rocking pump arm that you animated in Chapter 14, "Set Key Animation," doesn't have smooth action. It is as if it were catching on something as it pumps. Somebody has also left a tin oil can on the exhaust that falls to the grate, and an insect is flying around one of the lights that hangs from the ceiling.

It is not so bad that these things happen in the animation, but that they are not the way you want them to be. In this chapter, you learn to use graph editors for a more visual method of editing animation parameters in the scene.

First, you learn to use the Track View - Dope Sheet to make the falling oil can more convincing as it hits the hard grate. Right now, it just passes through the grate and stops. You will animate vertices to make it appear as though the oil can crushes as it makes contact with the grate.

You then learn to use the Track View - Curve Editor to investigate why the pump seems to have a catch in the action and to correct it to produce a smooth motion as the pump arm rocks back and forth.

Finally, the insect that is flying around the ceiling light has a flight pattern that is much too regular and consistent. You learn to apply an ease curve in the Curve Editor to superimpose a more halting motion as the insect nears the light itself.

Key Terms

- **Function curve**—These display the animation controller or constraint in graphical form over time.
- **Dope Sheet**—The term originates with traditional cel animation, showing dots or keys on a graph to represent action over time.
- **Tangent**—The amount of curvature on either side of an animation key that describes the velocity change approaching or leaving the key.

Graph Editors

The graph editors enable you to show similar information in two different ways: Track View - Curve Editor shows animation as a set of function curves on a graph; Track View - Dope Sheet shows animation keys on a graph.

Each graph editor enables you to assign new animation constraints and controllers to any component of a scene that can be animated or to change animation parameters of existing animations; in addition, you can see the relationships of multiple selected objects to compare their animation.

Familiarize yourself with the fundamentals of both graph editors so that you can choose the most appropriate way to adjust any particular animated scene.

Figure 16.1 shows the Graph Editors pull-down menu, from which you can choose one or the other type of editor.

note

In Chapter 15, "Controllers/ Constraints," you assigned animation constraints and controllers to the transformations of object in the Motion panel. Animated parameters for materials or lights, for example, can only be made in the graph editors.

Track views can be saved from this pull-down menu to make it faster to return to the same location deep within the graph editor hierarchy when editing the same parameters over and over, and those saved graph editors can be deleted when no longer needed.

FIGURE 16.1

From the Graph Editors pull-down menu, you can choose Track View - Curve Editor or Track View - Dope Sheet.

Track View - Dope Sheet

In Exercise 16.1, you open a scene of the engine room of your boat that has the added animation of a falling oil can and a flying insect as well as the animated pump arm from Chapter 14.

When the oil can hits the grate, however, it continues through it and appears to get stuck about halfway into the grate. This would not likely happen (unless, of course, you want it to...you are the animator), but instead, the oil can would bounce or crush as it hit.

You learn to make it appear to crush against the grate as it hits, crumpling the oil can and flattening one end. It is not actually the grate that makes the oil can appear to crush, but you use a grid helper object that has been placed at the top surface of the grate and animate the alignment of the oil can vertices that move beyond the surface of the grate to that grid plane.

However, the animated vertices start to appear to crush starting at frame 0 and be completely crushed at frame 45. You use Track View - Dope Sheet to adjust the start time of the animated vertices to frame 36, when the oil can makes apparent contact with the grate surface.

Exercise 16.1   Crushing an Oil Can and Adjusting the Animation in Track View - Dope Sheet

1. Open the file called Ch16_DopeSheet01.max on the CD-ROM. From the File pull-down menu, choose Save As, point to an appropriate subdirectory on your hard drive, and use the plus sign button to save a new file with the name incremented to Ch16_DopeSheet02.max.

2. Select the Oil_Can object sitting on top of the exhaust of the engine. Drag the Time slider to frame 38 and zoom in on the Oil_Can and Grate01 in the Front viewport. The Oil_Can is very close to striking the Grate01 at this frame (see Figure 16.2). Drag the Time slider to frame 45 and the Oil_Can stops halfway through the Grate01.

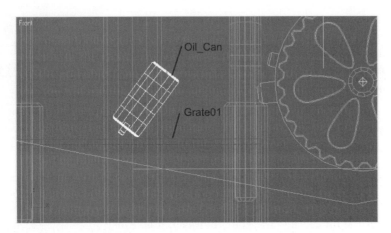

FIGURE 16.2   *Advancing the Time slider to frame 38 shows the Oil_Can very close to the top surface of Grate01.*

3. On the main toolbar, click Select by Name and double-click Crash_Grid in the list to select it. In the Front viewport, move the cursor over the top edge of Grate01 where the grid object sits and right-click. Choose Activate Grid in the Quad menu. You will use this grid as an alignment tool for the vertices of the can.

4. In the Front viewport, select Oil_Can. On the status bar, click the Auto Key button to activate that mode of animation. The button, the slider bar, and the viewport border highlight turns red. In the Modify panel, Stack view, expand Editable Mesh and highlight Vertex sub-object mode. Drag a selection window around all the Oil_Can vertices below the top edge of Grate01. You should see 176 Vertices Selected at the bottom of the Selection rollout (see Figure 16.3). At the bottom of the Edit Geometry rollout, click the Grid Align button. This moves all the selected vertices in a straight line to the active grid. Click Auto Key to disable it, exit sub-object Vertex in Stack view by clicking Editable Mesh, and click UVW Mapping modifier to return to the top of the stack.

5. Scrub the Time slider and you see in the Camera01 viewport that the Oil_Can starts to crush before it starts to fall from the exhaust and is fully crushed when it hits the Grate01. Drag the Time slider to frame 0.

6. Save the file; it should already be called Ch16_DopeSheet02.max.

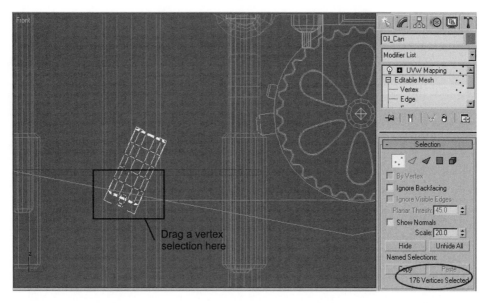

FIGURE 16.3   *At frame 45, with Auto Key animation mode on and, in sub-object Vertex mode, drag a selection window around all the Oil_Can vertices below the top surface of Grate01.*

Adjusting the Animation in Track View - Dope Sheet

In Exercise 16.2, you use the graph editor called Track View - Dope Sheet to adjust animation keys in time to correct the fact that the Oil_Can vertices that you aligned to the Crash_Grid start to move from frame 0, just as it falls from the exhaust pipe to the grate below.

If you were adjusting the animated position changes of the can itself, you might be able to simply use the track bar to move keys in time. Because it is only a subset of 176 vertices that are animated, however, a graph editor is the only method of accessing that level of the keys.

Exercise 16.2   Using Track View - Dope Sheet to Edit Oil_Can

1. Open the file called Ch16_DopeSheet02.max on the CD-ROM or from the preceding exercise. From the File pull-down menu, choose Save As, point to an appropriate subdirectory on your hard drive, and use the plus sign button to save a new file with the name incremented to Ch16_DopeSheet03.max. Drag the Time slider and observe in the Camera01 viewport that the top of the Oil_Can begins its

animation almost immediately. It should not begin to crush until it makes contact with the top surface of the Grate01.

2. In Camera01 viewport, select Oil_Can. From the Graph Editors pull-down menu, choose Track View - Dope Sheet (see Figure 16.4). The selected object, Oil_Can, appears at the top of the list in the panel on the left.

note

The gray cube to the left of the object name is highlighted yellow when the object is selected. You can select other objects in the scene by clicking their gray cubes.

Highlighting just the name of other objects or levels in the list does not select the object in the scene; you must highlight the gray cube itself.

FIGURE 16.4   *You can access Track View - Dope Sheet from the Graph Editors pull-down menu.*

3. Click the plus sign to the left of Oil_Can in the list to expand it, to show Transform, Modified Object, and Oil_Can materials in the list. Expand Modified Object. Expand Editable Mesh (Object). Expand Master Point Controller. This reveals the list of animated vertices below the Master Point Controller and their keys at frames 0 and 45 in the graph panel (see Figure 16.5).

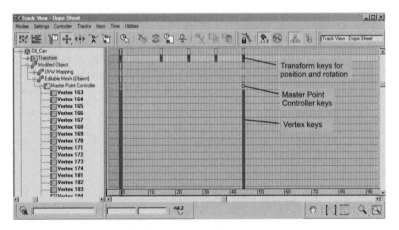

FIGURE 16.5   *Expanding Oil_Can in the left panel reveals animation keys for the vertices in the graph panel to the right.*

4. In the graph panel, to the right of Master Point Controller in the list, select the green key at frame 0 and drag the key to the right until the tooltip reads Time:36 Offset:36 to indicate that you want the vertices to start moving at frame 36 (see Figure 16.6).

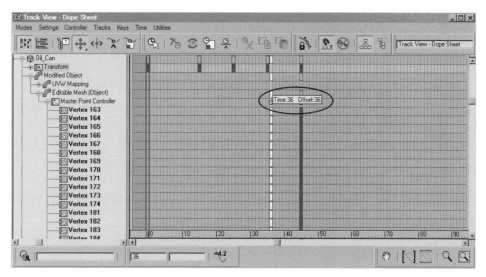

FIGURE 16.6 *Pick and drag the green Master Point Controller key from frame 0 to frame 36. The vertices now start to move at frame 36.*

5. Close Track View - Dope Sheet and drag the Time slider to see the resulting animation changes. The Oil_Can retains its shape until it makes contact with the Grate01 and crushes to frame 45 where that part of the animation ends.

6. In the Camera01 viewport, select Crash_Grid at the top surface of Grate01. Right-click in the viewport and choose Activate HomeGrid in the Quad menu.

7. Save the file; it should already be called Ch16_DopeSheet03.max.

caution

Leaving grid helper objects as the active grid can be confusing as you try to work in 3D space. Always activate the Home grid as soon as you have finished with any custom grid objects.

Track View - Curve Editor

In Exercise 16.3, you use a different form of graph editor, the Track View - Curve Editor, to remove a slight catch in the action of the Pump_arm as it rocks back and forth.

This is not something you specifically animated, but is the result of the type of default rotation controller tangency at the keys and the fact that the base animation from frame 0 to frame 20 is cycling over the full 100 frames in the scene.

It would be possible to correct the issue using Track View -Dope Sheet, but the problem itself and the solution would not be so visually obvious as it is when you use Track View - Curve Editor to display a function curve on a graph that describes the motion over time.

Exercise 16.3   Using Track View - Curve Editor

1. Open the file called Ch16_CurveEditor01.max on the CD-ROM. From the File pull-down menu, choose Save As, point to an appropriate subdirectory on your hard drive, and use the plus sign button to save a new file with the name incremented to Ch16_CurveEditor02.max. Click the Play Animation button and watch the Pump_arm pause slightly when it is horizontal before continuing its rocking motion. The pause is a bit more noticeable when the right side of the Pump_arm is traveling downward. Stop the animation and drag the Time slider to frame 0.

2. In the Front viewport, select Pump_arm. In the track bar, you see rotation keys that were set using the Set Key animation method you learned in Chapter 14, Exercise 14.2. The keys are from frame 0 to frame 20, but the animation continues to frame 100. This was also done in Track View - Curve Editor, as you will see. In the Graph Editors pull-down menu, choose Track View - Curve Editor.

3. The three rotation axes are highlighted in the left panel for the selected Pump_arm, and the function curves for each axis display in the graph panel on the right. The only animation is in the Y Rotation axis, so pick it in the left panel to highlight it only and to display the green function curve in the graph panel. The slight bump in the green curve at the gray 0-degree line indicates a change of velocity, which causes the pause (see Figure 16.7). The solid green curve is the actual keyed animation, the dotted green curve is created in the Controller pull-down menu of Track View - Curve Editor by setting the Out-of-Range Types to Cycle on the outgoing side of the existing animation (see Figure 16.8).

tip

The Graph Editor windows have their own zoom and pan tools at the lower left of the window that can help when working on sets of curves or keys.

Using Track View - Curve Editor Zoom Region might help with adjusting the tangents.

You can also use the mouse wheel when the Graph Editor is active.

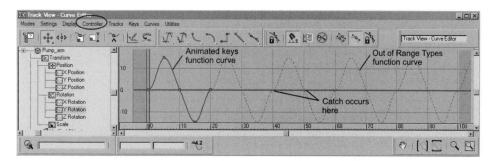

FIGURE 16.7   *With Pump_arm selected, Track View - Curve Editor shows green function curves for the Y Rotation axis. The solid curve is actual keyed animation and the dotted curve is set in Controller pull-down menu, Out-of-Range Types options.*

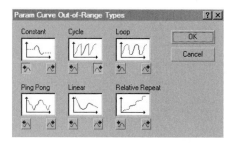

FIGURE 16.8   *The Param Curve Out-of-Range Types has been set to Cycle to continue the animation over the full range of frames in the scene.*

4. In the graph panel of Track View - Curve Editor, drag a selection window around the three keys on the 0-degree line. You see blue tangency handles that were set with the default Auto tangency when the keys were created. On the Track View - Curve Editor toolbar, click the Set Tangents to Custom button. The tangency handles turn black. Pick the control point at the end of each handle and position it over the green line to smooth the curve (see Figure 16.9). Close Track View - Curve Editor and play the animation to see the results.

5. Save the file; it should already be called Ch16_CurveEditor02.max.

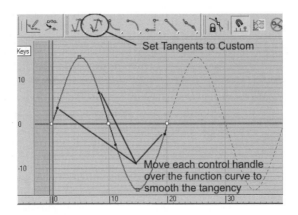

FIGURE 16.9   *By using Set Tangents to Custom and adjusting the tangency control handles, you can remove the animation pause caused by unwanted curvature in the function curve.*

Ease Curves and Velocity Control

Controlling the velocity of animated objects can be very important for convincing results. As you learned in Exercise 16.3, 3ds max 6 has defaults settings that assume certain parameters that are not always what you want in your animation.

In Exercise 16.4, you learn to apply an ease curve to an existing animation, a method that enables you to superimpose velocity changes onto the base animation. The function curve display of the ease curve provides visual feedback on the relative velocity of the object throughout the animation.

The prime advantage of applying the ease curve is that it does not change the base animation and can be removed at any time, or you can stack ease curve on ease curve to have subsequent levels of refinement to your motion. The ease curve is not a new controller type, so it does not replace the current animation. The ease curve must be applied in the Track View - Curve Editor.

Your animated engine room scene has an insect flying at a steady velocity near the light fixtures on the ceiling. An object called Bug_Dummy is animated with a path constraint that has been set to Constant Velocity. Bug_Dummy has a pair of flapping wings linked as children to it.

Your task, in Exercise 16.4, is to adjust the velocity of the Bug_Dummy so that it slows and pauses at the light on the left as seen in the Camera01 viewport, and then continues on its flight path.

Exercise 16.4   Applying an Ease Curve for Velocity Control

1. Open the file called Ch16_EaseCurve01.max on the CD-ROM. From the File pull-down menu, choose Save As, point to an appropriate subdirectory on your hard drive, and use the plus sign button to save a new file with the name incremented to Ch16_ EaseCurve02.max. Click the Play Animation button and you see the Bug_Dummy pull the wings at a steady velocity around the hanging light. Stop the animation and drag the Time slider to frame 0.

2. In the Front viewport, select Bug_Dummy. In the Graph Editors pull-down menu, choose Track View - Curve Editor. This displays a straight line in the graph panel to the right representing the constant velocity of the Path Constraint Percent field.

3. In the Curves pull-down menu of Track View - Curve Editor, choose Apply - Ease Curve. You won't see any apparent change in the Curve Editor. On closer observation, however, you might notice a plus sign to the left of Percent in the left panel. Click the plus sign to expand Percent. Highlight Ease Curve in the list to show the straight-line curve replicating the original percent curve (see Figure 16.10).

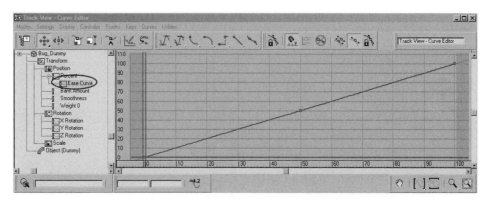

FIGURE 16.10   *Applying an ease curve to the percent of a path constraint and highlighting Ease Curve in the left panel shows a copy of the underlying function curve with an extra control key in the middle of the curve.*

4. In the Track View - Curve Editor graph panel, select the control key in the middle of the curve. In the Value field on the right side at the bottom left of the graph panel, enter 25 and press Enter (see Figure 16.11). At frame 50, the object will be at 25 percent along the path and the function curve will be flat at the left and get steeper toward the right. Play the animation and you see that Bug_Dummy is stopped where the curve is horizontal and increases velocity as the curve gets steeper.

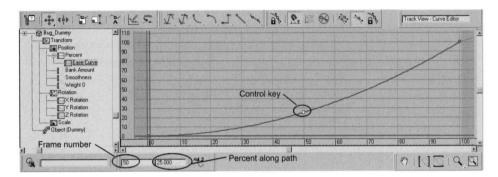

FIGURE 16.11 *Select the key in the middle of the function curve and enter 25 in the Value field at the lower left. Play the animation to see the change in velocity of Bug_Dummy.*

5. Now, add a key to the curve and adjust the velocity. On the Track View - Curve Editor toolbar, click the Add Keys button and click the function curve where it intersects with the vertical line near frame 60 in the horizontal time line. Click the Move Keys button on the toolbar to exit Add Keys mode. Enter 28 in the percent field and make sure the frame field is at 60 (see Figure 16.12). Play the animation and you see that the Bug_Dummy slows almost to a stop behind the light.

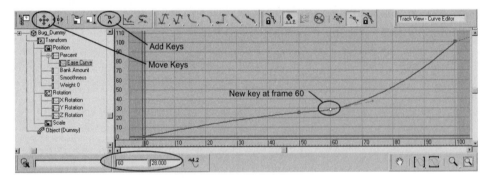

FIGURE 16.12 *By adding a new key to the function curve and adjusting the percent to 28, you can slow Bug_Dummy along the animation path.*

6. Select the control key at frame 50 and enter 30 in the Frame field and 40 in the Percent field. Play the animation and you see that where the curve slopes downward to the right, the Bug_Dummy goes backward on the path. Stop the animation.

7. Select the control key at frame 60 and enter 50 in the Frame field and 40 in the Percent field. Play the animation and, even though the two keys are set to 40 percent the curve is not flat and the Bug-Dummy does not stop, but still has a slight backward motion between frames 30 and 50. Stop the animation.

8. Right-click the control key at frame 50. In the Bug_Dummy\Ease Curve dialog, click and hold on the In Tangency button and choose the Linear button from the flyouts (see Figure 16.13).

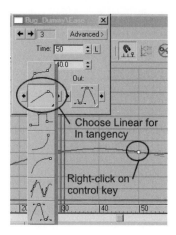

FIGURE 16.13   *Select the control key at frame 50 and right-click it. Click and hold on the In Tangency button and choose Linear from the flyouts.*

9. In the Bug_Dummy\Ease Curve dialog, click the black arrow to the left of the In Tangency button to copy the linear tangency to the out tangency of the control key at frame 30. This flattens the curve between the key at frame 30 and the key at frame 50 (see Figure 16.14). Play the animation and you see the Bug_Dummy stop completely between frames 30 and 50 and then continue the flight path. Stop the animation.

10. Close all dialogs and save the file. It should already be called Ch16_EaseCurve02.max.

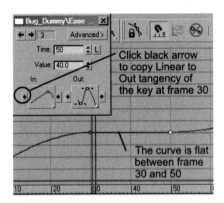

FIGURE 16.14   *Copying the linear tangency from the In side of the control key at frame 50 to the out side of the control key at frame 30 results in a flat curve to stop the object.*

Summary

In this chapter, you learned about these features:

- **Dope Sheet**—You learned that this graph editor presents the animation keys in a spreadsheet-like format, allowing you a broad view of animation relationships that can then be edited.

- **Curve Editor**—The Track View - Curve Editor displays animation with function curves shown on a graph to make editing easier to visualize (as you did when you learned to fix a pause in the Pump_arm animation).

- **Ease curves**—You learned that these function curves are superimposed on top of existing animation to fine tune the motion. The Ease Curves can easily be removed if the changes are not what you want without affecting the underlying animation.

PART V

Special Effects

CHAPTER 17

Reactor

In This Chapter

In this chapter, you learn some of the fundamentals of scene setup and calculation using the 3ds max 6 reactor feature, in which objects interact with each other and with environmental factors such as gravity and wind:

- **Rigid body collections**—You learn to set up rigid body collections to calculate the effects of colliding objects.

- **Cloth modifier and collection**—Some reactor collision detection requires that objects have special modifiers applied before being included in a collection for processing. You learn to apply a reactor Cloth modifier to simulate a hanging flag.

- **External forces**—You learn to apply external forces such as simulated wind to affect the movement of objects in a scene.

- **Baking collision data**—You learn to use reactor collision detection as a modeling tool by using the Snapshot tool to "freeze" copies of deformed objects in time.

Key Terms

- **Rigid body**—In 3ds max 6, rigid body objects are defined as having no surface deformation during collisions.

- **Cloth**—Cloth is an open-edged mesh with a special modifier that mimics soft, flexible surfaces deformed by simulated natural events or collisions with other objects.

- **Gravity**—Simulated gravity exists by default for all scenes in which reactor collision solutions are calculated.
- **Wind**—A force used in reactor calculations to simulate wind.
- **Snapshot**—A tool in 3ds max that creates copies of animated objects, including deformed objects, frozen in time.

Reactor

The reactor plug-in included with 3ds max 6 enables you to set up various types of complex physical reactions between objects or between objects and simulated forces.

An important first step to using reactor is to assign objects to reactor collections based on the physical properties that you want the objects to simulate. In this chapter, for example, you use collections of rigid body objects and cloth objects.

Rigid body objects only need to be included in a collection to be included in the calculations, but other types of simulations, such as cloth and rope, first must have a modifier applied to be recognized by the particular collection you need to add them to.

In this chapter, you learn to animate the Oil_Can object in the engine room scene with reactor to simulate a more natural motion than you could create by hand in a productive amount of time. In this case, the can will not crush as it hits the grate, but will be a rigid object that bounces naturally as it detects the surface of the Grate01.

The initial motion of the Oil_Can is caused by gravity, a force that is present by default in all reactor simulations. The Oil_Can has been positioned slightly above the exhaust pipe and gravity causes it to fall onto the round pipe and roll off to one side.

You also find a flag hanging in the engine room that will be fixed in place at its corners and allowed to drape naturally in a reaction to gravity's pull.

External forces can be added to a reactor scene for further interaction between objects. You learn to apply and adjust a wind force to create extra motion in the flag.

Although reactor is intended for animation, it is also a good modeling option when used with the Snapshot tool. You learn to make copies of the blowing flag that have been frozen in time as the wind deforms them. You could use similar techniques to make bedspreads and tablecloths or curtains for architectural scenes that do not require the animation but for which you want a natural and random appearance.

While working with reactor, you use the Hold and Fetch commands in the Edit pull-down menu extensively. The reactor calculations create animation keys on every frame for the objects in the simulation and that cannot be undone easily. Hold and Fetch allow you the freedom to experiment and return to the starting state in the scene much more easily.

Setting Up a Reactor Rigid Body Collision

In Exercise 17.1, you open a scene of the engine room of your boat that has a version of the Oil_Can (that will not crush) and a new flag suspended in space near the back wall.

You simulate the Oil_Can falling from the exhaust pipe to the grate below, bouncing naturally based on physical parameters set to define the colliding objects.

The pull of gravity is a default force within any reactor calculation, but you must assign specific properties to objects, such as mass or weight, elasticity values, and whether or not they can move or are fixed in space.

Before any calculations can be performed, you must assign objects to particular collections to define their overall properties. In this example, all colliding objects must belong to a rigid body collection.

Exercise 17.1   Rigid Body Collections and Object Properties

1. Open the file called Ch17_Reactor01.max on the CD-ROM. From the File pull-down menu, choose Save As, point to an appropriate subdirectory on your hard drive, and use the plus sign button to save a new file with the name incremented to Ch17_Reactor02.max. This scene is similar to what you saw in Chapter 16, "Graph Editors," with the animation removed from the Oil_Can on the exhaust pipe.

2. Right-click the main toolbar in a space between or below buttons and choose reactor from the menu (see Figure 17.1). This activates a new toolbar along the left side of the display with reactor buttons.

3. In the Camera01 viewport, select Oil_Can, Exhaust01, and Grate01 objects. On the reactor toolbar, click the Create Rigid Body Collection button. A new nonrenderable symbol appears in the viewports, and the Modify panel is activated to show the three objects defined as Rigid Bodies (see Figure 17.2).

note

The reactor toolbar is on by default in 3ds max 6, but was disabled and saved in the max-start.max file that you learned about in Chapter 2, "Important Fundamental Concepts in 3ds max 6."

FIGURE 17.1
Right-click the main toolbar in the empty space between or below buttons and choose reactor from the menu.

4. In the Camera01 viewport, select only Exhaust01. In the Utilities panel, click the reactor button. In the reactor panel that appears, expand the Properties rollout. In the Physical Properties area, check Unyielding (see Figure 17.3). This tells the object to be included in the reactor calculation as a rigid body, but not to be influenced by gravity. Otherwise, the exhaust pipe would fall in the simulation.

FIGURE 17.2
Selecting objects and clicking the Create Rigid Body Collection button places a symbol in the viewports and adds the selected objects to a list in the Modify panel, RB Collection Properties rollout.

FIGURE 17.3
Select Exhaust01 and, in the Utilities panel, reactor panel, set the object to Unyielding in the Properties rollout.

5. In the Camera01 viewport, select Grate01. In the reactor panel, Properties rollout, set the Elasticity to 0.5 and check Unyielding in the Physical Properties area. In the Simulation Geometry area, choose the Use Bounding Box radio button (see Figure 17.4). The increased elasticity setting makes objects that collide with the grate bounce more. The Use Bounding Box Simulation Geometry option simplifies the work the simulator must calculate by ignoring all the holes in the surface of the grate.

6. In the Camera01 viewport, select Oil_Can. In the Properties rollout, set the Mass to 3 kg and set Elasticity to 0.5. This object is not unyielding because you want it to fall when gravity is calculated.

7. In the reactor panel, World rollout, enter 1.5" in the Col. Tolerance field (see Figure 17.5). This collision tolerance number is how close an object must be to another object before the collision calculations start. Higher numbers make the objects float above other objects or appear not to collide before reacting. Smaller numbers take longer to calculate.

8. Save the file; it should already be called Ch17_Reactor02.max.

tip

It would be possible to check Use Bounding Box if calculation speed were important, but the handle at the top of the can would be ignored and the can might not bounce naturally. This scene is simple enough for even the slowest computers to calculate in a reasonable time.

caution

Col. Tolerance settings less that 1/40th the value of the World Scale (default 1 meter = 3' 3 2/8") can cause erratic behavior. If you need smaller Col. Tolerance values, you might need to reduce the World Scale value to compensate.

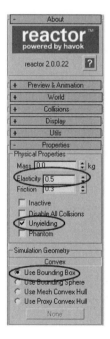

FIGURE 17.4
Set Grate01 to an Elasticity value of 0.5, make it Unyielding, and choose Use Bounding Box as Simulation Geometry type.

FIGURE 17.5
In the reactor panel, World rollout, set Col. Tolerance to 1.5" so that objects collide at smaller distances to other objects in the collection.

Calculating the Reactor Solution

In Exercise 17.2, you calculate the reactor solution to find that you need to move the can up slightly from the top of the exhaust pipe that it sits on. If you try a reactor solution before doing that, the can falls straight through the pipe when gravity begins to be calculated. This is because the can is closer than the 1.5" Col. Tolerance you set in Exercise 17.1.

You then process the calculation of the current reactor solution that you have set up. Again, this creates animation keys on every frame for each object animated in the scene and that cannot be undone. You will use Edit, Hold to save the current state of the scene in a buffer file so that you can use Fetch if the simulation needs modification.

Exercise 17.2   Creating a Reactor Animation

1. Open the file called Ch17_Reactor02.max on the CD-ROM or from the preceding exercise. From the File pull-down menu, choose Save As, point to an appropriate subdirectory on your hard drive, and use the plus sign button to save a new file with the name incremented to Ch17_Reactor03.max.

2. In the Utilities panel, reactor panel, Preview & Animation rollout, check the Update Viewports option. In the Edit pull-down menu, check Hold to save the current state of the scene in a buffer file. In the Preview & Animation rollout, click the Create Animation button. Click OK to the reactor dialog warning that includes This Action Cannot Be Undone. You are then presented with a World Analysis dialog indicating that there are interpenetrations between the Exhaust01 and Oil_Can (see Figure 17.6). This does not mean that they are physically touching each other, but that they are within the Col. Tolerance setting. Click Cancel to exit the dialog without processing.

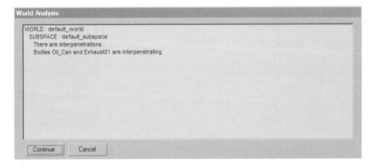

FIGURE 17.6 *Trying to create an animation at this point returns a World Analysis dialog reporting that two objects are interpenetrating. This means that they are closer than the Col. Tolerance setting and that they might not react as expected. They can fall through the exhaust.*

3. In the main toolbar, click the Select button and pick Oil_Can, then click the Select and Move button. On the status bar, toggle from Absolute Mode Transform Type-In to Offset Mode Transform Type-In. In the Z-axis transform type-in field, enter 1.5" and press Enter. The Oil_Can moves up off the Exhaust01.

4. In the Edit pull-down menu, choose Hold to save the new information in the buffer file and overwrite the previous file.

5. In the reactor panel, Preview & Animation rollout, click the Create Animation button. Click OK in the reactor dialog. The reactor solution is processed and, in the viewports, you see the Oil_Can fall to the Exhaust01, roll off, and bounce on the Grate01 before coming to rest. Click the Play Animation button to view the convincing motion. Stop the animation.

6. Save the file; it should already be called Ch17_Reactor03.max.

Cloth in Reactor

As mentioned earlier in this chapter, simulating the effect of a draping object such as cloth requires a slightly different approach to the process. Before objects can be added to a cloth collection in reactor, the mesh object must have the reactor Cloth modifier applied. It is in the reactor Cloth modifier that you set the specific parameters, such as mass and stiffness, for example.

Objects with the reactor Cloth modifier must be open-edged—a Plane primitive object is a good example—and have a sufficient number of vertices to allow deformation. You can add other modifiers, such as MeshSmooth or Tessellate, above the reactor Cloth modifier for more detailed deformations without adding to the reactor calculation overhead.

In Exercise 17.3, you include the flat plane called Flag01 suspended in space on the far side of the motor into a reactor cloth simulation. First, however, you must fix part of the Flag01 in space or it will just fall through the boat hull when gravity is calculated.

This is accomplished in sub-object Vertex mode of the reactor Cloth modifier by selecting vertices and declaring them as fixed in space. Then, gravity causes the Flag01 to drape naturally as if hung by its corners. You then learn to add a MeshSmooth modifier for a softer-looking cloth object.

tip

Closed-edged objects (a box, for example) could also be deformed similarly to cloth reactions, but you must use reactor SoftBody modifiers and collections.

Exercise 17.3   Making a Flag Drape Naturally

1. Open the file called Ch17_Cloth01.max from the CD-ROM. From the File pull-down menu, choose Save As, point to an appropriate subdirectory on your hard drive, and use the plus sign button to save a new file with the name incremented to Ch17_Cloth02.max.

2. Select Flag01 in the Camera01 viewport. On the reactor toolbar, click the Create Cloth Collection button. Nothing happens because the selected object does not have a reactor Cloth modifier assigned yet.

3. With Flag01 still selected, click the Apply Cloth Modifier button on the reactor toolbar. The Modify panel displays the Flag01 in stack view as a plane with a reactor Cloth modifier and a Properties roll-out displays the parameters for cloth (see Figure 17.7). You use the current parameters.

FIGURE 17.7
Adding a reactor Cloth modifier to Flag01 shows the Properties rollout in the Modify panel. You will use the default properties.

4. On the reactor toolbar, click the Create Cloth Collection button. A new cloth collection symbol shows in the display, and the Flag01 is listed under Cloth Entities in the Properties rollout in the Modify panel.

5. In the Edit pull-down menu, choose Hold to save the existing scene to the buffer file. In the Utilities panel, reactor panel, Preview & Animation rollout, click the Create Animation button. Click OK in the reactor dialog. The Flag01 falls because it is not attached to anything and there are no other objects in valid reactor collections for it to collide with. In the Edit pull-down menu, choose Fetch. Click Yes in the 3ds max dialog to fetch the file from the Hold buffer.

6. Select the Flag01 in the Camera01 viewport. In the Modify panel, Stack view, expand reactor Cloth and highlight Vertex (see Figure 17.8).

7. In the Camera01 viewport, select the vertex at the upper-left corner of Flag01, and then hold Ctrl and select vertex at the upper-right corner to add it to the selection set. In the Modify panel, Constraints rollout, click the Fix Vertices button. The list shows the Constrain To World message to indicate the vertices cannot move (see Figure 17.9).

FIGURE 17.8
In the Modify panel, Stack view, expand reactor Cloth and highlight Vertex. This enables you to select Flag01 vertices to be fixed in space.

FIGURE 17.9
Select the upper-corner vertices of Flag01 and click Fix Vertices in the Modify panel, Constraints rollout. The vertices are now fixed in space and do not move.

8. In the Edit pull-down menu, click Hold. In the Utilities panel, reactor panel, Preview & Animation rollout, click the Create Animation button. Click OK in the reactor dialog. When the calculations are finished, click the Play Animation button and you see that gravity pulls the Flag01 and it bounces and swings with its corners fixed in space.

9. From the Edit pull-down menu, choose Fetch and click Yes in the 3ds max dialog. Flag01 looks a bit like a stiff rubber sheet. You make some adjustments to soften it. Select Flag01 and, in the Modify panel, Modifier List, choose MeshSmooth. In the Subdivision Amount rollout, enter 2 in the Iterations field. This adds vertices to the final product after the initial calculations. In the Local Control rollout, clear the Isoline Display check box to see the new mesh (see Figure 17.10).

10. In the Edit pull-down menu, choose Hold. In the reactor panel, Preview & Animation rollout, click Create Animation. Click OK in the reactor dialog. Click the Play Animation button and see that the Flag01 has more flexibility as it sways and bounces.

11. Save the file; it should already be called Ch17_Cloth02.max.

FIGURE 17.10
Add a MeshSmooth modifier to Flag01 and increase Iterations to 2 for a more complex object. The original object is still used in the calculations for speed.

External Forces—Wind

The default external force of gravity is automatically applied in reactor calculations. You can also add wind as a force to influence objects in the scene. Rigid bodies could be made to blow around the scene or, as you will learn, the hanging Flag01 can blow as if there is air movement in the engine room from the cylinders.

In Exercise 17.4, you open the scene with the Flag01 set up as cloth, but with the previous animation removed. Some of the properties have been changed in the reactor Cloth modifier to make it appear lighter.

The location of the wind symbol does not affect its forces, but the direction it points is important. The symbol looks like a weathervane to enable you to aim it.

Exercise 17.4   Adding Wind as a Force

1. Open the file called Ch17_Wind01.max from the CD-ROM. From the File pull-down menu, choose Save As, point to an appropriate subdirectory on your hard drive, and use the plus sign button to save a new file with the name incremented to Ch17_Wind02.max.

2. Click the Create Wind button on the reactor toolbar. It looks like a rooster on a weathervane. In the Front viewport, pick to the right of the engine to place the symbol. The wind blows from left to right of the World X-axis (see Figure 17.11).

FIGURE 17.11   *Add the reactor wind symbol to the right of the engine in the Front viewport. Wind direction is from left to right in the viewport as seen by the weathervane.*

3. On the main toolbar, click the Select and Rotate button. On the status bar, enter 135 in the Y-axis Transform Type-In field. The wind now blows from the engine toward the flag at a 45-degree angle to its surface.

4. In the Modify panel, Properties rollout, enter 4' in the Wind Speed field and press Enter. In the Edit pull-down menu, choose Hold.

tip

In 3ds max 6, the wind has been improved to allow the parameters, such as wind strength, to be animated.

5. In the Utilities panel, reactor panel, Preview & Animation rollout, click the Create Animation button. Click OK in the reactor dialog.

6. Click the Play Animation button and see the Flag01 does not just hang and sway, but blows toward the back wall of the engine room and flaps from the force of the wind.

7. Save the file; it is already called Ch17_Wind02.max.

Using Snapshot to Copy Deformations in Time

In Exercise 17.5, you use the Snapshot tool to create several copies of Flag01 to capture mesh objects that are frozen in time during the animation you created in Exercise 17.4.

The Snapshot objects are no longer animation, nor are they part of the reactor Cloth modifier calculations, but are editable mesh objects that would be difficult to create modifying by hand.

Exercise 17.5   Snapshot and Reactor Cloth

1. Open the file called Ch17_Snapshot01.max from the CD-ROM. From the File pull-down menu, choose Save As, point to an appropriate subdirectory on your hard drive, and use the plus sign button to save a new file with the name incremented to Ch17_Snapshot02.max.

2. In the Front viewport, select Flag01. In the Tools pull-down menu, click Snapshot. In the Snapshot dialog, choose the Range radio button in the Snapshot area. This enables you to set the range of frames from which you want to freeze copies of the animated object.

note

There is not much motion in the flag from frame 0 to frame 20, and the copy at frame 0 would be a flat plane.

3. Enter 20 in the From field and 3 in the Copies field (see Figure 17.12). This creates three copies, one at frame 20, one at frame 100, and one halfway between. Click OK in the Snapshot dialog.

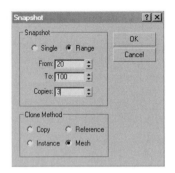

caution

Leave the Clone Method radio button set to Mesh. Otherwise, you will get copies of the Flag01 with all modifiers and animation included.

FIGURE 17.12 *In the Snapshot dialog, choose the Range radio button and enter 20 in the From field and 3 in the Copies field to make the Snapshot mesh copies.*

4. Use Select by Name and Select and Move from the main toolbar to move the Flag02, Flag03, and Flag04 to one side (see Figure 17.13). Drag the Time slider and you see that only Flag01 is animated.

FIGURE 17.13 *Use Select by Name and Select and Move to move the three new copies off to one side.*

5. Save the file; it should already be called Ch17_Snapshot02.max.

Summary

In this chapter, you learned about the following:

- **Rigid body collections**—You learned to set up rigid body collections to calculate the effects of colliding objects.

- **Cloth modifier and collection**—You learned to apply a reactor Cloth modifier and add the object to a cloth collection to simulate a hanging flag.

- **External forces**—You learned to apply wind as an external force to influence the movement of objects in the scene.

- **Baking collision data**—You learned to use reactor collisions as a modeling tool by using the Snapshot tool to "freeze" copies of deformed objects in time.

CHAPTER 18

PFlow

In This Chapter

In this chapter, you learn some of the fundamentals of using particle systems, specifically the new Particle Flow (PFlow) system in 3ds max 6 to create the illusion of animated smoke or steam and oil spilling from the can as it falls to the grate in the engine room scene. Some of the topics covered are as follows:

- **PFlow source**—You learn to create a basic Particle Flow source object and position it in your scene.

- **Particle View**—You learn to open Particle View and to edit the default event to change particle parameters and timing.

- **Materials and effects**—You learn to add a material to particles and to trigger special effects.

- **Decision branching**—You learn to set up decision branching in the particles to cause a new reaction based on particle age.

- **External forces**—You learn to apply external forces, such as simulated gravity and deflectors, to affect the movement of particles in a scene.

- **BlobMesh**—You learn to convert and adjust individual particles to form a moving contiguous mass.

Key Terms

- **Particle View**—This new dialog box enables you to create and edit complex hierarchical particle systems with visual feedback.

- **Events**—Particle operations that can be wired together to form a particle system.

- **Effects**—A post-rendering process to create special visual effects—in this case, Glow effects.

- **Forces**—A Particle View option to include external influences (gravity, for example) in a particle event.

- **Space warp**—An object type that can be placed in a scene as an external force (gravity and deflectors, for example).

PFlow—The Powerful New Particle System

3ds max 6 includes the new Particle Flow system that you can use to liven up the engine room of your boat with smoke escaping from a cylinder head and thick oil oozing from the can as it strikes the grate after falling.

With Particle Flow, you are able to visually manipulate events in a special dialog box called Particle View by dragging and dropping operators and wiring them into a complex system describing the behavior of the particles in the scene. Events are groups of operators that define the behavior of the particles.

The smoke will puff from the base of the cylinder as it compresses and then begin to rise more slowly as the older particles cool and expand.

With smoke and steam, the particles are so small they cannot be seen as individual objects with the naked eye. You simulate this with render effects and materials by making the particles themselves invisible but causing them to glow as a vaporous cloud in the scene.

You then link a new particle system to the Oil_Can object and set its timing to spray particles after it has hit the Grate01 below. You need external forces of gravity and a deflector to influence the motion of the particles. The particles in this event are made to represent a thick liquid that slowly spreads across the top of the Grate01 in a thick mass. This is accomplished by using the new BlobMesh compound object that connects individual particles into a flowing mass in which you can adjust the viscosity and affinity of neighboring particles.

Simulating a Leaky Cylinder Head

In Exercise 18.1, you place a Particle Flow source object at the bottom of the middle cylinder of the engine. You then open Particle View and adjust the parameters of the particles to cause them to burst horizontally at a time and speed that is appropriate.

Exercise 18.1   Creating and Adjusting a Particle Flow System

1. Open the file called Ch18_Smoke01.max on the CD-ROM. From the File pull-down menu, choose Save As, point to an appropriate subdirectory on your hard drive, and use the plus sign button to save a new file with the name incremented to Ch18_Smoke02.max.

2. In the Top viewport, select Cylinder02, the middle-finned cylinder head on top of the engine. In the Tools pull-down menu, choose Isolate Selection to hide all other objects in the scene. In the Create panel, Geometry panel, click Standard Primitives and choose Particle Systems in the list. In the Object Type rollout, click the PF Source button. In the Top viewport, click and drag a PF source icon (see Figure 18.1).

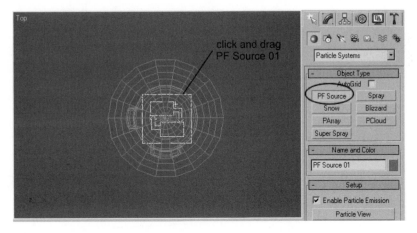

FIGURE 18.1   *In the Create panel, Geometry panel, Compound Objects, click the PF Source button and click and drag PF Source 01 in the Top viewport.*

3. On the main toolbar, click the Align button and pick Cylinder02 in the Top viewport. In the Align Selection dialog, click X Position and Y Position in the Align Position area. The Current Object and Target Object Center radio buttons should be selected by default. Click the Apply button to clear the options and place the

object. Choose the Pivot Point radio button in the Current Object column and Minimum in the Target Object column. Check the Z Position in the Align Position area to place the PF Source 01 icon at the bottom center of the Cylinder02. Click OK to finish the alignment.

4. Drag the Time slider. The particles spray downward from the emitter icon starting at frame 0 and stop being emitted at frame 30. Set the Time slider to frame 0.

5. In the Modify panel, Setup rollout, click the Particle View button. After a slight pause, the Particle View dialog appears with a window displaying the default PF Source 01 event wired to Event 01 that describes the characteristics of the particles. In a panel below the event window, you see a list of available operators for the particle system (see Figure 18.2).

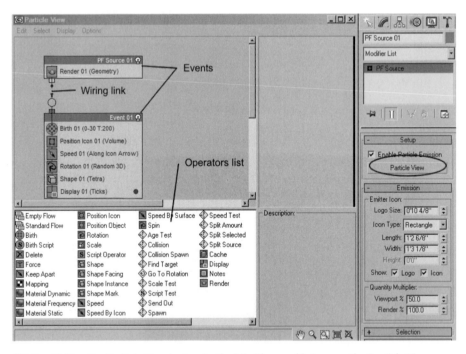

FIGURE 18.2   *Picking the Particle View button in the Modify panel brings up the Particle View dialog with the default source, events, and a list of available operators.*

6. The particles are emitted at frame 0 and you do not want them to show until frame 20, when the Cylinder02 starts its compression. In Particle View, click the Birth 01 operator in Event 01. In the Birth 01 rollout to the right, enter 20 in the Emit Start field and enter 40 in the Emit Stop field (see Figure 18.3). Two-hundred particles are emitted over 20 frames.

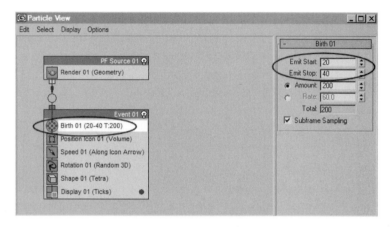

FIGURE 18.3 *In Particle View, highlight the Birth 01 operator in Event 01 and set Emit Start to 20 and Emit Stop to 40.*

7. To adjust the speed and direction of the particles, highlight Speed 01 in Event 01. In the Speed 01 rollout, enter 5'0" in the Speed field (5 feet per second). Click Along Icon Arrow and choose Random Horizontal from the list. Drag the Time slider and you see the particles shoot more slowly sideways from Cylinder02 (see Figure 18.4).

note

Setting the particle size in Shape 01 does not affect the display of the particles in the viewports, but only the rendered particle size. The Display 01 operator in Event 01 is set to show Ticks in the viewports for efficiency.

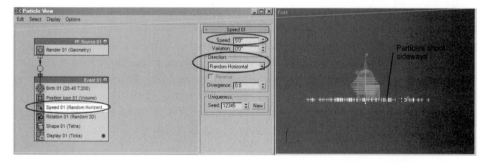

FIGURE 18.4 *By adjusting the particle speed and direction in the Speed 01 operator, you slow the particles and make them travel horizontally from the emitter icon.*

8. The size of the particles should be rather small for a Glow effect that will be applied in the next exercise. Highlight Shape 01 in Event 01 of Particle View. In the Shape 01 rollout, enter 0.5" in the Size field.

9. Close all dialogs, except Exit Isolation Mode. Save the file; it should already be called Ch18_Smoke02.max.

Adding a Material and Glow Effect

In Exercise 18.2, you view a material called Smoke in the Material Editor and assign the material to the particles with a Material Static operator. You use the Material Static operator because the material is constant and will not change over time. The material, however, will make the particles invisible in the rendered scene but will use an Effects Channel to cue a special-effect glow that processes immediately after the scene is rendered and applied to the image.

Exercise 18.2   Applying a Static Material to Cue a Glow Effect

1. Open the file called Ch18_Smoke02.max on the CD-ROM or from the preceding exercise. From the File pull-down menu, choose Save As, point to an appropriate subdirectory on your hard drive, and use the plus sign button to save a new file with the name incremented to Ch18_Smoke03.max.

2. On the main toolbar, click the Material Editor button. The highlighted sample window contains Smoke material that has opacity set to 0 to make it invisible. The Material Effects Channel is set to 1 (see Figure 18.5) and will cue a Render Effects Glow in a post-processing pass of a rendered scene.

3. Make sure PF Source 01 is the selected object. In the Modify panel, Setup rollout, click the Particle View button. In the Particle View dialog, drag the Material Static operator from the list to just below the Shape 01 operator in Event 01. You see a blue line to indicate that you can drop the operator. Highlight Material Static 01 in Event 01 and drag and drop the Smoke material from the Material Editor to the None button under Assign Material of Material Static 01 rollout. Make sure the Instance radio button is chosen in the Instance (Copy) Material dialog, and click OK. This assigns the material to the particles (see Figure 18.6).

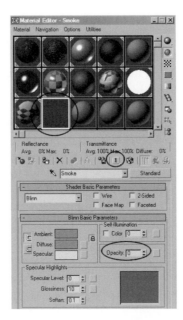

FIGURE 18.5 *Smoke is an invisible material with Opacity set to 0 and Material Effects Channel set to 1 to cue a Glow effect in post-processing.*

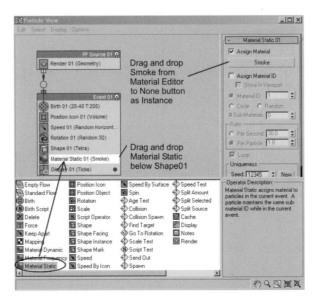

FIGURE 18.6 *Drag and drop the Material Static operator below Shape 01 in Event 01 and drag and drop the Smoke material as an instance clone onto the None button in Material Static 01 rollout.*

4. Now, apply the Glow special effect to the Smoke material. On the main toolbar, click Rendering, and choose Effects in the menu. In the Environment and Effects dialog, highlight Lens Effects in the Effects list. In the Lens Effects Parameters rollout, highlight Glow in the left pane and use the arrow button to push it to the right pane (see Figure 18.7).

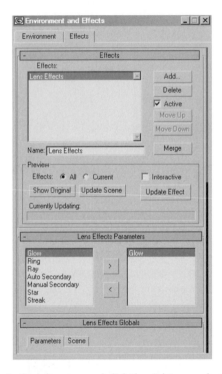

FIGURE 18.7   *Highlight Glow in the left pane, and click the right arrow button to push it into the right pane.*

5. Right-click in the Camera01 viewport to activate it. Drag the Time slider to frame 55. In the Environment and Effects dialog, Effects rollout, check the Interactive option. Camera01 viewport renders and displays in the Effects Preview window. This enables you to interactively adjust the settings for the Glow effect that you will cue on Material Effects Channel 1 of Smoke.

6. In the Environment and Effects dialog, Glow Element rollout, enter 1 in the Size field. Set Intensity to 20. Click the red color swatch in the Radial Color area and set it to blue (red=5, green=20, and blue=100) (see Figure 18.8). Close the Color Selector.

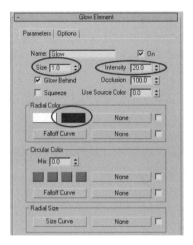

FIGURE 18.8   *In the Glow Element rollout, set Size to 1, Intensity to 20, and change the red Radial Color swatch to blue.*

7. Nothing is happening in Effects Preview because the Glow effect does not know what to use as a cue to apply it to in the scene. In the Glow Element rollout, click the Options tab. Check Image Centers in the Apply Element To area. This causes the Effects Preview window to refresh. In the Image Sources area, check Effects ID 1. This causes another refresh and, after a short calculation, displays the Glow effect on the invisible particles (see Figure 18.9).

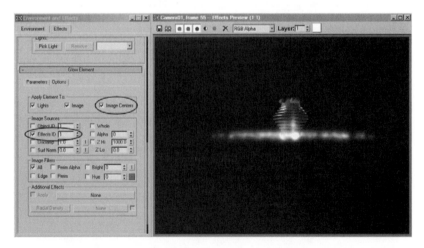

FIGURE 18.9   *The Smoke material Effects Channel 1 cues a Lens Effect Glow on all objects with that material in the scene. The interactive Effects Preview window shows the results after a short calculation.*

8. Close all dialogs except Exit Isolation Mode and save the file. It should already be called Ch18_Smoke03.max.

Decision-Based Test Operators

Usually, when smoke or steam is released into the air, it slows down and expands, which makes it rise into the air. PFlow has the capability of using decision-based test operators to make some particles behave differently from others in several ways. In this scene, you apply an Age Test operator to the Event 01 list to make all particles over a certain age available for other operators.

You then wire the Age Test operator in Event 01 with a new Event 02 that contains operators to slow them down and change their direction.

Exercise 18.3   Making the Smoke Rise

1. Open the file called Ch18_Smoke03.max on the CD-ROM or from the preceding exercise. From the File pull-down menu, choose Save As, point to an appropriate subdirectory on your hard drive, and use the plus sign button to save a new file with the name incremented to Ch18_Smoke04.max.

2. In the Modify panel, Setup rollout, click the Particle View button. In the Particle View dialog, drag the Age Test operator to just below Material Static 01 in Event 01. Highlight Age Test in Event 01 and, in the Age Test 01 rollout, enter 0 in the Variation field. This performs the age test for particles that are 30 frames old or older, but has no instructions on what to do with the older particles (see Figure 18.10).

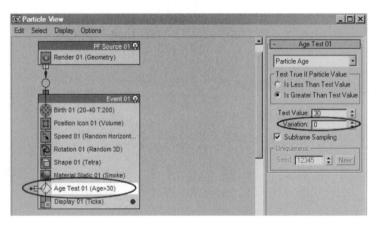

FIGURE 18.10   *Drag and drop an Age Test operator below Material Static 01 in Event 01, and set Variation to 0.*

3. Drag a Speed operator from the list into the empty panel space just below Event 01. This creates a new Event 02 with the Speed operator and a new Display operator. It does not know what particles to act on, however. Highlight the Speed 02 operator in Event 02 and, in the Speed 02 rollout, enter 1'0" in the Speed field and check the Reverse option to make the particles travel in the opposite direction of the Along Icon Arrow (downward in the scene) setting (see Figure 18.11).

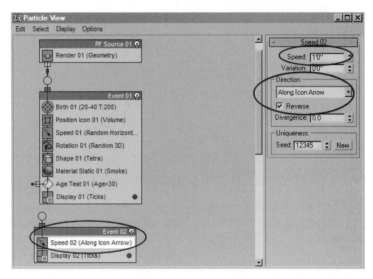

FIGURE 18.11   *A new Event 02 contains the Speed 02 operator with the Speed set to 1'0" and the direction reversed.*

4. The particles are still not affected by the new event because the age test has not been instructed to pass the results to Event 02. To the left of the Age Test 01 operator in Event 01 is a blue dot. Move the cursor over the blue dot to see the four-way arrow cursor. Drag to the large circle at the top of Event 02 to wire the two together and pass the age test particles into Event 02 (see Figure 18.12).

5. Scrub the Time slider and notice the particles stream horizontally from the emitter until they are 30 frames old, and then rise slowly toward the ceiling. Click Exit Isolation Mode to close it.

6. The Material Static operator is event specific. Highlight Material Static01 in Event 01, right-click, and choose Copy. Highlight Event 02 and choose Paste in the menu to insert a Material Static 02 operator after Speed 02.

The scene renders as normal, but you must wait before the Glow calculations are performed and applied to the image. On slower machines, this could take several minutes.

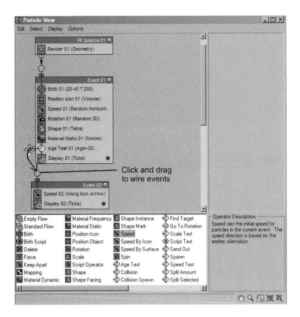

FIGURE 18.12 *Click and drag from the blue dot to the left of the Age Test 01 in Event 01 to the circle at the top of Event 02 to wire the events together. The Age Test 02 results are passed to Event 02.*

7. Set the Time slider at frame 90 and render the Camera01 viewport to see the particle smoke (see Figure 18.13).

FIGURE 18.13 *Rendering the Camera01 viewport at frame 90 shows the particles have started to rise toward the ceiling.*

8. Close all the windows and dialogs. Save the file; it should already be called Ch18_Smoke04.max.

Creating a Liquid PFlow System

In Exercise 18.4, you start a new PFlow source object that simulates thick gooey liquid flowing from the Oil_Can that falls onto the Grate01 in the engine room.

You learn about new operators that enable you to select external forces in the scene to change the behavior of the particles. The Force operator that you add to an event will cause a Gravity space warp to pull the particles downward as they emerge from the Oil_Can.

Exercise 18.4   Setting Up a New PFlow Source

1. Open the file called Ch18_Splash01.max on the CD-ROM. From the File pull-down menu, choose Save As, point to an appropriate subdirectory on your hard drive, and use the plus sign button to save a new file with the name incremented to Ch18_Splash02.max.

2. In the Top viewport, select the Oil_Can and Grate01 objects and, in the Tools pull-down, choose Isolate Selection. In the Create panel, Geometry panel, Object Type rollout, click PF Source. Click and drag in the Top viewport to create PF Source 02.

3. In the Modify panel, Emission rollout, set Logo Size, Length, and Width to 2". In the Top viewport, use Align and Select and Move from the main toolbar to align the PF Source 02 icon with the top of the Oil_Can, in the lower-left corner as seen from the Top viewport. Rotate PF Source 02 180 degrees in the X-axis to point the icon arrow upward (see Figure 18.14).

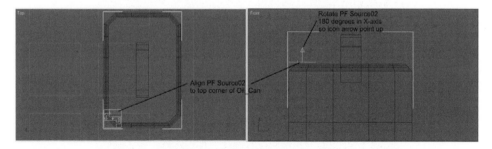

FIGURE 18.14   *Align PF Source 02 to the top of Oil_Can, lower-left corner as seen in Top viewport. Rotate PF Source 02 180 degrees in the X-axis.*

4. On the main toolbar, click Select and Link. Pick and drag from PF Source 02 to Oil_Can (see Figure 18.15), release to link the icon as a child to the parent Oil_Can. You will see the Oil_Can briefly flash white to indicate the link has occurred. If you scrub the Time slider, the icon will move with the animated can.

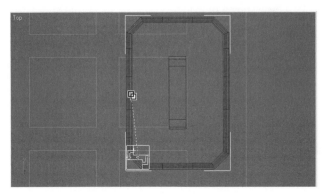

FIGURE 18.15 *Use Select and Link to drag from the PF Source02 to the Oil_Can. Release when you see the link cursor.*

5. Drag the Time slider to frame 45. In the Modify panel, Setup rollout, click Particle View. PF Source 02 shows in the Particle View dialog with a standard Birth Event 03. Highlight Birth 02 and, in the Birth 02 rollout, set Emit Start to 45 and Emit Stop to 100 (see Figure 18.16).

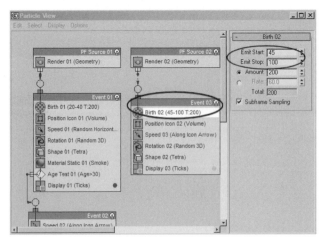

FIGURE 18.16 *Highlight Birth02 in Event 03 and enter 45 in Emit Start and 100 in Emit Stop in the Birth 02 rollout.*

6. In Event 03, highlight Speed 03. In Speed 03 roll-out, enter 1'0" in the Speed field and 20 in the Divergence. This makes a slow-moving spray with a 20-degree divergence as it leaves the icon. Drag the Time slider to frame 95.

7. The particles go straight out of the can, but you want them to fall to the Grate01. You need gravity to pull them down. In the Create panel, Space Warps panel, Forces, Object Type rollout, click the Gravity button. In the Top viewport, click and drag Gravity01 near the Oil_Can (see Figure 18.17).

The actual size and location of the Gravity01 icon has no meaning; however, the direction of the arrow in the icon indicates the direction of gravitational pull, in this case downward as seen from the Top viewport.

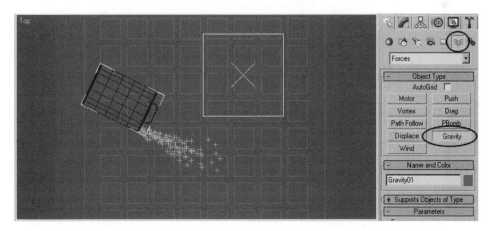

FIGURE 18.17 *From Create panel, Space Warps panel, click Gravity and click and drag near the Oil_Can.*

8. In the Particle View dialog, drag a Force operator from the list to below Speed 03 in Event 03. Highlight Force01 in Event 03 and, in the Force 01 rollout, click By List. Double-click Gravity01 in the Select Force Space Warps dialog to have it affect the particles (see Figure 18.18). Drag the Time slider, and you set that the particles fall through the Grate01 now.

9. Close all dialogs except Exit Isolation Mode. Save the file; it should already be called Ch18_Splash02.max.

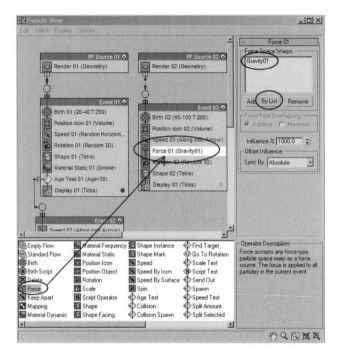

FIGURE 18.18   *Drag and drop a Force operator from the list to below Speed 03 in Event 03.*
In Force 01 rollout, click By List and double-click Gravity01.

Collision Detection

In Exercise 18.5, you learn to add a Collision operator to control the particles as they make contact with a Deflector space warp that keeps them from falling through the holes in the Grate01. A Send Out operator then advances the particles to the next event without performing any tests, and you adjust the behavior of the particles on the Deflector space warp.

Exercise 18.5   Collision Detection

1. Open the file called Ch18_Splash02.max on the CD-ROM or from the preceding exercise. From the File pull-down menu, choose Save As, point to an appropriate subdirectory on your hard drive, and use the plus sign button to save a new file with the name incremented to Ch18_Splash03.max.

2. Set the Time slider to frame 100. In the Create panel, Space Warps panel, click Forces, and choose Deflectors from the list. In the Object Type rollout, click the Deflector button, and, in the Top viewport, drag out Deflector01. In the Modify panel, make the size large enough to Oil_Can and particles with some room to spare, about 7'6" in width and 6'0" in length should be fine. In the Top viewport, use the Align tool to align the deflector with the top surface of Grate01 (see Figure 18.19).

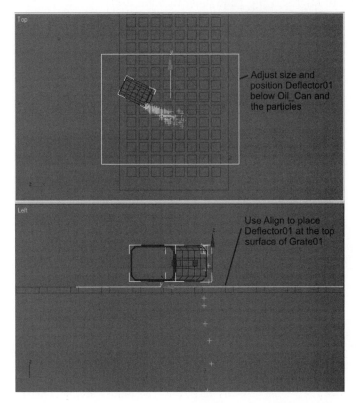

FIGURE 18.19   *In the Modify panel, adjust the size of Deflector01 to cover the Oil_Can and particles. Then, use Align to position it at the top surface of Grate01.*

3. To have the deflector work with the particles, select the PF Source 02 and, in Modify panel, Setup rollout, click Particle View. In the Particle View dialog, drag the Collision operator from the list to empty space below Event 03. This creates Event 04 with a Collision and a new Display operator. Highlight Collision 01 operator in Event 04 and, in the Collision 01 rollout, click By List. Double-click Deflector01 in the Select Deflectors dialog.

4. The Collision 01 operator has no effect because it is not wired to Event 03. There is nothing in Event 03 to pass the information forward, however. From the Operators list in the Particle View dialog, drag and drop a Send Out operator to below Display 03 in Event 03. Drag from the blue dot to the circle at the top of Event 04 to connect them and pass all particles to Event 04 (see Figure 18.20). Drag the Time slider and the particles now bounce off the deflector instead of falling through. Set the Time slider to frame 100.

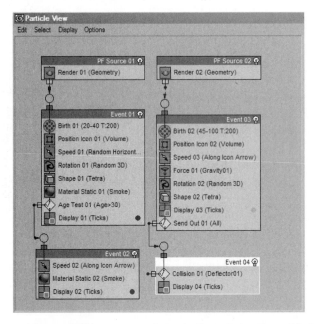

Figure 18.20   *Drag and drop a Collision operator from the list to below Event 03. Drag and drop a Send Out operator to the bottom of Event 03 and connect it to Event 04.*

5. In Event 04, highlight Collision 01. In Collision 01 rollout, choose Is Slow After Collision(s) radio button. In the Top viewport, select Deflector01. In the Modify panel, Parameters rollout, enter 0 in the Bounce field. Drag the Time slider. Most, but not all, of the particles fall to the Grate01 and slide slowly. You want all of them to fall.

6. In the Particle View dialog, highlight Force 01 and drag from Event 03 to the Event 04, just above Collision 01 (see Figure 18.21). The Force Gravity now acts on all particles sent to the Collision in Event 04. Drag the Time slider and all the particles slide slowly across the Grate01. Set the Time slider to frame 100.

7. Close all dialogs except Exit Isolation Mode. Save the file; it should already be called Ch18_Splash03.max.

BlobMesh

You adjust the size of the particles but no matter what you do, small, individual particles do not make a convincing flowing liquid. In Exercise 18.6, you learn to add a BlobMesh compound object to the scene and have it react with the particles to make a coherent mass with adjustable affinity around the particles.

Exercise 18.6   BlobMesh Compound Object

1. Open the file called Ch18_Splash03.max on the CD-ROM or from the preceding exercise. From the File pull-down menu, choose Save As, point to an appropriate subdirectory on your hard drive, and use the plus sign button to save a new file with the name incremented to Ch18_Splash04.max.

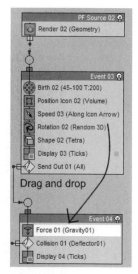

FIGURE 18.21
Drag and drop the Force 01 operator from Event 03 to the top of Event 04 to act on all particles.

2. Right-click in the Camera01 viewport to activate it, make sure the Time slider is set to frame 100 and, on the main toolbar, click the Quick Render button. The particles look like large crystals escaping from the can (see Figure 18.22). Close the Rendered Frame window.

3. In the Top viewport, select PF Source02. In the Modify panel, Setup rollout, click the Particle View button. In the Particle View dialog, highlight Shape 02 in Event 03. In the Shape 02 rollout, set Size to 1". Render the Camera 01 viewport. The particles are much smaller, but still look like crystals. Close all dialogs except Exit Isolation Mode.

4. In Create panel, Geometry panel, click Particle Systems and choose Compound Objects from the list. In the Object Type rollout, click the BlobMesh button. Pick in the Top viewport to create a BlobMesh object. The location does not matter; it disappears from the view when a blob is added.

5. In the Modify panel, Parameters rollout, set Size to 1". Set Tension to 0.01 to cause the blobs to stick together and form into a single mass. Check Off in Viewport.

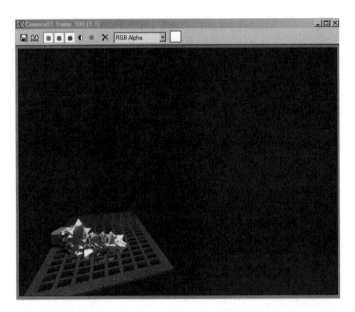

FIGURE 18.22   *Rendering the Camera01 viewport shows particles that look like large crystals.*

6. In the Blob Objects area, click the Add button and double-click PF Source 02 in the Add Blobs dialog (see Figure 18.23). In the Particle Flow Parameters rollout, All Particle Flow Events is checked to ensure that all particles are affected.

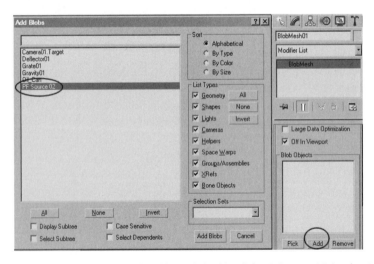

FIGURE 18.23   *In Blob Objects area, click Add, and double-click PF Source 02 in the Add Blobs dialog.*

7. Click the Exit Isolation Mode to bring back all the objects in your scene. Right-click in the Camera01 viewport to activate it and click the Quick Render button on the main toolbar. The Oil_Can looks like it is oozing a thick sticky liquid (see Figure 18.24).

FIGURE 18.24 *The rendered particles (without materials) look like a thick, sticky liquid because of BlobMesh compound object.*

8. Save the file; it should already be called Ch18_Splash04.max.

Summary

In the chapter, you learned about the following:

- **PFlow source**—You learned to create a basic Particle Flow source object and position it in your scene.

- **Particle View**—You learned to open the Particle View dialog and to edit the default event to change particle parameters and timing.

- **Materials and effects**—You learned to add a material to particles and to trigger special effects called Lens Effect Glow.

- **Decision branching**—You learned to set up decision branching in the particles by testing the particle age to cause a new reaction based on the particle age.

- **External forces**—You learned to apply external forces, such as simulated gravity and deflectors, to affect the movement of particles in a scene.

- **BlobMesh**—You learned to convert and adjust individual particles to form a moving contiguous mass.

Index

SYMBOLS

www.informit.com

YOUR GUIDE TO IT REFERENCE

New Riders has partnered with **InformIT.com** to bring technical information to your desktop. Drawing from New Riders authors and reviewers to provide additional information on topics of interest to you, **InformIT.com** provides free, in-depth information you won't find anywhere else.

Articles

Keep your edge with thousands of free articles, in-depth features, interviews, and IT reference recommendations— all written by experts you know and trust.

Online Books

Answers in an instant from **InformIT Online Books'** 600+ fully searchable online books.

POWERED BY

Catalog

Review online sample chapters, author biographies, and customer rankings and choose exactly the right book from a selection of more than 5,000 titles.

www.newriders.com

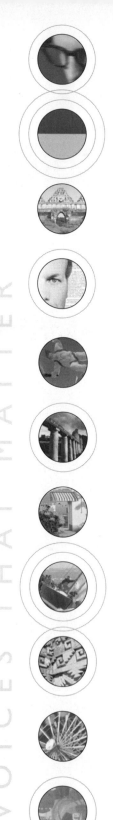

VOICES THAT MATTER

HOW TO CONTACT US

VISIT OUR WEB SITE

WWW.NEWRIDERS.COM

On our Web site you'll find information about our other books, authors, tables of contents, indexes, and book errata. You will also find information about book registration and how to purchase our books.

EMAIL US

Contact us at this address: **nrfeedback@newriders.com**

- If you have comments or questions about this book
- To report errors that you have found in this book
- If you have a book proposal to submit or are interested in writing for New Riders
- If you would like to have an author kit sent to you
- If you are an expert in a computer topic or technology and are interested in being a technical editor who reviews manuscripts for technical accuracy

- To find a distributor in your area, please contact our international department at this address. **nrmedia@newriders.com**

- For instructors from educational institutions who want to preview New Riders books for classroom use. Email should include your name, title, school, department, address, phone number, office days/hours, text in use, and enrollment, along with your request for desk/examination copies and/or additional information.
- For members of the media who are interested in reviewing copies of New Riders books. Send your name, mailing address, and email address, along with the name of the publication or Web site you work for.

BULK PURCHASES/CORPORATE SALES

The publisher offers discounts on this book when ordered in quantity for bulk purchases and special sales. For sales within the U.S., please contact: Corporate and Government Sales (800) 382-3419 or **corpsales@pearsontechgroup.com**. Outside of the U.S., please contact: International Sales (317) 428-3341 or **international@pearsontechgroup.com**.

WRITE TO US

New Riders Publishing
800 East 96th Street, 3rd Floor
Indianapolis, IN 46240

CALL US

Toll-free (800) 571-5840. Ask for New Riders.
If outside U.S. (317) 428-3000. Ask for New Riders.

FAX US

(317) 428-3280

0735711712
Mark Meadows
US$45.00

0735709181
Owen Demers
US$55.00

0735713863
Jon Bell
US$39.99
Coming soon

0735712433
Mark Giambruno
US$49.99

1532059548
Jeremy Birn
US$50.00

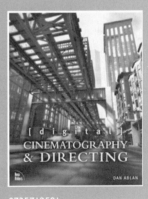

0735712581
Dan Ablan
US$45.00

VOICES
THAT MATTER™

New
Riders

WWW.NEWRIDERS.COM

1592730094
George "Fat Man" Sanger
US$35.00

1592730078
David Freeman
US$49.99

0735713634
Andrew Rollings
and Dave Morris
US$49.99

0735713677
Marc Saltzman
US$49.99

1592730019
Andrew Rollings
and Ernest Adams
US$49.99

0735713073
Marc Mencher
US$29.99